CARLO EMILIO GADDA
Contemporary Perspectives

Carlo Emilio Gadda (1893–1973) is considered by many to be Italy's most outstanding modern writer. Author of essays, novels, and short stories, Gadda has been awarded many literary prizes, particularly for his style, which has been compared to that of Joyce, Proust, and Musil. Because, however, his dense and complex linguistics tend to defy adequate translation, his work is not widely known outside of Italy. This collection of essays introduces Gadda's work at last to the English-speaking world.

Written by leading Gadda scholars, the essays capture the complexities that characterize Gadda's narrative. His plurilingualism, pastiches, and narrative entanglements are revealed both as a revolt against conventional literary style and as the expression of a chaotic, painful, and labyrinthine world inhabited by a fragmented subject. Gadda emerges as a transgressive novelist, a humorist, and a mannerist who continuously deforms language through parodic and comic modes.

No other work on Gadda in any language contains the variety of approaches and insights found in this collection. As well, the volume highlights interesting links between Gadda and a range of eminent writers, from Pirandello to Céline, thus opening his work to intertextual and comparative analysis and an international perspective.

MANUELA BERTONE is Maître de Conférences at Université de Savoie, Chambéry.

ROBERT S. DOMBROSKI is Distinguished Professor of Italian at the City University of New York.

MAJOR ITALIAN AUTHORS

General Editors:
Massimo Ciavolella and Amilcare A. Iannucci

EDITED BY
MANUELA BERTONE AND
ROBERT S. DOMBROSKI

Carlo Emilio
GADDA

Contemporary Perspectives

UNIVERSITY OF TORONTO PRESS
Toronto Buffalo London

© University of Toronto Press Incorporated 1997
Toronto Buffalo London
Printed in Canada

ISBN 0-8020-4171-X (cloth)
ISBN 0-8020-8033-2 (paper)

Printed on acid-free paper

Toronto Italian Studies: Major Italian Authors

Canadian Cataloguing in Publication Data

Main entry under title:

Carlo Emilio Gadda : contemporary perspectives

(Toronto Italian studies. Major Italian authors)
Includes bibliographical references.
ISBN 0-8020-4171-X (bound)   ISBN 0-8020-8033-2 (pbk.)

1. Gadda, Carlo Emilio, 1893–1973 – Criticism and
interpretation. I. Bertone, Manuela, 1960– .
II. Dombroski, Robert S. III. Series.

PQ4817.A33Z624 1997   853'.912   C97-931333-3

This book has been published with the financial assistance of the Goggio
fund.

University of Toronto Press acknowledges the financial assistance to its
publishing program of the Canada Council for the Arts and the Ontario
Arts Council.

Contents

Chronology

1893–1918

Carlo Emilio Gadda is born in Milan on 14 November 1893, the oldest son of Francesco Ippolito Gadda and Adele Lehr. His father was a business partner in the Ronchetti Silk Company, while his mother, who was half Hungarian, taught history and geography and served as principal of schools in several northern Italian towns. Carlo Emilio's paternal grandfather, Francesco, had married into the noble Ripamonti family; his son Giuseppe, Carlo Emilio's uncle, remembered for his achievements in the public sphere, served as minister of public works in the Lanza-Sella government from 1869 to 1873.

Throughout his works and in published interviews, Gadda refers to the important role his native city and social class played in his cultural formation. The values the nineteenth-century Milanese bourgeoisie handed down to the young Gadda were those of positivist science and technical and industrial efficiency, of productivity and competition in the best tradition of economic liberalism. He was taught to regard Milan as a model of enlightened rationality, the moral and cultural capital of Italy; his family, as a tranquil space and repository of deep feelings and emotions. But the specific circumstances of Gadda's childhood and adolescence opposed such an ideal image of family and society. Gadda obsessively remembers his youth as being thoroughly tormented, marked by continual frustration and the lack of affection. His father's imprudent investments, especially the expenses involved in the construction and maintenance of a country villa at Longone (Brianza), drained the family's financial resources, forcing it to the verge of bankruptcy. After the death of Francesco Ippolito in 1909, the Gadda family depended wholly on Adele's earnings as a public school teacher.

Gadda's early education was typical for someone of his social class and upbringing. In 1912, after taking his diploma at the Parini lyceum, he enrols in the then Istituto Tecnico Superiore in Milan, where he studies with the German physicist Max Abraham (1875–1922), remembered in *La cognizione del dolore* for his experiment of dropping a cat from the third floor of the villa to prove his theorem of impulse (*La cognizione del dolore*, 78; *Acquainted with Grief*, 38). In June of 1915, Gadda interrupts his second year in engineering to enlist in the army, sees action on several fronts, and, after Caporetto, is taken prisoner and sent to Celle Lager in Hannover, where he meets Ugo Betti and Bonaventura Tecchi. After the war, having returned to Milan, he learns that his brother, Enrico, an aviator, has been killed in the final months of the conflict. The memory of Enrico will haunt Gadda throughout his life as a writer; its presence is felt in practically all of his texts, but especially in *La cognizione del dolore*, where it is over-powering.

1919–1935

In 1919, Gadda returns to the Politecnico to finish his university studies, taking his degree in Industrial Engineering with a specialization in the design and application of electrical circuitry. As an electrical engineer, Gadda works in several Italian cities and abroad, spending more than a year in Argentina (December 1922 to February 1924), with the Compañia General de Fosforos. During his stay in South America, he begins to devote time to his literary pursuits, publishing a review of Ugo Betti's *Re pensieroso* in the Buenos Aires daily *Patria degli Italiani* (20 April 1923). A year later, he is back in Milan writing, but not finishing, his first novel, the *Racconto italiano di ignoto del novecento*, returning meanwhile to the Accademia Scientifico-Letteraria to study in the faculty of philosophy where he completes all his exams, but not the thesis he plans to write on Leibniz's *Nouveaux essais*. Financial difficulties force him to return to his profession and, in 1925, he moves to Rome to work for the Società Ammonia Casale, where he remains until 1931. A year later, he accepts a position with the Sezione Tecnologica dell'Ufficio Centrale dei Servizi Tecnici del Vaticano and is entrusted with overseeing the circuitry of the newly planned hydroelectric complex. He resigns in 1934.

During this period, Gadda writes *Meditazione milanese* (1928), *La meccanica* (1928–9), and three short narratives that will appear in 1971 under the collective title of *Novella seconda;* in 1931 he publishes his first book, *La Madonna dei Filosofi,* and in 1934 *Il castello di Udine* for which he receives the Bagutta Prize and the praise of such authoritative critics as Gianfranco Contini and Giacomo Devoto.

1936–1949

With the death of his mother in 1936, Gadda begins writing *La cognizione del dolore,* first published in instalments in *Letteratura* (1938–40). With his financial situation becoming increasingly precarious, he contracts with *L'Ambrosiano* and *Gazzetta del Popolo* to write a series of articles on science and technology, some of which he includes in *Le meraviglie d'Italia* (1939). In 1940, he moves to Florence, then considered the country's literary capital, where he makes the acquaintance of Montale, Vittorini, and Landolfi, among others. While in Florence, he publishes *Gli anni* (1943) and *L'Adalgisa* (1944), contributes to the weekly *Il Mondo* directed by Alessandro Bonsanti, and writes the initial chapters of *Quer pasticciaccio brutto de via Merulana,* also serialized in *Letteratura* (1946).

1950–1973

From 1950 to his death in 1973, Gadda's residence is Rome. Employed until 1955 as a literary journalist with the RAI's 'Terzo Programma,' he edits *Dalla terra alla luna* (1952) and *Norme per la redazione di un testo radiofonico* (1953), devoting himself almost exclusively to the management and publication of his works. He publishes *Il primo libro delle favole* (1952) and *Novelle dal Ducato in fiamme* (1953); in 1955, he begins reworking *Quer pasticciaccio brutto de via Merulana* which he publishes two years later with Garzanti. *I viaggi la morte* appears in 1958 and *Verso la Certosa* in 1961. In 1963, Einaudi publishes *La cognizione del dolore,* for which Gadda is awarded in the same year the Prix international de Littérature. Two texts prepared for radio broadcast, *I Luigi di Francia* (1964), *Il guerriero, l'amazzone, lo spirito della poesia nel verso immortale del Foscolo* (1967), the anti-Fascist pamphlet *Eros e Priapo* (1968), and the new edition of *La cognizione del dolore* (1970), containing previously unpublished chapters, complete the list of principal works published during Gadda's lifetime; the *Meditazione milanese* (1974), *Le bizze del capitano in congedo* (1981), and *Racconto italiano di ignoto del novecento* (1983) all appear posthumously.

Note on Texts and Translations

Given the uniqueness of Gadda's language and style, all quotations from Gadda's fiction and essays are from the Italian original, followed by bracketed translations; quotations from letters and collected interviews appear for the most part only in translation. For *La cognizione del dolore* and *Quer pasticciaccio brutto de via Merulana*, we have used, at times with slight changes, William Weaver's English translations: *Acquainted with Grief* (New York: George Braziller 1969) and *That Awful Mess on Via Merulana* (London, Melbourne, and New York: Quartet Books 1985), indicated in the text and notes as *AG* and *AM*, respectively. All quotations from Gadda's works, with the exception of letters and interviews, and unless otherwise indicated, have been taken from *Opere di Carlo Emilio Gadda*, published by Garzanti of Milan in five volumes under the general editorship of Dante Isella. The volumes are: *Romanzi e racconti I*, edited by Raffaella Rodondi, Guido Lucchini, and Emilio Manzotti, 1988; *Romanzi e racconti II*, edited by Giorgio Pinotti, Dante Isella, and Raffaella Rodondi, 1989; *Saggi Giornali Favole I*, edited by Liliana Orlando, Clelia Martignoni, and Dante Isella, 1991; *Saggi Giornali Favole II*, edited by Claudio Vela, Gianmarco Gaspari, Giorgio Pinotti, Franco Gavazzeni, Dante Isella, and Maria Antonietta Terzoli, 1992; *Scritti Vari e Postumi*, edited by Andrea Silvestri, Claudio Vela, Dante Isella, Paola Italia, and Giorgio Pinotti, 1993. The collection includes also a separate volume of bibliography and indices, edited by Dante Isella, Guido Lucchini, and Liliana Orlando, 1993. References in the text and notes are to the work and volume and are given with the following abbreviations:

Romanzi e racconti I = *RR I*
  La Madonna dei Filosofi = *MF*

Il castello di Udine = CU
L'Adalgisa – Disegni milanesi = A
La cognizione del dolore = CD
Romanzi e racconti II = RR II
   Quer pasticciaccio brutto de via Merulana = QP
   La meccanica = M
   Accoppiamenti giudiziosi = AccG
   Racconti dispersi = RD
   Racconti incompiuti = RIN
Saggi Giornali Favole I = SGF I
   Le meraviglie d'Italia = MI
   Gli anni = AN
   Verso la Certosa = VC
   I viaggi la morte = VM
   Scritti dispersi = SD
Saggi Giornali Favole II = SGF II
   Il primo libro delle Favole = PLF
   I Luigi di Francia = LF
   Eros e Priapo = EP
   *Il guerriero, l'amazzone, lo spirito della poesia nel verso immortale del
      Foscolo* = GAS
   Giornale di guerra e di prigionia = GGP
   Poesie = P
Scritti Vari e Postumi = SVP
   Pagine di divulazione tecnica = PDT
   Traduzioni = T
   Racconto italiano di ignoto del novecento = RI
   Meditazione milanese = MM
   I miti del somaro = MS
   Il palazzo degli ori = PO

CARLO EMILIO GADDA

Contemporary Perspectives

Introduction

MANUELA BERTONE and
ROBERT S. DOMBROSKI

Carlo Emilio Gadda is considered today to be the most original writer of twentieth-century Italian prose fiction. The impact of his language and style on both the work of his contemporaries and that of following genera-tions has been extensive. His works mark a crucial transition in modern literature from a poetics based on individualized styles, typical of early modernism, to one rooted in pastiche and satire. After Gadda, it can be said that a new age of narrative begins in Italy, one no longer anchored to the foundations of the novel established by Manzoni, nor to the various forms of realism that took hold in the first half of the twentieth century.

The difference between Gadda and other prominent Italian writers of this century consists in his ability to undermine convention. Such authors as Svevo and Pirandello imprinted their vision and narrative style on subsequent generations by introducing complexities of irony and am-biguity into standard bourgeois literary prose. Gadda's legacy runs deeper: it teaches his contemporaries to question all literary constructs (his own included), and thus to re-examine the tools of their trade, the institu-tions and conventions from which they derive, and the language in which they are crafted. Gadda's importance, however, consists much less in his influence than in the extraordinary power of his prose which, in its most intense moments, achieves, as Emilio Manzotti has remarked, a 'rare con-centration of expression, a "white hot" quality that inscribes itself on our memory with aphoristic conciseness' (Manzotti 1993, 17). This power of expression has earned Gadda the place he rightly deserves in the modern canon alongside Joyce, Kafka, Musil, and Proust.

Gadda's uniqueness was immediately recognized in the early thirties upon the publication of his first book, *La Madonna dei Filosofi*. From his entry into the Florentine literary milieu, he was praised and admired by a select group of literary intellectuals and critics who, in the words of Eugenio Montale, became indentured to him (Gadda 1993, 210). The appearance of Gadda's major novels in the late fifties and early sixties put him in contact with the general public, prompting widespread discussion of his work and its adoption by the neo–avant-garde as source and model for a literature of the future. Now there is no doubt that the young experimentalists of the Gruppo 63 had understood Gadda's seminal importance, for the Calvinos, Ecos, Tabucchis, Vassallis, Bufalinos, and Consolos of our day all appear to construct on, and over, the ruins left by his prose: upon the romantic, naturalist, aestheticist, and neorealist traditions it undermines, upon the void left by its parody of literary usage, and upon the confusion and fascination its schizophrenic character engenders. The eccentricity of Gadda's plurilingual and polyphonic texts remains, even in the light of today's more sober monolingualism, a sharp reminder of the limitless horizons of narrative; his life as a recluse outside the channels of political power and social distinction, a strong antidote to the taste for literary or intellectual celebrity.

Yet Gadda is still relatively unknown in the English-speaking world, despite the valiant efforts of literary critics and more popular writers to explain his unrivalled prose. Even the refrain that Gadda has much in common with Joyce, Proust, and Musil has done little to create much of an audience for his work on this side of the Atlantic. The main reason is that Gadda is largely untranslatable into English. Even such an expert hand as William Weaver confesses his frustration with Gadda's use of dialects and sub-languages that have no corresponding expression in English. The result being that, no matter how accurate and fluent the translation, the English-speaking reader finds himself trapped on the ornamented surface of Gadda's texts, unable to savour their extraordinary density or to enjoy their ensemble of grotesque imagery and relentless humour. Another reason is that of all modern Italian authors Gadda resists exportation the most, for his plurilingualism is rooted in the intricate tapestry of Italy's national culture, as well as in his own troubled personal life. His sentences are at times so thick with allusion that they must be read over and over again; his linguistic arsenal so varied and complicated that a broadly annotated text is an indispensable prerequisite for even the most expert of Italian readers.

Gadda's revolution in literature is essentially a revolt against simplicity. It consists of viewing the artistic text as the intersection of multiple codes, in which individual components, or systems, are part of a cognitive enterprise that privileges no one phenomenon or object of knowledge in itself (e.g., history, society, individual psychology), but rather the inter-action of these components and the global effect that such an interaction has on the stability of any preconceived systemic constraint. Not a mirror onto the world in the conventional, nineteenth-century, realist sense, nor a laboratory for the study of social reality, nor a circuit for transmitting unfathomable mysteries and secret and sublime correspondences, the lit-erary text for Gadda is a point of contact, a tangle or knot of an infinity of relationships, the site of at once the symbiosis and the disentanglement of the real. This site is the 'vortex' of Ingravallo's philosophical reasoning in *Quer pasticciaccio brutto de via Merulana*, the 'punto di depressione ciclonica nella coscienza del mondo [...] [Il] nodo o groviglio, o garbuglio, o gnommero' (*RR II*, 16) [cyclonic point of depression in the consciousness of the world ... the knot, or tangle, or muddle, or skein (*AM*, 5)]. The detective's philosophy is what regulates Gadda's writing which, like a 'vortex' or 'cyclonic point of depression' is made up of constant altera-tions, disturbances, and changes in tension and energy.

One episode in *La cognizione del dolore* provides an apt metaliterary directive to Gadda's method of writing: the description of the operation of the lightning rods on the Villa Bertoloni. Instead of harnessing the thunderbolt, controlling it, and thus reducing it according to their specific function, the rods initiate a violent chain reaction, a destructive un-ravelling and tangling in alternating directions of everything within the range of the lightning's fury. The result is what criticism has termed rightly a 'baroque,' 'manneristic,' or 'expressionistic' style, although these terms (and with them the adjectives 'grotesque' and 'macaronic') should be taken only as generic markers that from text to text maintain different grades of critical usefulness. In any case, Gadda's works are always to a greater or lesser degree the products of an aesthetic of expression. They all emit a cry of outrage that resonates into the reader's world, folding out into multiple, disymmetrical stratifications of meaning. These are the expressionistic projections of a hysterical subject for whom writing is essentially an act of deforming literary matter by means of linguistic pressure, caricature, and parody, and for whom literature is transgression, incompleteness, and ambiguity; convulsive movement around an ultima-tely unrepresentable object.

The task that this volume of essays proposes is twofold. It is intended to be a collective effort to establish a contemporary perspective on the greater part of Gadda's writing, and, at the same time, to facilitate the process of making that work familiar. The studies collected here all focus on one particular aspect of Gadda's work or on a problem of interpretation generated by recent critical debates and forums – intensified in 1993 by the celebration of the hundredth anniversary of the author's birth. They address, however, selected works and issues with varying degrees of specificity, from questions of narrative affiliation, philosophical influence, language, poetics, and style to psychological and ideological attitudes.

We begin with Gian Carlo Roscioni's groundbreaking essay on Gaddian humour, which succinctly illustrates the dimensions of Gadda's parodic style in relation to Lawrence Sterne and the tradition of Sternism in Italy. The mediating force in this relation is Ugo Foscolo who, through his translation of the *Sentimental Journey* and creation of the eccentric Didimo Chierico, provided Gadda with cogent examples of humorist writing, the most important elements of which are the construction of the humorist self and the technique of metacommentary. The relationship of Gadda to humorist writing, Roscioni is careful to underline, is not genealogical. Gadda does not descend from Sterne, but rather he shares with him, and his epigones, a distinct family resemblance.

The importance Roscioni places on Gadda's compositional notes included in the *Racconto italiano di ignoto del novecento* becomes the focus of Guido Guglielmi's study of Gadda's early reflections on narration and the form of the novel. Guglielmi carefully shows that Gadda is preoccupied with the question of entanglement from the very beginning of his work as a writer, and that as far back as 1928, with *Meditazione milanese*, he had established the philosophical principles on which all of his work would depend. Guglielmi pays special attention to the meaning of the fragment in Gadda's writings: it is not a simple part of the whole that reflects the cosmos in its particular configuration. Rather it is a self-enclosed, independent structure of a non-existent totality. It accounts for the open-endedness of Gadda's texts and the continual inflections and modulations of the narrative voice, including its self-irony and self-parody.

An important philosophical source for Gadda's conception of the fragment is Leibniz, from whom he takes the general frame of his ideas on multiplicity (the plurality of substances) and the monad (a term used by Leibniz to designate an autonomous unit of being). Reality is made up of self-enclosed, 'monadic' units, substances which, each in their own way, reflect the entirety of creation. But, in contrast to Leibniz, Gadda's monadic realities, or fragments, do not articulate the pre-established harmony of God's plan, but instead, as Roscioni deftly argued in *La disarmonia prestabilita*, are indices of infinite disorder and deformation. Robert S. Dombroski explores the relationship between the authorial self and the constantly shifting world of Gadda's multiple realities as an endless folding-out of linguistic and thematic materials in description. Drawing from Deleuze's study of Leibniz, *Le pli*, Dombroski examines the baroque structures of Gadda's writing practice, illustrating how Gadda engulfs the objects of his stories in description, how he employs the concept of entanglement to coordinate his fragments, and how he constructs and expresses the baroque subjects of his narratives.

Emilio Manzotti goes a step further in defining the architecture of Gadda's prose. His minute linguistic analysis of a passage drawn from *La cognizione del dolore* examines in fine detail two representative features of Gadda's writing: description by means of complementary variants and situations, and description that includes within itself some kind of digressive comment – the result being a form of prose in which rigorous structuring and dispersion exist side by side within a network of infinite references. Manzotti's essay, the most challenging for the non-specialist readers of this volume, is a compelling example of the best linguistic criticism on Gadda.

The theoretical background provided by these four studies will help the reader move on to more specific registers of critical discussion. In his essay on *L'Adalgisa – Disegni milanesi*, a collection of stories written in a blend of Italian and Milanese dialect, Gian Paolo Biasin demonstrates how Gadda seizes on the local mind of his native Milan to transform the city into a text. Examining an assortment of Gaddian narrative techniques, from enumeration and footnoting to parody, self-referentiality, and incompleteness, Biasin provides an invaluable blueprint of the many tools Gadda uses to penetrate the core of social life, interrupting its flow and exposing its myths and rituals.

Manuela Bertone addresses Gadda's fixation with the idea of matricide. Her purpose is to show the importance of the *Novella seconda* (an early, unfinished attempt to write a story based on a true matricide) as a paradigmatic text in the evolution of Gadda's fiction.The story of an unresolved murder, *Novella seconda* displays some of the main structural peculiarities of the major novels. By highlighting the matricide theme and showing, at the same time, the difficulties Gadda has in dealing with it, Bertone takes the reader into the complex area of autobiography and psychoanalysis, a terrain that is explored from different angles by two of the other essays in the volume.

Federica G. Pedriali shifts the emphasis Bertone places on the would-be death of the mother to the death of the brother. For her, Gadda's brother Enrico is a haunting presence in his work from his early poems to *La cognizione del dolore*. Like Bertone, she is concerned with the means Gadda employs to displace and disguise his feelings, whether through distinctly poetic imagery, irony, or sardonic humour. Attempting to unravel the complicated relationship between mother and son, Pedriali is the first to locate in Gadda's texts the deep inscriptions of his fratricidal fantasies, and thus offers an important complement to Bertone's analysis of the matricide theme.

While Pedriali steers clear of an explicit psychoanalytical reading of *La cognizione del dolore*, Carla Benedetti delves deep into the Freudian tradition to explain the relation between mourning and melancholy in the novel. She argues that Gadda's 'cognizione del dolore' has much in common with what Freud calls 'reality-testing': that is, to become 'acquainted with grief' the novel's protagonist, Gonzalo, must submit every object around him to a process of questioning and excavation, until he empties them of all meaning. From this 'reality-testing' derives Gadda's macaronic style, which is a cure for his resentment and grief. Crucial to Benedetti's study is her interpretation of Gaddian expressionism as anger directed against the negativity of the expressionistic subject who through laughter transforms meaningless fragments of reality into brilliant baroque fantasies.

Benedetti's detailed exploration of the Gaddian self finds ample support in Guido Lucchini's essay on Gadda and Freud. Establishing that Gadda had a firsthand knowledge of Freud, and that he possessed (and read in French translation) a significant number of Freud's studies in the thirties, Lucchini centres his discussion on the period, between 1946 and 1954, in which the question of narcissism comes to the fore in Gadda's essays. Lucchini shows that Gadda's Freudian culture was more substantial than was previously thought, and that the emphases he places on certain of Freud's ideas, while ignoring others, help us arrive at a more complete understanding of how, as a writer, Gadda approached the problems of self and subjectivity.

The place Gadda occupies in the development of the modern novel is surveyed by Wladimir Krysinski from the perspective of Gadda's affinity to Louis-Ferdinand Céline. According to Krysinski, Gadda and Céline refashion the novel in similar ways. They both view the genre as a medium for expressing the tensions inherent in the narrator, as opposed to the narrated. Feeling and emotion dictate the design of their prose, shifting the focus from the complexity of the object world, as seen in Joyce, to the modulations of the narrating subject. From such an approach derives a manner of writing that gives priority to fragmentation over narrative continuity. Behind their styles is the compulsion to reveal chaos. For Gadda it is the chaos of an entangled universe in which knowledge has been trapped and must be extricated. For Céline it is the chaos of death, destruction, and violence from which it is impossible to escape.

On the general question of Gadda and Fascism, Peter Hainsworth argues that Gadda was a convinced Fascist as far back as the early twenties and that his postwar denunciation of Mussolini and his regime was from a distinctly right-wing position. He dismisses the claims, made by a number of critics eager to enlist Gadda among the anti-Fascist writers, that his work during the years of Fascist rule was covertly anti-Fascist, showing that all of what could be taken for anti-Fascism was thoroughly compatible with Fascist rhetoric and ideology. But, more importantly, Hainsworth delves into the character of the anti-Fascist tirades of *Eros e Priapo*, *Quer pasticciaccio*, and *I miti del somaro*, focusing on their Freudian rhetoric and, especially, on their racism and the negative stereotype of woman which they contain. The ideological perspective he outlines is consistent with the early Gadda, a genuine nationalist who believed in the values of culture and civilization that Fascism was supposed to protect, but ultimately destroyed.

The last two essays in this collection are largely biographical in focus. Alba Andreini surveys the complicated history of the making of *Quer pasticciaccio brutto de via Merulana*, underlining Gadda's tendency to procrastinate, his tormented responses to the resolve of his friends and editors to deliver the manuscript for publication, and his reluctance to accept the fame and notoriety that the novel brought him. Andreini explores in detail the different phases of the novel's production from its instalments in *Letteratura* through its revisions for Garzanti and the screenplay *Il palazzo degli ori* which Gadda, prompted by financial exigency, wrote in 1947–8. Her reading of the screenplay in relation to the novel throws light on Gadda's social consciousness, an aspect of Gadda usually neglected by criticism.

The narcissism which Fascism embodied in the person of Mussolini carried over into the fifties and sixties in the form of publicity and fashion as Italy became transformed into a neocapitalist society. Paolo Archi's essay on how Gadda lived the passage from Fascism to modernity provides a suitable conclusion to our volume. Archi takes us on an excursion through Gadda's life in Rome, documenting his negative reaction to the cultural hegemony of the left, neo-Fascism, clericalism, and the newly born consumerism. Out of his interviews and journalism, Archi reconstructs in detail Gadda's experience as a humiliated and offended writer in the autumn of his life, forced, now more than ever, to compete in the cultural marketplace.

The close of Gadda's career in the sixties reveals an important dimension of his work, one that is relevant to our time. If it is not surprising that such a politically and socially reactionary writer like Gadda could produce, from the standpoint of language, style, and structure, the most 'revolutionary' body of works ever to appear in modern Italy, it should not surprise that his reactionary ideas can lend themselves to be usefully deployed in today's struggle against the various forms of market ideology. For there are few other writers whose ears could be more deaf to the rhetoric and suggestions of the 'fashion system.' Advertising representations and images, in all of their Fascistic configurations, have been the prime targets of Gadda's relentless scorn. Gadda's work is remarkable in that it displays all of its own reactionary ideology in public view. It thus undermines the potential of that ideology for becoming a metaphysics, materializing it in language, and, in so doing, divesting it of its value as a symbolic commodity.

References

Gadda, Carlo Emilio. 1993. *Per favore, mi lasci nell'ombra*. Milan: Adelphi
Manzotti, Emilio. 1993. 'Carlo Emilio Gadda: un profilo.' In Emilio Manzotti, ed., *Le ragioni del dolore – Carlo Emilio Gadda 1893–1993*. Lugano: Cenobio
Roscioni, Gian Carlo. 1975. *La disarmonia prestabilita*. Turin: Einaudi

Gadda as Humorist

GIAN CARLO ROSCIONI

In reference to what is, broadly speaking, the 'macaronic' matrix of Gadda's literary style, Gianfranco Contini specifies repeatedly that such a label does not allude to a documentable lineage. Folengo and Rabelais, he states, 'are obviously not Gadda's "sources," ' but rather colleagues of high stature [engaged] in a formal practice that could be defined as expressionistic mannerism,' and he goes on to say that Gadda 'owes nothing to Dossi and his descendants [...]; he belongs *naturally* to the line of benefactors that includes Folengo, Rabelais and the later Joyce' (Contini 1989, 82, 86, emphasis mine). In a word, Contini is referring to a typology, rather than a genealogy. For the most part, the lesson implicit in these clarifications has been taken to heart wisely, for no one, as far as I know, has attempted to define and measure Gadda's alleged indebtedness to the writers of the macaronic tradition.

I have underscored Contini's caution in this regard because my study is also based on findings and considerations that are essentially typological in kind. Moving from the premises of Contini's first decisive contribution to Gadda studies, entitled 'Carlo Emilio Gadda, o del "pastiche" ' (*Solaria*, 1934), I propose to suggest some possible implications. The result will be that, travelling along paths parallel to those charted by Contini, I will have the chance to encounter writers whom an unmistakable family resemblance permits us to relate to Gadda. I do not assume, however, that any future research into borrowings or specific comparisons can hope to be more promising than what has been unequivocally discouraged by Contini in relation to the macaronic.

A good point from which we can begin to discuss the pastiche in Gadda and other writers is provided in a footnote contained in Marina Fratnick's book *L'écriture détournée*, which draws our attention to the largely different use of the word *'pastiche'* in French and Italian criticism (Fratnick 1990, 106n). Once we have distinguished literary texts written *'à la manière de'* from those composed under the sign of multilingualism, it becomes apparent that only the latter, at least in Italy, have been studied. It is true that Contini has occasionally taken into consideration even the former, as is attested by the inclusion of Edoardo Calandra into his *Antologia degli scapigliati piemontesi*; but this is a wholly limited case. By contrast, multilingualism has recently been the subject of much discussion, indeed perhaps too much.

Multilingualism is of course a much more interesting phenomenon; but perhaps even literature 'in the manner of' deserves some attention: in the first place, because texts that imitate other texts with the prevailing, although not exclusive, intention to parody them are in fact less detached than one thinks from multilingualism (actually they could help us focus on some of multilingualism's more important aspects); secondly, because the comparison between what, to avoid confusion, I shall call *pastiches à l'italienne* and *pastiches à la française*, from a didactic standpoint (Gadda would say 'heuristic') can be useful as a means of orientation.

The first thing that comes to mind in this regard is that the most famous of Italian novels, *I promessi sposi*, begins with a pastiche, understood in the sense of 'in the manner of.' This did not escape Gadda's attention, for he mentions the introductory pages of *I promessi sposi* more than once, expressing a judgment that, admittedly, leaves me perplexed. In his opinion, Manzoni shows in the Introduction 'his fascination ... with baroque historiography and oratory' (*SGF I*, 1174). Everything leads us to believe the contrary: that, far from being attracted to the baroque, Manzoni intended to mimic a kind of writing which wavers – as we read in *Fermo e Lucia* – 'between what is at once awkward and affected, crude and pedantic' (Manzoni 1968, 7). But whatever may have been Manzoni's intentions, two considerations are in order.

The first is stylistic. Manzoni's mimetic powers do not prevent anyone in the least familiar with the vocabulary and rhythm of seventeenth-century prose from noticing the dissonances contained in the first two pages of *I promessi sposi*. This is not the place for a detailed analysis; let it suffice to say that instances of strained syntax or the use of forms extraneous – because either too ancient or too modern – to the writing practices of the· Seicento would discourage any relative expert from attributing unequivocally the passage to a writer of that century. Nor should it surprise us, since anachronisms and minor dissonances are inevitable when facing difficulties of this kind. Moreover, as a result of this, it is difficult to separate neatly the two varieties of pastiche. Actually one could say that in writings *à la manière de* there is no talent that holds sway, for – except in very short texts – the *pasticheur* always shows his hand. Put differently, the *pastiche à la française* tends often to become an unintentional and, most of the time, awkward *pastiche à l'italienne*. In any case, the objective difference between the two kinds of writing consists more in the author's intentions than in the results achieved.

Yet the scantness of the sample provided does not prevent us from considering Manzoni as an occasional *pasticheur* (in France, incidentally, there is not one scholar of this kind of literary activity who would refrain from mentioning the name of La Bruyère, author of a much shorter seventeenth-century pastiche). And the unexpected recruitment of such an illustrious writer into the ranks of the *pasticheurs* obliges us to reconsider the history and the very nature of a genre that many readers are inclined to treat either with diffidence or admiration, depending on one's perspective or the current cultural fashion. It is as if the writers devoted to the pastiche formed a sparse platoon of irregulars, misfits, or Bohemians, positioned next to solid battalions of orthodox, disciplined, and well-groomed troops.

But why is this an opportune moment to re-examine the history of the pastiche, be it either French or Italian? If Manzoni's contribution to the genre is very modest, the same cannot be said of a previous literary experience, also linked to the name of a famous novelist, which is no doubt significant. I am referring to Ugo Foscolo, author of the *Viaggio sentimentale di Yorick lungo la Francia e l'Italia*, who exhibits himself in a *pastiche à la française* with the Rabelaisian 'Fragment' contained on the sheet of paper with which La Fleur wrapped the butter for Yorick's breakfast. These are pages – Foscolo is intent on having us know – that 'Yorick did not translate into antiquated English,' (Foscolo 1951a, 148n) but that Didimo Chierico (that is, Foscolo) capriciously decided to render in an Italian midway between classical and archaic. If the language of Sterne's *Sentimental Journey* is anything but conventional, Foscolo does not hesitate to implant, here and there, in the English writer's story what at another time he called his *imposturette* (Foscolo 1951b, VI, 709n1). Nor should it be forgotten that the original translation project – as documented in a letter to Niccolò Bettoni of May 1806 (Foscolo 1952, *Epistolario*, II, 107) – foresaw the addition of pages to Sterne's text attributed to a certain Cookman: a name, not chosen by chance, which seems to allude, if not exactly to a pastiche, at least to a recipe of complex literary gastronomy.

It is not necessary to dwell here on the well-known fact that the translation itself of Laurence Sterne's *Sentimental Journey* is often carried out – either on account of allegiance to the original or by translator's licence – according to the principles, or with the ingredients, of a *pastiche à l'italienne* – alternating and mixing voices and forms uncommon to contemporary modes of expression.[1] If in the *Sesto tomo dell'io* Foscolo compared himself to a musical instrument 'capable of producing all kinds of sounds and made especially for modulation' (Foscolo 1991, 24), it is because even then he had in mind orchestrations quite similar to Sterne's, a writer whose 'fantasies' – Didimo Chierico explains – 'erupt altogether, simultaneously discordant and very disquieting, hinting at more than they state, and usurping sentences, words and orthography' (Foscolo 1951a, V, 40). The latter operation seems to contain embryonically some of the elements of what Gadda will call the 'spastic use' of language.[2]

The linguistic and stylistic characteristics of Foscolo's *Viaggio* were well known to Gadda who, presenting *Eros e Priapo* to Alberto Mondadori in 1945, wrote: 'The text is largely composed in an archaic, sixteenth-century Tuscan prose with various dialectal interpolations (Roman and Lombard). It thus recalls linguistically Balzac's *Contes drolatiques* or Foscolo's translation of Sterne's *Sentimental Journey*.'[3] However, such a wholly accidental reference is not what puts us on the track of would-be Foscolian imprints in Gadda's writing. My motives for insisting on Foscolo, or, better, on Foscolo's Sternism, are fundamental for other reasons.

A good starting point is the 'humoral tone' in which Gadda, writing to Mondadori, says he wants to record images and events. Not so long ago, in a lengthy digression on Gadda's numerous journeys during the 1920s, I mentioned how in the records and letters documenting these travels the author appears often as the protagonist of a 'sentimental journey,' a story, I maintained, 'in which the optic, humor and personality of the observer count more than the things observed' (Roscioni 1993, 3). But let Gadda himself explain how that kind of narrative takes shape. We read in 'compositional note' 33 of the *Racconto italiano di ignoto del novecento*:

Io vedo, io viaggiatore, che il capo-stazione fa questo e questo. E lo vedo ai miei fini, non ai suoi. E riallaccio il suo muoversi con i miei antecedenti e susseguenti, con i miei interessi, con le mie percezioni, non con le sue. Egli si muove 'per me,' nella mia intenzione e non 'per sé' e 'secondo sé.' (*RI*, 465)

[I, the traveller, see that the station master does this and that; I see him from my own point of view, not from his. I connect his moves to my former and subsequent objectives, to my personal interests, to my insights, not to his. He moves 'for me' according to my intentions, not 'for' and 'by' himself.]

Having discussed several times both the literal and the metaphoric role the journey plays in Gadda's works, and the literary tradition to which it belongs,[4] I should now like to better define its 'sentimental' character. But first we need to correct a mistaken notion. Sterne's title no doubt alludes to the protagonist's troubles of the heart, but perhaps not only to them. Like the word *sentimento* in classical Italian or *sentiment* in eighteenth-century French, the then English usage of 'sentiment' includes, besides emotional import in the modern and current sense of the word, other experiences and psychological processes. Among the more important meanings listed in the *Oxford English Dictionary*, we find 'mental attitude' and 'opinion or view.' Of these meanings 'opinion' strikes me as particularly important, because the word appears in another, no less famous, of Sterne's title pages. The complete title of *Tristram Shandy* is *The Life and Opinions of Tristram Shandy, Gentleman*. The novel is in fact based on one or more characters whose *opinions*, the title page states, count more than their actions. We are dealing with reasonable thoughts or judgments, shared, unfortunately, by only a few people; but also often with outlandish ideas, fixations, and paradoxical speculation, which, stated and analysed in more or less long digressions, end up forming the very substance of this outstanding story. Everyone remembers the relationship Sterne formulates between the name given to a person at baptism, or the shape of his nose, and his character and destiny.

An analogous eccentric and fastidious *habitus* of opinion and reflection runs through Gadda's stories. The characters Gadda deploys exclusively to express comic or tragic ideas on the nature of the world or on life and death (Cavaliere Digbens of *La Madonna dei Filosofi* or the 'buon Padre Lopez' of *La cognizione del dolore*) are in reality few and marginal. Yet, there are numerous protagonists in the novels and stories who air their *opinions* on disparate events and problems with systematic abundance. I am thinking naturally about those thoughts that stem from the 'rovello interno' [internal torment] of Gonzalo Pirobutirro or from some 'teoretica idea' [theoretical idea] of Detective Ingravallo 'sui casi degli uomini: e delle donne' [on the affairs of men, and of women] (*CD*, 607, and *QP*, 16). Enumerated quasi-didactically in a series of expositive propositions – 'Sosteneva, fra l'altro' [He sustained, among other things], 'Diceva anche' [He also would say], 'E poi soleva dire' [And then he used to say], 'Voleva significare' [What he meant was] – Ingravallo's opinions are interspersed with the comments of his listeners who are unanimous in emphasizing their unique character: 'sostenevano che leggesse dei libri strani' [they insisted that he read strange books]; 'Erano questioni un po' da manicomio: una terminologia da medici dei matti' [they were slightly crazy problems: his terminology was for doctors in looneybins] (*QP*, 16–17). But above all I have in mind the reflections and opinions of characters from other stories on themes much more futile or trivial. Some good examples are the problems discussed by the 'Captain on leave' relative to the mechanical pianos of travelling musicians or to the flush-mechanisms of the bathroom toilets: 'Stando alle sue opinioni' [According to his opinion]; 'secondo il modo di vedere del capitano Gaddus' [according to the point of view of Captain Gaddus]; 'Egli opinava che' [His opinion was]; 'Dacché il capitano Gaddus opinava altresì' [Since Captain Gaddus believed likewise] (*RD*, 969, 970, 973, 975). It goes without saying that the expression of these theories (*sentiments* and *opinions*) is accompanied, both in Gadda and in Sterne, by the often exhilarating description of the strange behaviour they inspire in those individuals who hold them.

Returning to Foscolo, it is unfortunate that Sterne's teachings (like the narrative or stylistic experiments undertaken in directions different from those signalled by *Ortis*), hold for us an almost solely historical interest. A quick appraisal: some meritorious attempts at different modes of writing, many works left in their initial stages, a good number of interesting projects, but few genuine results. *Il sesto tomo dell'io* is a title that promised much more than the text actually delivered. The translation of *Sentimental Journey* itself, in spite of its resonance throughout the nineteenth century, was more enterprising than convincing as a project. It is difficult not to subscribe – with greater indulgence, I hope – to the reservations advanced by Carlo Dossi, a writer hardly biased (at least in principle) against literary operations of this kind.

Yet taking account of the strengths displayed in these ventures, the one success Foscolo achieved was in the creation of Didimo Chierico, the progenitor of the Italian branch of a dynasty of characters whose most fortunate and successful descendants are precisely those opining and theorizing souls we encounter in some of Gadda's works. Portrayed with an eye attentive to British models, Didimo seems to have absorbed from the island fog a melancholic and ironic extravagance, a quaintness of behaviour (more than of speech) which will be handed down to Gonzalo and Captain Gaddus.

He held securely to [Foscolo writes in the *Notizia intorno a Didimo Chierico*] strange systems; and they seemed to be an integral part of him. From these systems and from the perseverance with which he applied them to his way of life derived a behaviour and system of beliefs that were the subject of laughter ... He had no love for cats because they seemed to him more taciturn than other animals; yet he praised them because, like dogs, they profited from society, and, as night owls, from freedom. He regarded panhandlers to be more eloquent than Cicero in perorating and more expert phrenologists than Lavater. He did not believe that anyone who lived next door to a butcher or near the gallows was trustworthy. He believed in prophetic inspiration and actually presumed to know its sources. He blamed a wife's first infidelity on her husband's nightcap, dressing gown, and slippers. (Foscolo 1951a, V, 177–8)

It should be noted that, notwithstanding 'the subject of laughter,' these 'sentences' presuppose a disconsolate vision of human life and a radical pessimism in regard to the effectiveness of the means available to confront it: 'He once said to me that many tortuous paths cross the great valley of life,' etcetera: 'Human reason, Didimo used to say, labours with mere abstractions; it begins unwittingly from nothing; and after a lengthy journey we return with open eyes terrified by the nothingness.' 'Moreover, it seemed to me that he felt somewhat of a dissonance in the harmony of the world' (ibid., 177, 179, 185).

In spite of the obvious differences between Didimo (Yorick and Tristram, as well) and Gonzalo or Captain Gaddus, it seems that there is enough in these remarks and attitudes to recognize the family resemblance referred to above. In both cases we have characters who are not only different from the rest of human kind, but, on account of their changeable behaviour and moods, are at times different from themselves. Is there any better way of representing them than in a falsetto mode, through artificially produced tones, beyond the normal range? If an expedient appropriate to this end is writing in a language that doesn't exist (because it is arbitrarily made up of different languages), another no less pertinent means is to attribute to these characters abstruse beliefs regarding the most concrete things, and rigorous theories regarding life's most frivolous accidents. The sentences they pronounce thus affirm the solitary and cantankerous wisdom of someone who does not want to be part of the multitude, while denouncing the bitter, ridiculous experience of an individual who opines and speculates on life and forgets to live.

Furthermore, when the *Racconto italiano* was published, the attention of many readers, forewarned by the volume's editor, was drawn to the particularly interesting 'compositional notes' which constitute a veritable incunabulum of Italian narratology. There have even been attempts to compare these notes to then contemporary, or subsequent, reflections of theoreticians and writers from other countries. If we ask ourselves what made Gadda consider certain questions, we come up with different, but not necessarily contradictory, answers. For example, one could bring up Gadda's experience in civil engineering, for is not the development of a plot in some way a problem of construction theory? It is equally legitimate to suppose that the young writer's theoretical and epistemological propensities led him to delve into what he calls (in the same composition-al note) 'il *punto di vista* "organizzatore" della realtà complessa' (*RI*, 461) [the 'organizational' *point of view* of reality in its entirety].

For a writer like Gadda to discuss so meticulously problems of narrative organization could at first sight seem incongruous. Doesn't he himself propose (in the above-cited letter to Alberto Mondadori) a book in which the reader encounters images and events 'recorded in a humoral tone'? The fact of the matter is that there is a tight connection between those *organizational* problems and the author's humours. In the first article published on the *Madonna dei Filosofi*, Gadda is defined (in its very title) *Un umorista* [A Humorist] (Linati 1931). Carlo Linati's definition, shared at that time by other reviewers, is just as fitting now. But, regrettably, these critics and Linati himself to a certain degree, speak of *humour* in the now current usage of the term. We should not forget that up until then, as Linati certainly knew, the word had a fundamentally different meaning. Dossi writes that 'a humorist, according to the dictionaries, is a person who is fickle and bizarre' (Dossi 1988, 103, n1759). In other words, the word denoted a person who from time to time fell prey to one of the four *humours* of Galen: sometimes melancholic, sometimes cheerful, sometimes apathetic, sometimes irascible; also capable of combining in one disposi-tion humours that appear totally incompatible. Dossi states: 'Bruno's motto "in tristitia hilaris, in hilaritate tristis" could be the motto of humour' (ibid., 197, n2416).

Gadda has often spoken of his humours. For example, in a letter to Ambrogio Gobbi (25 August 1916), he writes: 'Cosa vuoi che ti dica di me? Sono sempre il Gaddus, sempre più balogio che mai, sempre più mer-luzzo, sempre più sconclusionato, svirgolato, sfessato ma sempre più bilioso e pieno d'invettive contro tutti' (Gadda 1983, 30–1) [What do you want me to say about myself? I'm always Gaddus, always as much of a dullard as ever, always more of a nerd, always more incoherent, miser-able, downhearted, but always more irascible and full of invectives against everybody]. However, it is the literary rather than the psychological dimension of humour that interests us here. In this regard, Dossi, who under the influence of Jean Paul had planned to write (but never did) a book devoted entirely to this subject, has made some decisive pronouncements.

Two fundamental presuppositions are clearly stated in the *Note azzurre*. The first concerns the object of the story: 'A humorist,' Dossi writes, 'describes himself rather than his heroes'; the second is instead technical in kind: with most contemporary writers 'the concern is purely in the story, while with the humorists, it is in the fabric of the story' (Dossi 1988, 325, n3210; 213, n2490). From the standpoint of composition, the humorists' favourite theme (autobiography) is one of the most delicate. As scholars of autobiography have attested, speaking about oneself gives rise to various problems, beginning with the decisive question of the relationship between the author of the book and the voice in the story that says 'I.' Moreover, writers like Sterne or Gadda portray themselves in ways wholly different from other writers. The autobiography of the humorist is, so to speak, hyperbolic. It is the self-portrait of a person who looks at himself in a circus mirror that makes things look either bigger or smaller than they actually are. Why are the 'Viaggi di Gulliver, cioè del Gaddus' titled so? Because Gaddus, just like Gulliver, feels, from the time of the experiences recorded in his *Giornale di guerra*, much bigger or much smaller than those around him; in any case, very different from them.

The humorist, however, also enjoys looking at himself in such other mirrors as those found, say, in tailor or barber shops, mirrors that multiply his image, at times ad infinitum. 'The "I" of *Tristram Shandy* is at once Laurence Sterne and his two creations Tristram Shandy and Parson Yorick; and it is all three simultaneously and turn by turn.'[5] In Gadda's stories, we witness much less a duplication of the subjects identifiable with whoever says 'I,' than processes of superimposition or doubling, often accompanied by strange name games. This happens in *La Madonna dei Filosofi*, where the story of Gadda's brother Enrico, who was killed in the war, becomes absorbed in the story of a boy called (what a coincidence) Emilio, in which are mixed the traits and experiences of the Gadda brothers. And how about the comparison Gadda institutes in an 'exemplum' of the *Meditazione milanese* between the opposite war behaviour of two soldiers whose names are Carlo and Emilio? (*MM*, 695–6) The humorous matrix of such an operation is clearly manifest. Did not Carlo Alberto Pisani Dossi assign to Carlo Dossi the task of writing the *Vita di Alberto Pisani*?

Apart from the game itself, it is useful to recognize in exercises of this kind a need that, already transparent in Sterne and other writers, becomes explicit in Gadda. One of the teachings we find in the compositional notes of the *Racconto italiano* is that the creation of characters – the first, fundamental act of every narrative – is secondary to the 'necessità di creazione di una personalità dell'autore' (*RI*, 479) [need for the creation of an authorial personality]. We must not confuse this position with the apparently similar one held by the romantics. In Gadda's case, as confirmed by other experiences at that time in literature and theatre, the author's search for himself is, in some way, internal to the work and, thus, 'ironic'; it contributes to shifting the emphasis from (to use Dossi's formula) the 'story' to the 'fabric of the story.'

The shift is realized by introducing a metalinguistic component, or at least a reflexive, *opining* dimension, into the narrative, which alters the traditional pre-eminence of the 'story' over its accompanying elements. 'The humorist writer,' we read in another 'blue note,' 'must render the plot barely interesting, so that the reader in his desire to devour the book does not skip over all those minute and acute observations that constitute humour' (Dossi 1988, 135, n2174). Although Gadda is hardly inclined to sacrifice plot, he indulges in every kind of 'observation' and 'diversion,' both in the text and in the footnotes; nor does he refrain from including explanatory notes where one would least expect to find them.

As for his overriding disposition to metacommentary, it does not appear only in the novels and in the 'compositional notes.' It suffices to leaf through the *Giornale di guerra* to find the following consideration, dated 20 September 1918: 'Credo che il modo migliore per notare queste cose sia il rappresentarle cronologicamente e dal mio punto di vista, da spettatore insomma' (*GGP*, 812) [I think the best way of taking note of these things is to represent them chronologically and from my point of view, in sum, as a spectator]. The desperate recluse of Cellelager finds therefore a way of dwelling on the narratological problem *par excellence*, namely, point of view, and doing so even in writings and circumstances that are the least suitable.

Let us venture a conclusion. Disparate texts and documents seem to prove that a narratological problematic is intrinsic to stories written in the Sternian or humorous vein. Naturally, not all writers are aware of it to the same degree, as not all are interested in discussing the theoretical and technical aspects of composition. In Gadda this interest was so acute that we should not be surprised by the questions and discussions that accompany or recur in his records or fictions. Given the personality of the protagonists and the kind of events narrated, that kind of speculation on

the 'fabric' of the fable constitutes, in reality, the most natural of complements to the fable itself.

Although writers like Foscolo, Dossi, and Gadda have taken part in the
affairs of Italian Sternism, the balance sheet regarding this experience is,
on the whole, not a positive one. Reconstructing the history of Sternism,
more than seventy years ago, Giovanni Rabizzani called Foscolo 'the first
modern Italian humorist' (Rabizzani 1920, 107). His assessment is essentially correct. One wonders, however, why Foscolo knew how to give us
only a small portrait of Didimo Chierico. Was it perhaps because the
forces that urged him to follow different paths got the best of him?
Probably yes. Among the good and bad reasons that provoked Gadda's
tenacious contempt in Foscolo's regard, there is an issue to which Dossi,
without mentioning Foscolo, calls our attention: 'Humour in Italy' – he
writes in another 'blue note' – 'had much difficulty developing. Glorious
family traditions often led the family to ruin. Italy always believed too
much in Greece and Rome' (Dossi 1988, 148, n2269).

I truly believe that if Foscolo did not write his own *Tristram Shandy* the
principal reason was that at that time, in Italy, there was neither a sound
and respected tradition in the novel to parody, nor, above all, a reading
public capable of understanding Sterne's ironic signals. This does not
detract from the fact that even Foscolo's numerous and different pursuits
had contributed to the whimsical and episodic character of his humour.
The problem interests us to the extent to which Gadda, the Italian writer
who has travelled the farthest on the paths created by Swift and Sterne,
had to work within a notably unreceptive literary and cultural milieu,
tackling problems not always in consonance with the poetics of humour
and, at times, actually opposed to it.

In his review of *La Madonna dei Filosofi*, Linati, having evoked the figure
of Dossi ('this Monseigneur of humour'), makes incidental reference to the
so called *'extravagants'* from the other side of the Channel. Seventy years
later, both references, although pertinent, appear inadequate in relation
to the phenomenon under examination. When I was writing the piece
mentioned above on Gadda's continual changes of residence during the
twenties, on the conflicts with his landladies, and on his perpetual search
for new places to live, I came across by chance a page in the *Viaggio
sentimentale di Yorick* on the wanderings of Smelfungus. We read in
Foscolo's translation:

He left with hypochondria and irascibility, and every object he touched became
discoloured and deformed; and he had to narrate an odyssey of disastrous

incidents ... and that they had skinned him so that he defied Saint Bartholomew and diabolically roasted him alive at every tavern he visited ... 'And I'll tell it,' Smelfungus used to cry out, 'I'll tell it to the world.' 'Tell it to your doctor,' I replied, 'it would be better.' (Foscolo 1951a, V, 68–9).

This reference to the doctor as the only person capable of understanding the things that pass through the mind of the neurotic traveller will remind Gadda's readers of the episode in *La cognizione del dolore* in which Gonzalo – quasi-accepting the invitation extended to Smelfungus in the *Viaggio sentimentale* – decides to entrust to a doctor truths about himself that are suggestive of a malady very similar to Smelfungus's hypochondria and irascibility.

However curious it may seem, this coincidence separates rather than unites the two texts. That which for Sterne is a quip, for Gadda and the culture of his age was a very serious problem. If more than two chapters of the *Cognizione* are devoted to Gonzalo's visit and conversation with the doctor, it is because the doctor has become Gonzalo's only possible, albeit inadequate, interlocutor. Problems that once fell to the competence of the moralist, if not the theologian, are now the prerogative of science. As a result, Gadda, rather than a 'sentimental traveller,' is a 'minimissimo Zoluzzo di Lombardia' (*AN*, 243) [miniature Zola from Lombardy] who, besides talking about himself, talks about many other things; and he does so, when the occasion is right, with the spirit, objectivity, and language of science.

It would take too long to disclose all the instances and reasons impelling Gadda to separate himself from Sternian prototypes and their Italian epigones. It cannot be denied, however, that a certain Sternism, however unwitting – Contini would call it *natural* – constitutes an essential part of his art. If Gadda knows how to handle successfully any subject, it is above all when he talks about himself that his pages are inimitably brilliant. Dossi's receipt for humour, in his case, works exceedingly well.

Let me add that comparing Gadda to other humorists or 'sentimental' writers contributes to better verify and justify aspects of his work and poetics which, if considered by themselves, would lose much of their significance. Among these aspects one can actually find unsuspected hierarchies. While Sternism – as attested by the examples of Foscolo and Dossi (as well as other Italian and foreign authors) – seems to involve, or favour, a certain dose of the macaronic or of the pastiche, the opposite does not hold true. Neither the macaronic in itself nor the pastiche have ever been capable of sustaining narrative thematics or, much less, narratological problematics of any kind whatsoever. Might then humour be the catalysis of phenomena regarded up to now as chapters of different stories that, inadvertently, converge in Gadda's work?[6]

Translated by Robert S. Dombroski

Notes

1 To give some idea of the spirit animating Foscolo's literary operation, let us recall what he had written in one of the first drafts of the 'Notizia intorno a Didimo Chierico' about two of the alleged translations of the *Sentimental Journey*: 'The second [translation] is in a Boccaccesque style with many long verbal transpositions, which is bothersome, but not bad; what is bad in my opinion is the large number of antiquated words that, although not found in Boccaccio, are scattered here and there in writers preceding him. The third [translation] is written so that whoever translates into French doesn't have to change a syllable; moreover, it resembles many contemporary books' (Foscolo 1951a, V, 229).

2 I have cited various passages written by Gadda on this theme in *La disarmonia prestabilita*, 17.

3 Letter dated 25 Nov. 1945, cited by Giorgio Pinotti in *SGF II*, 995.

4 See my review of the new edition of Contini's *Antologia degli scapigliati piemontesi*, edited by Dante Isella, entitled 'Gli antichi padri di Joyce e Gadda' (*La Repubblica*, 15 Feb. 1992: 3).

5 See John Cowper Powys's introduction to *Tristram Shandy* (London: Macdonald 1949, 29).

6 A brief postscript. The role I have attributed to Foscolo in this study is not intended to confuse those readers who see in Sterne's Italian translator above all the target of *Il guerriero, l'amazzone, lo spirito della poesia nel verso immortale del Foscolo*. As I have already remarked, there is more than one Foscolo. His more assiduous readers know that among the 'Prose originali' contained in the manuscript 'Piano di studi' we find the following title: 'L'uomo e la verità. Saggio filosofico sotto il nome di Olocsof' (Foscolo 1951b, VI, 6). Well, if Gadda detested Foscolo, a secret affinity perhaps linked Alì Oco de Madrigal to Olocsof.

References

Contini, Gianfranco. 1989. *Quarant'anni di amicizia. Scritti su Carlo Emilio Gadda*. Turin: Einaudi

Dossi, Carlo. 1988. *Note azzurre*. Milan: Adelphi

Foscolo, Ugo. 1951a. *Prose varie d'arte* (= *PV*). Vol. V. Edited by Mario Fubini. Florence: Edizione nazionale delle opere di Ugo Foscolo
– 1951b. *Scritti letterari e politici dal 1796 al 1808* (= *SLP*). Vol. VI. Edited by Giovanni Gamberin. Florence: Edizione nazionale delle opere di Ugo Foscolo
– 1952. *Epistolario*. Vol. II. Edited by Plinio Carli. Florence: Edizione nazionale delle opere di Ugo Foscolo
– 1991. *Il sesto tomo dell'io*. Vol. V. Edited by Arnaldo Di Benedetto. Turin: Einaudi
Fratnik, Marina. 1990. *L'écriture détournée. Essai sur le texte narratif de C.E. Gadda*. Turin: Albert Meynier
Gadda, Carlo Emilio. 1983. *Lettere agli amici milanesi*. Edited by Emma Sassi. Milan: Il Saggiatore
Linati, Carlo. 1931. 'Un umorista.' *L'Ambrosiano*. 9 May
Manzoni, Alessandro. 1968. *Fermo e Lucia*. In Alberto Chiari and Fausto Ghisalberti, eds, *Tutte le opere*, Vol. II. Milan: Mondadori
Rabizzani, Giovanni. 1920. *Sterne in Italia*. Rome: Formiggini
Roscioni, Gian Carlo. 1975. *La disarmonia prestabilita*. Turin: Einaudi
– 1993. 'Gadda cerca casa.' *La Repubblica*, 14 Aug.
Sterne, Laurence. 1949. *Tristram Shandy*. London: Macdonald

Gadda and the Form of the Novel

GUIDO GUGLIELMI

In his preface to the Einaudi edition of Gadda's *Racconto italiano di ignoto del novecento*, or *Cahier d'études* (1924), Dante Isella reminds us that in *Les faux-monnayeurs* (1925) Gide laid the theoretical foundation for a kind of novel no longer conceived as a *tranche de vie* and no longer based on plot, but rather constructed *en largeur* and *en profondeur* (as opposed to *en longueur*). In addition to self-reflection, the materials making up the new novel were the attendant circumstances of its composition. The notebook is itself the novel, to the extent of being a notebook of a notebook. Gide's protagonist and spokesman puts it as follows: 'I would like to include everything in the novel. I shall not cut any of its substance for effect. For more than a year I've been working on it, I put nothing into it that I did not experience and I did not want to include; everything I see, everything I know, everything I learn from others' lives and from my own' (Gide 1958, 1082).

The novel in Gide's formulation is conceived as a heterogeneous work in progress. Whether he himself succeeded in creating such a novel is another question. His reflections on the matter, nevertheless, are pertinent to Gadda.[1]

The nineteenth-century classical novel is a structured, yet organic, work that does not want to appear as an artistic construct; its form, its unifying principle, is its disguise. It presents itself as anti-rhetorical, or rhetorically impalpable, designed wholly in relation to the realities it describes, comments on, and narrates. Although its claims are pluralistic, it creates its own materials, homogenizes and reduces them to a formal and thematic unity, imposing, so to speak, order on chaos. By contrast, the new novel described by Gide belongs to a lineage that dismantles form, which can be called mannerist in the broad sense of the term. The text discloses its own strategies, enlarges particular details, dwells at length on the disorganic and the fragmentary, counterposes disharmony to harmony, converts simplicity into complexity and identity into difference. In its rejection of unity, the pictures it presents are unfinished. For example, Svevo, it is commonly agreed, created in effect only one character and wrote only one novel. But only *La coscienza di Zeno* represents a new kind of novel. Each of its chapters enjoys – the same could be said of Joyce's *Ulysses* – full autonomy in that it recounts the character's entire life on the basis of a single theme. The chapters are not linked together in a functional relationship, organized according to plot, nor do they blend into a superior, 'epic' unity of meaning. Their governing principle is coordination, rather than subordination.

Pirandello called our attention to such a principle in his essay on *Humor*, a text that, in its inventory of humour, details some of the main characteristics of Gadda's art, such as the priority of dialect over rhetorical and humanistic monolingualism, the eccentricity of style, a writing technique based on splitting and doubling, and the humorist's disdain for idealizing syntheses and moral edification. Pirandello believed that the major obstacle to the development of a humorist art in Italy was rhetoric (Pirandello 1960, 107). Lombard Romanticism – the movement to which Manzoni belonged in principle – represented in his view the last stronghold in the battle of the will and emotion against a literature of 'abstract rules and compositional norms' (ibid.). Humorist writers spoke for the unofficial, subterranean line of literature. They were all solitary spirits, intolerant of rhetoric and fond of dialect. Humour, he remarks: 'by virtue of its intimate, specious, essential process, *decomposes* and disintegrates, while art, as we learn in school and from rhetoric, is above all formal *composition*, a logically ordered harmony of parts' (49).

It is then not difficult to understand why in *Meditazione milanese* Gadda refers to Pirandello as il 'nostro grande tragico' (*MM*, 815). In Gadda, the humorist coordination by incongruous contrast, as outlined by Pirandello, becomes coordination by polarity, that is, the disjunction of points of view, and noetic dissociation. I do not mean to imply that Gadda had found already in 1924 the path he was to follow. The *Racconto italiano* is a search for method. We sense the presence of a great writer, but all we have are notes. The poetic art that makes *Quer pasticciaccio* the masterpiece it is has yet to be found.

In 1923, Giuseppe Antonio Borgese had published *Tempo di edificare*, a work which in proposing a return to nineteenth-century narrative models captured the general feeling that the novel's time had come. The *Racconto italiano* is further verification of this new moment. Following the realist and naturalist traditions, Gadda invents numerous characters and explores the possibility of ordering them within an organically conceived plot. The protagonist (Grifonetto), a Fascist architect with whom the narrator identifies (in Gadda's project notes), ends up killing himself, involved as he was, à la Foscolo's *Ortis*, in a tragic emotional and political love affair. Gadda sees his novel as the expression of social and political actuality, a chronicle of contemporary history. But in direct reference to the Manzoni classical narrator, who has to keep the threads of his story together lest they unravel, Gadda experiences the principal difficulties associated with narration. He finds the job difficult, especially the construction of the kinds of plots we find in the 'vecchi romanzi' that the 'nuovi romanzi' disdain (*RI*, 460). Gadda, therefore, is already aware of the existence of new novels, and, while he considers the ways of linking together and activating his narrative materials, he realizes that these materials escape him because they constitute life itself, and life, for him, has no orderly construction, but instead is entangled intrigue ('ingarbugliato intreccio' [ibid.]). Gadda sidesteps, momentarily, the problem of expanding his story through the addition of characters, and prefers to invent several parallel stories to be reserved for future use. His tack is to steer clear of a one-track plot. But it soon is evident that the more his novel grows in length, and the more thematically complex it becomes, the more its end is out of reach. While the stories multiply, only traces remain of their possible conclusions. Gadda is far from realizing a complex design that incorporates all of the stories; all he has given us is a need for inquiry and analysis.

It is symptomatic that Gadda switches his emphasis from plot to point of view. The question he poses is whether the novel should be written *ab interiore* or *ab exteriore*. Indicative of his position is his refusal to consider the use of *ab interiore* dramatic language, like that deployed by Verga in *I Malavoglia*, and he never mentions Flaubert. Nor does it occur to Gadda that there might be an internal logic to reality which only needs to be given voice. But, Gadda no doubt understands, the *tranche de vie* in fact eludes the problem of where to effect the narrative cut. Verga distances an intensely emotional subject matter by adopting the authority of writer, scientist, and quasi-ethnologist who, at the same time, is a participant in the story. Gadda, by contrast, is not interested in such a technique, simply because he does not see reality as an inexorable process of cause and effect. For him, no single series of causes determines whether behaviour is normal or abnormal. The normal and the abnormal coexist; good and evil are reciprocally interactive polarities: 'L'immoralità sussiste in quanto sussiste la moralità e viceversa, il crimine in quanto sussiste il giusto, e reagiscono a vicenda' (RI, 407) [Immorality exists to the degree that morality exists and vice versa, criminal actions to the degree that there are, reciprocally, just actions].

Here, it seems, Gadda is making use of Leibniz, but it is a Leibniz deprived of the concept of theodicy. Gadda does not believe in the vindication of divine justice in the face of the existence of evil. The crucial term of his equation is not God, but rather life itself in all its contradictions and obscurity. Life expresses things and their opposites: 'Se la necessità sociale ha creato un determinato tipo sociale, nella vita rientra anche il dissociale' (ibid.) [If social necessity has created a particular social type, in life we find also the sociopath]. Nor is it simply a case of objective necessity; instead, necessity is internal to life. Gadda has read Leibniz no doubt through the filter of Bergson, for whom life is élan, expansion, but also contraction, arrestment, matter. Life is 'dissoluzione' (470), Gadda states, the loss of organic connections, atavism, ego involution.

Putting aside the question of impersonal narration (the narrator's abstention from judgment, his 'critical reserve,' as it were), we find that Gadda's ideas on narration are still far from being fully developed. Moreover, a narrator who refers to himself as a 'minimissimo Zoluzzo di Lombardia' (AN, 243) could never delight completely in his own lyrical inclinations, nor be content with his own perception of reality or 'momento conoscitivo,' as he puts it. Rather, he has to invade his characters' perception and reasoning, as well as their practical activity (RI, 461). Gadda cites D'Annunzio's Il piacere as an example of a novel written ab interiore. D'Annunzio, however, does not suffice, and it is no wonder, for his novels are the product of a single idea and only one point of view. His is a simple solution unsuitable for the kind of complex, dialectical novel Gadda wants to write: a 'romanzo psicopatico e caravaggesco' (411) [a psychopathic and Caravaggesque novel].

Gadda's reflections on interior and exterior narration fill tormented pages of his notebook. At stake is nothing less than the fundamental question of how to write a polysemic novel:

Passando dal semplice al complesso, dall'uno al molteplice (e io ci dovrò passare essendo il mio romanzo della pluralità), come viene il gioco 'ab interiore' trattandosi di più personaggi? Quali sono le possibilità di sviluppo rappresentativo e drammatico? (ibid., 462)

[Passing from the simple to the complex, from the one to the many (something I have to do because my novel contains a plurality of meanings), how does one create the 'ab interiore' effect with more than one character? As a matter of fact, with numerous characters; what possibilities are there for representation and drama?]

Such a novel demands movement outward to where 'il dotto parla da dotto, il delinquente da delinquente' (ibid., 475) [the learned speaks like the learned, the criminal like a criminal]. The author must put himself into the minds of others, into other alien languages. Here Gadda recalls a primary mechanism, at once magical and mimetic. Otherness reveals the unrealized possibilities within us; the Other is what we are. Thus the masculine includes the feminine, and vice versa: 'noi siamo degli "onni-potenziali"' (463) [we are omnipotential].

The novelist must therefore become the characters he creates, while maintaining his own specific difference, in the same way that becoming the other sex does not eliminate gender barriers: male remains male, female, female. The novelist must intuit what others intuit; he must know his characters' knowledge, while, at the same time, knowing the self-reflective nature of all life from his own narrative standpoint. This is the point when the internal and external novels merge. There is no clear alternative between the two forms of narration. Furthermore, the author may in fact function as character (ibid., 474), with the possibility, however, that later on in the novel the need may arise to create a distinct authorial personality. Thus Gadda reverses completely the naturalist theory of impersonality, opting therefore for a multiperspective interior novel (*ab interiore*), but one having the active presence of the author and, perhaps, even of the author-character (*ab exteriore*).

The novelist Gadda looks to for his narrative model is no doubt Manzoni. As writers, Manzoni and Gadda, to be sure, are worlds apart, yet similar in certain respects. The fact that the 'Apologia manzoniana' resonates in the *Cahier* can only mean that Manzoni for Gadda is an essential point of reference. *I promessi sposi* is always implicitly present in Gadda's narratives. I am not referring to a surface likeness, but rather to Gadda's absorption of stylistic and parodic forms common to Manzoni: chiefly, his critique of language and his tendency towards the macaronic. For example, think of chapter 14 of *I promessi sposi*. It is a day of rebellion and defiance of authority. Renzo refuses to sign the tavern register and gets angry at the custom of signing one's name, feeling it is just another way for the masters to keep the common people in tow. And in reply to his drinking companion's quip ('those gentlemen are the ones who eat all the geese, and they have so many quills to get rid of' [Manzoni 1972, 274]), Renzo remarks 'the fellow must be a poet.' The poet is thus seen from below, and Manzoni takes advantage of Renzo's mockery to poke fun at him from his sophisticated dialogic and ironic point of view. Here Manzoni's 'poet' is no other than the Gaddian 'figurino del vate' (*RI*, 431):[2]

To understand poor Renzo's nonsense, the reader must realize that the common people of Milan, and still more those who live in the surrounding country, do not use the word 'poet' as the gentry do, to mean a consecrated genius, dwelling on Parnassus, a pupil of the Muses. For them, it means a hare-brained, eccentric fellow, whose actions and words are governed, not by reason, but by an odd, penetrating low cunning. For those meddling common people have the nerve to ill treat our language, and give words a meaning poles apart from the real one! What, I ask you, is the connection between being hare-brained and being a poet? (Manzoni 1972, 274-5)

This is an example we all remember. And it is hardly necessary to rehearse, in addition to the remarkable pastiche found in the novel's Introduction, Manzoni's erudite exposition of the edicts, his ironic commentary, Azzeccagarbugli's speech and Renzo's misunderstanding, and the dispatch issued by the Captain of Justice for Renzo's arrest, written in Latin, but interspersed with the vernacular. Thus Renzo's genuinely macaronic speech comes as no surprise at all. Language is deceit, 'trufferia di parole,' as Manzoni puts it in reference to the plague which no one was willing to accept as real:

In the beginning, then, there had been no plague, no pestilence, none at all, not on any account. The very words had been forbidden. Next came the talk of 'pestilent fever' – the idea being admitted indirectly, in adjectival form. Then it was 'not real pestilence' – that is to say, it was a pestilence, but only in a certain sense; not a true pestilence, but something for which it was difficult to find another name. Last of all, it became a pestilence without any doubt or argument – but now a new idea was attached to it, the idea of poisoning and witchcraft, and this corrupted and confused the sense conveyed by the dreaded word which could now no longer be suppressed. (582-3)

Like Manzoni, Gadda too believed that false speech falsifies the spirit, 'la parlata falsa ne falsifica l'animo' (*RI*, 445). And with respect to language, he is equally suspicious, condescendingly subscribing to the general opinion that there is nothing easier than manipulating words or, in more genuinely Gaddian terms, getting stuck 'in un caramello di modi di dire' (*VM*, 451) [in a caramel of idioms].

The similarities between Gadda and Manzoni are not limited to representational modes. They extend to both characterization and plot. For example, in *La Madonna dei Filosofi*, Engineer Baronfo, the bibliophile, comes across a nineteenth-century rarity while perusing the book stalls along the Seine: a *bouquin* in which, in reference to a certain Ismaele Digbens, Gadda remarks: 'Egli fu [...] benemerito della filosofia (dogmatica) e più specialmente di quel ramo di essa chiamato settecentescamente pneumatologia o pneumatica, ovverosia scienza dell'anima' (*MF*, 89) [He was ... accomplished in (dogmatic) philosophy, in particular in that branch called in eighteenth-century terminology pneumatology or pneumatics, meaning the science of the mind]. And he goes on to parody the philosopher's magisterial arguments:

> Era benemerito altresì della filologia e della fisica. Contro il 'lockiano' Burner, accumulò dodici prove dell'esistenza di Dio: quattro chiamò metafisiche, quattro fisiche, e quattro miste [...] Inoltre aveva dimostrato che le bestie non posseggono ragione, salvo in alcuni casi specialissimi [...] ammetteva che esistessero regioni dello spazio vuote di materia, ossia insostanziali [...] Invece il cervello dei minorati, degli idioti nati e dei morti senza battesimo era un pieno o sostanza, ma scarsamente dotato di attitudini modali [...] L'anima concepiva come un essere o sostanza semplice. (89–90)

> [Cavalier Digbens was] also accomplished in philology and physics. In arguing against the 'Lockeian' Burner, he accumulated twelve proofs for the existence of God: four he referred to as metaphysical, four physical and four mixed ... In addition, he had demonstrated that animals do not possess reason, save in some special cases ... He maintained that there existed regions in space deprived of matter, meaning unsubstantial ... While [according to him] the brain of the mentally handicapped, of born idiots, and of those who died without baptism was a fullness or substance, but hardly endowed with modal aptitude ... He conceived of the soul as a being or simple substance.]

Ismaele Digbens believes in the same kind of vacuous syllogisms and scholastic terminology as Manzoni's Don Ferrante who, we know, is the husband of Donna Prassede, herself indirectly the subject of parody by Gadda in the short story 'San Giorgio in casa Brocchi.' Like Donna

Prassede, Countess Giuseppina is an enterprising and zealous woman, watchful of her family's morality (especially her son Gigi's acquaintances), and sensitive to the disorder and crassness of contemporary life. Her brother, zio Agamennone, is a literatus engaged in writing a book that he has promised to Gigi on his nineteenth birthday: a treatise 'da servire di guida, all'entrar della vita, per i giovani delle più cospicue famiglie' (*AccG*, 651) [to serve as a guide for boys from the best families as they enter into adulthood]. But besides zio Agamennone, the target of an amusing pastiche is none other than Cicero himself, author of the *De officiis*, a text, it turns out, of questionable utility for his nephew who, the day he receives his uncle's gift, is introduced to the life of the senses by Jole, the servant who brings him the book. Zio Agamennone is of course a caricature of Cicero, who also had dedicated his book on the subject of duty to his son Marco: 'Cicerone era un classico, lo zio era il neoclassico' (690) [Cicero was a classic, zio Agamennone a neoclassic]. Cicero is for Gadda the Azzeccagarbugli of antiquity who composes 'un minestrone di fagioli stoici, di verze accademiche e di carote peripatetiche' (673) [a minestrone of stoic beans, of academic cabbages and peripatetic carrots] and, moreover, in times of personal and public hardship:

Erano ormai scaduti i bei giorni, quando i mille Renzi d'Italia recavano all'Azzec-cagarbugli urbano [più autorevole forse e più coraggioso dell'autentico] il vistoso imbonimento de' lor grassi capponi. (675)

[The beautiful days had passed when the thousands of Italian Renzos used to bring to their urban Azzeccagarbugli (perhaps more authoritative and courageous than the original) their ostentatious bounty of fat capons.]

Manzoni has no doubt an acute sense of reality's dialectical complexity and is gifted by a subtle sense of humour. Gadda is aware of the way he takes note of the contradictions and obscurity of life, making even the most penetrating of analyses subject to them. But in Manzoni the knot of contradiction is destined to unravel, and obscurity in the last instance is clarified. His novel includes a sphere that transcends history, in which all evil is annulled. This is its romantic vein. At the same time, it is the very inaccessibility of such a sphere that allows Manzoni to foreground history's negative aspects, its profound entanglements, and its factual nudity. Manzoni's great paradox is that his religious spirit is the prime condition of his realism. His humility in front of history prohibits him from elaborating reassuring equations to counter ignorance and evil. Lucidity of mind and a Gaddian sense of the world's complexities make him the great realist and incomparable historian he is. Hence Gadda is right to stress the disharmony of Manzoni's vision and its wholly Pirandellian sense of incongruity:

La mescolanza degli apporti storici e teoretici più disparati, di cui si plasmò e si plasma tuttavia il nostro bizzarro e imprevedibile vivere, Egli ne avvertì le derivazioni contaminantisi in un'espressione grottesca. (*RI*, 591)

[He singled out the grotesque derivations of the mixture of the most disparate of historical and theoretical elements that informed and continue to inform our bizarre and unpredictable lives.]

In spite of such affinities, Manzoni and Gadda offer diametrically opposed forms of writing. Gadda, in fact, is well aware of what separates him from his mentor: 'Manzoni concetto morale-civile / Io concetto più agnostico-umano' (ibid., 397) [Manzoni, moral-civil writer / Me more agnostic-individual oriented]. Here 'agnostico-umano' should be taken to mean 'as within human limits' and 'within the boundaries of the world and time.' For Manzoni, as for all the great classical realists, the reconciliation of the disparate aspects of human life, although never realized, is none the less posited as possible. It is something both ideally necessary, yet impossible to achieve. Manzoni moves in the direction of synthesis; whereas Gadda's totally different itinerary points him in the direction of experimentation, and his novel project provided a solution, although it was not the one he was looking for: 'Uno studio è già una cosa completa, finita, se pur riveste i caratteri del tentativo' (576) [A study is already something complete, finished, even though it may be tentative]. Gadda's theoretical reflections are experimental. Manzoni was the kind of writer who wanted to 'arrivare al pubblico *fino* attraverso il grosso' (*Novella seconda*, in *RR II*, 1318) [to reach a refined public by means of the public at large]. He was motivated, if not by common sense, by a common good sense, and thus he needed to create a *koinè*, a unitary language for a new reading public. In so doing, he adopted a polytonal, monolingual idiom; whereas Gadda employs an explosive plurilingualism. To illustrate, there is an image in Manzoni that can be taken as a supreme example of restraint. In chapter 30, we learn that, after don Abbondio's town had been sacked by the imperial soldiers, the priest returns home to find in his fireplace the charred remains of pieces of furniture all jumbled together. At which point, Manzoni compares these signs of destruction to 'the many implied ideas in an allusive period penned by an elegant writer.' (Manzoni, 1972, 561) This is a good example of Manzoni's art of ironic dissimulation. Gadda would no doubt have made these implied ideas surface. While Manzoni suspends the contradictory aspects of reality in a desire for meaning, Gadda sharpens their definition, rendering them strident or 'spastic.' The former is looking for the superior comprehension of a refined readership; his is a synchronic ideal of possible communication. The latter refuses to accept any communicative economy whatsoever, moving as he does along a diachronic axis. Simply put, Manzoni is a classical writer, who exacts a perfect harmony between literature and communication. Gadda, by contrast, is a mannerist: he deforms language and dismantles words.

At this point it is useful to take up the question of 'expressionism,' since Gadda refers to his writing as an instrument of vengeance:

Nella mia vita di 'umiliato e offeso' la narrazione mi è apparsa, talvolta, lo strumento che mi avrebbe consentito di ristabilire la 'mia' verità, il 'mio' modo di vedere [...] lo strumento in assoluto del riscatto e della vendetta. (*VM*, 503)

[In my life as someone who has been humiliated and offended, narration has often appeared to me as the tool that would give me the opportunity to state the truth of *my* life, of *my* way of seeing things ... the ultimate means of vengeance and vindication.]

This is certainly indicative of Gadda's sense of the intimacy of style (an intimacy that Pirandello attributed to humorist writers). Expressionism, however, as Gadda understands it, rejects the word as mediator, namely, the delay it forces on the urgency of expression and the intensity of experience. Gadda, we repeat, is a mannerist rather than an expressionist. What separates him from early-twentieth-century expressionism is his passion for writing. He is a hyperliterary author (something Manzoni refused to be). Like Joyce, he is an artist of the word and an artist of the novel.

As a writer who jealously, almost pathologically, holds on to his intimacy, Gadda is a most sagacious *artifex*, an extraordinary manipulator of words who plays with language to reveal unpopular truths. Freud's concept of the joke comes to mind in this regard: a joke derives from the pleasure taken in the use of words – from the play of incongruity and equivocation – and is the bearer of deep and secret meanings. A remark from the *Cahier* states 'mantenere omonimità per accrescere confusione' (*RI*, 1269) [maintain homonymy to increase confusion], which is a precise definition of the spastic word. Moreover, it is worth remembering that among the five manners Gadda attributes to himself, the fifth has perhaps not received the attention it deserves:

Finalmente posso elencare la quinta maniera, che chiamerò la maniera cretina, che è fresca, puerile, mitica, omerica, con tracce di simbolismo, con stupefazione – innocenza – ingenuità. E' lo stile di un bambino che vede il mondo (e che sapesse già scrivere). (ibid., 386)

[Finally I can add to the list a fifth manner which I shall name the manner of cretins; it is fresh, puerile, mythical, Homeric, and contains traces of symbolism mixed with wonder, innocence and naïveté. It is the style of a child who sees the world (and could already write).]

Gadda ridicules writers who think of themselves as creators; he does not believe that words are of their very nature 'expressive.' He is a *pasticheur*, someone who works with already existing languages and styles and adopts conventional, accepted linguistic codes in order to undermine them. Take, for example, one of the *disegni* included in *L'Adalgisa*, 'Claudio disimpara a vivere,' where the main character is thrown out of the house of a famous structural engineer and professor on account of his having used the word 'crollato' [collapsed] in reference to a bridge built under the professor's supervision and which caved in while his students were examining its structure, causing several injuries to the students themselves. In addressing the idiocy of the world, Gadda derives his 'timbro perverso' (*VM*, 437) [perverse imprint] – his fundamental, childish and exaggerated tone – from the different dialects and inflections of common speech. It is only through the world's many idioms that he can modulate his own unique voice; his singularly original expression that comes from narrating the expression of others.

Gadda always re-produces the word of the other in ways that range from parody to high-mimetic stylization (his fourth manner of writing). The word is never pure; it never aspires to an original or absolute resonance, but rather echoes spastically; it can thus be regarded as pragmatic and ethical. Unmasking the senselessness of all idioms, Gadda forces the reader to look at reality with a critical eye. Reality tends towards involution, stasis, and paralysis. The idiocy of the world consists in its inoperativeness. In turn, languages tend to crystallize in stereotypes. To be brought back to life, they have to be used dialectically – an artistic and ethically motivated procedure that produces works as reflective and critical as they are creative. It is important, therefore, that we see Gadda's theoretical reflections as an integral part of his work as a writer and not as something found exclusively in the *Meditazione milanese*, the work that provides the foundation and justification for Gadda's grotesque licence. Like all great novelists, Gadda gives us both the novel and its theory; action registered and reflected on. And just as behind a writer like Sterne we find Hume's radical empiricism, behind Gadda we find the early-twentieth-century problematics of knowledge and science. Only in this sense can we understand why his novels are all unfinished at the same time as they are aesthetically complete. The state of being unfinished is itself a formal feature; it adheres to a narrative model that belongs to a tradition whose history is no less rich than its well-made, organically structured counterpart.

As documented in *Meditazione milanese*, Gadda's program of reconstruction entails a complete overhauling of philosophical positions dear to classical rationalism. He corrects his favourite authors, Leibniz and Spinoza, in the theoretical foundation of their thought, where they display their greatest certainty in reason and in the world order:

Qualcuno fra i molti razionalisti del secolo 17°–18° sarà stato certo della 'finitezza in sé' del sistema della conoscenza. Bastano a smentirlo le trovate del secolo 19° e 20°. Non ripetiamo noi lo stesso errore. (*MM*, 743)

[Some of the many rationalists of the seventeenth and eighteenth centuries were no doubt convinced of the 'completeness' of the system of knowledge. The discoveries of the nineteenth and twentieth centuries are sufficient to disprove their arguments. Let us not make the same errors.]

Factual data definitely exist, but they are the effect of millennial fragmentation. The datum is the material trace, the present recognition of past ruins. Although aware of the weight that data carry, Gadda believes, following Bergson, that the world exists in a state of becoming. Only the idle mind represents the world as something at rest and fully defined. Knowledge has no definite and stable limits. Hypotheses can be formulated to determine boundaries, but they are only hypotheses, conceived according to historical contingency. Even the most rigorous of scientific languages is riddled with contradictions:

Ciascuna scienza pone da sé i suoi termini, belli, lindi, certi, finiti, ben pettinati, indiscutibili, senza perplessità, senza angosce, senza nuvolaglie filosofiche e circondata da così indiscutibili e ben pettinati perché, siede Regina del mondo. (*MM*, 740)

[Each science establishes its own terms, neat, pretty, finite, well-groomed, indisputable, unambiguous, stable and philosophically univocal, and surrounded by such indisputable and well-groomed questions, it sits Queen of the world.]

Scientific principles themselves are subject to continual transformation: 'Non esiste una ragione fissa ed eterna con le sue categorie immutabili' (733) [There is no one fixed and eternal reason having categories that are unchangeable]. The systematic arrangement of factual data, rather than leading to certainty, reproduces what is already known; it is not a heuristic device aimed at discovery. Gadda juxtaposes the systematic arrangement of data to investigation and, from this Bergsonian perspective, he takes his leave of nineteenth-century science and positivism.

From Spinoza, summarily stated, Gadda appears to derive the idea of the identity of extension and thought, of the *ordo rerum* and the *ordo idearum*, but in a pragmatic manner for which being is doing (*res* becomes *pragmata*). In fact, when he speaks of a system, he refers at once to a system of theory and a system of things in the world. If 'conoscere significa deformare' [to know means to deform], then the object of knowledge – he writes – is in perennial deformation: 'noi siamo convinti di una cosa sola: che qualcosa accade e per accade intendiamo si "deforma"' (ibid., 742) [we are convinced of one thing alone: that something happens, and that by 'happens' we mean 'is being deformed'].

From Leibniz, Gadda derives his concept of multiplicity: the infinity of monads. Leibniz, however, comes to Gadda, as we have said, via Bergson. His life-world is animated by forces of ascent and involution; it is both a world of forever more complex structures and one that contracts itself, becomes paralysed and breaks up into fragments. The difference between Gadda, on the one hand, and Leibniz and Spinoza, on the other, consists in what they regard respectively as science. Gadda gives priority to change, not systematization. Using the terminology of Thomas Kuhn, we could say that he opts for an 'exceptional,' as opposed to an ordinary, science. In these terms, rational decisions must take into account the changing nature of the data relative to the problem. From the uncertain data, we must pass on to a datum of the second degree. There are no pre-established ends:

In realtà l'idea di un fine (come modello tematico per uno sviluppo o lavoro) implica in sé una conoscenza teoretica del punto da raggiungere, che è assolutamente smentita dai fatti nel caso del bene di 2° grado. (761)

[In reality the idea of an end (as a thematic model to be developed or worked on) implies in itself theoretical knowledge of the point to be reached, which is entirely disproved by the facts in the case of a second-degree good.]

In addition to finalistic conceptions of the world, Gadda rejects also traditional concepts of causality. The universe is a 'flusso deformatore' (ibid., 760) [a flux that deforms]. And in the 'corrente sacra del gran fiume causale' (865) [sacred current of the great causal river] causes are infinite. Thus, with an expression from Musil that parodies Leibniz, we can speak of a principle of 'insufficient' cause. Gadda problematizes his positivist heritage: criticizes its rationalist program by depriving it of its internal logic, thus completely reformulating it.

Every closed system has only the appearance of completeness, for it contains a defect, a gap, that makes it incoherent. As far back as 1928, Gadda had established the principle of the 'impossibile chiusura di un sistema' (ibid., 741) [impossible closure of a system] in opposition to those 'weak-hearted' thinkers who, in need of the reassurance of reason, maintained that the world existed within fixed parameters. But what is the relationship between pre-existing matter and the theorizing mind that gives it order? Order, for Gadda, is but a provisional moment, a pause in the vital flux. Only chaos is absolute. Gadda takes the example of the bookcase: at its centre, the books are in a vertical position; as we move away from the centre, their position becomes more angled until, at the ends of the shelf, it is horizontal. As long as the books support each other they are in a dialectical relation; where that relation does not hold we are at the limit: nothingness (error, darkness, death), determined not by the finiteness of understanding nor by the shortsightedness of theory, but rather by the finiteness of our capacity to act. Reality fades into darkness at the point at which we can no longer act.

In philosophical terms, one could say that for Gadda ethics holds priority over the intellect, praxis over thought. Pure theoretical inquiry is, in fact, possible if the world is conceived already as system; it is impossible if it is subject to being systematized. And systematizing the world carries the burden of experience; it must come to grips with the fundamental instability of experience:

Io non vedo [...] né il fondo dell'abisso né l'assoluto cielo: ma partendo dal traballante ponte della realtà data cerco di estendere la conoscenza nelle (due) direzioni (ascensionale e involutiva.) Aliter: non parto da un culmine assoluto né da un fondo assoluto, ma dal dato che è un punto del coesistente. E l'indagine si allarga come una chiazza d'olio sulla superficie sferica. (ibid., 667)

[I see ... neither the depths of the abyss nor the entire sky. But moving ahead from the rickety bridge of reality as it is given I try to extend my knowledge in (two) directions (outwardly and inwardly). *Aliter*: I do not move from either an absolute end or an absolute origin, but from the datum which is a point of coexisting forces. And the investigation broadens like a drop of oil on a round surface.]

Here, no doubt, instead of Manzoni, we have the 'più agnostico-umano' Gadda.

The *Meditazione milanese*, however, is not just a philosophical text. Its rational arguments are cast as narratives that are 'intellectual' in the Pirandellian sense, thus not subject to the kinds of spontaneous emotional outbursts and automatism characteristic of the mature Gadda. It is a writing mediated by theory and developed from lived experience. The *Meditazione milanese* gives sufficient proof that Gadda, with his belief in deformation, could not follow in the classical tradition and thus was left with no other recourse than to abandon his novel of Grifonetto and Maria. Compact narrative structures could not satisfy him. The task of activating and linking together his chosen materials would turn out to be unproductive. Already the proliferation of characters and the confusion of names heralded another project: a kind of story that included discontinuous 'cognitive moments,' as Gadda would phrase it, therefore at once massing together and dissolving narrative realities, as opposed to creating well-calibrated combinations. In the *Racconto italiano* Gadda already announces his poetics of entanglement. Let us return for a moment to Manzoni. We know that although Gadda admired the final corrected version of *I promessi sposi*, he did not share the rationale behind Manzoni's process of revision. It was the mixing not the sorting out of things that interested Gadda the most; he did not share Manzoni's idea of final perfection. He would want the corrected version of the novel revised, and the revised text still corrected once again, and so forth (*MM*, 712). Of course, Manzoni was the first to be convinced of his novel's imperfections; he believed in literature a lot less than Gadda did. But what separates him significantly from Gadda is his belief in the existence of an appropriate and suitable literary form that can be achieved.

Manzoni, like all great classical writers, believed in formal perfection, just as he believed in one substantial truth in which all partial verities are justified and become law. Whether we refer to this law as God, or World Spirit, or destiny and natural necessity, does not matter. Formal perfection is an ideal to be pursued. The writer's task is to capture as much as possible of this truth. Gadda speaks of systems and takes his position against them; in the same way he speaks of totalities, meaning a more comprehensive reality, but he excludes the possibility of attaining such a totality. Heuresis, he writes:

è dunque l'autodeformazione del reale [...] e sembra non possedere modelli o temi teoretici finali, non aver fini in senso teoretico stretto (chiamate finali) pur 'andando verso il diverso.' Potremo chiamare questo diverso il 'vieppiù differenziato' [...] sebbene esista anche, come ho lumeggiato, il venir meno, il rilassarsi dei sistemi di relazioni: (cioè il deformarsi in regresso). (ibid., 783)

[is therefore the self-deformation of reality ... and it appears to have no models or theoretical objectives, no ends in the strict theoretical sense of final causes, yet it 'moves towards difference.' We could call this a differential surplus ... even though there exists, as I have pointed out, a lessening, or slackening of the relational system, that is, a regression of deformation.]

There is therefore no closure, no finality. All movement progresses towards difference and differentiation; regression towards that which is undifferentiated or unreal. Gadda thus can only work with fragments. His two novels, *Quer pasticciaccio* and *La cognizione del dolore*, can be regarded as a unification of fragments, composed and selected according to the principle, stated beforehand in the *Racconto italiano*, of polarization and differentiation. He expands his writing not by means of linear syntagmas but by the massing together of paradigms. It is important to pay attention to the meaning of the fragment in Gadda, where the boundary between cosmos and chaos is constantly shifting to the point where all closure is precluded. The fragment is not, as with the Romantics, a part of the whole, but rather a fragment of a non-existing totality that cannot be ideally posited. The fragment is the structure itself. Narrative form is therefore nothing other than a pause. The object in itself, Gadda writes later on, is but the 'corpo morto della realtà, il residuo fecale della storia' (*VM*, 630) [the corpse of reality, the fecal residue of history].

Corpse and residue are also the self. Gadda does not spare his contempt for the illusions of selfhood: the masks we wear, the consistency in which we take pride. The self is a constantly changing, plural entity. The role of the narrator is also posed in these terms. In the *Racconto italiano* it is a question that concerns not only the relationship between narrator and character, but also that between narrator and reader. According to what criterion are characters to be judged? How do they gain the respect of the reading public? With what authority does the narrator address the reader? In this regard, Gadda distinguishes among three modes of narration.

First of all there is the Homeric mode. Homer speaks to a public that is hearing things it already knows. By recounting them, he makes his public remember. As representative of the mind of a single humanity, he realizes what is universally human. But since we do not live in Homeric times, we do not partake of one unified humanity. Another example he gives is Dante. Dante can speak with supreme authority by virtue of the strength of his personality. But 'una pesante casa non può poggiare sopra una *pietra mal ferma*' (*RI*, 477, my emphasis) [a heavy house cannot rest on a wobbly foundation]. And 'il signor grigiastro qualunque dei qualunqui' [the insignificant man in the masses], as Gadda refers to himself hypothetically, is not a Dante. While the Homeric mode is impossible to achieve, the second manner can be found in writers who become advocates of common belief, that is to say, fashionable writers of the moment. Then 'il termine universale può essere sostituito da un termine non universale, ma a larga base' (479) [the universal term can be substituted by a term that, although not universal, has a broad base]. But this is entertainment literature, and Gadda rejects it the same way he rejects the 'Straussism' of D'Annunzio (sparkling images meant to dazzle and seduce), a writer whom he otherwise respects. But there is a third mode in which the 'qualunque dei qualunqui,' the man in the mass, confirms his own existence. The most powerful of modern authors has become the historical and moral consciousness of such a 'man without qualities.' He, as writer (and character), is the wobbly foundation on which the unstable house is built. Not being able to exit from the infinite web of relations, he cannot assume the position of judge; his opinions are one with his reactions and hold no judicial authority. His irony, therefore, is self-irony, his parody, self-parody. His words echo the word of the Other (all the ancient and modern languages of the world) according to an intention both his own and provisional; he speaks in two spasmodic voices.

Gadda speaks of his own identity as being that of someone lost and wounded, 'dissociato noetico' (*VM*, 431) [intellectually dissociated], conflating affective and intellectual experience, *pathos* and *logos*. Reason is affected by emotion; the *logos* does not exist outside of life's flux:

D'intorno a me, d'intorno a noi, il mareggiare degli eventi mortiferi, il dolore, il lento strazio degli anni. Il concetto di volere si abolisce, nel lento impossible. L'oceano della stupidità. (ibid.)

[Everywhere around me, around us, the tide of dying things, sorrow, the slow dismemberment of (passing) years. The concept of willing is abolished, in impossible delay. The ocean of stupidity.]

Here we have the melancholic side of Gadda that exhibits his sense of mortality and that unites the sublime and the grotesque under the sign of excess. His 'awareness of grief' is the awareness of absolute error, of 'the ocean of stupidity,' of darkness. In Gadda's world, it is absurd to try to give order to life's negative (regressive) pulsations. At a certain point, reason is found to be infinitely at fault. Comedy is transformed into its opposite; laughter, in all its festivity and vitality, blends with mannerist sorrow.

Translated by Robert S. Dombroski

Notes

1 On Gide and Gadda, see Bertone 1993, 11–14.
2 On Manzoni's parody, see Raimondi 1990, 81–110.

References

Bertone, Manuela. 1993. *Il romanzo come sistema. Molteplicità e differenza in C.E. Gadda*. Rome: Editori Riuniti
Gide, André. 1958. *Romans, récits, soties et oeuvres lyriques*. Paris: Gallimard
Manzoni, Alessandro. 1972. *The Betrothed*. London: Penguin Books
Pirandello, Luigi. 1960. *Saggi, poesie, scritti varii*. Edited by Manlio Lo Vecchio Musti. Milan: Mondadori
Raimondi, Ezio. 1990. *La dissimulazione romanzesca. Antropologia manzoniana*. Bologna: Il Mulino

Gadda and the Baroque

ROBERT S. DOMBROSKI

An obsession with knots, a penchant for extravagant verbal chemistry and intricate style, a desire to distort and pervert, a philosophical intelligence that seeks out obscure correspondences, and a fascination with labyrinthine narrative structures, fragmentation, unpredictability, and obscurity, these are the characteristic features of Gadda's art that, from early on in his literary career, earned him the title of 'baroque,' a designation he vigorously defended against all pejorative associations, not the least being false and grotesque pedantry and, what amounts to the same, an excessive concern for artifice and ingeniousness. Gadda's defence of style, which serves both to ward off potential detractors and to set himself apart from his contemporaries, takes three intersecting tacks. The baroque (equated with the macaronic) is Gadda's weapon against all that in life and in literature is counterfeit, artificial and spurious: against the hollowness of 'la retorica dei buoni sentimenti' (VM, 434; my emphasis) [the rhetoric of noble feelings] and 'le parole della frode' (VM, 496; my emphasis) [the language of fraud]. It is also his means of avenging what he calls repeatedly a cruel destiny of unspeakable hardships (CU, 119–22). And, most importantly for this discussion, he sees the baroque as a quality of external reality; it exists in things, in history, and in nature.

Of the arguments Gadda employs in defence of his baroque manner, the most developed is contained in the imaginary dialogue with his editor ('L'editore chiede venia del recupero chiamando in causa l'Autore') that prefaces the first Einaudi edition of La cognizione del dolore (1963). Faced with the spectacle of lies, deceptions, and disorder of a diseased society (another commonplace of the historical baroque), the writer, Gadda argues, is stirred to derision which occasionally takes on hysterical proportions. His polemics, mockery, intolerance, general cruelty, and misanthropy, his 'baroqueness' and 'grotesqueness,' are all affected by the radically contradictory and uncertain reality in which the life of the subject unfolds. Thus, if Gadda is 'baroque,' he is so not on account of a love for artifice and ornament, but rather because the world itself is baroque; as a writer, his task is to represent the reality of its baroqueness:

Il barocco e il grottesco albergano già nelle cose, nelle singole trovate di una fenomenologia a noi esterna: nelle stesse espressioni del costume, nella nozione accettata 'comunemente' dai pochi o dai molti: e nelle lettere umane o disumane che siano: grottesco e barocco non ascrivibili a una premeditata volontà o tendenza espressiva dell'autore, ma legati alla natura e alla storia [...] Talché il grido-parola d'ordine 'barocco è il G.!' potrebbe communicarsi nel più ragionevole e più pacato asserto 'barocco è il mondo, e il G. ne ha percepito e ritratto la baroccaggine.' (*CD*, 760)

[The baroque and the grotesque dwell already in things, in the individual discoveries of a phenomenology external to us: in our very customs, in the 'common' sense of the few or the many: and in letters, be they humane or unhumane. Baroque and grotesque are not attributable to the author's premeditation or expressive propensities, rather they are linked to nature and history ... So much so that the rallying call 'G. is baroque!' could be expressed in the more reasonable and serene assertion 'the world is baroque, and G. has perceived and depicted its baroqueness.']

And to those scholars who view the baroque as a category of the spirit or historical constant (Croce and Eugenio d'Ors, for example), Gadda remarks that:

La natura e la storia, percepite come un succedersi di tentativi di ricerca, di conati, di ritrovati, d'un Arte e o d'un Pensiero che trascendono le attuali nostre possibilità operative, o conoscitive, avviene faccino a lor volta un passo falso, o più passi falsi: che nei loro conati, vale a dire nella ricerca e nell'euresi, abbino a incontrare la sosta o la deviazione 'provvisoria' del barocco, magari del grottesco. (ibid.).

[Nature and History are perceived as the continual inquiry (attempts, corrections and reformulations) of an Art or Mind that transcends our current operative and cognitive faculties, at times falling into error or errors. In the effort to understand, namely, through the investigatory or heuristic process, one encounters the baroque, even the grotesque, an obstacle or momentary detour.]

Gadda goes on to say that the question of the relation between order (Arte e Pensiero) and disorder (the baroque and the grotesque) is internal and reciprocal. The baroque (disorder, disharmony, deformation, etcetera) is therefore not the opposite of order but a deep structure within a complex system. Faced with of this 'universal reality,' the subject of knowledge and discovery is caught in the labyrinth ('intrappolatosi in reiterate impasses'), and once he appears with great difficulty to have found an exit ('divincolatosi poi a mala esperienza esperita'), he becomes entangled again and once again he attempts to free himself ('se ne sbroglia del tutto e di nuovo tende la via libera'); so he moves along a pathway towards 'la infinita, nel tempo e nel numero, suddivisione-specializza-zione-obiettivazione del molteplice' [the infinite, in time and number, subdivision-specialization-objectification of multiple realities].

What may appear here as random speculation are propositions constituting a philosophical position, developed early on, in the *Meditazione milanese*, into a cognitive mode that justifies a particular kind of *affect* or emotional reaction to the world, disclosed even in Gadda's earliest fictions and in the manifest anxieties of the *Giornale di guerra e di prigionia*. The self-reflexivity, parody, distortion, and infinite entanglements and references that characterize all of Gadda's texts, their excesses and instabilities, as well as their tendency to break down or dissipate in repetition, are at once symptoms and procedures, designed to distance and differentiate the writing subject from the national (and popular) cultural activity of his time. In certain respects, Gadda's writings (criticism and essays included) embody what, in a perceptive study of the Spanish literary baroque, has been called an 'aristocratic fetish of a highly wrought art form' (Beverley 1993, 59). The comparison is of course by way of analogy and could be extended to other forms of literary modernism (D'Annunzio, for example). In Gadda's case, we are obviously not dealing with exactly the same kind of ideological practice that characterizes the different forms of the historical baroque.[1] Yet, there is little doubt that Gadda's texts – as opposed to *prosa d'arte* and neorealism – are intended to escape the understanding of the masses and that they place themselves in stark opposition to popular bourgeois cultural practices by virtue of the uniqueness of the writer's biography and experience, which accounts for the singularity of his style:

Come non lavoro. Che dà egual frutto, a momenti, nella vicenda oscillante d'uno spirito fugitivo e aleatorio, chiamato dall'improbabile altrettanto e più che dal probabile: da una puerizia atterrita e dal dolore e dalla disciplina militare e di scuola delabante poi verso il nulla, col suo tesoro d'oscurità e d'incertezze. (*VM*, 427)

[How I do not work. Which gives equal results, at times, in the unsteady life of a transitory and alterable spirit, summoned by the improbable more than by the probable: by a terrifying childhood, by grief and by military and academic discipline stumbling then towards nothingness, with its stock of obscurity and uncertainty.]

This quotation begins an essay, published in *Paragone* in 1949, written by Gadda in response to an invitation extended to several writers to expound on the principles behind their literary practice. It is inscribed, to use the words Contini reserves for all of Gadda's essays, on the 'chaotic register of viscous darkness' (1963, 14). The experience it describes, because of Gadda's usual restraint before the concrete factuality of his life, hovers on the border between history and myth.

The self which Gadda constructs throughout his fiction can in many respects be termed a 'baroque self,' in that it stretches a life beyond its precise historical limits into infinite partitions or inflections. This life does not crystallize in independent phases or points, but blends into a series of figures inscribed in propositions predicated of an individual subject. The numerous reflections on the authorial self that we find in Gadda's writings from Captain Gaddus and Engineer Baronfo to Gonzalo Pirobutirro, Don Ciccio Ingravallo, and Alì Oco De Madrigal constitute a folded-out personal unity, a repository of propositions that contribute to the modelling of a fully shaped allegorical figure, a figure that both reveals and contains (protects) the author.

An approach to Gadda from the standpoint of his baroque aesthetic is justified by the importance the baroque holds both in the genesis of modernity and, in particular, for post-structuralist criticism. In this respect, Gilles Deleuze's *Le Pli. Leibniz et le Baroque* (1988) [*The Fold: Leibniz and the Baroque* (1993)] carries special weight because it elaborates the notion of a neobaroque[2] in relation to one of Gadda's more important philosophical sources.[3]

Deleuze's discussion of Leibniz's philosophy provides some valuable insights into Gadda's own readings of the *Monadologie* and the *Théodicée*, particularly into what Deleuze calls the baroque concept of the story. Deleuze argues that Leibniz's philosophy can be conceived as an allegory of the world. He regards the *Théodicée* as a foundational narrative of the Roman Empire, in which Sextus and Lucretia, rather than being symbolic abstractions of particular concepts, contain those concepts within their figures; their story 'combines figures, inscriptions or propositions, individual subjects or points of view with their propositional concepts' (Deleuze 1993, 174). For Deleuze, Leibniz has thus provided a paradigm for the baroque story: 'The Baroque introduces a new kind of story in which ... description replaces the object, the concept becomes narrative, and the subject becomes point of view or subject of expression' (ibid.). Although these traits may be found in all allegories, they stand out in Gadda's work as distinctive formal features that make possible the absolute conflation of subjective and objective perspectives, a *modus operandi* that produces the 'Omnis in unum' effect of stories enclosed one in the other as different modulations of the same thematic refrain. The basic unity of *La cognizione del dolore* and *Quer pasticciaccio brutto de via Merulana* consists, in fact, not in the narration of realities that form a relevant body of knowledge, but rather in the descriptive process that engulfs those realities, suffocating them to a point where they drop out altogether as signifying elements. Georg Lukàcs's well-known distinction between narrating and describing would certainly not obtain in Gadda's case. For description in Gadda is neither digression nor static contemplation; nor is it a question of whether description is extrinsic (naturalism) or intrinsic (realism) to his plots. The simple reason is that there are no plots in Gadda, no centre from which the narrator can stray. In his narratives, description of the object world is itself the story and thus acts as a surrogate for another story that has been withdrawn or repressed. Description also takes the place of plot and character, overturning the classical functions of setting and mood. For example, *La cognizione del dolore* begins with what looks like an attempt to establish a narrative frame of reference (the setting for the action). Yet the described world of Maradagàl is so replete with objects that attract the narrator's eye that it cannot hold its own as the centre of attention. As soon as it is evoked, it gives way in rapid succession to a multitude of solicitations. Take, for example, the idea of crop diseases, which sets in motion a description that exceeds the objective referential frame, taking on a life of its own:

Paventata, piú che ogni altra [malattia], la ineluttabile 'Peronospera bazanvoisi' del Cattaneo: essa opera, nella misera pianta, a un disseccamento e sfarinamento delle radicine e del fusto, proprio nei mesi dello sviluppo: e lascia ai disperati e agli affamati, invece del granone, un tritume simile a quello che lascia dietro di sé il tarlo, o il succhiello, in un trave di rovere. In talune plaghe bisogna poi fare i conti anche con la grandine. A quest'altro flagello, in verità, non è particolarmente esposta la involuta pannocchia del banzavois, ch'è una specie di granoturco dolciastro proprio a quel clima. Clima o cielo, in certe regioni, altrettanto grandinifero che il cielo incombente su alcune mezze pertiche della nostra indimenticabile Brianza: terra, se mai altra, meticolosamente perticata. (CD, 571)

[Feared above all others was the ineluctable 'Peronospera banzavoisi' mentioned by Cattaneo: it causes in the hapless plant, a drying and crumbling of the little roots and stem in the very months of development: and for the desperate and the hungry, it leaves, instead of corn, a powder similar to that left behind by the termite, or a gimlet, in an oak beam. In certain regions hail also had to be taken into consideration. This last scourge, to tell the truth, doesn't have a great effect on the wrapped ear of the banzavois, which is a kind of sweetish maize proper to that climate. Climate or sky, in certain regions, as hail bearing as the sky that hangs over certain half-acres of our own unforgettable Brianza: a land, if there ever was one, carefully acred out. (AG, 3)]

Using Deleuze's terminology, we can refer to such inflections in the narration as descriptive folds. The line they determine is not finite, that is to say, the solicitation is not delimited or partitioned in the form of an illustration or particularization of a general idea, but instead moves between the surface of the narrative and some interior space, or subtext, bringing the spirit of the author in contact with the matter summoned to express it. It forms, in other words, a texture that bridges the dichotomy between author and text. Description in Gadda is then a means of reconciling the inside and the outside, the high and the low (Deleuze 1993, 35), spheres, independent of one another, that through description are integrated.

In terms of literary architecture, Gaddian description is the façade consisting of an explosive, exacerbated language; a complicated decoration shrouding a closed interiority, incapable of direct speech or communication. In La cognizione such a process is materialized in the metatextual referent of the Pirobuttiro villa, whose walls contain literally the autobiographical soul of the narrative. Behind them, the inseparable existences of Mother and Son unfold and fold out into the world. Put succinctly, the autobiographical object, the self as centre and principle of unity, is replaced by description, intertwined into the labyrinth of matter; it unwinds descriptively from the standpoint of others, including the narrator who takes leave of his own autobiographical identity in adopting the third person to force a separation between himself and Gonzalo. The motif of the Nistitúos folds out into the bizarre, carnivalesque account of the life of Gaetano Palumbo alias Pedro Mahagones alias Manganones, which in turn folds into the story of the merchant, which in turn folds into the description of Peppa, Beppina, and Pina, then into that of the villas ('Di ville, di ville!; di villette [...]').

Within these descriptive folds we find the multifold 'pleats of matter,' an indefinite stretching out of the description's constituent parts to form a labyrinth. These pleats envelop what has now become the object of narration, forming 'little vortices in a maelstrom' (Deleuze 1993, 8). To illustrate fully the stylistic complexity of such a procedure would exceed the limits of this essay. Let it suffice to look at one unit or 'pleat' (itself relatively lengthy) of the story of Gaetano Palumbo (Pedro), the Nistitúos guard assigned to watch over the Pirobuttiro villa: the physical description of his face:

Era, sopra la corpulente imponenza della persona, e sul collo chiuso dell'uniforme, una faccia larga e paterna dai corti baffi, a spazzola e rossi, dal naso breve, diritto: gli occhi affossati, piccoli, lucidi, assai mobili con faville acutissime e d'una luce di lama nello sguardo, cui la visiera attenuava ma non poteva spegnere interamente. Quando levava il berretto, come a lasciare vaporare la cabeza, allora la fronte appariva alta, ma piú stretta degli zigomi, e fuggiva con alcune modulazioni di tinta nella cupola del cranio calvo, bianco, e, a onor del vero, assai pulito, cioè senza lentiggine di crassume e di polveri impastati assieme. Allora, senza visiera, gli occhi rimanevano soli al comando, ferivano l'interlocutore con una espressione di dover assolutamente pagare qualche cosa, una specie di multa virtuale, per legge: perché così voleva la legge: ricevendone in adeguato concambio uno scontrino rosa, o cilestro, come ricevuta, spiccato da un libercoletto a matrici ch'egli sapeva estrarre da una tasca laterale della giubba con una naturalezza straordinaria. Tutti, o almeno quasi tutti, d'altronde, nella zona di Lukones, s'erano messi d'impegno e di buona volontà, visto che pagare avevano pagato, a farsi un'idea di quelle pericolose ronde nel buio: e avevano finito per mandar giú anche l'importanza e la delicatezza dell'incarico che gravava sulle sue spalle, per quanto è lunga e buia la notte, e tutti ormai ci credevano, all'importanza: dacché non sempre la buona fama di un uomo, nel Sud America, o la notorietà di un funzionario, dipende dalla inutilità delle sue mansioni. (*CD*, 576)

[It was, above the imposing corpulence of his person, and resting on the buttoned collar of his uniform, a broad and paternal face with a clipped red bush of a moustache, and a short, straight nose: the eyes were sunken, tiny, glistening, darting, with the bright sparks of a blade's flash in his gaze, attenuated by his visor, which however couldn't extinguish it entirely. When he took off his cap, as if to let his cabeza steam, his forehead then appeared, high but narrower than the cheekbones, and receding with some modulations of hue into the dome of the white, bald cranium, which was, truth to tell, very clean, that is without freckles of dust and grease kneaded together. Then, visorless, his eyes remained alone in command; they wounded the interlocutor with an expression of demand and expectation; one had the sensation of absolutely having to pay something, a sort of virtual fine, by law – because this is what the law required – receiving in return for it a pink or pale-blue chit, as a receipt, detached from a little book with counter chits which he could draw from a side-pocket of his tunic with extraordinary naturalness. Everyone, or almost everyone, in the Lukones area had tried hard and with all the will in the world, since they had paid up, to form an idea of those perilous rounds in the dark: and they also had swallowed the importance and the delicacy of the assignment that weighed on his shoulders, through all the length and darkness of the night, and everybody now believed in it, in this importance: since a man's good name, in South America, or an official's notoriety doesn't always derive from the uselessness of his duties. (*AG*, 10–11)]

The units of this description are stages that allow the reader to pass from one level to another: from the material phenomenon (the face) to the inside (the soul) to the outside (the world). Each unit contains several subunits (smaller pleats, potentially infinite in number). What is baroque about the portrait is that each of its units (or subunits) is an open linkage, not governed by any one principle of narrative identity that fixes it with a particular function in relation to an overriding (metaphysical) unity. Rather each unit is a kind of vein that gives definition to an unfinished block of marble – the metaphor is also Deleuze's – but does not determine its form; its destiny is repetition and endless proliferation. Pedro's story can go on indefinitely, given Gadda's belief in the interrelatedness of things and the fact that it contains, instead of one specific object, only differential relations. In fact, when it incorporates the story of the cloth merchant, displacing itself onto another potentially endless trajectory, the authorial voice comically intervenes, stating it is time to stop – 'esaurire questa stupida storia e potercene sbarazzare una volta per tutte' (*CD*, 580) [exhaust this stupid story and be rid of it once and for all (*AG*, 15)].

Another distinguishing feature of this description is that it is infinitely receptive to authorial solicitation and thus capable of being deflected spontaneously. This trait is sustained through the unspecified citation of a stylistic model (Manzoni), repeatedly destabilized through comic interruption (e.g., 'Quando levava il berretto, come a lasciare vaporare la cabeza, allora la fronte appariva alta ...') or through authorial glosses ('a onor del vero,' 'perché così voleva la legge,' 'o almeno quasi tutti') that establish the parodic tone of the description.

In *Quer pasticciaccio* the same holds true. Description operates to transform what is planned as a detective story, thus what is meant to conform to certain laws of equilibrium and order, into a pastiche. The elements of plot, all present initially in the text, are continually made subject to secondary linkages that end up by destabilizing a seemingly organic structure, converting it into incoherent aggregates that depend for their form on authorial impulses conditioned by the solicitations evoked by material references, the most notorious being that of Mussolini and Fascism. Contrary to traditional crime fiction, *Quer pasticciaccio* proliferates, rather than condenses, meaning. The text exceeds its pre-established frame, radiates in every direction, invading, it seems, every surface. The generic convention, according to which the formal coordinates (crime, criminal, detective, collectivity) define the intersecting lines of final causes and moral necessity, converges with a material universe of disorder. Each of these coordinates is assimilated to an 'infinite curvature of inflection' (Deleuze 1993, 101) in such a way that every one of them expresses a complex of differential relations, a general diffusion of meanings within a structure in which meanings are normally condensed. This is what Calvino is referring to when he describes *Quer pasticciaccio* as an inquiry into the world conceived as a 'system of systems' in which 'every element of a system contains within it another system; each individual system in turn is linked to a genealogy of systems. A change in any particular elements results in a breakdown of the whole.'[4] It is useful to emphasize, however, that each element of the convention or system, if considered abstractly, is a world unto itself, a designated zone of meaning and inquiry, a 'pre-established harmony,' which submits to the impression, and thus expression, of authorial impulse. Hence, through desciption, the object of narration spills over the boundaries of its frame (take, for example, the initial description of Don Ciccio) to join a broader cycle of meaning.

To illustrate the relationship of concept to object in Gadda, it is useful to consider, albeit schematically, the composition of the objective world in realist fiction, and how such a world is expressed through its characters. Manzoni's Don Abbondio, for example – a figure, incidentally, particularly dear to Gadda – is one among many object realities the author creates to convey a particular sense of the world. As the personification of moral weakness and private interest, his form constitutes a particular frame that, existing side by side with other frames, operates to complete the systematic expression of the world as Manzoni sees it. Although Don

Abbondio interacts with other characters, he retains his specific difference and never encroaches on their space. He speaks in a voice totally commensurate to his moral figure and in his actions combines momentary reality and universal concept. The narration of this concept (Abbondio in all of his negative and lovable qualities) is, of course, the character in all its being and action, distinct in quality and extension from all the other characters and subsumed to Manzoni's moral and aesthetic ideas. The narrative, or story, constitutes, in other words, a universal frame that incorporates particular concepts of reality; the horizontal axis is centred in the vertical.

In Gadda's baroque world, the individualized realist frame loses all of its autonomy. The unity of the one in the many is replaced by a point of view that projects downward from the top, permeating the text at every level. What appear as fragments or unspecified spaces are coordinated by means of the overriding concept of entanglement. This gives rise to a vision of the world in which all boundaries are transgressed and where the authorial self is externalized into a series of figures and events.

In *La cognizione*, the concept (of entanglement) that engulfs the narrative is conveyed first and foremost by the novel's title. For it directs the reader's attention to the subject in which the faculty of acquiring knowledge resides, while at the same time emphasizing knowledge as process: the continual perception of the knowing subject. At the same time, it posits the existence of a referent that defies specification because it is one and the same with life itself. Hence the title, rather than referring to a particular object of narration, evokes the unique condition of the point of view from which that narration will unfold. There is an inevitable cause of human suffering that the subject alone can understand: he alone has the gift of deep perception into a complicated and confused reality; he alone has the insights and the power to extend his concept of chaos into narration.[5]

In *Quer pasticciaccio*, we see even more clearly how entanglement gives texture to the narration and thus constitutes its unifying principle. Right from the beginning the narrative shows its own capacity for radiating in all directions in the search of some one thing that will define a specific object of perception. But immediately we realize that such a procedure has been sanctioned by the point of view of Don Ciccio, the very character it is engaged in describing:

Sosteneva, fra l'altro, che le inopinate castastofi non sono mai la consequenza o l'effetto che dir si voglia d'un unico motivo, di una causa al singolare: ma sono come un vortice, un punto di depressione ciclonica nella coscienza del mondo, verso cui hanno cospirato tutta una molteplicità di causali convergenti. *(QP,* 16)

[He maintained, among other things, that unforeseen catastrophes are never the consequence or the effect, if you prefer, of a single motive, of *a* cause singular; but they are rather like a whirlpool, a cyclonic point of depression in the consciousness of the world, to which a whole multitude of converging causes have contributed. *(AM,* 5)]

Hence the narrative point of view is taken from the detective whose work is destined never to finish because, like that of the narrator, his philosophy raises the fabric of the world up to infinity. The 'nodo,' 'groviglio,' 'garbuglio,' or 'gnommero' can never be disentangled, but just folded out endlessly. The narration, in other words, because it is one and the same with its own guiding concept, can never be concluded, but only interrupted.[6]

If we shift our focus from the concept that becomes the narration to the subject of the narration, we see that the authorial point of view and the subject of narrative are one and the same. The manner in which they are linked, however, is not typical of either classical autobiographical narratives or 'autobiografismo.'

By the term 'subject' I am referring to the text's controlling consciousness, the point of view that produces the reality to which it sub-jects the reader. In other words, this 'subject' creates the text's ideology by providing the knowledge necessary for placing the reader in a position appropriate to an understanding of the story. It does so by elaborating a discourse that gives the story its particular form. The story's discursive organization is then subject to a metadiscourse which supervises and regulates the development of the elements and procedures it adopts in order to convey its vision. Such a 'vision' in classical narrative is motivated by a desire for unity.[7] In traditional autobiographical narrative, the same relation between discourse and story holds true. The self (or the surrogate that stands in for the self in 'autobiografismo') that speaks is the subject that organizes the text to give it its patina of truth and spontaneity.

In Gadda, the controlling subject occupies a position of control, but it cannot in effect control the meaning it produces. The position of the author is generally assumed by the narrator who, while attempting to organize the materials of his story, cannot distance himself sufficiently from them in order to promote either the illusion of objectivity or, by contrast, of subjective involvement. His attachment to the objects of his narration can best be described as 'schizophrenic.' The object world is for him the source of confusion. It contains a multiplicity of positions which he cannot control by excluding or absorbing. His status as narrator is problematic because he cannot sustain the discourse he has initiated. And it is equally problematic because it cannot maintain its position of control. As a result, the authorial voice, or metadiscourse, to which the narrator's point of view is subject, becomes itself subjected to the material impulses it has generated, literally left to the mercy of the world it has created. Put differently, the inner world of the author prevents the novel from being written for the simple reason that it undermines any and all pretensions to unity or resolution. The effect is that the subject has difficulty focusing on the object; it cannot establish the correct distance from which to view the object; it is unable to establish a criterion of relevance that may serve to underpin its ideology. While Gadda's texts express conservative political and social beliefs, they do so without a principle of ideological transcription, that is, those beliefs are not represented 'innocently' as reality or truth. The breakdown in the construction of subjectivity is a breakdown in the epistemology that makes ideological closure possible. In the baroque conflation of the subject with the subject of expression, the burden of truth is borne not by a controlling consciousness but rather by expression.

Through expression, the object of narration in Gadda takes on a new status. It no longer refers back to a content that has been given an objective shape. Instead it exists in a continual state of modulation determined by its convergence with the narrating subject. The object is, in other words, at the mercy of the teller of the story who envelops it in the constant flux of his moods and impulses. The result of this diffusion of the subjective viewpoint into the object is the transformation of the character into a labyrinth or knot.[8]

To illustrate this process let us take the figures of Son and Mother in the second chapter of Part Two of *La cognizione*. The narrator begins by describing an image of Gonzalo: his silhouette as seen on the terrace from the open French door of the villa: 'L'alta figura di lui si disegnò nera nel vano della porta-finestra, di sul terrazzo, come l'ombra d'uno sconosciuto' (*CD*, 685) [His tall form was outlined, black, in the frame of the French window, from the terrace, like the shadow of a stranger (*AG*, 148)]. The initial effect of an objective perspective established by a would-be omniscient eye is immediately lost by the incorporation into its position of the mother's emotional response at the sight of her son whom she regards as a stranger in her house. The narration then folds out into a wholly lyrical reference: 'Diòscuri splendidi sopra una fascia d'amaranto, lontana, nel quadrante di bellezza e di conoscenza: fraternità salva!' (CD, 685) [Splendid Dioscuri over a stripe of amaranth, distant, in the quadrant of beauty and of knowledge: saved fraternity! (AG, 148)]. The narrator has now become the dark figure in the window, who, gazing at the constellation Gemini, is reminded of the immortality shared by both Castor and Pollux, whereas he, Gonzalo, unlike Pollux, cannot intervene to bring his dead brother back to life. The narrator has then encroached on the space both of the mother, who desperately needs to relate to her son, and of Gonzalo who is obsessed with the death of his brother; the narrator has forfeited his potentially strong position on the outside because he cannot separate his frame of interrogation from that of his characters. At the same time, he does not relinquish a certain degree of distance afforded him by the authorial perspective he voices. While the lyrical reference to the myth of Castor and Pollux evokes an experience on the borders of the ineffable, it does so parodically by mimicking Gonzalo's (and Gadda's) need to sublimate his grief into literature. This parodic instance is prefigured by the equally parodic insertion at the beginning of the passage of 'di' before 'sul' which destabilizes the objective description, echoing a procedure common to Leopardi and Carducci. Hence, three boundaries are crossed in the space of two sentences: author, narrator, and character are tangled in such a way that it is practically impossible to distinguish one from the other. The tangle becomes even more intricate as the narrator returns to focus on Gonzalo: 'Egli allora entrò, e recava una piccola valigia, la solita, quella di cartone giallo da quaranta centavos, come d'un venditore ambulante di fazzoletti' (CD, 685–6) [He came in then, and was carrying a small valise, the usual, the one of yellow cardboard costing forty centavos, like a travelling peddler of handkerchiefs (AG, 148)]. Now the narrative voice blends with that of the chorus of townspeople for whom Gonzalo is an eccentric misanthrope, and the image of the travelling peddler returns as another obsessive reference to what Gonzalo believes is his mother's excessive liberality.

The blurring of perspectives brings together the different worlds that make up the book (the worlds of Gonzalo, his mother, the doctor-colonel Di Pascuale, the townspeople), resulting in a new kind of harmony that issues from the polytonal recentring of the different viewpoints into one overriding conceptual refrain. From now on the reader must recognize that with the narrator he is trapped within a labyrinth from which there is no exit; it is the labyrinth of authorial consciousness and cognition. As the narrator recounts the mother's need to please her son by proving that the villa is functional, he becomes by degrees at once both character and author. He begins by reflecting what the mother could have been thinking as she prepared supper for her son: that at the slightest provocation he would burst into tirades against everything associated with the villa he so hated. But, as soon as the circuit, so to speak, of the mother's possible thoughts and fears is established, the narrator overloads it with an endless description of the objects of Gonzalo's invectives: 'Egli avrebbe colto quel pretesto,' 'Avrebbe ripetutamente scorbacchiato,' 'Sarebbe trasceso alle bestemmie' (CD, 686) [He would have seized upon that pretext ... He would have repeatedly ridiculed ... he would have cursed' (AG, 149)], folding thus an apparently objective perspective with distinct frames of reference into an infinite series of converging singularities (the villa and every association that it elicits in Gonzalo's paranoiac consciousness). We witness a vast play of expression which fills the holes of the protagonist's emptiness with a formidable excess:

La Idea Matrice della villa se l'era appropriata quale organo rubente od entelechia prima consustanziale ai visceri, e però inalienabile dalla sacra interezza della persona: quasi armadio od appiccapanni di De Chirico, carnale ed eterno dentro il sognante cuore dei lari. A quella pituita somma, recondita, noumenica, corrispondeva esternamente – gioiello o bargiglio primo fuor dai confini della psiche – la villa obbiettiva, il dato. Operando in lei, durante quarant'anni, gli ormoni infaticabili della anagenesi; ciò che donna prende, in vita lo rende: quella costanza imperterrita, quella felice ignoranza dell'abisso, del paracarro, sicché, dàlli e dàlli, d'un cetriolo, arrivano a incoronar fuori un ingegnere; la formidabile capacità di austione, di immissione dello sproposito nella realtà, che è propria d'alcune meglio di esse; le piú deliberate e di piú vigoroso intelletto. Tali donne, anche se non sono isteriche, impegnano magari il latte, e la caparbietà di tutta una vita, a costituire in thesaurum certo, storicamente reale, un qualsiasi prodotto d'incontro della umana stupidaggine, il primo che capiti loro fra i piedi, a non dir fra le gambe, il piú vano: simbolo efimero di una emulazione o riverenza od acquisto che conterà nulla: diploma grande, villa, sissignora, piumacchio. C'è poi da aggiungere che il piú degli uomini si comportano tal'e quale come loro. Ed è una proprio delle meraviglie di natura, a volerlo considerare nei modi e nei risultati, questo processo di accumulo della volizione: è l'incedere automatico della sonnambula verso il tuo trionfo-catastrofe: da un certo momento in poi l'isteria del ripicco perviene a costituire la loro sola ragione d'essere, di tali donne, le adduce alla menzogna, al reato: e allora il vessillo dell'inutile, con la grinta buggerona della falsità, è portato avanti, avanti, sempre piú ostinatamente, sempre piú inutilmente, avverso la rabbia disperata della controparte. Sopravviene la tenebra liberatrice, che a tutte parti rimedia. (CD, 687)

[The Matrix Idea of the villa she had appropriated for herself as a rubescent organ or prime entelechy consubstantial with the womb, and therefore inalienable from the sacred wholeness of her person: like a wardrobe or hatrack of De Chirico, carnal and external within the dreaming heart of the lares. To that pituitary sum, recondite, noumenical, there corresponded externally – jewel or prime cock crest beyond the confines of the psyche – the objective villa, the datum. Operating in her, during forty years, were the tireless hormones of anagenesis – what woman takes, in life she gives back – that unperturbed constancy, that happy ignorance of the abyss, of the curbstone, so that, never say die, from pumpkinhead, they manage to produce an engineer; the formidable capacity for absorption, for introduction of absurdity into reality, which is characteristic of some of the best of women – the most resolute, the most vigorous of intellect. Such women, even if they aren't hysterical, impound their milk, and the stubbornness of a whole life, to constitute a thesaurus certain, historically real, a commonplace product of the encounter with human stupidity: the first that they find at their feet, not to say between their legs, the vainest: ephemeral symbol of an emulation or a reverence or an acquisition which will count for nothing: large diploma, villa, yes Madame, plume. It must be added also that the majority of men behave exactly like them. And it is really one of the wonders of nature, if you choose to consider it in its methods and results, this process of accumulation of volition. It is automatic progress of the somnambulist toward her triumph-catastrophe: from a certain moment on, the hysteria of pique succeeds in forming their sole reason for existence; in such women, it leads them to falsehood, to crime, and then the banner of the useless, with the fraudulent mug of falsity, is borne forward, forward, more and more obstinately, more and more uselessly, against the desperate anger of the other side. The liberating darkness arrives, which remedies all sides. (*AG*, 150–1)]

The development of this passage, which for reasons of space I have excerpted from a much larger context, depends on the subordination of the narrative (and historical) truth (the mother's pride and identification with the villa) to the creative potential of that truth. The truth holds what Deleuze calls an 'infinité de petites perceptions' (1988, 122) the value of which consists not in whether they are true, but in the fact that they gain privileged status in expression. Samples of the perceptions constituting the passage just cited include: 'La Idea Matrice': the villa as mother or womb; 'l'organo rubente': the villa as phallus; 'entelechia prima consustanziale ai visceri': the mother's desire for self-fulfilment in the villa; 'armadio od appiccapanni di De Chirico': the kinds of inalienable objects that occupy the domestic space of the villa, which in De Chirico's art are metaphysical values; 'pituita somma': hormonic fatality perceived as noumenon: the villa as thing in itself; 'anagenesis': the villa as compensation for the loss of a son (Gadda/Gonzalo's brother); 'costanza imperterrita [...] ingegnere': the mother's predisposition to surrender to the phallus.

These perceptions are not meant as a rational illustration of a general theme or idea through particular examples; they do not serve to define the relation between villa and mother; nor are they qualities of a physical reality that excite the mind of the narrator. Rather, they find unity only in the narrative unconscious; they are in effect unconscious perceptions articulated by free association: the folds of the villa/mother as idea embedded in the monadic inner world of a hysterical subject. They rise from the depths of his being and take on the quality of hallucinations.[9]

The autobiographical subject in all of its inflections cannot then disentangle itself from its inner world of a 'dolore' it cannot explain but only express. At the same time it is aware of the liability accompanying its own expression: namely, the impulse to dissolve the grief into literature which for Gadda is both expression and disguise. Gadda's profound awareness of his own potential for literary entrapment is one of the most distinctive features of his art. It enables him to exit, however slightly, from the anxieties and obsessions that characterize his paranoia and thus to take some degree of distance from his own baroque expressionism. It makes possible the comedy and the spectacle, the thorough materialization of systems within systems.

In conclusion, to understand Gadda's baroque, one must keep in mind Gadda's stated premise that the universe is baroque, while rejecting the implication that his texts are that world's mimetic transcription. Gadda ceases to transmit the exterior world at the very moment he engages in self-reflection and inspection. Yet in so doing he takes a position at the opposite extreme of that espoused by contemporary theoreticians and practitioners of the neobaroque. By exposing the self as the sole arbiter of meaning, he prevents himself from moving beyond his own chaotic representations. The vibrations and oscillations of the narrative psyche that, as we have seen, shatter traditional language boundaries and framing structures are not made to exemplify in the least an indeterminate process of meaning production. Rather the complexity that Gadda's self-referentiality highlights is the reduction of the world and of all its chaos and fragments to authorial intention and, therefore, to one infinitely communicable experience: the quintessential experience of 'wordless pain within the monad,' as Fredric Jameson writes in reference to Edvard Munch's painting *The Scream*, the cathartic projection and externalization of 'gesture or cry, as desperate communication and the outward dramatization of inward feeling' (1992, 11–12).

Notes

1   In the case of the Spanish baroque, with 'a seigneurial, Catholic ruling class that needs to differentiate itself from the sordid world of commerce and manual labor' (Beverley 1993, 59).

2   A concept of the neobaroque has also been developed by Omar Calabrese as an effective substitute for the term 'postmodernism.' In Calabrese's view, the neobaroque refers to the recurrence in contemporary art and culture of forms that recall the historical baroque. Calabrese is careful not to impune the specificity of the historical moment or the singular case, factors that condition the expression of either the baroque or classical formal constant. At the same time, his rigorously formalistic procedure focuses exclusively on the text's underlying morphologies. Calabrese's approach has a particular relevance for Gadda in that it theorizes the baroque as a modern cultural and literary trope. Morover, by considering the baroque as a cultural system displaying specific formal characteristics, Calabrese's discussions place us squarely within Gadda's own referential arena. As regards postmodernism, Gadda's use of parody and citation have no doubt something in common with postmodern literary practices, but his ongoing fascination with the depth and difficulty of his subject matter and with a hermeneutic based on cognition, investigation, and decipherment sets his work apart from postmodernism's most important constitutive features.

3   The formative influence of Leibniz on Gadda can be attested to by the *Meditazione milanese* and by Gadda's decision to write his doctoral thesis on Leibniz's theory of knowledge in the *Nouveaux essais*, a study he never completed.

4   See Italo Calvino's introduction to *That Awful Mess on Via Merulana*, v.

5   On the novel's title, see Emilio Manzotti: 'Gadda *La cognizione del dolore*' in *Opere* (IV, 2) of *Letteratura italiana* (Turin: Einaudi 1994), 201–337. Manzotti argues most convincingly that Gadda took his title directly from Schopenhauer's *The World as Will and Representation*, which he read in Italian translation. Manzotti's discussion of the novel's title is the most thorough to date.

6   See Calvino's perceptive remarks in *Six Memos for the Next Millennium* (1988): '[In Gadda's novels] the least thing is seen as the center of a network of relationships that the writer cannot restrain himself from following, multiplying the details so that his descriptions and digressions become infinite. Whatever the starting point, the matter in hand spreads out, encompassing ever vaster horizons, and if it were permitted to go on further and further in every direction, it would end by embracing the entire universe' (107).

7   In Italian literature, such a category would include writers as different from one another as Alfieri and Svevo. The constitution of the subject of narrative

and its functions in the history of Italian narrative fiction up to Gadda remains essentially the same in that it is based on the premise that the purpose of narration is to give unity and thus to resolve the contradictions in the social order from which the fiction ultimately derives.

8   On the knot and the labyrinth as baroque figures, see Calabrese 1992, 131–43.

9   *'Every perception is hallucinatory because perception has no object.* Conscious perception has no object and does not refer to a physical mechanism of excitation that could explain it from without: it refers only to the exclusively physical mechanism of differential relations among unconscious perceptions that are comprising it within the monad. And unconscious perceptions have no object and do not refer to physical things. They are only related to the cosmological and metaphysical mechanism according to which the world does not exist outside of the monads that are conveying it' (Deleuze 1993, 93–4).

References

Beverley, John. 1993. *Against Literature*. Minneapolis and London: University of Minnesota Press

Calabrese, Omar. 1992. *Neo-Baroque*. Translated by Charles Lambert. Princeton, N.J.: Princeton University Press. Translation of *L'età neobarocca*. Rome and Bari: Laterza 1987

Calvino, Italo. 1988. *Six Memos for the Next Millennium*. Translated by Patrick Creagh. Cambridge, Mass.: Harvard University Press

Contini, Gianfranco. 1963. 'Saggio introduttivo.' In Carlo Emilio Gadda, *La cognizione del dolore*. Turnin: Einaudi

Deleuze, Gilles. 1988. *Le pli. Leibniz et le Baroque*. Paris: Les Éditions de Minuit

– 1993. *The Fold: Leibniz and the Baroque*. Translated by Tom Conley. Minneapolis and London: University of Minnesota Press

Jameson, Fredric. 1993. *Postmodernism, or, the Cultural Logic of Late Capitalism*. Durham, N.C.: Duke University Press

Description 'by Alternatives' and Description 'with Comment': Some Characteristic Procedures of Gadda's Writing

EMILIO MANZOTTI

It has been observed, on the basis of an oft-cited passage from *I viaggi la morte*, that representation in Gadda tends to a kind of diachrony, a kind of historicization of the fact, thus superimposing upon the contingency of the present characteristics of the past and hypothetical developments of the future. The present condition of the object or event in representation appears simultaneously laden with its past and pregnant with its future.[1] Fragments of reality, more than circumscribed contingencies, are 'moments of a process of becoming,' 'intervals of a deformation as it is happening.'[2]

Thus, in the month of March, as described in *Quer pasticciaccio brutto de via Merulana*, the trees on the side of a Roman road are cultivated in the 'critical moment of transition between winter's past, which is no longer, and the future of "spring's rebirth," which has not yet arrived' (Manzotti 1993, 18). 'I platani e i rami della Merulana furon selva, allo svoltare, intrico, per lo sguardo, sul discendere parallelo dei fili, di cui si alimentavano i tramme: *ancora scheletriti nel marzo, con di già un languore in pelle in pelle, tuttavia, na specie de prurito* per entro la chiarità lieta e stradale della lor còrtica, fatta di scaglie e di pezze' (*QP*, 264, my emphasis) [The plane-trees and the boughs of Merulana were a forest, as the car turned, a tangle to the eyes, on the parallel descent of the lines which nourished the trams: still skeletal in March, with already a skin-deep languor, nonetheless, a kind of itch within the happy, street-lining clarity of their bark, made of scales and patches (*AM*, 370)]. The modifiers thus, inscribe in the present, as signalled by the symmetrical adverbs *ancora* (still) and *di già* (already), clearly visible traces of the past and delicate anticipations of the future.

Something analogous also occurs (and this time with a kind of microscopic diachrony, embedded in the adjectives) in a passage of *Cugino barbiere,* the first story of *Accoppiamenti giudiziosi,* regarding the lettuces with which the curious neighbours of Zoraide pretend to be busy.[3]

Zoraide aprì finalmente ed uscì lei sul terrazzino, decisa. Sui terrazzini da lato e di fronte, nel sole tepido, c'erano già per qualche loro occorrenza altre diciasette donne, quale appoggiata alla ringhiera e quale in sulla porta come per entrare od uscirne, e quale con un rugginoso coltello *dal defunto manico* a rimestare dentro vasi o cassette di *probabili lattughe* o di garofani: intenzionata poi a dacquarli, tanto per concludere. (*AccG,* 599; my emphases)

[Zoraide finally opened the door and strode out decisively onto the balcony, herself. On balconies to both sides and across from her, in the warmth of the sun, there were already for whatever reason another seventeen women, some leaning against the railings, some in the doorways as if about to go in or go out, and some gripping rusty knives by *their defunct handles* to dig up the soil in the vases or boxes planted with *probable lettuces* or carnations: as if intending then to finish up by watering them.]

The first pole of the binary alternative *lattughe/garofani* (lettuces/carnations) is qualified with 'probable': they are lettuces, God willing, to be, while the instrument of domestic horticulture is a knife with a *defunct* handle: colloquially, the handle is 'history.'

As is well known, this kind of collocation of diachronically distinct moments manifests a more general tendency of Gadda's prose towards 'infinite metonymy.'[4] It manifests also what we might otherwise call the 'representative kaleidoscope,' that is, a tendency to refract the whole within the individual unit, to wrap the individual entity in that network of associations which, in a relational conception of the world, constitutes its identity. Furthermore, even on the narrative level, this principle has novel implications; particularly in its aperspectivism, in that seeming absence of a hierarchy among the tesserae of narrative discourse which was so acutely observed by Pietro Citati at the time of the re-release of *La cognizione del dolore.*

In this essay, I propose to designate two modes of the Gaddian 'kaleidoscope' which until now, as far as I know, have been passed over in silence. Limiting myself to the sphere of description in the strict sense, I will distinguish two recurring representative procedures entirely characteristic of the author: (1) description 'by alternatives' and (2) description 'with comment.' Concerning both I will analyse in detail a brief passage drawn from *La cognizione del dolore.* The results of such an effort, however, are applicable more generally to Gadda's literary and journalistic production as a whole; indeed, the results are equally valid for his representation of actions, processes, and situations as well as that of description.

Description 'by alternatives' gathers together diverse aspects of the represented object with the varying of specific dimensions and parameters. If, as in the case that we shall discuss, the object represented is a path, and if one privileges, among those dimensions possible, that of 'travelling along the path,' we shall then obtain from time to time new assertions by introducing and varying the parameters such as (a) the means of locomotion, (b) the direction, (c) the frequency of travel, (d) the sex of the travellers, (e) their profession or social status, and so on. One thus generates not a finite, contingent, or static description, but a summation, a plurality of descriptions, a sort of description of unlimited potential, one capable of passing through a whole series of possible concrete manifestations. This is, in other words, description carried out 'by alternatives,' that is, by means of variants, situations, and manifestations complementary to each other. Their very abundance and variety, together with the superimposition and clash of different parameters, opens the way to the typically Gaddian play between the poles of order and disorder, between a meticulous listing by genus and species on one side, and chaotic combination on the other.

For its part, description 'with comment' is a description achieved through non-homogeneous layers with respect to the textual type or level. More specifically, and in elementary terms, it is a description that includes within itself some form of digressive comment. There are, that is, jumps in the level of representation. At certain points in the narrative, notations are inserted, as apparent digressions, which comment, justify, generalize, and so on, at a clearly higher level of discourse, upon the notations of the first level. This counterpoint of description leads to, among other effects, a palpable slowing of descriptive velocity, and above all it relativizes, or even denies, the narrative value of individual notations.

However, in the course of the following analyses, it should be kept in mind that the foregoing descriptive types are almost never purely expressed as the one and only organizing procedure of a description. Upon each (and the two are often combined) Gadda superimposes his usual techniques of disharmony, which have already been noted and more or less extensively described by other critics. Those techniques include thematic drift through chains of anadiplosis, the progressive loosening of syntactic linkages, the unbalanced elements of a parallel structure, the mutation and multiplication of differentiating criteria among successive elements of an opposition, and so on. Some of these techniques will be discussed briefly as the occasion arises.

1 Description 'by Alternatives'

We begin by examining a single instance of the type of description which we defined as 'by alternatives,' that which has been alluded to above as similar to a road or path. This choice is by no means arbitrary, if we take into consideration that, for Gadda, streets, like large buildings, are a concentration of *vie* (à la Perec), the privileged sites of the 'pandemonio della vita' (*MI*, 45) [pandemonium of life], the true and proper generators, through the infinite possibilities of chance, of new combinatorial events. This choice, then, like all choices, presupposes a paradigm, and an extremely extensive one at that. Once our attention has been drawn to this phenomenon, we seem to find nothing else as we read Gadda's work, page after page. It will be sufficient here to produce two passages, without failing to mention the one from the *Accoppiamenti* already cited above, where the anaphora of *quale* introduced three alternatives of feigned behaviour in a narrative unit packed with covert motives (curiosity). The first extract is from 'Mercato di frutta e verdura.' Here, there are bicycles 'aggruppate a quindici a quindici come dei muli all'addiaccio' [grouped dozen upon dozen like mules in a corral], that 'paiono non altro attendere se non robusti galloni ed i glùtei saluberrimi del proprietario' [appear to be waiting for nothing other than the broad stripes and bulging gluteals of the owner]:

Il quale, ammantellato e baffuto, le riconduca alla nativa cassina. *Fendendo* col naso la nebbia, dove si sperde, al passare, ogni salice dopo il compagno. *O* nel sereno splendore della primavera, dimesso il mantello, *avvistando* dietro i filari de' pioppi un campanile, poi l'altro, poi l'ultimo: capisaldi trigonometrici (per il redattori del catasto e dei mappali di base) sopra il rinverdire di ogni pioppo. (ibid.; my emphases)

[who, cloaked and mustached, rides it back to his native hamlet. *Cleaving* the fog with his nose, where, in passing, every succeeding willow is lost after its companion before it. Or in the serene splendour of the spring, cloakless, *spying* beyond the lines of poplars a belfry, then another, then the last: trigonometric steeples (for the compilers of the land registry office and the editors of city maps) towering above the regreening of every poplar.]

The second of the two gerunds (*Fendendo ... avvistando*) is placed in a separate sentence and lengthened by the recapitulatory apposition (of the various *belfries*) *capisaldi trigonometrici*, a specific example of linear thematic progression by means of anadiplosis. In the same story, there is an even more striking example, with an elaborate hierarchy of alternatives, which are, seemingly, lined up:

tra le infinite carrette vagano pochissime ombre, le tuniche semoventi di alcuni conduttori: *sàgome allampanate* d'un color *piombo o marrone scuro*. Tra il Goya e il Magnasco, con un[a] flanella cinerea che gli infagotta il collo e la gola tossicolosa, col naso che gócciola: *o sono invece dei gobbetti membruti*, e trascineranno il loro carretto ai mercatini lontani lamentando a scatti, con urli ritmati, e per quanto duri tutto il tragitto, i rinviliti prezzi dell'üga bell'üga; *o dei nani*, i quali fermi a un cantone con il negozio, ti guardano: e nell'adunca mano *sorreggono un pomo da poterlo lustrare di gomito: o hanno una spazzola-caravella*, da spazzolare, ai primi di agosto, la prima pubertà della pesca agostana. (ibid., 44; my emphases)

[a few shades wander among the endless two-wheeled carts, the self-propelled tunics of several vendors: *gaunt silhouettes* of *lead-grey or dark brown* hue. Between Goya and Magnasco, with an ash-grey flannel scarf wrapped around their necks and throats prone to a constant cough, with dripping noses: *or they are instead strong-limbed hunchbacks*, and they will go dragging their carts to outlying marketplaces lamenting jerkily, with rhythmic shouts, and for however long it takes to make the trip, the slashed prices of their grapes, choice grapes; *or dwarves*, who, having set up for business on the corner, stand there watching you: and with crooked hand *they pick up an apple so as to polish it with their elbow: or they wield a brush*, to dust off, in the early days of August, the first pubescent fuzz of the August peach.]

There are also instances, in this tendency to exhaust all possibilities, of alternatives that are poorly integrated into the context. The *aut aut* seems, then, to be an a priori form of thought, superimposed like a perceptual stamp upon the reality described, without concern for that piece of reality's own intrinsic constitution. That is, for example, what happens in 'Terra lombarda,' one of the pieces collected in *Gli anni* (*SGF I*, 211–12). In the following quotation, cues for the alternatives are written in upper-case italics and counterposed assertions in lower-case italics:

Ricordo che gli uomini camminavano [...] Il contadino dalle scarpe grevi e chiodate percorreva gravemente la strada campestre: taciturno [...] Tra *due siepi di spino O due file di salci O d'alti pioppi*, quando il fosso adacquatore lungheggiasse, col suo dolce filo, il consueto andare della polvere. *La chiarità d'estate si infarinava di bianche miglia*, in cima alle quali erano le cose necessarie e solenni, la compera, la vendita, la pluralità degli esseri addobbata de' suoi scuri panni, la silente preghiera, la Messa cantata: da tutti. *O*, dopo lungo pensiero, *il disco del sole si tuffava negli ori e nei carmini, dietro scheletri d'alberi, come in una pozzanghera di liquefatto metallo*. La cimasa delle pioppaie veniva celandone l'estrema dipartita: solo, qualche *frustolo d'oro, O una goccia*, di quel fuoco lontano, durava a persistere nell'intrico nero delle ramaglie.

D'estate, *INVECE, il popolo dei pioppi, unanime, trascolorava nella sera*: le raganelle, dai fossi, dalle risaie, sgranavano dentro il silenzio il dolce monile della sera: con un cauto singhiozzo la rana, per più lenti intervalli, salutava lo zaffiro della stella Espero, tacitamente splendida. S'era affacciata alla ringhiera dei pioppi. (*AN*, 211–12)

[I remember that the men were walking ... The peasant with his heavy hobnail boots was trudging down the country road: taciturn ... *Between two thorn hedges OR two rows of willows OR of tall poplars*, when the irrigation ditch ran alongside, with its gentle trickle, the usual trail of dust. *The clarity of summer was powdered in the dust of white miles*, at the end of which were things necessary and solemn, buying, selling, the plurality of beings decked out in their sombre clothing, the silent prayer, the Mass intoned: by all. *OR*, after long thought, the disc of the sun would dive into the golds and carmines, *behind skeletons of trees, as if into a puddle of molten metal*. But the heights of the poplar groves would end up hiding its ultimate departure: only, some *wisps of gold, OR a drop* from that distant fire, would manage to penetrate the black tangle of the branches.

In the summer, *ON THE OTHER HAND, the population of poplars, unanimous, would turn pale in the evening*: the tree frogs, from the ditches, from the rice paddies, husked the dulcet jewel of sunset in silence: with a cautious hiccup the bull frog, over more prolonged intervals, greeted the sapphire star of Hope, which shone tacitly splendid. It had appeared beyond the poplars as if at the railing of a balcony.]

Leaving aside the minor, subordinated alternatives in the first paragraph, the specific difference between the two poles of the alternative is reconstructible at first sight as that between two moments of a summer day: the noon hour (chiarità dell'estate) is being counterposed to sunset. But the *scheletri d'alberi* and l'*intrico nero delle ramaglie* immediately impose a second factor of variation, and that is the season: summer versus winter. Even so, immediately after, in the paragraph that follows, an unexpected *invece* reintroduces almost *ex novo* the summer season, even while maintaining the time of day constant. It is thus possible to summarize the oppositional scheme as follows:

(DAY + SUMMER) → (EVENING + WINTER) → (EVENING + SUMMER)

This scheme is, at least to a degree, circular, and one of its effects is to introduce into the description an idea of completeness, of having exhausted all the possible manifestations of the real.

The passage which we will now examine in detail presents a complex logical architecture that, especially in the second paragraph, is based essentially on the combinatorial possibilities offered by the concatenation of alternatives. It is drawn from one of the lyric heights of *La cognizione del dolore*, the final section of the seventh 'segment' (the third of the second part, the segment that concluded the first version in *Letteratura*, and the first edition of the novel in 1963). It concerns the minute description of the country path that runs along one side of the Pirobutirro property, a description (whose archetype is, when scrutinized, already set down in the *Racconto italiano* [425–6]), summarily sketched out in the first part of *La cognizione* during the conversation between Gonzalo and the doctor (C, 191–2)[5] and taken up, as we shall see, more extensively a third time in the last segment (C, 442–7). The passage is as follows:

Di là dal muretto, una stradaccia. Ghiaiosa, a forte pendenza, con lùnule di piatti infranti, o d'una scodella, tra i ciòttoli, od oblio di un rugginoso baràttolo, vuotato, beninteso, dell'antica salsa o mostarda: tratto tratto anche, sotto il livido metallo d'un paio di mosconi ebbri, l'onta estrusa dall'Adamo, l'arrotolata turpitudine: stavolta per davvero sì d'un qualche guirlache de almendras, ma di quelli! ... da pesarli in bilancia, diavolo maiale, per veder cosa pesano; parvenze, d'altronde, che la magnanimità del nostro apparato sensorio, aiutata da onorevole addobbo di circostanze, non può far altro, in verità, se non fingere di non aver percepito.

Percorsa da pedoni radi, la strada: e talora, in discesa, da qualche ciclista da campagna con bicicletta-mulo; o risalita dal procaccia impavido, arrancante sotto pioggia o stravento, o zoppicata non si sa in che verso da alcuni mendichi ebdomadarî, maschi e femmine, cenciose apparizioni nella gran luce del nulla. Vaporando l'autunno, vi sfringuellavano battute di ragazzi birbi, a piè nudi, en busca de higos y de ciruelas, che arrivano a divinare per telepatia di là d'ogni chiuso: d'orto (salvo l'orto del prete) o di signorile giardino. Vi si avventurava pure, col settembre, qualche puttanona d'automobile sfiancata dagli strapazzi, dagli anni, imbarcando magari tutta una famiglia gitante, con due litri di pipì a testa in serbo per la prima fermata, pupi e pupe, e il chioccione di dietro, sparapanzato a poppa, che soffocava con la patria potestà del deretano i due fili d'erba delle due figliolette maggiori. Pareva che una Meccanica latrice di prosciutti si avventasse contro l'assurdo, ruggendo, strombazzando, schioppando, sparando sassi da sotto le gomme, lacerando con ruggiti del motore e con gli strilli de' suoi sbatacchiati Argonauti-donne il tenue ragnatelo di ogni filosofia. (*C*, 380–2)

[On the other side of the little wall, an awful little road. Gravelly, steep, with lunules of broken plates, or of a bowl, among the pebbles, or the oblivion of a rusty can, emptied, of course, of its ancient sauce or mustard: here and there also, under the livid din of a pair of fat drunken flies, the shame extruded from Adam, the coiled turpitude: yes, this time for sure the product of some guirlache de almendras, but of the good kind! ... the kind that have to be put on the scale, for chrissakes, to see what they weigh; appearances, furthermore, that the magnanimity of our sensory apparatus, aided by honorable adornment of circumstances, can do no more, in truth, than to pretend not to have perceived.

Traveled by rare pedestrians, the road: and at times, in descent, by some backroad cyclists with their mule-bikes; or ascended by the fearless rural postman, trudging along against rain and high winds; or limped over who knows in which direction by a few hebdomadal beggars, male and female, ragged apparitions in the great light of nothingness. As autumn misted away, bands of roguish boys would run about, jabbering, barefooted, en busca de higos y de ciruelas, who manage to divine through telepathy the contents of every enclosure: of garden (excepting the priest's garden) or of lordly park. There ventured also, with September, a few whorish old automobiles, exhausted by their excesses, by their years, having taken aboard perhaps a whole excursive family, with two quarts of peepee apiece in their tank saved up for the first stop, kiddies boys and girls, and the old rooster in back, sprawled in the poop, who stifled with the paternal authority of his behind the delicate green shoots of his two eldest daughters. It seemed as if a Mechanics, bearer of hams, were hurling itself against the absurd, booming, bombinating, firing stones out from beneath its tires, lacerating, with the roars of its motors and the cries of its battered Argonaut-women, the delicate web of all philosophy. (*AG*, 183–4)][6]

Graphically, the description appears to be articulated in two paragraph-moments, each of whose *incipit* exhibits identical phenomena in parallel: the ellipsis of the verb (an existential *v'era*, at first, and the auxiliary of the passive, later) and above all the dislocation to the right of the subject, a stylistic shift, which, as Terracini once pointed out, was dear not only to Pirandello, but also to lyric prose writers at the beginning of this century. Of the two moments, the first enumerates intrinsic aspects of the referent (treating, that is, a sort of physical geography, into which the presence of man is none the less already intruding), the second lists the modes of utilization – in a word, the human geography: it concerns the road in so far as it is used by different types of passersby. Let's begin with a few words on the first moment, before concentrating our attention on the second.

After opening with a detached phrase that poses the descriptive theme (and places it spatially, and evaluates it disparagingly: *stradACCia*), the first moment is composed, schematically, of a ternary list of qualifiers: three juxtaposed assertions of the descriptive theme, one adjectival, one adverbial, and one complexly prepositional (composed, that is, by a coordination of prepositional syntagmata)

$$\left\{ \begin{array}{l} \text{Ghiaiosa} \\ \text{a forte pendenza} \\ \text{con lùnule} \end{array} \right.$$

Here, it seems, we are well within the bounds of the classical syntax of the textual type known as 'description': after an introductory existential phrase, comes a series of assertions. When scrutinized, however, the usual descriptive syntax appears as a sort of pretext or, better, a sort of useful point of departure for manoeuvres that solicit various modes of reading. In particular, this happens through the imbalance caused by the dimensions of the last assertion (*con lùnule*). The latter, decidedly more lengthy and complex than the preceding two, and provided with two harshly dissonant digressive codas, contains, in effect, another ternary coordination with a final destabilizing element, whose first element is in its turn binary in its specification (*di piatti infranti / d'una scodella*). We can represent the resulting disjunctive scheme as follows:

$$\left\{ \begin{array}{l} \text{con lùnule} \left\{ \begin{array}{l} \text{di piatti infranti} \\ \text{o d'una scodella [...]} \end{array} \right. \\ \text{od [con] oblìo d'un rugginoso baràttolo [...]} \\ \text{[con] tratto tratto anche [...] l'onta estrusa [...]} \end{array} \right.$$

Particularly noteworthy, in this disjunctive scheme, is that its different elements are subjected to an extraordinary syntactical and semantic elaboration, whose artificiality contrasts and redeems its own insignificance, the leaden weight of the brute fact. This is a virtuoso performance which, let it be said in passing, the translations all tend more or less, for no good linguistic reason, to conjure away. Sticking to the 'bare facts,' that is, setting aside the superimposed elaboration, the three referents named and located *tra i ciottoli* (the last of which is *tratto tratto*, which is to say, at intervals, thus present iteratively) are nothing other than insignificant or unpleasant appearances (*parvenze*). These are described in the following order: (1) slivers of plates and bowls; (2) an empty can (or perhaps several, given the attractive force of the other plurals); and finally, (3) faeces. However, to begin with, Gadda, like Plato's God, 'geometrizes': he geometrizes the humble and formless reality of the slivers of plate, by representing them as instances of the noble geometric shape, consisting of the intersection of two unequal arcs, which is called the *lùnula*. This is a shape, it should be noted, that is especially dear to the author, who recycles it from the distant past of the *Racconto italiano* – 'quelle caratteristiche lùnule di terraglia' (*RI*, 426) [those characteristic lunules of earthenware]) – and uses it another two times in *La cognizione*. Beyond the occasion on which it is used to describe the bags under the doctor's eyes: 'Le occhiaie gonfie, a lùnula' (*C*, 468) [swollen rings under his eyes, in the shape of lunules], it appears precisely in the redescribing (which we have already mentioned) of the same road about fifty pages farther on (*C*, 443). In two other occurrences outside of *La cognizione*, the term is, on the contrary, provided with an erudite gloss. In 'Crociera mediterranea,' we read:

Lùnula, detta di Ippocrate, è la porzione del piano definita da un arco di circonferenza e dalla semicirconferenza che curerai tracciare prendendo a diametro la corda di quello. Questa figura è quadrabile (per comparazione e diffalco) senza il sussidio del calcolo integrale. E la sua quadratura occupò anche Leonardo nel 'De ludo geometrico.' (*CU*, 216, n57)

[The lunule, attributed to Hippocrates, is the portion of a plane defined by an arc and the semicircle obtained by using the arc's chord as diameter. This shape can be squared (by comparison and reduction) without the need of integral calculus. Leonardo too addressed the squaring of this shape in his 'De ludo geometrico.']

And in *L'Adalgisa*, the term is again associated with plates – 'aveva ridotto in lùnule una trentacinquina di piatti' (*A*, 319) [some thirty-five plates had been reduced to lunules]:

Lùnula è la superficie piana definita da un arco di circonferenza e dalla semicirconferenza costruita sulla corda di quello, assunta per diametro. (Teorema di Ippocrate sulle lùnule del triangolo retto). (ibid., 340, n27)

[The lunule is the planar surface formed by an arc whose chord is taken as the diameter of a semicircle constructed to intersect the arc. (Theorem of Hippocrates on lunules and the right triangle).]

Pursuing the same line of attack, though with a change in stylistic register (from technico-scientific to poetic), the *baràttolo*, the second humble *parvenza* related to the road, is presented obliquely through the hypostatization of one of its past and present qualities: that of having been abandoned, or that of lying now in desolate abandonment (*oblìo*), with its antidiphthong accent mark. This slash of symbolist literary sensibility is then immediately contradicted by the *clin d'oeil* of *beninteso* applied to an 'idiot' notation (but notice the alternative of *antica salsa o mostarda*), this turning of the quality (that is, the condition of the can as 'forgotten' or 'abandoned') into the noun *oblìo* moreover introduces the harmonies of poetic memory into the description. *Oblìo*, I believe, seems to allude with caricatured extremism to the use (already somewhat strained) Pascoli made of it in the first verse of *Nella macchia* (*Myricae*): 'Errai nell'oblìo della valle / tra ciuffi di stipe fiorite, / tra querce rigonfie di galle' [I wandered in the oblivion of the vale / among clumps of flowered scrub / among oak trees swollen with gall].

Not dissimilarly, the third appearance is (at first) designated by a distancing circumlocution hinged upon the abstract *onta* (which also appears at the end of the first passage, 'Onta, per lui, e rammarico immedicabile' (C, 102–3) [Shame, for him, and unmedicable regret ...]: 'l'onta estrusa dall'Adamo' [the extruded shame from Adam], with its symbolist syntax homologous to that of *oblìo* and extended moreover also to the antecedent circumstantiation: 'sotto il livido metallo d'un paio di mosconi ebbri' [under the livid din of a pair of fat drunken flies].[7] The designation is then immediately after taken up again by an apposition which is also impressionistically periphrastic: *l'arrotolata turpitudine*. Just as for *oblìo*, in the word *onta* it is almost obligatory to read a literary reference. In this case it is to D'Annunzio, whose *Elettra* Gadda boasted knowing completely by heart. I am referring to the arched coupling of 'A Roma' (vv 186–7), 'di contro all'Onta / dell'Uomo' [against the Shame / of Man] (where *l'onta* is counterposed to *Potenza*), especially if one considers that in Gadda's syntagma *l'onta estrusa d'Adamo*, the article in front of *Adamo* revives[8] the etymological 'uomo' which in Hebrew is *adham*. The elaboration of this description holds still other surprises. After the appositional refrain already mentioned (*l'arrotolata turpitudine*), the colon introduces a sibylline and trivial explanation concerning the origin of the *merde*: due presumably to the indigestion of some almond nougat[9] (in Spanish, *guirlache de almendras*), genuine nougat this (cf *stavolta sì*), and not figurative like the broken glass (*schegge di bottiglia*) of the preceding paragraph. Simultaneously, however, these *merde* are a 'torrone di mandorle,' in the same way as those *mandorlate-piantate* left behind by other roguish boys upon the Milanese *rovine dei fortilizi spagnoli* [ruins of the Spanish fortresses], ruins, one should note, that are described as 'sgretolate come torroni secchi' (*C*, 406) [crumbling like dried blocks of nougat]. And this suggests a startling metonymic analogy to certain *frantumi di tegoli* [fragments of tiles] which in the archetypal description of the *Racconto italiano* (*RI*, 426–7) a passerby on the *stradaccia* removed with his *bastoncello* [little cane]. The image seems to be hatched right out of Manzoni: 'e buttando con un piede verso il muro i ciottoli che facevano inciampo nel sentiero' (*I promessi sposi*, ch. 1) [and kicking towards the wall the stones that obstructed the path]. There then follows a final comment in an abstract, psychological-philosophical tone reminiscent of James, initiated by a new apposition (*parvenze*), which generalizes upon the contingent *turpitudini* of the road: it is quite dissimilar in tone to the development to which it is attached.

Though constructed upon a simple and symmetrical framework, the first paragraph becomes difficult to enjoy as description. Inevitably, the accumulation of 'the ornate' and of collateral information masks the structural elements. It is worthwhile to compare the different treatment that is given to the image of the *stradaccia* nearly halfway through the ninth and last segment (*C*, 442–7). The schema of this 'description B' is very close to the schema of the one discussed above (which for clarity we shall call 'description A'): the first two qualifiers (*ghiaiosa, a forte pendenza*) having been fused in the predicate *è una cateratta di pietrisco e ciottoli*, the third reappears in its prepositional format (from the same starting point: *con lùnule di piatti*), though acquiring along the way a fourth and final addition (*uno o due spazzolini*):

Un sentierino lo taglia quel campo [= 'un breve campo di banzavóis'] e immette sulla civica strada, già descritta, che costeggia il già descritto muro dei susini: questo ente civico, designato nei mappali catastali come 'Civica strada alla costa,' dove lambisce il muriccio dei susini è una specie di cateratta di pietrisco e ciottoli grossi come bocce, e alcuni anzi come cocomeri, ma molto più duri, con *lùnule* di piatti rotti e fondi di bicchieri e bottiglie assai taglienti, *qualche barattolo vuoto, diverse merde* di colore e consistenza diversa, e *uno o due spazzolini frusti da denti,* abbandonati al destino delle cose fruste, beninteso.

Nessuno mai vi transitava di notte, perché la stradaccia, che in definitiva e dopo assai rigiri e sassi e guizzi di lucertoloni dai roveti, discende a Lukones, non congiunge in modo diretto dei centri abitati. Disserve solo qualche campicello di banzavóis macilento e le ville con mutria di Svizzera, occupate, *ecc.*

Nessuno dunque passava da quella strada nelle ore mute della notte: o forse, talvolta, con la bicicletta senza fanale, il Palumbo, che doveva infilare il bigliettino in una qualche punta de' cancelli, una villa sì e una no. (My emphases)

[A little path cuts through that field [= 'a small field of banzavois'] and comes out onto the civic road, already described, that runs along the already-described wall with the plum trees: this civic institution, designated on the official maps as 'Official road to the coast,' is a kind of cataract of rubble and crushed stones the size of bocce balls, some actually as big as watermelons, though much harder, *with lunules* of broken plates and chunks of rather jagged glass, *a few empty cans, diverse defecations* of different color and consistency, and *one or two worn-out toothbrushes*), abandoned to the fate of all things shabby, naturally.

No one ever traveled there at night, because that miserable road, in the end and after endless twists and rocks and slitherings of lizards amongst the bramble-bushes, descends to Lukones, without joining up directly with any of the populated centers. It serves only some patchy fields of emaciated banzavois and the haughty-faced Swiss villas, occupied ... etc.

So nobody passed along that road in the silent hours of the night: or maybe at times, on a bicycle with no headlamp, Palumbo might, whose duty it was to stick his little slip of paper into a hole in the gates, some villas yes, some villas no. (*AG*, 218–19)]

Despite the relatively pervasive presence of digressing notes in the tone of the comic *naïf* (I mean in particular the comparison and correction of *come cocomeri, ma molto più duri*, the recycling of *beninteso* and the somewhat stale play on the word *fruste*), the description here appears to be more readable, even if it is also surely more banal. Its referentiality is not, all told, impaired by the superimposition of a different key. The humour (in its low form) and the heterogeneity of certain ingredients (for example, the pedantic use of *assai* to intensify *taglienti*, together with the deprecation of *diverse merde*) do not lead the reader too far off the track of the traditional descriptive syntax of the list. The informed reader of *La cognizione* will recall that the elaborative level of the final two segments belongs to an earlier draft, which has simply been tagged on to the rest of the text, out of an understandable editorial decision to present the work as completely as possible. In *Letteratura* and in the first edition of Einaudi's

Supercoralli, *La cognizione* ended with this segment, just one page beyond the passage that we are analysing here. In description A, on the other hand, the greater degree of elaborative care leads to the explosion of the individual descriptive units in autonomous directions: autonomous in style and in elaborative processes. One outstanding component of that autonomy seems to be, in fact, the different method of connecting the units, which in the less elaborated description B is the conjunctive type, while in the more highly elaborated A, we find the alternative type.

We arrive now at the second paragraph, in which, as has already been noted, the human geography is foregrounded. First depicted as *ghiaiosa, a forte pendenza*, the road is now *percorsa, risalita, zoppicata* etc.; and that by a multiplicity of users,[10] almost in antithesis to the *Nessuno mai vi transitava [...] la notte* of description B, that has only the hypothetical, though significance-laden, exception of Manganones on his bicycle: 'Nessuno dunque passava da quella strada nelle ore mute della notte: o forse, talvolta, con la bicicletta senza fanale ...' [So nobody passed along that road in the silent hours of the night: or maybe, at times, on a bicycle with no headlamp ...]. But the isolated rustic path that leads to the Piro-butirro villa, a true and proper umbilical cord that ties it to the external world, appears to be narratively animated even before, even outside of this description. In a brief span of time, the reader finds first, on his way up, the doctor, walking, even though a potential cyclist: 'Tentava il buon medico, i primi ciottoli della postrema sassonia: una stradaccia affossata nei due muri y por suerte nelle ombre delle robinie e d'alcuni olmi, per l'ultima pazienza de'suoi piedi eroici' (*C*, 97) [The good doctor started up the first pebbles of the last rocky stretch: a little road sunk between two walls y por suerte in the shadows of the locusts and of some elms, the ultimate trial for the patience of his heroic feet (*AG*, 46)]; he finds there 'Battistina in discesa' (*C*, 116) [Battistina on her way down], who has a long conversation with the doctor on the path; then Gonzalo's mother herself, who has gone down ('con queste strade!' [with these roads!]) to the cemetery; also the 'nipotino del Di Pascuale' [young nephew of Di Pascuale] (163–4) and a little later Manganones on his bicycle, going up and coming back down. The passage that we are analysing is thus a kind of generalizing compendium of all this commotion.[11]

The first qualification of the *stradaccia* in the second paragraph is that it is simply, with an anodyne verb, neutral in respect to the particular means utilized, *percorsa*: passed along by *pedoni* without further individuation (thus travelled on foot) and with reduced frequency (*radi*). To this first very general descriptive note is added by means of coordination (note: with the word *e*) a doubling of the complement of the agent (= e [...] *da qualche ciclista di campagna con bicicletta mulo*). As often happens in Gadda's prose, the result (thanks to the morphology of *qualche* and to the shift of the quantifier from adjective, *radi*, to adverb: *talora*) is a more individuating, more precise annotation than the first. Its specific difference consists (beyond its many variations of linguistic realization) in the choice of bicycle as means (recall that the doctor is another potential user-cyclist of the *stradaccia*), counterposed to the absence of means, and in the specification, also absent at first, of the direction of travel: *in discesa*. It is also necessary to call the reader's attention back to the adverb *talora*, a sort of stylistic signature of the author, his instrument of choice for inserting particular events into a habitual practice, and vice versa for varying the fixity of it: in short, for describing that which is contingent over the backdrop of a paradigm of alternatives.[12]

The paragraph's opening appears to be dominated by the verb of motion at its beginning, expanded by a pair of coordinated, piled-up complements, which we will call *a* and *b*. With the disjunction *o*, the development that follows (= *c*) introduces an alternative (singular) in respect to *b* and to *a*: passing along the road is now the *procaccia* (= mailman), in place of the backroad cyclists and the pedestrians. But at the same time, given that the verb *risalita* incorporates the direction that first was expressed adverbially (= *in discesa*), *c* works also as alternative to the verb *percorsa* of *a*, which is no longer simply implied as it was in *b*. Syntagma *c* is thus attached to both *b* and, on a higher level, *a*, or better to the unit formed by *a* and *b*. The variation in the passage from *b* to *c* is, moreover, multiple, and not merely binary: beyond the agent (i) and the direction (ii), the numbers (iii) and definition (iv) of the agents change; and again (v) their frequency (*talora*, versus the absence of indications); (vi) the means: the *bicicletta* versus (presumably) 'on foot'; and (vii) the modality: the absence of modality (unless one may read it into *bicicletta-mulo* versus the participial specification (*arrancante*, etcetera) of one. The apparently simple alternative based on a binary opposition in effect turns out to be a chimera of heterogeneous oppositions. With a classically crescendoed closure, the final development of the sentence (= *d*) multiplies the differential elements (again, as in *b*, a plural, again the mention of the frequency, and so on). In particular it integrates in the verb, from which by compensation the directional component is given, the modality that first was external: *zoppicata* (limped over) and the question of direction thus raised is declared unknown (*non si sa in che verso*). Finally, a hermetically symbolist apposition reformulates the description of the agent (*cenciose apparizioni nella gran luce del nulla*).

The complex system of permanences and variations in the first part of the paragraph can be visualized schematically in the following table:

verb of motion	frequency	direction	mode	agent	number	means
traveled	——	——	——	those on foot	rare	(On foot – integrated in the agent)
[traveled]	at times	in descent	expressed by mule-bike	(some) backroad cyclists	some	on bicycle
ascended (includes direction)	——	ascending (in verb)	trudging in the rain, etc.	fearless mailman	one	(on foot – but not explicit)
limped over (includes mode and means)	hebdomadal	unknown direction	(limping integrated in verb)	beggars	a few	(on foot – integrated in verb)

A simple syntactic module of 'participle + complement of the agent + dislocated subject' thus furnishes at the beginning of the paragraph the woof of a process, which is reiterated with mounting complexity, within which the individual photograms of the *stradaccia* progressively acquire autonomy. In other words, the description appears to be executed from various perspectives, constructed by juxtaposition and summation of independent tesserae.

The autonomy of the component images also becomes syntactical in the second part of the paragraph, in which appear two elaborated *tableaux* (*d* and *e*) of *battute* and country outings, now introduced by predicates *vi sfringuellavano* and *Vi si avventurava*. The first, a happy image of unbridled freedom, I would venture, means more than the contextually incongruous 'vociare, cicalare' [shouting, jabbering] set down in the lexicons. In my opinion, the meaning of *vi sfringuellavano* is closer to 'move about, from place to place, like finches'; in other words, it integrates the movement and its modality. But the most salient aspect of the new development *d* is not so much in the verbal neologism or in the dash of Spanish it contains as in the gerund *Vaporando l'autunno*, which adds a further factor of variation, that of the season, to the preceding series, a factor that has been retained and specified (= *col settembre*) in the concluding development of the passage. That same development is itself a description completely articulated in two moments, the second analogical, at least in the beginning (*Pareva*) if not in the final gerunds of the series,[13] and the first referential, but with an extended modality ('imbarcando magari tutta una famiglia gitante') which isolates once again an alternative hypothetical episode. The conclusion returns the descriptive excursus to the *particular* of the novel's protagonist, distracted in his refuge from the noble idlings which the silence induces.

In conclusion, the second paragraph, as is moreover somewhat the case in the first, with its focalizations of diverse segments, offers the road with a description not in the usual sense of the word: that is, a representation of the contingency of an entity or of a situation. Rather, the second paragraph furnishes the reader what might be called a 'summation' of various possible contingencies: the juxtaposition of several or many of the different aspects, among them alternatives, of a kaleidoscopic reality. It therefore provides a description 'by alternatives,' a description which condenses into one the usually disjointed, rather than concomitant, manysidedness of reality.

2. Description 'with Comment'

As has been said above, description 'with comment' is a description consisting of dishomogeneous layers; it includes moments at a higher level, one of almost metareferential comment, providing justifications, generalizations, and so on, with respect to the normal descriptive plane. This type of description, I believe, responds to a widely (and quite successfully) deployed tendency in Gadda's writing: the juxtaposition of precise observations on contingent facts along with their 'valuation,' which is to say, a sort of comment on the datum, or an 'abstraction' drawn from it. Moreover, the speculative aspect, dominant in certain parts of Gadda's work, is never altogether absent; implicitly or explicitly, it is found also in the parts which are more decidedly narrative, and can, as in *Quer pasticciaccio* and *La cognizione*, attain important dimensions. Thus, the technique involves continual excursions, starting from contingency and moving towards a representative plane of greater generalization, and successive brusque returns to the preceding level. Such a tendency, which according to the author is deeply rooted in his method of work, in his constant attempt to impose a 'poetic idea' upon 'many injections of classical readings' (Gadda 1993, 49), seems to respond (to name a few of the causes) to Gadda's incapacity in principle to limit himself to a single thread, to the single 'voice.' Or, positively, it may respond to a profound need for polyphony, for the paradigmatization of the individual fact (whence the plurality of perspectives) according to an approach similar to that of Tacitus in history and morals (whence the type of plurality). The result is a representation with levels which are grafted on, one of which is often that of the maxim, of the apothegm. There is, to take an example from the catalogue of Gonzalo's cruelties,[14] that famous paragraph about the falling cat, about the cat thrown from the third floor of the villa for experimental purposes, or out of a sadistic impulse. (This is a passage that attracted the critical attention of Pasolini, and that finds, beyond its parallel with *The Brothers Karamazov*, which has been written about extensively, another surprising as well as fortuitous correspondence with Buchner's *Woyzeck*.)[15] In and of itself, the act has no such implications, at least not that Gonzalo is aware of; it is merely aimed at functionalizing a very general principle of rational mechanics (the theorem of impulse or of the conservation of momentum: 'impulse equals the change of momentum' $<I = MV>$), which he intends to check through a concrete application. But, beyond that, the paragraph is sealed by a second principle formulated in the mode of a maxim ('Perché' etcetera), isolated for greater strength in a separate sentence: 'Poiché ogni oltraggio è morte.' This is a formula that grasps a further abstraction which can be drawn from the concrete fact, this time related to the moral mechanics of the protagonists, human or animal, of *La cognizione* or of life, and so intuitively self-evident as not to require any verification at all.

Now, however, let us turn to a particular instance of description by comment with a detailed consideration of the opening of the second segment of the first part of *La cognizione*, a selection characteristic of Gadda's intensely 'written,' semantically concentrated prose:

Al passar della nuvola, il carpino tacque. E' compagno all'olmo, e nella Néa Keltiké lo potano senza remissione fino a crescerne altrettanti pali con il turbante, lungo i sentieri e la polvere: di grezza scorza, e così denudati di ramo, han foglie misere e fruste, quasi lacere, che buttano su quei nodi d'in cima. La robinia tacque, senza nobiltà di carme, ignota al fuggitivo pavore delle Driadi, come alla fistola dell'antico bicorne; radice utilitaria e propagativa dedotta in quella campagna dell'Australasia e subito fronzuta e pungente alla tutela dei broli, al sostegno delle ripe. Fu per le cure d'un agrònomo che speculava il progresso e ne diede sicuro il presagio, vaticinando la fine alle querci, agli olmi, o, dentro i forni della calcina, all'antico sognare dei faggi. Dei quali non favolosi giganti, verso la fine ancora del decimottavo secolo, era oro e porpora sotto ai cieli d'autunno tutta la spalla di là della dolomite di Terepáttola, dove di qua strapiomba, irraggiando, sulla turchese livellazione del fondovalle, che conosciamo essere un lago. La calcina, manco a dirlo, per fabbricare le ville, e i muri di cinta alle ville: coi peri a spalliera. (*C*, 111–15)

[The passing of the cloud, the hornbeam fell silent. It is companion to the elm, and in Nea Keltike they relentlessly despoil it of branches until it has grown into so many turbaned stakes along the paths and the dust: rough-barked and stripped thus of boughs, it has wretched, worn, almost tattered, leaves which burst out into those knots at the crown. The locust was silent, without nobility of song, as unknown to the fugitive fear of the dryads as to the syrinx of the ancient two-horned one: utilitarian and propagative root introduced into that countryside from Australasia and immediately thick-leaved and pungent in the guardianship of enclosures, and in the support of slopes. It was here thanks to the attentions of an agronomist who speculated on Progress and gave its prospects as certain, predicting an end to oaks, to elms, and, inside the lime kilns, to the ancient dreaming of the beeches. From which nonfabulous giants, even toward the end of the eighteenth century, it was gold and purple under the autumn skies across the entire flank on the other side of the dolomites of Terepattola, and where on this side it drops precipitously, radiating out upon the turquoise flattening of the valley bed, which we know to be a lake. The lime, it goes without saying, was to build the villas, and the garden walls of the villas – with espaliered pear trees. (*AG*, 51)]

Inserted in its context, this passage, despite its isolated position at the beginning of a 'segment,' takes the form of a descriptive stop related to a broader unit that in turn sets the stage for the first major scene of the novel: the 'philosophical' dialogue between the 'good' doctor and his patient.[16] 'Ripresa descrittiva del paesaggio e satirica' (*C*, 350) [Return to the landscape's description and satire] is how Gadda labelled it. The doctor's progress, to the same degree as other durational actions in other places, keeps being reactualized at regular intervals so as to furnish, together with the character's equally recurrent reactions or comments, a solid framework for (by nature) disordered reflections. The representation is thus articulated in two superimposed and parallel 'layers': one external, elemental, progressive, and the other mental and associative. This second layer contains within itself departures from homogeneity: the thoughts of the doctor, which, though they essentially keep turning towards his patient, display a process of alternation, with recurring increments of abstraction or generality, belonging to the type that we have discussed above. In these thoughts, the doctor, even if his voice is at times indistinguishable from that of the author, indulges in considerations of general validity; he philosophizes ('filosofeggia'), for example, meditating aphoristically upon alimentary habits (as the precocious disciple, in this regard, of Dr Bircher-Benner), or in the mawkish accents of a moralist, he intones upon the fate of mankind. This is where, in particular, the justly celebrated passage concerning the 'cammino delle generazioni' is found: 'Oh! lungo il cammino delle generazioni, la luce!...che recede, recede.... opaca....dell'immutato divenire. Ma nei giorni, nelle anime, quale elaborante speranza!...e l'astratta fede, la pertinace carità. Ogni prassi è un' immagine,.....zendado, impresa, nel vento bandiera....' (C, 97–8) ['Oh! what light along the roadway of the generations! ... which fades, fades ... opaque ... of the immutable process of becoming. But through the days, inside the souls, what elaborate expectancy and hope! ... and the abstract strength of faith, the pertinacity of charity. Every praxis is an image, ... a silken emblem, a venturing forth, flag fluttering in the wind ... (AG, 46)].

The passage under scrutiny, which is, as has been said, a tessera of a larger unit organized through parallel and superimposed layers, belongs, with its comprehensive description of natural events (and so, with extremely slackened narrative thrust), to the 'low' narrative layer. This layer consists of the chronological relation of minor actions (or really of their textual reactualization, of their being renamed), actions of minimal relevance to the plot, which are none the less implied by other actions which are really quite central. We shall now see that this 'low' narrative layer, or at least the segment with which we are dealing, is organized, and even more visibly so, according to a scheme homologous to that of the mental excursus. That is to say, it is organized by regular alternations between the specific and the general, with a sinusoidal trajectory with respect to the generality of the themes touched upon and the references made.

One will notice, to begin, that our passage essentially depicts a sudden silence in the countryside, an impromptu pause in the duration 'senza termini' [without end] (strictly speaking, 'without spatial limits,' which is to say, spread over the entire countryside) of the cicada's song. The cicadas, suddenly,[17] 'fall silent' (tacciono) – with an almost technical verb, in the literary Koiné, for the interruption of a durational activity (just recall the adynaton in Ovid's Ars I, 271, 'vere prius volucres taceant, aestate cicadae'). Those who fall silent in the representation are in reality not so much the cicadas, which are not named anywhere in the paragraph, but metonymically, the trees in which the cicadas are perched, with which they are completely at one (as was suggested in the compositional note mentioned above, with its juxtaposition of 'carpino-cicala'). In fact, only two, among all the types of trees, fall silent: the *carpino* and the *robinia*, and they do so, in the text, at a distance, the hornbeam in the first and the locust in the third sentence, that is, in a discontinuous way despite the isochronic nature of the event.

As a coded representation of the cicadas 'falling silent,' of the country-side's becoming quiet, the passage turns out to be tightly tiled in with prior and subsequent moments of the promenade: it is joined to a note on the surroundings found on the first page: 'la cicala sull'olmo senz'ombre [note here the pairing of two singular genera] friniva a tutto vapore[18] verso il mezzogiorno, dilatava la immensità chiara dell'estate' (*C*, 105) [the cicada, upon the elm without shadows was chirping full-steam towards midday, it dilated the crystal immensity of the summer (*AG*, 49)], and taken up again and pursued in its turn pages later by an analogous nota-tion on the surroundings (this time with a plural): 'Le cicale, risveglie, screziavano di fragore le inezie verdi sotto la dovizie di luce, tutto il cielo della estate crepitava di quello strìdio senza termini nell'unisono d'una vacanza assordante' (*C*, 123) [The cicadas, reawakened, speckled with their din the green motes beneath the abundance of light; all the summer sky was crackling with that endless noise, in the unison of a deafening vacancy (*AG*, 57)]. Thus, in succession: the song of the cicadas, its sudden cessation in our passage, and its eventual resumption (where *risveglie* presupposes the twin *tacque*) and duration – with the usual iterative actualizations: for example, on pages *C*, 128, 'Il toccare delle undici e mezza [...] metallo immane sullo stridere di tutte le piante' [the striking of half-past eleven ... monstrous metal over the creaking of all the trees]; 129, 'Il crepitìo infinito della terra pareva consustanziale alla luce' [The infinite crackling of the earth seemed consubstantial with the light]; 143, 'la luce della campagna; screziata di quella infinita crepidine' [the light of the countryside, speckled with that infinite crackling]; 144, 'E le cicale, popolo dell'immenso di fuori, padrone della luce' [And the cicadas, populace of the immensity outside, masters of the light (*AG*, 60, 61, 68)].

The silencing, or better, the alternation of song and silence, appears to be synchronized in this passage with an alternation of another sphere of perception: that between light and shadow over the landscape. The cicadas, 'bestie di luce' (*C*, 151), fall silent each time the passing clouds project a shadow over the countryside.[19] This passing of clouds overhead is recurrent (see, for example, the innovative space-time adverbial: 'come se parlasse tra sé e sé, o tra una nuvola e l'altra' (146) [as if a conversation were taking place between sky and earth or between one cloud and an-other (*AG* 70)], and belongs to the perceptual stereotypes of the author, who is sensitive to every rhythmic scansion of time and space (ranging from that, in *La cognizione* and elsewhere, of the 'giro breve' [brief journey] of the woodworms to that, in *C*, 384, of the 'numero di bronzo' [bronze number], 'dopo desolati intervalli' [after desolate intervals], and that, in *Gli anni*, 210–12, of the frog, which 'per più lenti intervalli' [for longer intervals] with respect to the tree frog, greets with its 'cauto singhiozzo' [cautious hiccup] the 'zaffiro della stella Espero, tacitamente splendida' [sapphire star of Hope, tacitly splendid]). It is worth noting that this perceptual and representational scheme may already have been prefigured in the goliardic onomastics of the unpublished 'Villa in Brianza,' even if there it was only (partially) implied:

Nuvole strane *trasvolavano nel* torrido *cielo*, da Bergamo sopra l'Albenza, da Lecco, bel nome lombardo, come anche Menaggio e Chiavenna. I cumuli enormi si morulavano, come a simboleggiare future tempeste. *La cicala immensa, a tratti, taceva* e più lontane e remote cicale dicevano malinconiose desolazioni della terra, popolata di brianzoli.

[Strange *clouds were sailing across* the torrid *sky*, from Bergamo above Albenza, from Lecco, a beautiful Lombard name, like Menaggio and Chiavenna, too. The enormous cumuli were dividing and multiplying like morulae, as if omens of future storms. *The immense voice* of the *cicada* would *at times fall silent* and cicadas farther on and more remote would take up the discourse on the melancholic desolations of the earth, populated by the people of Brianza.]

(The relevant parts are in italics; the 'beautiful Lombard name' is an obvious reference to Carducci's *Odi Barbare*, 'Per la morte di Napoleone Eugenio,' v. 33: 'Ivi Letizia bel nome italico.')

To return to the passage under discussion, linguistically the synchronization is not so much asserted as suggested by the circumstantial 'Al passar della nuvola' (implied in the third sentence), which compresses, by eliminating the usual intermediary term, the overly explicit formula of the first draft version with its double circumstantiation: 'Nell'intermettere della cicala, trasvolando la nuvola, si tacitò il carpino' [In the intermission of the cicadas, while the cloud was passing over, the hornbeam fell silent] (a version which, in the order *b-a-c*, foregrounded the standard *b* term and the figurative *c*).

At the passing of each cloud, therefore, the chirping of the cicadas ceases, and, figuratively, the 'vocal' trees fall silent. It will not be overlooked that the context here has led to the insertion of the singular represented event into a series of events of the same kind (it is Gadda's tendency, to which we have already referred apropos the adverb *talora*, to place the single fact within series of similar facts). But it is above all important at this point to bring out how the alternation and synchronization of lights and sounds correspond elsewhere in the text to a pattern (so to speak) of engaging in speculation, and are essential to our comprehension of *La cognizione*. Many pages and segments farther on, in a different scenic unit, but in a similar temporal and psychological situation, Gonzalo, on the terrace of his villa, contemplates the passage of the clouds: 'Nubi transitavano, dalla montagna, in quel cielo, così sereno e ampio da parere infinito' (*C*, 420) [There were clouds moving across from the mountains in that sky, so serene and wide as to appear infinite (*AG*, 207]. And at 'ogni ombra,' in the suspension of time, there comes from the depths of the countryside, 'ritenuto e profondo come la cognizione del dolore' [extended and profound, like the cognition of grief], the 'desperate cry' of the cuckoo:

Per intervalli sospesi al di là di ogni clausola, due note venivano dai silenzî, quasi dallo spazio e dal tempo astratti, ritenute e profonde, come la cognizione del dolore: immanenti alla terra, quandoché vi migravano luci ed ombre. E, sommesso, venutogli dalla remorta scaturigine della campagna, si cancellava il disperato singhiozzo. (*C*, 421–3)

[At intervals, suspended beyond any resolution, two notes came out of the silences, as if arising out of abstract space and time, extended and profound, like the cognition of grief: immanent in the earth, whenever light and shadow migrated across it. And, softly, having come to him from the remote source of the countryside, the desperate sob died away. (Cf *AG*, 208.)]

Beyond the confines of different scenes which are nonetheless similar, an identical scansion rules over the flow of immobile days: intervals of light and pauses of shadow, and correspondingly, on the sunny countryside, the deafening unison of infinite cicàdas; and, in the shade, the solitary voice, the extended cry of the cuckoo hidden in the thickets. The structuring of natural perception thus finely reflects the oppositions on which *La cognizione* is built: that between plurality (the others, the *many*, the *everybody*, the faceless multitude of *calibans*) and singularity, and those between sociality and solitude, between the natural and the cultural, between clamour and silence, between act and thought. At one of the poles, there is the solitary *cuculo*, Gonzalo, in one of his darker moments of existence (despite the sunny moments of verbal outpourings, which alternate with the saturnine).

Let us now return, after these contextual excursuses, to the representational organization of our paragraph. In it, the miniscule event of a sudden sonorous clouding over of the countryside, subsequently reversed, as seen from the re-emergent *risveglie* (C, 123), is depicted in two discontinuous temporal moments, and the more important of these is flooded with bits of information which are placed on a clearly more significant level of generality. Schematically, the paragraph can be outlined with the formula:

$$A\ B\ A'\ B,'$$

or more analytically:

$$[\text{---}]\ \ [\text{------}]\ \ [\text{---}]\ \ [\text{------}]$$
$$A\ A \qquad B\quad B \qquad A'\ A' \qquad B' \qquad B'$$

in which the 'reflective' moments B and B', which are of greater length, are inserted after the two moments A ('Al passar della nuvola, il carpino tacque') and A' ('La robinia tacque') of concrete representation. This further alternation is prolonged through hysteresis even if less rigorously, in the following paragraph and in the beginning of a moment C ('Quella straduccia che il medico doveva risalire andò a lungo nell'ombre, non già dei carpini radi, ma delle robinie senza fine. *Etc.*'). Moment C is homologous to moments A and A'; it is developed in its turn after a long descriptive insertion about the locust, by a further reflective moment D' ('La sua mediocre puzza la fece considerare utile ai molti; etc.') in series with B and B', only to come back down finally to E: 'Un quadrupedare tra i ciottoli tolse il dottore ai pensieri: levò il capo *etc.*' [A quadrupeddaling among the pebbles disturbed the doctor from his thoughts: he raised his head *etc.* (AG, 52)]. What results is a trajectory that might be called sinusoidal, which can be illustratively transposed into a two-levelled scheme which visually displays the upswings into generalization in a protracted alternation between the concrete and the general:

$$B\ B'\ D'$$
$$A\ A'\ C\ E.$$

As a fragment of a prior draft (the only one, in fact, to have been preserved) attests, the scheme described here seems to have been present from the beginning, or at least from a very early stage. This is a fact that is not irrelevant for understanding the genesis of Gadda's writing. The fragment is presented here with the standard editorial markings:

Nell'intermettere della cicala, trasvolando la nuvola, si tacitò il carpino. E' una sorta d'olmi, nella Néa Keltiké potati senza remissione, fino a crescerne altrettanti pali del telegrafo lungo i sentieri o >le strade il polverone delle strade le strade< la polvere. Di grezza scorza, e così diradati di ramo e di fronda, con foglia povera e frusta, quasi lacera. Si tacitò la robinia senza nobiltà di passato, né studio <di rustico [*p. ill. cassata*] veterano>, né >canto< lode >di antica buccolica bucolica< di faunesca fistola o >di smarrita< canto [*p. ill.*] di>malinconiosa< smarrita bucolica: radice utilitaria e propagativa dedotta in quella campagna dall'Australasia e subito fronzuta e padrona d'ogni ripa, d'ogni brolo. Fu per le cure d'un agronomo progressivo >ch'ebbe< che diede sicuro il presagio: >e< <egli> <su quel fondamento [?]> scontò la fine alle querci, agli olmi >;< : o, dentro i forni della calcina, all'antico sognare dei faggi; dei quali non favolosi giganti, verso la fine ancora del >decimosettimo< decimottavo secolo, era oro e porpora sotto ai cieli >dell'< d'autunno tutta la spalla di là della dolomite di Terepàttola, dove di qua strapiomba, e <dorata> splende, <come >apparizione< muro di regni non >tocchi< valicati> sulla >chiarità< livellazione turchese del lago. La calcina, manco a dirlo, per fabbricare le ville: e i muri di cinta delle ville: coi peri a spalliera

[In the intermission of the cicada, while the cloud was passing overhead, the hornbeam fell silent. It is a sort of elm, in Nea Keltike pruned relentlessly, until it grows into so many telegraph poles along the paths or >the roads the dust of the roads the roads< the dust. Rough-barked, and so stripped of branch and frond, with miserable and worn-out leaves, almost tattered. The locust fell silent without nobility of past, nor study of <rustic [p. ill. cassata] veteran> , nor >song< praise >of ancient buccolic bucolic< of faunish fistula or >of lost< song [p. ill.] of >melanchonious< lost bucolic: a utilitarian and propagative root introduced into that countryside from Australasia and immediately thick-leaved and guardian of every slope and every enclosure. It was thanks to the attentions of a progressive agronomist >who had< who ensured the presage:>and< <he><on that basis [?]> it made up for the end of the oaks, the elms >;<:or, inside the lime kilns, the ancient dreaming of the beeches; from which nonfabulous giants, even towards the end of the >seventeenth< eighteenth century, it was gold and purple under the skies >of the< in autumn the entire flank on the other side of the dolomites of Terepattola, and where on this side it drops precipitously, and <golden> shines, <as>apparition< wall of realms not >touch< crossed> on the >clarity< turquoise flattening of the lake.The lime, it goes without saying, was to build the villas: and the walls surrounding the villas: with espaliered pear trees. (Cf *AG*, 51.)]

We now come to a minute examination of the articulation *A B A' B'* of the paragraph, and especially of the two so-called reflective moments *B* and *B'*. In *A* and *A'*, thanks to the personification imposed through the deployment of the verb 'tacere,' the protagonist is the countryside, of which (merging narration and description into one: the verb is in the past tense – specifically, 'passato remoto,' or 'distant past' – remote from the narration of events) a specific alteration is presented. The interposed elements *B* and *B'*, with a sudden leap to the level of generalization, lead instead away from the narration-description, to a level that is less concrete, and more abstract: in order to introduce what might be called encyclopaedic information about the referents, in order to load these referents with history and knowledge: of economic, botanical, literary, and mythological culture. The hornbeams that fall silent in *A* are those named somewhat affectedly with a singular 'generic' noun ('Il carpino') which are planted along the *stradaccia* being travelled by the doctor, or along other nearby paths. But suddenly, in *B*, the reference is extended generally, with the implied subject of the new sentence ('É compagno ...'), to all the hornbeams of Nea Keltike (Lombardy, the Po Valley) and correspondingly, the assertion becomes habitual, with the use of the factual present tense (from *tacque* to *e compagno*, to *lo potano*, etcetera), and in fact is applied after the colon, with a third metamorphosis of the reference, to the plural of *carpini-pali*, which is to say, the condition to which the 'care' of the peasants reduces the defenseless *popolo*. Underneath the virtuosity of the mutating denotation and the thematic kaleidoscope (evident in the progressive diminution of focus right down to the leaves of the trees) there are, in contrast to what is contingent, solid notions of botany and agronomy, not unworthy of the pages of a 'Politecnico': the hornbeam, 'companion' to the elm, and not simply 'associated' with it (although the elm does accompany the doctor on his way [*C*, 97]), tends to be treated as a thicket (in particular, the sparse fronds, 'foglie misere e fruste, quasi lacere' [wretched, worn, almost tattered leaves] had been utilized as feed for the livestock. Pascoli's *Viola*, too, 'facea brocche di carpino e d'ontano' [made jugs out of hornbeam and elder]), denuded of all their lateral branches, thus producing the appearance of 'pali con il turbante' [turbaned poles]; also, the qualification of the bark, *grezza*, is reminiscent of the 'cortice [...] scabro' in the line of Forcellini, which bears testimony, moreover, with references to Pliny and Cato, to the plant's noble, bucolic history.

The *robinia*, which in *A'*, analogously, falls silent, is instead, for its part, a new tree, without tradition, propagated during the eighteen hundreds to supplant the autochthonous flora of the Po Valley for (according to the narrator) primarily economic reasons. A tree without qualities (the first three are negative: *senza* + negative noun and twice *ignota* + positive noun), the locust catalyses the polemical *vis* of a narrator who completely forgets about his character. A remark from an incomplete and earlier text, 'Viaggi di Gulliver,' is recycled and inserted here: the 'arbore pungentissimo' [highly pungent arbour] of locusts was the sixth 'generazione di felicità' [generation of happiness] 'infitta nella felice Breanza' [grown thick in happy Breanza]: 'più feconda che non le mosche sopra al risotto o i pesci gobbi in Eupili' [more prolific than the flies hovering over the *risotto* or the humpbacked fish in Eupili]. And in both places, Manzoni is charged for his real or purported propagation of the locust (*RR II*, 965).

Two trees, therefore, in the two 'referential' moments *A* and *A'*; or better, two types of trees, associated by their practical role but in a certain way counterposed. The first, the ancient one, is seen as the victim of ruthless necessity ('lo potano senza remissione') yet also the cause of its own tendencies to humility ('foglie misere e fruste, quasi lacere'); and the second is seen as the triumphant creature of utility. One thus discovers again an opposition homologous to that between light and shadow, between cicadas and cuckoo.

We have thus far analysed the binary architecture of our passage, which alternates between description and comment, an architecture noteworthy for its complex correspondences and patterns, and one which is certainly unusual in twentieth-century Italian prose. How typical it is of Gadda's writing is further illustrated by the superimposition of procedures which disrupt the equilibrium of the logical schemes so as to compromise their consistency from within, introducing a spontaneous playfulness in the very place where rationality seemed to rule supreme. One might consider, in particular, the pattern of the symmetrical *dispositivo A B / A' B'*. The formal rigidity of the pattern is mitigated in at least two ways. On one side, more subtly, the syntactic modality of the transition from *A* to *B* and from *A'* to *B'* intervenes: this is done first across the boundaries of the sentences ('il carpino tacque. É compagno all'olmo'), and later, in a more insidious manner, within the same phrase or sentence, straddling the boundaries of syntagma ('La robinia tacque, senza nobilità di carme'). Irregularity is thus grafted upon regularity, the former feeds off the latter. And on another side, the mitigation is effected by means of a more obvious asymmetry between *B* and *B'*. The *B'* segment

turns out to be longer and above all more complex than the B. This complexity derives from several characteristic (characteristic not by their nature but in their mode, frequency, and mass) techniques of expansion:
i) essentially digressive progression or linear thematic 'drift' (of which we have already spoken above, at the beginning of section 1);
ii) progression through *expolitio* of parallel subthemes.
The juxtaposition of qualifying negatives ('senza nobilità [...] ignota al [...] come alla [...]') and positives (part of which are conceivable as justifications of the negatives: 'senza nobilità di carme [...] perchè dedotta [...]') with which B' begins is in effect developed, after a period, by a new sentence. The new sentence returns to and elaborates one piece of the new, significant, rhematic information – on the first level of the preceding sentence: 'dedotta in quella campagna [...] Fu per le cure di [...]' In other words, having started from the locust's introduction into Europe from distant lands (Australasia – here Gadda is confusing the locust and the acacia) he arrives at speaking of the person mainly responsible for that modification, which had such a great impact upon the ecosystem. And he then continues in the same way, taking up again and developing the element, or one of the rhematic elements of the preceding unit in a new syntactic and semantic unit. The rhematic enumeration 'alle querci, agli olmi, o [...] all'antico sognare dei faggi' is rethematized at the beginning of the new sentence with 'Dei quali non favolosi giganti, [...]' and the new sentence reproduces within itself twice more the process of linear thematic progression. Now, however, it occurs under the strictest anadiplosis by contact, antecedent + relative: 'della dolomite di Terepattola [= Resegone or rather, I believe, Grigna, near Terepattola-Lecco] dove [= *'mentre essa,'* cioè *'la quale invece'*] di qua strapiomba [...] del fondovalle, che conosciamo essere un lago.'
The quadruple thematicization of rhematic elements takes the reader far away from the initial theme of B', the locusts of a plainly utilitarian present: it takes one back in time to the 'popolo senza frode' of the great trees – *querci olmi faggi* – of the Lombard countryside of the 'nineteenth century,' not without a hint of Ariosto (see *Orlando Furioso* I, 33: 'Il mover de le frondi e di verzure, / che di cerri sentia, d'olmi e di faggi'; moreover, even the return 'dei quali non favolosi giganti' seems to remind us generically of the *Orlando Furioso*); or it takes us, as in the opening of the *I promessi sposi*, to the affectionate present of a countryside dear to the author's own gaze, like the 'turchese livellazio del fondovalle, che conosciamo essere un lago.' In contrast to the drift of these themes, the second expansion technique named above, progression through *expolitio*

of parallel subthemes, takes over at this point. In other words, the author decides to go (partially) back up the digressive chain, recycling the new theme – 'La calcina' – from the same sentence from which the beeches and other 'non favolosi giganti' had been extracted:

vaticinando la fine alle querci $_a$, agli olmi $_{a'}$ o, dentro i forni della calcina $_b$, all'antico sognare dei faggi $_a$. Dei quali non favolosi giganti $_{a'}$ verso la fine ancora del decimottavo secolo, era oro e porpora sotto ai cieli d'autunno tutta la spalla di là [...] La calcina $_b$, manco a dirlo, per fabbricare le ville, e i muri di cinta alle ville: coi peri a spalliera

(the single/double underlinings and the subscripts illustrate the scheme with which the return is constructed, which is, comprehensively, of the type: $a_1, a_2 b, a_3 / a_{1-3} b$, or more simply: $a b / a' b'$). The last and briefest member of the segment B' is thus forced, instituting a parallelism, to re-establish the equilibrium compromised by a progressive marginalization of the centre of gravity.

The same thing is evident in the opening paragraph of *La cognizione*, which, having set out in a direct line to establish in detail the historical and spatial coordinates of the narration, soon pours forth in an unstoppable cascade of anadiplosis, marked at moments by feigned attempts to climb back up the thematic chain. This procedure is simultaneously a narrative beginning and a parodic caricature of the techniques of narration. Analogous phenomena of thematic drift occur in many other places, confirming the importance for Gadda's style of centrifugal forces which are meant to balance, on the level of writing and of cognition, the *ratio* of syntax, logic, and other values. The following passage is an example for one and all:

l'immagine del vecchio colonnello medico, che lui pure aveva avuto occasione di conoscere, se non proprio all'Ospedale Militare Centrale di Pastufazio. Del vecchio medico, e colonnello nonostante tutto, dal mento quadrato, dal colletto insufficiente al perimetro, col piccolo gancio ogniqualvolta sganciato, sul collo: che appariva quasi bendato dalla bianca benda militare. bende ch'egli aveva visto, egli Gonzalo, ai distesi: non mai bianche, nel monte. (*C*, 245)

[the image of the old medical colonel, whom he too had occasion to know, if not exactly at the Central Military Hospital of Pastrufazio – the image of the old doctor, and colonel in spite of all, with the squared chin, the collar insufficient to the perimeter, with the little hook every so often unhooked, around his neck, so that he seemed almost wrapped in a white military bandage. Bandages that he had seen, he Gonzalo, on those lying outstretched; but never white, on the mountains. (*AG*, 127)]

The combining into linearity of concrete observations of reality and excursions into commentary results, as has already been said about the amassing of ornate elements in the passage analysed in Part 1 of this essay (and as is true, furthermore, for the elements of every complex alternative structure), in a palpable slowing down of the text, which in a complex way devalues the narrative relevance of the very description contained within it. In this process, secondary themes acquire autonomous resonance, and harmonic notes associated with the principal themes are amplified. That is what, I believe, happens in our passage in regard to the 'song of the cicadas' theme. This theme, which in the representation of the noon hour returns innumerable times in the *La cognizione* (one of Gadda's 'greatest metaphoric orchestrations' according to Pietro Citati),[20] can hardly be said to have no more significance than a mere descriptive fact. On one side, it resonates with rich literary allusions – recall what has been said about the author's method of work – firstly, his similarities with Ariosto – for example, the memorable verses in *Orlando Furioso*, VIII, 20 'sol la cicala col noioso metro / fra i densi rami del fronzuto stelo / le valli e i monti assorda, e il mare e il cielo' (Gadda's locust, too, is 'subito *fronzuta*') which Carducci in 'Risorse *di San Miniato al Tedesco*' (well known to Gadda, as a letter to Contini attests) had referred to in an ironic polemic within a lovely eulogy to cicadas: 'Nelle fiere solitudini del solleone, pare che tutta la pianura canti, e tutti i monti cantino, e tutti i boschi cantino: pare che essa la terra dalla perenne gioventù del suo seno espanda in un inno immenso il giubilo de' suoi sempre nuovi amori co 'l sole' [In the fierce solitudes of the dog days, it seems as if the whole plain is singing, and all the mountains and all the woods are singing along with it: it is as if the very earth is bursting forth from its perennially youthful bosom in an immense hymn of jubilation for its ever-renewed love affair with the sun].

But on another side, the vigilant omnipresence of the cicadas does not seem extraneous to a certain mannered Hellenism – one thinks, moreover, of a page of the *Meraviglie d'Italia* in which the light of Hellas is evoked: 'quella luce che già vide Zeusi, immota ed immensa tra le foglie digitate e setose, assordata dal disteso frinire' (*MI*, 49) [that light which Zeus once saw, motionless and immense among the digitated and bristly foliage, deafened by the prolonged chirping] – with perhaps as well an explicit allusion to one of the most famous myths of Plato's *Phaedrus*. In it, the cicadas are fated to be the ears of the Muses, to whom they carefully report concerning how the Muses are being honoured by men: in particular, they reveal to Calliope and Urania those who 'pass through life philosophizing.' Thus, for many reasons, Socrates concluded, 'we must continue our discourse and not abandon ourselves to the noonday sun.' And, in fact, 'Per non dormire ...' [So as not to fall asleep ...] is precisely the exclamation Gonzalo uses in acceding to the doctor's story (in *C*, 227): which is certainly a D'Annunzian expression, but one spoken by a protagonist who cultivates his philosophical musings: who reads the *Parmenides* (386), the *Symposium* and perhaps the *Laws* (411), and who rejects the clamour and the surrounding appearances of the world because they do not allow him to 'raccogliersi ne' suoi studi filosofici o algebrici' (492) [gather himself in his philosophical or algebraic studies]. The 'bestie della luce' are thus the faithful witnesses to Gonzalo's 'not abandoning himself to the somnolence of the midday'; witnesses, in fact, of his philosophical dialogue with the doctor, in which the alternation of theoretical and plainly quotidian sections (the latter entrusted mostly though not entirely to the doctor) seems to reproduce the alternation of song and silence, of light and shadow, in the introductory description.

A few words in conclusion: reading (the descriptions of) Gadda. In the preceding pages, we have individuated two descriptive techniques, that of 'description by alternatives' and that of 'description with comment,' which are particular to Gadda's prose. We have also maintained that such techniques are traceable to a tendency to 'infinite metonymy,' to seeing in every parcel of reality the network of relations, the 'web of infinite references' (*VM*, 638) which constitutes it. An identical motivation links the two descriptive techniques to well-known phenomena such as the superabundance (sometimes) of footnotes, or the jumps in tone or even in language, in the arrangement of the words in a sentence. Without exaggeration, it is legitimate to affirm that all of Gadda's prose is governed by a principle of generalized association, which systematically subjects his writing, line by line, word by word, to a 'metonymic explosion.'

However, the natural consequence of this fact, if we want to follow the author's multiple excursions, is that the average speed of our reading is necessarily greatly diminished in comparison to that for a hypothetical standard turn-of-the century narrative. It could be said that Gadda's pages demand a reading that is slow, painstaking, and attentive to detail. In effect, many of Gadda's narrative constructions are often, as has been said about the *La cognizione*, 'static structures,' 'more essay or treatise and confession than narration.' And particularly static are many of the descriptions, where there is no sense in trying to find the usual narrative functions (to establish the framework of the action, to create a *Stimmung*, to introduce indices of judgment, and so on). While this is altogether true, there are different modalities of slow-paced reading. I think it is quite mistaken to think of Gadda as a writer to approach solely 'on a small scale,' because of his lingerings, deviations, and returns, exploring minutely and without pre-established itineraries the associative meanderings of his sentence structure and lexicon. That is to say, it is mistaken to approach his work by employing a reading which is essentially astructural, antinovelistic in its atomism. In Gadda's writing, the static quality and the associated metonymic explosion are in reality a calculated result of an undaunted structuring will: they are one aspect of the unstable equilibrium between the two counterposed forces of order and disorder, of structure and dispersion.

As a result, an adequate reading of Gadda's descriptions (and of his writing in general), requires, beyond a total readiness to abandon oneself to its spontaneous excursions, its leaps of associative fantasy, the effort to reconstruct the rigorous architecture that potentiates and triggers off its opposite: an aleatory centrifugality. This architecture is certainly manifested on a small scale, within the paragraph and portions of it, as has been seen in parts 1 and 2 of this paper; none the less, it is also manifested in the macrostructures, and an attentive reading should always depart from the latter. A description like that which opens the second segment – 'Al passar della nuvola, il carpino tacque' – acquires meaning and function only if we insert it, as we have endeavoured to do in the first paragraphs of part 2, into the narrative context that justifies it and that it in turn relativizes. Reading certain descriptions by Gadda correctly is thus equivalent to doing justice simultaneously to their static quality and to their negated dynamism, to their character of being both fragment and indispensable tessera in the narrative mosaic.

Translated by William Hartley

Notes

1 'Cose, oggetti, eventi, non mi valgono per sé, chiusi nell'involucro di una lor pelle individua [...] : mi valgono in una aspettazione, in un'attesa di ciò che seguirà, o in un richiamo di quanto li ha preceduti e determinati' (*VM*, 629) [To me things, objects, events, enclosed in the husk of their individual skins,

are not valuable in themselves ... : what interests me is the sense of expectancy, an expectation of what is about to follow, or the echo of what has preceded and determined them]. The observation is Gian Carlo Roscioni's: see Roscioni 1975, 3 ff.

2 From a passage in *Meditazione milanese*, cited by Roscioni 1975, 16.

3 Cf Manzotti 1993, 19, which also gives details on the different versions in the *Meccanica*.

4 'Every stone, every object, every fact is therefore susceptible to innumerable meanings. Objects are points of departure for ... infinite rays ... To name them thus means to describe them and, even more, to join them and relate them to other objects. Gadda's very frequent recourse to metonymy is not the product of an exasperated search for literary expressivity, but obeys instead a need to arrive at deeper levels of knowing' (Roscioni 1975, 7–8).

5 All quotations from *La cognizione del dolore* are taken from the Einaudi 'Struzzi' edition, Turin 1987; henceforth referred to with the letter 'C.'

6 Quotations from Weaver's translation of *La cognizione del dolore* have been modified in various degrees.

7 For which we are reminded at the very least of: 'una qualche carogna di cavallo [...] : le quattro zampe all'aria, un corteggio di mosche verdi' (*MI*, 108) [a horse carcass or two ... : with its four hooves sticking up into the air, a cortege of green flies'].

8 As in 'la spada fiammeggiante, che scaccia di paradiso l'Adamo' (*AccG*, 826) [the ... flaming sword, that chases Adam out of paradise]; Cf also Manzotti 1993, 35, n37.

9 See also *C*, 431: 'dei torroni, dei colpi di gomito, delle frittelle, delle arachidi brustolite che precipitano il mal di pancia alle merde' (*AccG*, 211) [some nougat candies, some elbow blows, some fried dough pastries, some roasted peanuts which prompt the aching stomach to precipitate turds].

10 This is analogous to many other roads in Gadda's work. See, for example, those in 'Notte di luna' in *L'Adalgisa* (and in the *Racconto*): 'La sera vi passano senza rallentare altri ciclisti e pedoni' (*A*, 294) [At night other cyclists and pedestrians go by there without slowing down], and that of 'Ronda al Castello': 'Ciclisti d'ogni qualità e costume fendevano la greve consistenza dell'aria' (*MI*, 97) [Cyclists of every calibre and costume cleaved the heavy consistency of that air].

11 With reference to this episode see also, *C*, 73, 97, 115, 162–3, 222, and 225.

12 Among the many other examples, see *A*, 417, and *C*, 260, 261, and 268–9. Undoubtedly, we are dealing with a method used by Manzoni; cf chapter 1 of *I promessi sposi*: 'Diceva tranquillamente il suo ufizio, e *talvolta* tra un salmo e l'altro, chiudeva il breviario, tenendovi dentro, per segno, l'índice

della mano destra [...]. Aperto poi di nuovo il breviario, e recitato un altro squarcio, giunse ad una voltata della stradetta, dov' *era solito* d'alzar sempre gli occhi dal libro, e di guardarsi dinanzi: e *così fece anche quel giorno'* (my emphases) (Manzoni 1972, 27) [He was peacefully reciting his office. From time to time, between one psalm and another, he would shut up his breviary, keeping the forefinger of his right hand tucked into it as a bookmarker ... Then he reopened his breviary and recited another passage, which took him to a bend in the track, where *it was his habit* to raise his eyes from the book, and look straight ahead, *as he did on this occasion*]. This method was also adopted by D'Annunzio.

13 It should be recalled that the series of juxtaposed instrumental gerunds is typical of Gadda; indeed, it is even used at times to introduce alternatives. Minimally, it was so used in the passage cited above (*Fendendo, avvistando*); more complexly, it appears alongside the instrumental syntagma 'con' + definite article + infinitive in *C*, 247–8.

14 See Manzotti 1984, 332–56.

15 In the fragment called *hH: Der Hof des Professors*: 'meine Herren, wenn ich diese Katze zum Fenster hinauswerfe, wie wird diese Wensenheit sich zum centrum gravitationis gemäss ihrem eigenen Instinct verhalten.'

16 The habitual qualification of the doctor as 'good' constitutes an ironic allusion to nineteenth-century modes of narration: Cf *C*, 400, and the related note.

17 Somewhat following the lead of a sonnet by Zanella, which Gadda doubtless had memorized: 'Il suo stridor sospeso ha la cicala' (*Astichello*, XV, v 1), if not of one of Pascoli's *Temporale* ('É mezzodì. Rintomba. / Tacciono le cicale / nelle stridule seccie').

18 The adverbial clause, when closely considered, is a brilliant 'technological' corrective to the onomatopoeic and lexical insufficiency which Carducci's 'Risorse di San Miniato al Tedesco' lamented in regard to the word 'frinire' (the substitute 'strillare,' for example, is experimented with in 'Ebre di sole strillan le cicale,' in *Per la sospensione del 'Don Chisciotte.'*

19 This is an alternation which is by no means literarily innovative. See, for example, D'Annunzio's *Poema Paradisiaco*, 'Nell'estate dei morti' (in which one also finds the pairing of *purple/gold*): 'Guarda le nubi [...] . Dense come tangibili velari / scorrono il piano le lunghe ombre loro. / Entro splendonvi or sì or no le vigne / pampinee, le pergole, i pomarii, / e le foreste da la chioma insigne, / e tutte quelle sparse cose d'oro, / come entro laghi azzurri e solitarii.'

20 Citati, 'Il male invisibile,' in *Il Menabò* 6 (1963): 37. On this theme, see also the observations of Carlo De Matteis (1985, 36–7), with his proposals for a

symbolic interpretation: 'The meeting of the doctor and the son is prepared for and accompanied by a thematic correspondence emanating from the synesthetic identification of the light and the cicadas' song, which are manifestations of the outer world, placed beyond the penumbra and silence of the villa. The howling [sic] of the cicadas is assimilated into the blinding summer light, into endless counterpoint of the earth, in a notion of infinite presence and of absolute certainty, the proof of the pre-existence of an immutable worldly plenitude: "being in itself," enfolding with its irreducible density the emptiness of the villa and the perplexed consciousness drawn towards nullity which is closed up inside it. The first appearance of the cicadas prepares for the meeting with the son, the chirping of the cicadas is projected into a figure of symbolic spatial dimension.'

References

Citati, Pietro. 1963. 'Il male invisibile.' In *Il Menabò* 6

De Matteis, Carlo. 1985. *Prospezioni su Gadda*. Teramo: Lisciani and Giunti

Gadda, Carlo Emilio. 1970. *La cognizione del dolore*. Edited by Emilio Manzotti. Turin: Einaudi

– 1993. *'Per favore mi lasci nell'ombra.' Interviste 1950–1972*. Edited by Claudio Vela. Milan: Adelphi

Manzotti, Emilio. 1984. 'Astrazione e dettaglio. Lettura di un passo della *Cognizione del dolore*.' In *Cenobio* 32

Manzotti, Emilio, ed. 1993. *Le ragioni del dolore – Carlo Emilio Gadda 1893–1993*. Lugano: Edizioni Cenobio

Roscioni, Gian Carlo. 1975. *La disarmonia prestabilita*. Turin: Einaudi

Of Bards, Lombards, and Longobards: Narrating Milan in *L'Adalgisa*

GIAN PAOLO BIASIN

'È la Milano che dispare: e quale la lasceremo non era, e qual'era neppur più la ricordo: la forme d'une ville – change plus vite, hélas! que le coeur d'un mortel[32].' [This is the Milan that is disappearing, and it was not such as we will leave it, and the way it was I don't even remember any more: la forme d'une ville – change plus vite, hélas! que le coeur d'un mortel]. We find this sentence towards the end of 'Quando il Girolamo ha smesso ...' (*A*, 326), the second of the ten pieces that make up Carlo Emilio Gadda's *L'Adalgisa – Disegni milanesi* (1944), one of its author's major novelistic achievements.

Although this sentence is not particularly striking for any stylistic feature, it can none the less serve as an important introduction to Gadda's project and mode of writing. It indicates his favourite subject matter – his city, with the surrounding region of Lombardy; the passing of time, with the imprints left by a long history going back to the Longobards and beyond; and the self-awareness of the writer who stages himself as narrator and uses intertextual quotations and literary references to illustrious predecessors ranging from Baudelaire (here) to Rabelais, Manzoni, and many others (elsewhere). The quotation from *Les Fleurs du mal* is incorporated into the Italian text without marks or italics, as just another element of the all-pervasive literariness of the whole, a quality that bespeaks the European and universal, not provincial, import of Gadda's work: the shape of Milan and of any other city changes more rapidly, alas, than the heart of Gadda or that of any other mortal being.

Furthermore, the number '32' at the end of the quotation marks one of the many authorial footnotes that both enrich the principal text and make up another set of texts, micro-essays, and encyclopaedia entries that sustain and support the main 'story' (if we can still speak of a 'story' at all) with an indissoluble network of historical, geographic, scientific, cultural, sociological, and linguistic notions. This sentence is also an indirect reply to the question posed by the anthropologist and architect Franco La Cecla in his *Mente locale: per un'antropologia dell'abitare*: 'Is it possible to transform a city into a text, a narration?' (La Cecla 1993, 63)[1] – a question that, besides being particularly relevant for Gadda, has to do with the human shaping of space:

To inhabit is the diachronic dimension of presence, this presence lengthened in time, looking backwards (as if inhabiting were a light that projects the shadow of our presence behind us) in order to find its points of reference not only in the surrounding space, but in lived space. This is why to describe a city is difficult, because the synchronic and diachronic dimensions intersect and merge, and every narration of a city is a narration of a presence in it. (73)

In other words, in all human settlements and particularly in a city, geography is intertwined with history, and the one cannot exist without the other. The 'anthropology of inhabiting' is the latest effort to understand the human condition in terms of both space and time, by focusing on the peculiarities of a given place which both shape and are shaped by its local inhabitants, their language or dialect, their mentality, their attitudes, their customs (or habits, hence in-habitants). Narration, then, is related to *mente locale*, the 'local mind' or knowledge of local ways, in so far as the latter is, in La Cecla's words, 'a competence and the use of this competence. A narration is a competence that makes a discourse' (74).

L'Adalgisa is, first and foremost, Gadda's Lombard and Milanese 'competence' become 'discourse.' It is his effort to narrate Milan, and, more specifically, to transform Milan into a novelistic narration. Yet the subtitle of the book, 'Milanese drawings,' not 'a Milanese novel' or 'a Milanese story,' while harking back to Manzoni's subtitle for *I promessi sposi*, 'Storia milanese del secolo xvii,' clearly indicates another characteristic of Gadda's writing – the pluralism and fragmentation that mark his entire oeuvre and seemingly prevent him from 'completing' or 'finishing' such novels as *La meccanica, La cognizione del dolore*, or *Quer pasticciaccio brutto de via Merulana*.[2]

To transform a city into a narration does not mean to set a story against a cityscape or an urban background – Balzac's or Zola's Paris, Dostoevski's St Petersburg, Joyce's Dublin, Svevo's Trieste, or Manzoni's Milan. It means to make the city itself the subject of the story, with its inhabitants, its topography, its institutions, its monuments, its slaughterhouses, its markets, its canals, and even its sewers. And this is what Gadda does explicitly and systematically in *L'Adalgisa* (but also in other scattered pieces from *Le meraviglie d'Italia* and *Accoppiamenti giudiziosi*).[3]

'The Milan that is disappearing' is, for example, the Milan of 'La Confidenza,' a firm specializing in house cleaning and particularly in wood floor ('parquet') polishing and waxing for well-to-do bourgeois families like the Cavenaghi. It is the Milan of horse-drawn carriages in the park, of concerts that become social occasions for endless gossip, of engineers graduated from the local polytechnic, of maids from the Brianza region, of collectors of stamps, minerals, and coleopters, of widows and opera singers, small crooks and butchers' errand boys. It is the Milan of interiors in bad taste, leaking faucets, hexagonal tile floors, public libraries and private clubs, ladies' purses and gentlemen's vests, boiled beef and radishes, and statesmen and bankers and doctors – like the ineffable Doctor Piva who takes care of many characters' families by ordering olive oil in the simplest cases, 'el comandava l'oli d'oliva,' in rhyme and dialect (*A*, 468).

But lest the reader be led into believing that he is nostalgically looking back towards lost times, Gadda provides ironic comments and judgments that sharply distance his *alter ego* narrator from the limitations and bigotries of his characters, while revealing an affective complicity, a sort of love-hate relationship with them that only the act of writing shows and clarifies. Gadda displays a dizzying array of linguistic and stylistic devices to make sure that his reconstruction is indeed 'the narration of a presence' rather than the re-evocation of a past. His Milan includes bourgeois interiors, courtyards, streets, shops, theatres, parks, public gardens. And these places are animated by a gallery of characters, mostly from the bourgeoisie, culminating in the portrait of the eponymous Adalgisa – Adalgisa Borella, the widow of the accountant Carlo Biandronni. A Gaddian interior might be reminiscent, *mutatis mutandis*, of Guido Gozzano's 'le buone cose di pessimo gusto' [the good things in very bad taste], and certain of his cityscapes might hark back to Aldo Palazzeschi's 'La passeggiata' (a poem made up of ironic lists of shop signs and names).[4] But what is really important is that Gadda's narration of Milan is truly the novel of a city, comparable perhaps to Carlo Porta's portrait of Milan in his dialect poetry (for instance, 'Lament del Marchionn di gamb avert' or 'Desgrazzi de Giovannin Bongee,' to quote two memorable characters), or (returning to the contemporary scene) to what Giorgio Bassani has called *Il romanzo di Ferrara* – that is, a novel in which the places are at least as important as the stories of the characters, and the histories of the city's institutions and customs take up a great narrative space of their own.[5] History and geography become literally stories, and these interconnected and intertwining stories are the very texture of *L'Adalgisa*. (I am tempted to suggest that a contemporary filmic equivalent of Gadda's 'Milanese drawings' might be the Los Angeles of Robert Altman's *Short Cuts*, for both its formal fragmentation – 'short cuts' in a technical sense – and moral stance – 'short cuts' as a metaphor for the characters' actions and omissions.)

It is impossible to give an adequate account of *L'Adalgisa*, of the subplots, figures, events, and voices recurring in the stories and giving the book its multiple unity. While I shall extrapolate a few examples, I intend to highlight above all some of the techniques and the stylistic and structural traits of Gadda's writing: the use of catalogues and chaotic enumeration; the network of references and connections in the text and in the footnotes, which are truly an institutionalized system of digressions; the Bakhtinian polyphony of different registers of Italian, Milanese dialect, and foreign languages; the open-endedness of the stories; and the self-awareness of the narrator.[6] These traits constitute the modernity of Gadda's writing and seem to illustrate the conception of the novel as an essay and as a complex tool of knowledge.[7] They are also the formal counterpart of Gadda's world-view: the catalogue and the chaotic enumeration mimic the open-ended order-disorder of the world; the fragmentation of the plots and the network of relationships point to the complexity of causes and effects, to the impossibility of total knowledge and closure.

Italian critics, from Arnaldo Ceccaroni (1970) and Gian Carlo Roscioni (1969) to Alberto Arbasino (1971), the self-styled 'nipotino dell'Ingegnere' or Gadda's little grandchild, have emphasized the importance of accumulation and the list in Gadda's work. *L'Adalgisa* is no exception. To start with, the text is literally filled with family names relating the characters among themselves (within and among the drawings) as well as with the narrator who at one point is called 'Gaddus.' A good example, among the many possible, of a list of typically Milanese family names is the following:

Questi, nel giorno di domenica 28 aprile 1931 di Nostro Signore, alle ore 16 precise, questi erano i Lattuada, i Perego, i Caviggioni, i Trabattoni, i Berlusconi, i Bambergi, i Dadda, i Frigerio, i Tremolada, i Cormanni, i Ghezzi, i Gnocchi, i Gnecchi, i Recalcati, i Ghiringhelli, i Cavenaghi, i Pini, i Tantardini, i Comolli, i Consonni, i Repossi, i Freguglia. Coniugati fra loro, imparentati fra loro, associati fra loro (*A*, 468).

[These, on the day of Our Lord, Sunday, April 28, 1931, at 4 pm sharp, were the Lattuadas, ... the Freguglias. All married among them, related among them, associated among them.]

This list seems to be propelled forward not so much by the relations among the families as by the power of the rhymes (Caviggioni-Trabattoni-Berlusconi, Pini-Tantardini) and the assonances (Ghezzi-Gnocchi-Gnecchi, Comolli-Consonni). As for 'Gaddus,' he is a member of the 'Biblioteca Linguistica' along with 'due Corbetta, tre Perego, e sei Caviggioni' [two Corbettas, three Peregos, and six Caviggionis]: the homonymies are complicated by 'toponomàstica urbana: il Perego di Via Giulio Carcano si chiama Filippo e il Perego di Via Filippo Carcano si chiama Giulio. Il Perego di Piazzale Giulio Cesare non si chiama né Giulio né Cesare, ma Pompeo' (413–14) [urban toponymy: the Perego of Giulio Carcano Street is named Filippo and the Perego of Filippo Carcano Street is named Giulio. The Perego of Giulio Cesare Place is named neither Giulio nor Cesare, but Pompeo]. The linguistic *divertissement* is quite obvious.

The same linguistic emphasis and pleasure are present in a list of 'authentic' (so the narrator assures us) dialect nicknames of small crooks on page 329, followed by an appropriate footnote on page 342 with the explanation: 'el Gildogratta' [Gildo the thief], 'el Biscella' [Curly], 'el Pistòla' [Teen-ager or annoying Bully], 'el Scirésa' [Cherry, meaning Baby], 'el Baüscia' [Messy], 'el Cascivít' [Screwdriver, meaning Good-for-Nothing].[8] Then, scattered throughout the text and the footnotes, there are the accumulations of technical terms related to various kitchen gadgets or electrical utilities or art criticism, the scientific terms of chemistry, physics, mechanics, mathematics, and biology, and even what I have elsewhere called 'a chaotic but structural enumeration' of alimentary and gastronomic referents throughout the 'drawings' (Biasin 1993, 87).

One of the best examples of catalogue turned into chaotic enumeration is perhaps at the beginning of 'Quando il Girolamo ha smesso ...': the scene is the interior of the Cavenaghi house, where the agents of the floor-polishing firm are at work, moving all the furniture and the objects from their usual positions in order to do a thorough job of cleaning:

in un battibaleno avevano bell'e che messo a soqquadro tutta casa: seggiole, cuscini, tavolini, lettini: la chincaglieria del salotto e il bazàr del salone, e la pelle d'orso bianco con il muso disteso e gli unghioni rotondi (che solevano gracchiare sul lucido appena pestarli), e i comò e i canapè e il cavallo a dòndolo del Luciano, e il busto in gesso del bisnonno Cavenaghi eternamente pericolante sul suo colon-nino a torciglione: e bomboniere, Lari, leonesse, orologi a pendolo, vasi di ciliege sotto spirito, orinali pieni di castagne secche, il tombolo di Cantú della nonna Bertagnoni, rotoli di tappeti e batterie di pantofole snidate da sotto i letti, e tutti insomma gli ingredienti e gli aggeggi della prudenza e della demenza domestica: dapprima scaravoltati gambe all'aria, poi simultanati, razionalizzati in una nuova e capovolta ragione, in una nuova e mirabile, per quanto imprevedibile, sintassi. (*A*, 301)

[In a flash they had already turned the whole house upside down: chairs, cushions, small tables, small beds: the trinkets of the sitting-room and the bazaar of the living-room, and the white bear skin with its spread-out muzzle and the big round nails (that used to screech on the shining floor when threaded upon), and the chests of drawers and the sofas and Luciano's rocking-horse, and the plaster bust of great-grandfather Cavenaghi, eternally in danger on its small twisted column: and *bonbonnières*, Lares, lionesses, pendulum-clocks, jars of cherries in alcohol, night pots filled with dry chestnuts, grandmother Bertagnoni's Cantù lace-pillow, rolls of rugs and batteries of slippers taken out from under the beds, and in sum all the ingredients and the gadgets of domestic prudence and folly: first turned upside down with their legs in the air, then simultaneously rationalized in a new, topsy-turvy reason, in a new and admirable, however unforeseeable, syntax.]

The chaotic enumeration is justified by the needs of the job to be done, but becomes a delightful catalogue of the turn-of-the-century tastes and idiosyncrasies of the Milanese bourgeoisie, or, as the narrator comments, 'of domestic prudence and folly'; not to mention the fact that the apparent disorder caused in the house and on the page by the strange grouping of so many disparate and even unusual or little-known objects turns out to be a different kind of order, a new 'syntax,' literally – it is as if the narrator were calling attention to his own syntax, with an ironic wink to the reader.

Actually, Gadda's irony is all-pervading, and can be perceived at the lexical and linguistic level in his widespread use of Milanese dialect and regional Italian, beginning with the very title of the book, *L'Adalgisa*, and the title of the piece, 'Quando il Girolamo ha smesso ...,' in both of which the definite articles precede the proper feminine and masculine names, a usage which is typically Milanese. Dialect and Milanese expressions are uttered by all the characters in both direct and indirect speech, and are placed as well in key positions by the narrator on his own, to echo, emphasize, or criticize his characters. In a 1953 essay, 'Il terrore del dàttilo' (*VM*, 515–21), Gadda describes the 'tonalità celtica' [Celtic tonality] of the

Milanese dialect and its 'nasalità gallica' [Gallic nasality], specifying that
the Longobardic component is not lexical (since the lexical basis is neo-
Latin) but pertains to the phonetic level and reveals or embodies a pragmatic and direct attitude of the speakers who are accustomed to doing
rather than telling – the brevity of oxytone words and iambic verses is
juxtaposed to the relative length of paroxytone nouns and dactylic metres
(517, 519–20).

Such technical considerations have an ironic and narrative counterpoint
throughout *L'Adalgisa*, as, for example, when the narrator states that 'I
cromosòmi gallici e i langobardici si scontravano e ribollivano dentro vene
ricche, potenziati da rimota lügànega' (*A*, 452) [The Gallic and Longobardic chromosomes clashed and boiled inside the rich veins [of the Milanese
people], made powerful by remote sausages]. Since it is impossible to
render the dialect – with its abundance of Longobardic 'k' sounds and
Gallic 'oeu's and 'eu's – into English, I shall not quote any example, and
will choose instead a passage in which the polyphony is particularly
evident and effective. After describing and mocking the fears of certain
bourgeois ladies about being robbed of the diamonds set in their earrings,
with the consequent laceration of the ear-lobes, the text goes on to compare the act of illicit appropriation by such a hypothetical and 'adorable'
thief with another, famous historical gesture:

Magari col cipiglio e con l'atto che usò in Duomo il piccinella, pallido e glabro e
incomptis capillis[10], quei quattro che gli rimanevano, e indaffarato ovunque verso
le fanfare e la gloria: quando prese su lui stesso dal cuscino cremisi (francese
cramoisi) la corona del re Agilulfo che gli veniva oblata, e con una risolutezza
spavalda se la pigiò sulla capa lui stesso, cointeressando l'Onnipotente alla ben
nota millanteria.

Questa rottura, questo cracking[11] della nenia e querimonia procedurale, esercita
un fascino incredibile sull'animo delle donne: stupendo tatràc, repentino gitto
della lama e della punta fuora del guscio, del coltello a serramànico. (305)

[Perhaps with the frowning and the act that Shorty used in the cathedral, he who
was pale and smooth and incomptis capillis[10], what little was left, and busy
everywhere towards fanfares and glory: when he himself took up from the
crimson cushion (French *cramoisi*) King Agilulf's crown that was offered him, and
with bold determination pressed it on his own head himself, involving the
Omnipotent in his well-known boast.

This breaking, this cracking[11] of the lullaby and procedural ceremony exerts an
incredible appeal on women's souls: a stupendous tatràc, a sudden thrust of the
pointed blade out of its shell, of the jack-knife.]

It is needless to remark that here Gadda is alluding to Napoleon's gesture, upon being crowned King of Italy in 1805, when he put the crown on his head and said: 'God gave it to me, woe to the one who dares to touch it!' And it is equally needless to emphasize that the comparison with the thief, coupled with the language used in the telling of the episode, has devastating satirical effects. In fact, next to the courtly language of historians and Romantic literati (such as 'pallido e glabro' [pale and smooth], or 'le fanfare e la gloria' [fanfares and glory] there are the contrasting references and connotations of 'Il piccinella' [Shorty] and 'indaffarato' [busy] that belong to a mocking and disparaging register. The same can be said for the Latin 'incomptis capillis,' whose disorderly connotation contrasts sharply with its own classic aura and with the official and royal French 'cramoisi' – while the dialectal 'la capa' (instead of the elevated 'il capo' or the average Italian 'la testa') for 'head' further diminishes the solemnity of the occasion and prepares the reader for the final blow, the Omnipotent God involved by Napoleon in his well-known boast. Incidentally, Gadda exercises his satirical power and displays his moral indignation not only against Napoleon, but also against other historical characters guilty of the same type of braggadocio, like Ugo Foscolo, in *Il guerriero, l'amazzone, lo spirito della poesia nel verso immortale del Foscolo* and Mussolini, in *Eros e Priapo (da furore a cenere)*. Then Gadda's irony shifts to 'the soul of women,' who allegedly – in his misogyny – are fascinated by similar violent acts. And these acts are compared to the process of 'cracking' (in English in the text) in oil refineries, and expressed onomatopoeically by the 'stupendous tatràc' of a jack-knife blade.

The preceding quotation is also important because it clearly reveals the structure or the construction of *L'Adalgisa*, with two footnotes that the reader must read in order to derive all the implications from the (main) text. Gadda's footnote number 10, in particular, is a five-page, small-print, historical and satirical account of Napoleon's crowning in Milan's cathedral (ibid., 331–6). It begins with a dutiful acknowledgment of Horace's Latin 'incomptis capillis' for 'disorderly hair' and contains references to the educator Rousseau, the political theorist Babeuf, the painter David, the poet Carducci, the scientist Freud, the novelist Manzoni, the historian Paolo Warnefrido, plus a dozen or so historical characters connected in various ways with Bonaparte, including two popes and the Longobard king and queen Agilulf and Teodolinda. Thus, history becomes a story, a digression from the main story – if we may call 'main story' the one from which the 'footnote' originates. Up to this point, the main story deals with the following 'events': floor polishing, casual chats between the lady of the house and the old worker ('il' Girolamo of the piece's title), her fears for her diamonds, and the narrator's comparison between the hypothetical thief and Napoleon. Even more, it is as if Gadda were repeating the Manzonian choice of reducing 'Historie' to 'story' in a more definitive and radical way,[9] in that here official history is told as a literal subtext to both a private story and a local geography – the parquets and the cathedral.

This is the kind of narrative itinerary that is typical of L'Adalgisa, in which a character's gesture or thought or dress triggers an entirely different story that provides the necessary background – historical, scientific, or environmental – to understand that particular dress or thought or gesture. For example, the tears (or almost tears) with which the old Girolamo says goodbye to Signora Elsa Cavenaghi, after waxing her parquets for one last time, are due to his retirement which in turn is due to the bankruptcy of his firm 'La Confidenza' and are the culmination of a ten-page story of how that bankruptcy came about, with bank scandals, frauds, swindlers, lawyers, Royal carabinieri, patriotic rhetoric, Michelangelo, and the Bible (ibid., 309–20). Adriano Seroni has rightly emphasized the importance of footnote number 8 in the last 'drawing,' which provides a detailed account of Milan during the 'positivistic period' as an integral part of the portrait of 'il povero Carlo,' the beloved late husband of Adalgisa and a true embodiment of that period in the present of the narrative (Seroni 1969, 52–5).

The examples could be multiplied, but in any case this is the kind of narrative structure that made Italo Calvino choose Gadda (with a passage from *Quer pasticciaccio brutto de via Merulana*) as a primary example of 'multiplicity' in *Six Memos for the Next Millennium*, indeed, as 'an excellent introduction' to 'the contemporary novel' conceived 'as an encyclopedia, as a method of knowledge, and above all as a network of connections between the events, the people, and the things of the world' (Calvino 1988, 105). Relying on Gian Carlo Roscioni's ground-breaking work *La disarmonia prestabilita*, Calvino describes how Gadda 'tried all his life to represent the world as a knot, a tangled skein of yarn; to represent it without in the least diminishing the inextricable complexity or, to put it better, the simultaneous presence of the most disparate elements that converge to determine every event' (106). The result is that

in each episode in one of Gadda's novels, the least thing is seen as the center of a network of relationships that the writer cannot restrain himself from following, multiplying the details so that his descriptions and digressions become infinite. Whatever the starting point, the matter in hand spreads out and out, encompassing ever vaster horizons, and if it were permitted to go on further and further in every direction, it would end by embracing the entire universe. (107)

But obviously there must be some limit to the representation of the real, and Gadda solves the problem by leaving his works unfinished, open-ended, suggesting rather than achieving infinity and the universe, much as an encyclopaedia does. After all, he had explicitly contemplated and clearly suggested the idea of writing as encyclopaedia back in 1929, in 'Le belle lettere e i contributi espressivi delle tecniche' (*VM*, 475–88), in which he arrives at his 'modesto pensiero' [modest thought] by way of his preoccupation with precision (and not by chance, 'precision' is another of Calvino's literary values to be saved for the next millennium): 'se la precisione espressiva dovesse tener dietro alle tecniche meticolose [...] ogni scrittore diverrebbe l'Enciclopedia' (478) [If expressive precision should follow the [many] meticulous techniques ... then each writer would become the Encyclopaedia]. This is why *L'Adalgisa* is made up of ten stories (two of which, 'Strane dicerie contristano i Bertoloni' and 'Navi approdano al Parapagàl,' originally published in *Letteratura*, were later incorporated in *La cognizione del dolore*, also unfinished), but it could have been made up of nine, or twenty, or sixty-four, or maybe ninety-nine, like the chapters in Georges Perec's *La vie mode d'emploi* – not one hundred, because, as Calvino suggests, 'this ultra-completed book has an intentional loophole left for incompleteness' (Calvino 1988, 121). And this is why a parquet in the Cavenaghi household becomes the centre from which a network of relationships develops, encompassing Milan, and Italy, and Europe, as well as literature, history, and philosophy, not to mention engineering and entomology – much as a simple trash bin is enough for Calvino to trace a stupendous, truly anthropological description of Paris in his 'La poubelle agréée' (Calvino 1990, 87-116).

Ultimately, it is Gadda's *mente locale* that governs the whole process. And such *mente locale* is by definition open, because it is rooted in the past but is projected towards the future, is anchored in a specific place but also yearns to discover others. It is no coincidence, I believe, that in his desire to name things exactly, with scientific precision, and to be all-encompassing while being minutely descriptive, Gadda at a certain point of 'L'Adalgisa' (the piece that gives the title to the book) mentions the *garbo*, the tool used in 'costruzioni navali' [ship building] to achieve the best possible shape for hulls, but relates it to the tapered form of the water coleopter *Dysticus* chased by Carlo Biandronni in the countryside around Milan (*A*, 520–1) – just as a section of La Cecla's *Mente locale* is devoted precisely to the *garbo* of Sicilian fishermen and boat builders, and their relationship to their geographical location and social position – their beach and their village (La Cecla 1993, 105–15).

But the competence of *mente locale* becomes discourse when an author

begins to narrate a city, and it is to Gadda's literary discourse that I have
to turn my attention now. We may recall that, in the initial quotation of
my essay, the narrator of L'Adalgisa says, 'I don't even remember any
more.' In saying so, he places himself at the centre of the text as narrator,
as he does also on numerous other occasions, as for instance when he
shifts his narration from the bankruptcy of the floor-polishing firm 'La
Confidenza' to another, 'più grave fatto' [more serious fact] that 'aveva
portato la costernazione in tutta la nobile famiglia' [had brought dismay
to the whole noble Cavenaghi family]: 'Mi dispiace proprio, ma è una
storia che bisogna risucchiarla fin dal principio' (A, 318) [I am really sorry,
but it is a story that must be chewed from the very beginning]. Besides
serving as linkages between the many subplots of the story, such self-
reflexive acts by the narrator enhance the literariness of his writing and
oblige the reader to recognize it immediately and repeatedly throughout
the 'drawings.'

But from this point of view there is no doubt that Gadda's very choice
of footnoting his text is also the result of a self-referential attitude, of a
metaliterary discourse that is delightfully ironic as well as illuminating.
It is not by chance that many of the footnotes of L'Adalgisa focus on the
language, in fact the languages, used in the book – almost an illustration
of Gadda's theories expounded in such essays as 'Come lavoro' (VM,
427–43), 'Le belle lettere e i contributi espressivi delle tecniche,' (VM,
475–88) and 'Lingua letteraria e lingua dell'uso' (VM, 489–94), whose very
titles underscore some of the linguistic materials used by Gadda in his
literary construction.

In these footnotes there are numerous and detailed translations into
Italian and punctilious explanations of Milanese dialect terms, worthy of
Francesco Cherubini's 1814 Vocabolario Milanese-Italiano, the same
dictionary that such critics as Ezio Raimondi and Luciano Bottoni have
used to document the Milanese layer of Manzoni's lexicon in I promessi
sposi.[10] Such linguistic footnotes are another homage-challenge, à la
Harold Bloom, that Gadda pays to his great Milanese predecessor and
bard – not to mention the obvious harking back to the other great
Milanese bard, Carlo Porta (suffice here to recall that Adalgisa was called
'la Tettòn, à la Porta' by the narrator and his friends when she was a
desirable young lady endowed with a generous bosom even before becoming a 'signora,' [A, 529]).

Then there are ironic disclaimers, such as: 'Le locuzioni e i vocaboli di
lingua straniera (1928) sono adibiti a riprendere il tono (cioè rifare il verso)

a certa conversazione colta o medio-colta dell'ambiente e dell'epoca: non devono attribuirsi a difetto di possibilità lessicali da parte dell'autore o a menomato ossequio della madrelingua' (ibid., 419) [The expressions and nouns in foreign languages (1928) are used to take up the tone of (to mimic) a certain, learned or medium-learned conversation of the milieu and the period: they should not be attributed to a lack of lexical possibilities in the author or to a lessened reverence towards his mother tongue], or 'Vocabolario dell'Adalgisa' (560) [This is Adalgisa's vocabulary (– not mine)]. Even more importantly, there are true critical analyses of Gadda's own 'principal' text, such as the following:

L'orditura sintattica, le clausole prosodiche, l'impasto lessicale della discorsa, in più che un passaggio, devono perciò ritenersi funzioni mimetiche del clima, dell'aura di via Pasquirolo o del Pontaccio: che dico, dell'impetus e dello zefiro parlativo i quali dall'ambiente promanano, o prorompono. E ciò non soltanto nel dialogato, ma nella didascalia e nel contesto in genere, quasicché a propria volta l'autore si tuffi nella bagnarola e nell'acqua medesime ove poco prima erano a diguazzare i suoi colombi. (374–5)

[The syntactic texture, the prosodic clauses, the lexical mixture of the discourse in more than one passage must be considered as mimetic functions of the climate, the aura of via Pasquirolo or of the Pontaccio neighbourhood; what am I saying, of the impetus and the speaking zephyr issuing from, bursting out of that milieu. And this is true not only in the dialogues, but in the captions and the context in general, as if in his turn the author had plunged into the same bathtub and water in which his doves were splashing about a bit earlier.]

This note is a sharp critical description of Gadda's own text. It is extremely modern, almost mimicking the modes of narratology *ante litteram*, and in doing so it highlights precisely the self-awareness of the narrator as narrator. But it also demonstrates how Gadda's writing goes well beyond his asserted mimesis: it is a deformation, a grotesque and 'baroque' transformation of reality that, no matter how 'baroque' it may be to start with, becomes even more complex under Gadda's scrutiny and in his vision of a tangle of multiple and simultaneous co-causes (explored, in fact, in his philosophic treatise bearing the seemingly incongruous but revealing title *Meditazione milanese*).[11]

In the last quotation above, the narrator shows himself as partaking of the same milieu as his characters, splashing about in the same bathtub and water as his doves: Gadda's authorial irony has epistemological, as well as moral, tones that make his writing unmistakable. But, as he said in 'Le belle lettere e i contributi espressivi delle tecniche':

La tecnica d'uno scrittore tallisce in certa misura da uno sfondo preindividuale che è la comune adozione del linguaggio vale a dire il consuntivo semantico (signiferatore) d'una storia-esperienza che sia stata raggiunta e consolidata: e se ne forma e si congegna per accettazione o per antitesi, per arricchimento o per denegazione di determinati modi espressivi. L'adozione del linguaggio è riferibile a un lavoro collettivo, storicamente capitalizzato in una massa idiomatica, storicamente consequenziato in uno sviluppo, o, più generalmente, in una deformazione; questa esperienza insomma travalica i confini della personalità e ci dà modo di pensare a una storia della poesia in senso collettivo. (*VM*, 475)

[A writer's technique, to a certain extent, grows out of a pre-individual background that is the common adoption of language, that is the semantic stock (bearer of meaning) of a history-experience already realized and consolidated. This stock is formed and articulated through acceptance or antithesis, by enrichment or negation of certain expressive modes. The adoption of a language should be referred to a collective work, historically capitalized in an idiomatic mass, historically consequential in a certain development or more generally in some sort of deformation. In sum, this experience goes beyond the boundaries of a single personality and allows us to think of a history of poetry in a collective sense.]

If we project these assertions onto the screen of *L'Adalgisa*, it becomes evident how the very substance of the book, the Lombard and Milanese *mente locale* with its Longobardic ancestors and its bards Manzoni and Porta, is crucial in understanding Gadda: Milan is the place where the writer is rooted; the language, experience, and history of the city are the pre-individual humus and the collective competence out of which the individual discourse is born, 'through acceptance or antithesis,' 'in some sort of deformation.' And through the local history-experience of his Milan, expressed in his unique discourse, Gadda significantly enriches the history of Italian, and indeed world, literature.

Notes

1 All translations in this essay are the author's.
2 In a recent study, Ferdinando Amigoni has persuasively demonstrated that

Quer pasticciaccio is actually concluded with a clear indication of the murderer. See Amigoni 1995, 34–6.

3 A footnote in *L'Adalgisa* (330) explicitly recalls 'Una mattinata ai macelli' from *Le meraviglie d'Italia* (*MI*, 19–30); at least one other piece from the same book should be mentioned: 'Mercato di frutta e verdura' (38–51), and, from *Verso la Certosa*, 'Risotto pàtrio. Rècipe' (*VC*, 369–71).

4 The differences, however, are obvious. Gozzano recalls aristocratic interiors in *fin de siècle* Turin with the nostalgic, self-ironic tone that has since been known as 'crepuscular.' Palazzeschi uses a joking, even futuristic, technique; it is interesting to note that a 'ribbon and braid' shop appears at the beginning of the poem, just as it is the locale of an episode in *L'Adalgisa* ('Seterie e Passamanerie Milanesi Carugati & Bondanza' [366]).

5 See Carlo Porta, *Le poesie* (1964) and Giorgio Bassani, *Il romanzo di Ferrara* (1990).

6 Ernst Robert Curtius deals with the epic function of the catalogue in *European Literature and the Latin Middle Ages* (1953), while Leo Spitzer analyses the role of chaotic enumeration in modern poetry in 'La enumeración caótica en la poesia moderna' in *Linguística y historia literaria* (1961). The notion of polyphony (eteroglossia, dialogism) is especially important for Mikhail Bakhtin's critical discourse in *The Dialogic Imagination* (1981).

7 The references are in particular to Thomas Harrison, *Essayism: Conrad, Musil and Pirandello* (1992) and Gene Moore, *Proust and Musil: The Novel as Research Instrument* (1985).

8 Another example is the list of scientific terms on pages 520–1: 'Carlo aveva meticolosamente infilzato gli Scarabei' [Carlo had meticulously pinned the *Scarabaei*], with the ensuing names of the numerous families of beetles and all the detailed operations necessary to preserve them – a precise and ironic documentation of Carlo's positivistic background, attitude, and methods contrasted with Adalgisa's matter-of-fact and down-to-earth practicality.

9 The reference is to the well-known introduction of Alessandro Manzoni's *I promessi sposi*, 'L'historia si può veramente deffinire,' rendered as 'Historie may be verilie defined ...' by his English translator, Archibald Colquhoun: *The Betrothed* (New York: Dutton 1961), xi.

10 See Ezio Raimondi's and Luciano Bottoni's presentation, notes, and commentary in Alessandro Manzoni, *I promessi sposi* (1988).

11 *SVP*, 615–894. The debate centring on mimesis, expressivity, and the baroque is articulated in both Gianfranco Contini's introduction to the first edition of *La cognizione del dolore* (Turin: Einaudi 1963) and in Gadda's own 'L'editore chiede venia del recupero chiamando in causa l'autore' (*CD*, 759–66).

References

Amigoni, Ferdinando. 1995. *La più semplice macchina. Lettura freudiana del 'Pasticciaccio.'* Bologna: Il Mulino

Arbasino, Alberto. 1971. *Sessanta posizioni.* Milan: Feltrinelli

Bakhtin, Mikhail. 1981. *The Dialogic Imagination.* Translated by Caryl Emerson and Michael Holquist. Austin: University of Texas Press

Bassani, Giorgio. 1990. *Il romanzo di Ferrara.* Milan: Mondadori

Biasin, Gian Paolo. 1993. *The Flavors of Modernity: Food and the Novel.* Princeton: Princeton University Press

Calvino, Italo. 1988. *Six Memos for the Next Millennium.* Translated by Patrick Creagh. Cambridge, Mass.: Harvard University Press

– 1990. *La strada di San Giovanni.* Milan: Mondadori

Ceccaroni, Arnaldo. 1970. 'Per una lettura del "Pasticciaccio" di Carlo Emilio Gadda.' *Lingua e stile* 5, no. 1 (Apr.)

Curtius, Ernst Robert. 1953. *European Literature and the Latin Middle Ages.* Translated by Willard Trask. New York: Pantheon

Harrison, Thomas. 1992. *Essayism: Conrad, Musil and Pirandello.* Baltimore: Johns Hopkins University Press

La Cecla, Franco. 1993. *Mente locale. Per un'antropologia dell'abitare.* Milan: Elèuthera

Manzoni, Alessandro. 1988. *I promessi sposi.* Milan: Principato

Moore, Gene. 1985. *Proust and Musil: The Novel as Research Instrument.* New York: Garland

Porta, Carlo. 1964. *Le poesie.* Edited by Carla Guarisco. Milan: Feltrinelli

Roscioni, Gian Carlo. 1969. *La disarmonia prestabilita. Studio su Gadda.* Turin: Einaudi

Seroni, Adriano. 1969. *Gadda.* Florence: La Nuova Italia

Spitzer, Leo. 1961. *Lingüística y historia literaria.* Madrid: Gredos

Murderous Desires: Gaddian Matricides from *Novella seconda* to *La cognizione del dolore*

MANUELA BERTONE

Gadda appears literally obsessed with the idea of matricide to the extent that his major narratives are all in some way affected by this compulsion. Yet he refrains from following through with his impulse, ultimately removing the matricide solution to the margin of his texts, sheltering it, so to speak, in a space of partial darkness, in equivocation and ambiguity, while his stories break off, unfinished and unfulfilled.

Novella seconda[1] is a story inspired by a sordid newspaper account: the case of a boy indicted for having murdered his mother. At first, Gadda thinks of giving his novella the title of *Matricide*, but ends up choosing *Novella seconda*, simply a 'second story' that follows in order of composition *La maliarda ereditiera*, published in 1931 as *La Madonna dei Filosofi*. Gadda's decision to change the story's title is most likely due to the fact that during the actual trial it was established that, although present at his mother's murder, the boy, Renzo Pettine, had not killed her. Gadda interrupts *Novella seconda* before the murder takes place, even though he no doubt had read complete accounts of the crime in the newspapers and, more importantly, despite the fact that he had sketched out a conclusion in his notebook. His projected ending includes the mother's death (but not at the hands of her son), as well as the last moments of her life in which she, unable to identify her killer, believes that it may be her son.

La cognizione del dolore, with its compositional notes ('note costruttive') is constructed similarly: while Gadda underscores the possibility/certainty that the señora has recognized her son as her killer, he does not rule out the likelihood that someone else (that is, Manganones, the 'scemo di guerra' who resembles Gonzalo) may be the actual murderer. Here, once again, the drama of an unresolved plot or 'open ending' derives from the tension generated by a double truth: namely, the killer is at once a mysterious stranger and/or an uncanny son.

Quer pasticciaccio brutto de via Merulana, also the story of an unresolved murder, can be seen to be based on matricide.[2] Paradoxically, the victim, Liliana Balducci, is sterile, but, nevertheless, she is killed by one of her 'adopted children-domestics' who reside in her Via Merulana apartment as stand-ins for the real children she could never have. The killer's identity is never truly established, in spite of the suspicion that it might be the boyfriend of one of the victim's domestics. At the same time, Ingravallo, the detective assigned to the case and Gadda's principal voice in the text, may be seen to be 'guilty' of Liliana's death, in the sense that he abandons the central, geographical, terrain of the investigation for his own fixed idea of Signora Balducci as a maternal figure. In other words, what is technically not a matricide, through Ingravallo's reflections (and repressed desires), becomes, allegorically, the death of maternity at the hands of the narrator (Gadda/Ingravallo). Once again we are faced with a 'real' and an 'ideal(ized)' criminal.

This brief cross-reading of the three stories elicits some crucial questions. First of all, why is it that Gadda, after developing his narratives in the direction of matricide (punishment by killing of a [the] mother), is so reticent about writing the 'double truth' ending he has so carefully planned? Why are both *Novella seconda* and *La cognizione del dolore* aborted as they reach their climax? Second, why does Gadda never choose to conclude with a genuine matricide, opting instead for a hybrid crime that has only the appearance of a matricide? And third, why, in *Quer pasticciaccio*, does Gadda manipulate a simple homicide so that it takes on the appearance of a matricide? The fundamental question is why the disguise.

To attempt to answer all of these questions in detail would take us beyond the scope of this essay. Instead, I shall limit myself to a close reading of the archetypal text of matricide, *Novella seconda*, hoping at least to locate the principles that guide Gadda in his treatment of the matricide theme. I shall try to show why the story created by the matricide subject results in the transfiguration of matricide and, accordingly, in the interruption, or mis-conclusion, of the narrative.

I shall approach the text as autobiographical discourse, that is, as a self-reflective cognitive act (cf Neppi 1992, 7–44) organized and produced by Gadda, although it would be perfectly legitimate to investigate Gadda's habit of 'violently resorting to autobiography' (Contini 1989, 12). As for the text's psychoanalytical content, let it suffice to say that Gadda's literary language is not the same thing as the non-communicative language of Gadda's unconscious mind. I therefore do not regard the text as a symptom of, as Robert Dombroski has put it, 'something external to it, and, what is more, as a sort of pathology' (Dombroski 1987, 153). But a psychoanalytical response is required when a story has 'a distinctly Freudian character' that allows us to conclude 'not that underneath the literal meaning lies a latent psychoanalytical content and that the text stands there to prove it, [but] rather that the literal meaning and the psychoanalytical content are equivalent' (Dombroski 1987, 154).

In the notes Gadda appends to *Novella seconda*, we read: 'Voglio fare sulla novella una prova per arrivare poi al romanzo' (*RR II*, 1318) [I want to experiment on the short story to then approach the novel]: a test in view of *Racconto italiano di ignoto del novecento*, a novel, begun in 1924, which he had hoped to submit in competition for a prize then announced by Mondadori. And in another note (10 October 1928), included in a project entitled 'Temi per novelle' (itself a part of the 'quaderno climaterico'), Gadda refers to still another project: 'una elaborazione più fine [del] tema tragico della novella 2.ª (matricidio) e farne una novella-romanzo di circa 100 pagine a stampa' (1309) [A more refined elaboration [of the] tragic theme of the novella 2.ª (matricide) in view of a novella-novel of about 100 printed pages]. Gadda has yet to realize that the matricide story would come in handy for even more ambitious projects. Moreover, *Novella seconda* provides Gadda with the opportunity to test both his 'Sherlock Holmes-ism' (1317), an approach he will rely on later in *Quer pasticciaccio brutto de via Merulana*, and the 'spunto quasi shakespeariano' (1314) [quasi-Shakespearian thrust] he deploys throughout *La cognizione del dolore*.

Within the small, two-page space devoted to his program, Gadda makes three references to Shakespeare and three to Conan Doyle. While he admires the latter's talent for logical reconstruction and his ability to realize all the fictional potential of murder, he is attracted by the former's skill in remaking historical, personal, emotional, and moral disputes. Yet it is significant that Gadda plans to break away from his models and follow his own narrative inclinations. Referring to the Pettine trial, he notes how Shakespeare is there in himself but also in his 'possibili deformazioni' (ibid., 1314) [possible deformation] and, later, when he mentions the creator of Sherlock Holmes, he adds 'Differire però da lui perché ormai il pubblico lo sa a memoria e non ci si diverte più' (1317) [Differ from him because readers know him by heart and are no longer amused]. The very essence of *Novella seconda* rests on these references to deformation and difference. In fact, Gadda, on the one hand, goes on to dismantle the tragic support sustaining the mother-son relationship in Shakespeare's plays (particularly in *Hamlet*), and on the other, removes the investigative support that makes possible the detective-criminal confrontation in Doyle's mysteries.

Shakespeare and Conan Doyle are no doubt operative in *Novella seconda*, but there is also another text of which Gadda makes ample use: Sophocles' *Women of Trachis*.[3] Gadda takes directly from Sophocles the name Dejanira (Deianeira) which he assigns to his female protagonist. The name is particularly fitting for Gadda's character, since it means 'she who destroys her spouse.' The Sophoclean heroine appeals to Gadda also because she is a woman who 'without meaning to ... has caught Heracles in the poisoned trap of Nessus' shirt,' but she is also the person who, urged by her son Hyllus, 'turns to the sword for a quick death' (Loraux 1987, 10). The bloody legacy of the woman of Trachis is thus passed on to the girl born across the river Piave. Gadda even allows her to introduce herself as 'Denira,' a quasi-nickname, surely, as he thought, an appropriate self-inflicted deformation for so provincial a character.

In view of the static character of Gadda's literary culture (cf Lucchini 1988), it is not surprising that *Novella seconda* is influenced by certain crucial readings after which Gadda will never change his mind about matricide. These are literary antecedents in which matricide was only virtually or metaphorically committed and expiated by an innocent son. Gadda appears satisfied in alluding only to presumed matricides, adopting mechanisms and features of tragedies whose structures allude to or suggest the idea of matricide, representing it as a possibility, while withholding or repressing the crime proper. He seems unresponsive to the most natural of antecedents, Aeschylus' *Oresteian Trilogy* and *Electra* in both the versions of Euripides and Sophocles, as they contain plots in which matricide is planned, described, and represented as inevitable.

But in the final analysis, Gadda does not opt for either real or metaphorical matricides, but instead for matricide as a kind of paradoxical mixture of the two: in Gadda's stories, there is no real matricide, but someone believes that there is. Such a solution, however, is doomed to failure simply because Gadda does not provide his subject with a narrative and psychological background solid enough to justify and support such an ambiguous turn in the plot.

In composing *Novella seconda*, Gadda works as usual on two narrative registers: he recounts his story, and at the very same time he notes his thematic objectives and compositional strategies. At the outset of the manuscript, we have a note that refers to the trial in Milan where Renzo Pettine is found guilty and sentenced to fifteen years' imprisonment; this is followed by a reference to the above-mentioned literary models and to the possible ways of transforming the case into fiction. Gadda knows that the mentally deranged boy has not committed the crime, yet in the first note he refers to him as the 'matricide' (also simply as 'the young man' ['il giovane'], and earlier on as 'uno sciagurato demente' [a wretched psychopath]), while in the following note this unfortunate and depraved boy is called a 'victim' who did not kill his mother, but who was just there ('aveva presenziato'), unable to help her, a passive witness to her death (*RR II*, 1318). The attributes used in describing the boy vary from factual references ('il giovane,' 'il matricida') to their qualification by means of such psycho-behavioural nuances as 'sciagurato' and 'corrotto.' Gadda is at a loss how to respond to this potential criminal: should he be indignant or sympathetic; should he pity or condemn him? The dilemma is resolved in the paradox contained in the second note where Gadda does not describe the facts of the case as such, but rather plans their fictionalization. Becoming an author, he transforms the criminal into a victim, thus revealing the gap between legal simplification and an event 'tragicamente intimo, familiare, psicologico' (1316) [tragically intimate, private, psychological].

Gadda's first note ends with reasons one could evoke to exculpate the young man:

Bisogna parlare di lui come un essere fuori dell'umanità e della ragione [...] Non può darsi che il trauma morale inerente alla tragica scena, abbia sconvolto la sua anima già debole, tarata, malata? (ibid., 1316)

[One should speak of him as someone existing beyond the norms of humanity and reason. Could it not be that the moral trauma inherent in the tragic scene has upset his weak, depraved, sick mind?]

This does not come as a surprise, for it follows Gadda's lengthy description of the late twenties as a time of deep moral corruption (ibid., 1315). Gadda is full of zeal for the guilty boy's good cause. He is a victim of both his corrupt times and his very fragile mind. As for the true victim of the crime, the mother, Gadda shows little compassion. Actually, she is hardly a part of his reflections at all, entering his line of vision only in the second note, but deprived of the extenuating circumstances Gadda reserves for her son:

La madre è vanesia, letterata, troia: povera vuol parere ricca [...] Ella ama i tipi perversi, potenti nel mondo, ecc. (1318)

[The mother is a vain and educated whore; she's poor but wants to appear rich ... She loves criminal types with power, etc.]

The profile he draws of the mother confirms his wish to overturn the situation in favour of the son. His narrative will unfold towards a conclusion intended to demonstrate that the mother is guilty and the son is innocent. He will show how the mother leads her son into the crime, how the boy suffers the murder, how the mother deserves to be killed, while the son should not be held responsible for his mother's crimes.

In the first note, Gadda's praise of the *guilty victim* is preceded by the following statement:

Dai resoconti dei giornali io non ho potuto farmi un'idea profonda della verità. Ma ho l'impressione che una eccessiva durezza di giudizio ha colpito lo sciagurato [...] *Sento* questo. (ibid., 1315)

[The newspaper reports have not allowed me to develop a strong opinion about the truth of the case. I have the impression, however, that the judgment taken against the wretched boy has been excessively tough ... This is what *I feel*.]

Gadda's reference to his impression, the use of the verb 'sentire,' the emphasis placed on 'sento' are at least surprising. For they come from a writer who, in writing the story, will be extremely careful to separate 'il logicamente connesso e consequenziato dall'uterinamente avventato' (1041) [what is logically connected and consequential from what is ute-rinely reckless], who vigorously stresses the opposition between a disinterested critical posture and unexpected circumstances ('imprevedute rotazioni'), and who, accordingly, is perfectly capable of excluding the mother from his own feelings. The mother, in fact, seems to enter the frame of the story only because her presence is necessary to counter the tragedy of the real trial and to make the plot more complicated as a fiction (1317). She is necessary in order to:

interessare il grosso pubblico. E cioè arrivare al pubblico *fino* attraverso il *grosso* [per] interessare la plebaglia per raggiungere e penetrare un'altezza espressiva che mi faccia apprezzare dai cervelli buoni. (1318)

[hold the attention even of the common man. That is, reach a refined audience by means of ordinary people ... Interest the rabble in order to reach and to penetrate to a certain expressive level so that refined spirits can appreciate me.]

Did Gadda repress his emotions in order to privilege rationality when he moved from his program to the story itself? It should be noted that a considerable amount of screening and cover-up took place in the very short time between the writing of the note and the writing of the story, particularly if we recall that the story is packed with dubious philosophical and scientific references that are somewhat positivistic and Lombrosian in kind. These were included not only because 'they were required by the events that inspired the story' and not only because Gadda wanted 'to acquit the son' (Ferretti 1987, 11). They were included because Gadda wanted to see the son acquitted on purely rational grounds in order to conceal his own feelings.

Moreover, we should keep in mind that a story tightly bound in biological and social materials is a story that bears no more signs of personal involvement. Let us not forget that Gadda has appropriated a titillating newspaper story. He even confesses in his note that he could not attend the trial because the courtroom had been assailed by the curious: 'Il processo ha destato morboso interesse, specie nelle donne isteriche' (*RR II*, 1314) [The trial had awakened a morbid interest especially in hysterical women]. Clearly, if Gadda had tried, unsuccessfully, to attend the trial, it means that *his* 'morbid interest' was aroused just as much as that of Milan's hysterical females. What about Gadda's own hysteria? Instead of exposing this typically feminine disorder, he conceals it behind a highly philosophical and scientifically ordered plot.

Although his project is partially developed, he plans to set the son at centre stage: 'Non allontanarsi da Renzo Pettine, che deve essere il centro, il fulcro del romanzesco' (ibid., 1318) [Don't leave Renzo Pettine behind; he has to be the centre, the fulcrum of the fiction]. And so it will be for Gadda's future matricide stories. The axis around which the entire plot of *La cognizione del dolore* rotates is Gonzalo, the son, with all his neurosis, depression, melancholy, transgressions, and numerous character failings – all due, as with Renzo Pettine, to poor upbringing. The mother is responsible for all of her son's foibles and misdeeds, since the father has been long dead. The same holds true for the more complex case of *Quer pasticciaccio*. At its centre stands a male character, badly loved by a woman who is apparently 'lily-white,' but who is guilty like all other women of using wrongly her womanly and maternal attributes.

The protagonist of *Novella seconda*, Denira, is born in a remote town in the Veneto region, the ninth child of a local woman and a well-educated physician. The story actually begins 'quando il pondo ascoso di Denira era per anco celato nel grembo materno' (ibid., 1030) [when Denira's hidden body was still concealed in her mother's womb]. Her mother dies four months after her birth, her father eighteen years later of alcoholism. After losing her brothers at war and a good part of her inheritance, she sets off to seek her fortune in Milan. There she falls in love with a certain Lieu-tenant Dalti who, as fate would have it, is shot dead in a political revolt, Denira being left only with his son to whom she gives the name 'Doro.' Lonely and grief-stricken, and after an exhausting pilgrimage to her be-loved's grave site in the Marche region, Denira marries Aristide Manni, a well-to-do middle-aged man who had previously courted her. This is the extent of the action. The notes written in the margins of these pages in-clude a number of hypotheses about possible expansion. What follows are two short scenes (not the four Gadda had planned), simply called 'Scena I' and 'Scena II,' that are also embellished by marginal notes containing more suggestions on how the story might be further developed.

After completing the story as summarized, Gadda notes that he has come to the end of his work's historical antecedent. He has recounted the facts that explain his protagonist's social and psychological development: her birth, upbringing in an unstable environment, an unsupervised adolescence that leads to her giving birth to an illegitimate child and, finally, to an arranged marriage. Gadda presents all of these events in a sincere, benevolent tone that, at times, becomes amused and condescend-ing. In any case, Denira's life gradually worsens as Gadda lines up along its trajectory a row of corpses, either real (her parents, brothers, lover), or metaphorically displaced on a series of deadly events: a funereal marriage which makes the world leave her in peace (ibid., 1061) and the delivery of a child that takes place 'in pace ... quanto lo consentivano gli strazianti ricordi del passato, la desolazione presente e il buio futuro' (1056) [in peace ... as far as her dreadful memories, her present desolation, and the dark future could allow for peace]. At the celebration of her eighteenth birthday, Gadda portrays her as 'piena di sangue' [sanguine], a sanguin-ary synthesis that, in retrospect, sounds like a prophecy.

When Denira's son breaks into the story, Gadda's intentions become clearer. It is worth reading the passage devoted to his birth in its entirety:

Il bambino nacque nervoso: è difficile cogliere nei primi mesi di vita i segni di certe tare che la natura si riserba di rivelare negli anni futuri [...]

Concepito dalla figlia d'un alcolizzato nel tumulto della rissa civile, portato nel dolore spasmodico e nell'oscuramento dell'anima, quando il suo amore glie lo assassinavano così, già i liquori erano più che una distrazione innocente od un semplice aperitivo chiamato giù dallo stomaco vivo, ad americanizzare un po' il sangue, nato nell'affanno d'un'esistenza incerta contro cui già si chiudevano tutte le porte della *pruderie* ufficiale e della carità benpensante, Doro Dalti non poteva sortire dalle viscere materne, neanche a volerlo, il tema armonioso e sereno, nucleante di serenità, armonizzante la vita. (ibid., 1056–7)

[The child was born nervous. It is difficult to capture in the first months of life the signs of the defects nature prefers to reveal in future years ...
Conceived by the daughter of an alcoholic in the midst of civil riots, borne in convulsive grief and in a darkened mind, when her love was being killed like that and drinking was becoming more than an innocent distraction, more than a simple apéritif imbibed by an active stomach to americanize her blood a bit. Born to the stress of an uncertain life, shut off from official *pruderie* and the charity of the well-meaning, Doro Dalti could not exit from the maternal entrails as a harmonious and serene theme, bursting with serenity and the harmonizing energy of life.]

This short passage includes everything the story had already recounted in full: a catalogue of the mother's defects and the child's portrait developed as a reflection of his mother's and without any reference whatsoever to the father's genetic heritage. Gadda is constructing a perfect alibi for the son's future transgressions, ascribed a priori to the faulty female mould, just as if Doro's birth had come about by spontaneous procreation. In Denira's case, too, Gadda mentions only the depraved side of her ancestry, that of her alcoholic father, while her mother's seemingly perfect constitution goes unmentioned (after all, she had borne nine healthy children before dying). For Gadda, birth is a time when defects are passed on. He actually reverses the traditional claim about child-bearing as a strengthening time for a women's body. Not allowed a pause in physical and moral stress, Denira is imprisoned in her condition as a woman, a biological and psychological makeup outside of which she cannot be imagined by Gadda. In fact, the picture of tragic birth had already been sketched out when Denira entered the world. Her birth was an event only to her father, registered on her mother's record only with the sentence that contains the announcement of the latter's death ('Così morì quattro mesi dopo che Denira *le* era nata' [ibid., 1031]), and not before her death is grieved by the father (la moglie *gli* morì'[1030]), that is, at the same time when he lost his cow ('morì *anche* quella' [1030]).

Denira (a sort of mother-murderer herself) goes on from being a victim of sorrow 'che distrusse in lei ogni luce' [that extinguished in her every ray of light] to becoming the subject of a 'maternità dolce e accorata' (1055) [a sweet and heartfelt maternity]: an impracticable transition, indeed, and Gadda decides to turn motherhood into the very cause of its impracticability, for once the child is born, its mother is driven by an 'odio folle [...] per ogni aspetto della vita' (1057) [mad hatred ... for every feature of life].

Doro, the innocent fruit of (de)generation, is condemned naturalistically to the reproduction of the disharmony that formed him. Not only is he without his father and only his mother's son, but he is actually forced to live her identity, a kind of *Doppelgänger*, deprived in advance of his own genetic characteristics. The son does not have a form of his own, he is like his mother.

Gadda does not engage the identity motif solely in connection with the Pettine case. The idea of developing the son's story around the mother's genealogy is one of his obsessions, and a very productive one at that, for it surfaces in both his major novels. In fact, *La cognizione del dolore* is a thorough investigation into the psychological tragedy of a son who cannot detach himself from his mother's identity. His refusal of normality is founded on his stubborn desire to identify with his mother as a means of recovering the part of his self he believes is missing. At the same time, the novel exhibits the anguish and anger that derive from the son's inability to free himself from being imprisoned within his mother's selfhood (cf Dombroski 1987, 148, and 1994, 135).

To return to *Novella seconda*, we should point out that what is contained in the 'antecedent facts' and in the two final scenes occurs at a great distance in time. Denira has become a well-to-do bourgeoise whom we find in her drawing-room, in splendid company, but without her son. Where is he? We are told he left the scene of his mother's world, and, thus, he enters the story for the first time only by name: he is a non-presence: 'Jole Veretti [...] non cessò di guardare tratto tratto l'uscio dietro cui era sparito Doro Dalti' (*RR II*, 1063)[4] [Jole Veretti ... kept watching the door behind which Doro Dalti had disappeared].

Now the identity motif has been replaced (both in the story and in the protagonist's life) by role reversal, a literal reversal of mother-son roles to be added to the metaphorical role reversal Gadda established when he assigned innocence to the son and guilt to the mother. The mother strikes the reader as being too sociable and worldly; the son, by contrast, as being reserved, restrained, and introverted. With respect to the space she occupies, the mother takes on masculine characteristics, bridging the gap that separates the home (sanctuary of femininity and the only possible territory for a woman's activity) from the outside world. Her son, instead, is now compelled to protect the integrity and peace of the home, taking on the responsibilities his mother has relinquished. From Denira's drawing-room come coarse laughs and vulgar cries. The mother revels in her world, 'stretta da tanti' (ibid., 1062) [hugged by many], while the son sits still in his melancholy (1064).[5]

Starting in 1928, Gadda estranges the figure of the son from the Oedipal model of development (see Lucchini 1988, 111 and 121), framing him within a structure of primary and absolute narcissism, that is, in the pre-Oedipal stage that precedes the constitution of the ego. Unable to sever the primary bond that connects him to his mother, the son seeks to recover the state lost at birth and reattach himself to the *matrix*.[6]

But compared to *La cognizione*, *Novella seconda* leaves the motif of role reversal somewhat underdeveloped. The novella differs from the novel also as far as the conception of the mother, the son, their relationship, and the environment are concerned. Unlike Denira, the señora (the fictional embodiment of Gadda's real mother, Adele Lehr) is not a degenerate and fast woman; Gonzalo, a homely and mature man, is far more neurotic, lonely, and desperate than Doro. This is so because *La cognizione* investigates at a more extensive and much deeper level than *Novella seconda*.

Yet one cannot help noticing the degree to which the setting and framing of the novella gets projected on to the novel, even in its minimal details. First, the quarrels between mother and son are sparked by the unnatural enlargement of the mother's territory: they all break out under the same circumstances and result in identical solutions. Denira becomes patron to Ermenegildo, a young electrician whom she protects and to whom she gives piano lessons (*RR II*, 1062); Gonzalo's mother occupies herself with the Colonel's dull grandson to whom she gives French lessons. Both mothers attend to the feelings of strangers, while treating their own sons with detachment. Denira loves Doro from a distance, as if he were a lost object (1065); the señora, according to Gonzalo, cares only about others, opening her house to all sorts of rabble, thus denying Gonzalo sole possession of her. Denira, too, opens her house to visitors and accepts being cheated by her servants. Doro tries to take refuge in his study in much the same way as Gonzalo, only to find intruders there on whom both sons vent their anger. In Denira's drawing-room circulate trays loaded with all kinds of fresh food, while Doro is presented with a supper of leftovers (1064). So it is with Gonzalo who, as a child, is given a thin slice of boiled beef, while his parents pour all the family money into

the villa; as an adult, too, he is forced to dine on soup and three 'peperon-
cini verdastri, vizzi' (*CD*, 336) [greenish, withered peppers] (*AG*, 162),
while the peons feast on mushrooms, chicken, and fish.

The notes Gadda writes in the margin of *Novella seconda* spell out even
more clearly the story's relation to *La cognizione*. Gadda mentions a quarrel
between Doro (Gigetto in the notes), his mother, and a guest, which ends
with the dismissal of a servant. The very same scene is announced in a
note to *La cognizione*: Gadda plans to discharge an intrusive peon in order
to create a tangle of collateral tensions necessary to the murder theme. In
Novella seconda he writes: 'La madre vuole accopparlo' (1324) [His mother
wants to kill him]. Moreover, in 'Cui non risere parentes,' a verse from
Virgil, used as the title of a fragment appended to *La cognizione*, Gadda
speaks of a maternal sadism that leads the señora so far as to threaten her
son's life: 'La madre avrebbe dovuto stozzarlo [...] Bisognava essere molto
severi con lui [...] percuoterlo ferocemente, minacciarlo di morte' (*CD*,
530n) [The mother should have strangled him ... It was necessary to be
very severe with him ... beat him ferociously, threaten him with death].
The enigmatic, menacing words, included in the notes to *Novella seconda*,
a forewarning that something is bound to happen, correspond to the ad-
monitions of Battistina to the doctor on their way to the villa, just as
Gigetto-Doro's departure for the countryside (*RR II*, 1325) is analogous to
Gonzalo's travels away from the scene of the crime (*CD*, 461).

In a similar way, Gonzalo's foreboding dream corresponds, *in nube et
in aenigmate*, to Gadda's cryptic announcement of Gigetto's dream (*RR II*,
1324) in a note following 'Scena I.' Interestingly enough, both dreams are
positioned parenthetically between the premeditation of the crime and its
realization. This deliberate narrative choice echoes a scene from *Julius
Caesar* in which Shakespeare allows Brutus to reflect on the moments preceding his treacherous act:

> Between the acting of a dreadful thing
> And the first motion, all the interim is
> Like a phantasma or a hideous dream:
> The Genius and the mortal instruments
> Are then in council, and the state of a man
> Like to a little kingdom, suffers then
> The nature of an insurrection.   (II.1. 63–9)

The first three of these verses are translated freely by Manzoni at the end
of chapter 7 of *I promessi sposi* ('Tra il primo pensiero d'una impresa

terribile, e l'esecuzione di essa [...] l'íntervallo è un sogno pieno di fantasmi e di paure' [Manzoni 1971, 161]) in reference to Lucia who 'had been in the throes of just such a dream for many hours now' (Manzoni 1972, 141), and are accompanied by an ironic allusion to Shakespeare: 'to quote a barbarian who was not devoid of genius' (ibid.).

It is most likely, however, that Gadda, although aware of Manzoni's cryptic reference, took inspiration directly from *Julius Caesar*, for, in *La cognizione*, he translates literally 'phantasma' and 'hideous dream' into 'fantasma' and 'sogno spaventoso' (*CD*, 167). Moreover, Gadda includes *Julius Caesar* among the works he needs to read in view of writing 'Novella terza,' which was supposed to deal with Caesar's tenth legion. We can thus assume that Gadda had direct knowledge of Shakespeare's play by the time he was writing *Novella seconda*.

If we turn to the crime itself, it is easy to see that between *Novella seconda* and *La cognizione del dolore* Gadda's plots had not undergone significant changes. Regarding the former text, he writes in a note (24 March 1928):

E' uccisa da amanti volgari che sono: 1.º) Stufi di lei non potendola più sfruttare. 2.º) Mandanti di un amante potente che ella ha recentemente conquistato, mentre il mondo li crede rivali. (Vedere poi ... come è possibile combinare il minestrone.) (*RR II*, 1318)

[She is killed by common lovers who are 1) sick of her because they can no longer exploit her. 2) assassins hired by a powerful lover whom she had recently seduced, while everyone thinks they are rivals. (See then how to mix it up.)]

Gadda will not mix up the pieces after all, as he opts for the matricide suspicion, observing, in another note, that there is only one possibility:

(Scena tragica della madre morente che sente il figlio di là e lo chiama: non capisce. Crede che il suo figlio sia complice. Muore.) – Mi hai uccisa ... (oppure al buio non ha visto il Pesautti?) Disperazione di lui, che impazzisce [...] Lui pazzo, confessa di aver ucciso la madre ... (*RR II*, 1325).

[(Tragic scene of the dying mother who hears her son in the other room and calls him: she does not understand. She thinks her son is an accomplice. She dies.) You've killed me ... (or perhaps on account of the dark she didn't see Pesautti?) Desperation of the boy who goes crazy ... Mad, he confesses to having killed his mother.]

In *La cognizione*, Gadda has in mind the same kind of ambiguous conclusion. His notes read:

Il senso tragico del matricidio deve essere soltanto nel terrore degli ultimi momenti della madre, che pensa al figlio come esecutore: ma poi esclude lei stessa, morendo. E nell'angoscia del figlio che pensa che la madre abbia potuto sospettare di lui. -Mantenere vagamente la probabilità della guardia. (*CD*, 555)

[The tragic sense of matricide must be seen only in the terror of the mother's final moments when she thinks of her son as her executor. But ultimately when dying she excludes that possibility. And in the son's anguish, when he thinks that his mother might have suspected him. Vaguely keep present the probability that the guard might be guilty.]

Risolvere con la supposta uccisione della madre e con la pazzia. (ibid., 556)

[Conclude with the supposed killing of the mother and with madness].

In una scena terribile la signora è assalita dal Manganones mentre è in letto. Ella crede Il figlio. Statura eguale [...] Sopraggiungono i due peones e la salvano [...] In una terza scena si ha l'agonia e la morte della signora-che crede nel delirio di essere stata uccisa dal figlio. Il dolore eterno. (ibid., 563).

[In a terrible scene, the señora is assailed by Manganones while in bed. She thinks it's her son. Same physique ... Two peones arrive and rescue her ... In a third scene, we have the agony and death of the señora who, in her delirium, thinks she was killed by her son. Eternal grief.]

In both stories, Gadda exploits ambiguity: the presence of the stranger (the real murderer) provokes the tragic misunderstanding of the mother's uncertainty. In both plots, the son's madness is the direct consequence of these occurrences and the note on which the story ends.[7]

If we turn now to *Quer pasticciaccio*, we can understand even better the importance of *Novella seconda* as the source of Gadda's fictional itineraries. A short time before the murder of Liliana, a domestic named Virginia is dismissed by the Balducci family. Liliana's husband, Remo, the only non-transitory male figure in her life, is, like Doro and Gonzalo, away from home at the time of the murder. Here, too, at the locus of the murder yet to be committed in Via Merulana 286, the dark staircases and halls allow for equivocation. A petty thief, guilty only of having robbed Signora

Menegazzi, is constantly referred to as an assassin before Liliana is killed two days later: an oversight that recalls the sibylline references in *Novella seconda* and Battistina's forewarning in *La cognizione*. Ingravallo himself points out how allusive and meaningful this slip of the tongue is when he asks: 'ma qua' assassine si nun ce stà 'o muorto' (*QP*, 29) [but what murder if there is no dead body (*AM*, 24)] and when, influenced as he is by what the others are saying, he sets himself the goal of catching not a thief but a murderer.

As far as *Novella seconda* is concerned, one wonders whether Gadda deletes the matricide from his register just to be faithful to what happened in court, or whether it was just an accident that he left unfinished and unassembled the different pieces of a rather brilliant story. Of course, one can take Gadda's usual excuses about his discontinuous work as a writer forced to spend valuable time on professional engagements. But it is unlikely that whatever Gadda wrote of *Novella seconda* between 23 March and 8 April 1928 (together with many other plans for novels and short stories) was just casually left in a drawer and just as casually fused into *La cognizione* and *Quer pasticciaccio*. We know for a fact that, after 1928, Gadda tests his ability at telling the story of a son as if it were the story of a mother, while simultaneously hiding behind numerous narrative screens. Gadda is actually less interested in the sufferings of Renzo Pettine than in the destiny of his weak and depraved soul (*RR II*, 1316). This is probably why Gadda, upon describing what is left of Doro's love for his mother, shifts from the disjunctive plural object pronoun 'loro' to the impersonal relative 'chi' and then to the first-person-plural disjunctive 'noi,' as if he were becoming more and more implicated:

Nulla vi era più di reale in *loro*, come in *chi* vivesse per automatismo, per un'arida concatenazione di effetti, senza più desiderio, né pensiero che *lo* allacci alle cose, al mondo [...] Il mondo appare allora come un rotolamento di effetti, il suo contenuto è già stato enunciato al di fuori di *noi* un'orrenda petraia rovina giù senza fine. Ogni volere è smarrito. Non *siamo* che cose. (1065; emphasis mine)

[Nothing real was left in *them*, as in *someone who* went on living like an automaton, through a dry concatenation of effects, without any more desire, nor manner of thinking that could link *him* to things, to the world ... The world appears then like a rolling of effects and its content has already been announced outside of *us* as a horrendous wasteland. The power of willing is lost. *We are* nothing but things.]

These words are similar to those Gadda wrote in his *Giornale di guerra e di prigionia* to record his state of mind after he had returned from the front to discover that his brother Enrico had been killed, and in the midst of quarrels with his mother:

Automatismo esteriore e senso della mia stessa morte (*GGP*, 850)

[Exterior automatism and the sense of my own death]

La mia vita è inutile, è quella d'un automa sopravvissuto a se stesso, che fa per inerzia alcune cose materiali, senza amore né fede [...] finirò la mia torbida vita nell'antica e odiosa palude dell'indolenza che ha avvelenato il mio crescere mutando le possibilità dell'azione in vani, sterili sogni. (867)

[My life is useless, it is the life of an automaton that has survived its own death, which does by force of inertia some material things, without either love or faith ... I shall end my torpid life in the ancient and odious swamp of indolence that has stunted my growth by turning the possibilities of action into vain, sterile dreams.]

In *La cognizione del dolore* the terms become clearer:

Il figlio pareva aver dimenticato al di là d'ogni immagine lo strazio di quegli anni, la incenerita giovinezza. Il suo rancore veniva da una lontananza più tetra, come se fra lui e la mamma ci fosse qualcosa di irreparabile, di più atroce d'ogni guerra: e di ogni spaventosa morte. (*CD*, 317)

[The son seemed to have forgotten, beyond all imagining, the torment of those years, youth reduced to ash. His rancor came from a grimmer remoteness, as if between him and his mother there were something irreparable, more atrocious than any war: and than any frightful death. (*AG*, 156)]

Time and again Gadda raises the issue of the mother and, implicitly, of her death, to the degree that it becomes his principal, albeit disguised and undeveloped, theme. Disguised and undeveloped because encased within it is the issue of the son's life.

'What is to become of the son?' is *the* question Gadda cannot answer, either in 1928 or in 1936. His principal difficulty seems to lie in writing about what follows the abrupt exit of the mother from the life of her son (and from the story). Gadda aborts his story not because he feels guilty for having designed the murder of a mother by a son with whom he identifies, nor because he cannot see her being killed by a stranger. The story actually stops before it shows a mother dying. No doubt this amounts to a punishing, symbolic act of self-castration, but it is one that is useless, for it destroys the conclusion of a novel that has yet to complete the destructive phase of the mother-son relationship. What matters is that the story be stopped before the beginning of the son's survival in a motherless world. In *Novella seconda*, the son is like an embryo unable to live apart from his mother. Therefore, if the matricide took place, it could be perpetrated only by a third party, not because he is unable to kill his own mother but because killing her would put an end to his total symbiosis with the body that begot him and, thus, it would amount to killing himself. Gadda's decision to forgo the matricide stems from his need to conceal the self-destructive (masochistic) component in which he imprisons both the story and its protagonist. His notes demonstrate that even the surrendering of the deed to a third party would not be sufficient to free his protagonist, upon and beyond the death of his mother, from the bonds of identification. For Doro-Gigetto, Gadda anticipates madness: a madness caused by the very same doubt his mother could not dispel before dying. Just as in the woman's case, the presence of a supposedly guilty stranger means the certainty of being caught in a misunderstanding that it is too late to clarify. The son is a matricide because his mother thinks he is, and he cannot define himself otherwise (remember 'he confesses he has killed his mother' [*RR II*, 1325]); he is left there, mad, to live in the dread of pain their knowledge engenders, in the 'cognizione' of their shared 'dolore.'

The relationship that joins mother and son in life makes the latter's loss irreparable. Theirs is a primary, absolute, and destructive narcissistic bond, fuelled by ruinous impulses, which dissolves the unity of the self into an undifferentiated state of identity and antagonism. No matter how it comes about, the mother's death always implies the son's loss of omnipotence, that is, his destruction or at least the destruction of the biological and existential unit formed by two perfectly interconnected beings. Gadda portrays this union as a common thanatological destiny when he writes that 'La madre [...] a quel ragazzo gli voleva un bene lontano, come a una cosa perduta. Era un ben immaginario, stanco, come se fossero due sprettri, già tutti e due' (ibid., 1065) [The mother ... loved the boy with a distant kind of love, like that of a lost object. It was an imaginary kind of love, as if they were two ghosts, already, both of them]. The matricide therefore must be left outside the narrative frame, lest the author suffocate his protagonist, making him disappear before he comes into being. André Green has offered an apt commentary on the above:

Destruction is beyond the subject's reach. He does not have available the kind of investments necessary to re-establish a lasting objective relationship and to engage progressively in a profound personal implication, for which the ability to care for the other is required ... A curse is on him, that of the dead mother who does not stop dying, who keeps a hold on him, as if he were her prisoner. Grief, a narcissistic feeling, surfaces again. (1983, 234; translation mine)

Meanwhile, while Doro is not given the opportunity to express and develop his desire to kill his mother in the story, Gadda's desire, by contrast, is fully constructed and unfolded. Should we say then that, given the failed representation of the murder, Gadda pursued in vain the fulfilment of his desire? On the one hand, it is true that the fact of having planned the murder is a way of perpetrating it; in this sense, despite the story's open-endedness, Gadda got his wish. On the other, we must not forget that Gadda planned and carried out repeatedly the very same crime, which suggests we are dealing with a complex question that cannot be answered with a simple yes or no. The construction of the death scene and its re-elaboration are shaped in time not only by the killing of the mother, but also, above all, by her return to life. The son-writer is constantly giving and re-giving birth to his mother. His stubborn return to the dead mother allows us to outline a peculiar configuration in the so-called process of reparation, one based on an inversion with respect to the former dependence of the son on his mother. Now the mother is dependent on her son who

spends his life nurturing the dead, as if he were the only one in charge. Guardian of the tomb, sole possessor of the key to the burial place, he plays the role of the parent who nurtures secretly. He keeps his dead mother imprisoned, she remains his property. The mother has become her child's child. It is up to him to treat the narcissistic wound. We are confronted with a paradox: if the mother is mourning, dead, she is lost to the subject, but at least, even if hurt, she is there. The subject can take care of her, he can try to wake her up, to bring her to life, to cure her. But if, once cured, she wakes up, she is back to life, she lives, then the subject loses her again, because she leaves him to go about her own business and to invest in other objects. Therefore, we are dealing with a subject who is caught between two losses: death with her, life without her. From here comes the extreme ambiguity inherent in the wish of re-bringing to life one's own mother. (Green, 244–5; translation mine)

Gadda must overcome the ambiguity and ambivalence inherent in this anomalous process of reparation. He must manage to go beyond the harsh censorship he imposes on himself for having expressed not a simple desire but the guiltiest desire of all. In order to realize it fully he must stop resurrecting the mother he wants dead. He must give concrete shape to his phantasm of self-sufficiency at the same time as he must put an end to his habit of giving priority to his phantasm of dependence.

Despite numerous pauses and interruptions, Gadda keeps searching for a story that will allow him to construct the identity of a son dis-identified with his mother, or, at least, an individualized being capable of surviving until the end of the story, able to live even after having accepted responsibility, directly or indirectly, for a mother's death. Gadda reaches such a goal in *Quer pasticciaccio brutto de via Merulana* by means of a filial character who is not a son, but who lives as one, differentiated and detached from the dead object. Hence Gadda realizes finally his murderous desires.

Notes

1 I do not share Dante Isella's view that *Dejanira Classis* should be taken as the title of this work in progress. Although Dejanira is at the centre of the parts of the story that Gadda managed to develop, the novella, as I shall argue, is about the son, not the mother. If Gadda had wanted to entitle his text *Dejanira Classis*, he would have done so in 1970, when the work was first published. Quotes from *La cognizione del dolore* refer to Emilio Manzotti's 1987 edition of the novel published by Einaudi.

2 On the problem of matricide in *Quer pasticciaccio*, see Manuela Bertone 1993 and Denis Ferraris 1992.

3 An analysis of Gadda's use of Sophocles' text cannot be developed here, but my general view is that in organizing Denira's life and death, Gadda had in mind Sophocles' development of the character of the mother, the mother-son relationship, and the mother's killing. On Sophocles' Deianeira, see Nicole Loraux 1985/1987.

4 'Jole,' just as 'Dejanira,' is a name that refers to the scene of action in Sophocles' *Women of Trachis*. Although unnamed in the play, Jole is present on the stage: she is Eurytos' daughter and Heracles' young seductress whom he sends to Trachis before his own arrival. In Gadda, the name 'Jole' is associated with seduction also in the short story 'San Giorgio in casa Brocchi,' Jole being the pretty maid who seduces Gigi.

5 By a very simple combination of factors (heredity plus trauma), Gadda represents, perhaps unintentionally, Freud's view on the aetiology of neurosis, according to which 'the psychic constitution of the child is formed

by a combination of his personal and hereditary predispositions and the events of early childhood' (Green 1993, 249). As Guido Lucchini has pointed out, Gadda's works that involve psychoanalysis in some way belong – with the exception of 'Una tigre nel parco' – to the post-Second World War period, and 'Gadda's interest in Freud is to be situated between the 30s and the 40s' (Lucchini 1988, 113). But in light of the coincidence just mentioned, and particularly in light of the whole mother-son discourse developed in *Novella seconda*, it would be necessary to push back in time Gadda's interest in Freud, or, indeed, attempt to verify how much and which Freud Gadda might already have read in 1928.

6   As far as the mother is concerned, Gadda recycles the conventional and stereotypical pattern inspired, via Freud, by Sophocles' Jocasta: a mother who is far from being excluded from the narrative project (as feminist criticism has often suggested), a mother who is actually all too present, who drives her son to his tragic deeds. Gadda does not question the tradition. He, in fact, ignores the fact that the son's problem is his inability to break off not with his mother, but with a given ideology of motherhood. Motherhood is represented as a condition bound to express itself either as unselfish love or as unpardonable error, either as the extolling of maternal instinct or as the perversion of the natural essence of it. On the question of the literary stereotypes associated with motherhood, see Christiane Oliver 1980.

7   Gadda's notes contain a particularly cautious hypothesis: 'Per quanto riguarda la morte della madre, evitare il delitto, troppo disgustoso: ammettere il furto dei diamanti (visto anche come punizione della avidità del figlio), ma la madre muore di morte naturale, per la nota malattia' (*CD*, 554) [As regards the mother's death, avoid the crime, it's too disgusting; allow for the theft of her diamonds (seen also as a way of punishing her son's greed), but the mother dies a natural death on account of her known illness.]

References

Bertone, Manuela. 1993. *Il romanzo come sistema. Molteplicità e differenza in C.E. Gadda*. Rome: Editori Riuniti

Contini, Gianfranco. 1989. *Quarant' anni d'amicizia*. Turin: Einaudi

Dombroski, Robert S. 1987. 'La dialettica della follia: per un'interpretazione sociale del dolore gaddiano.' In *Gadda. Progettualità e scrittura*, 143–55. Rome: Editori Riuniti

– 1994. *Properties of Writing: Ideological Discourse in Modern Italian Fiction*. Baltimore and London: Johns Hopkins University Press

Ferraris, Denis. 1992. 'On tue une mère.' *Narrativa* 2: 61–74

Ferretti, Gian Carlo. 1987. *Ritratto di Gadda*. Rome and Bari: Laterza

Green, André. 1993. *Narcissisme de vie, Narcissisme de Mort*. Paris: Editions de Minuit

Loraux, Nicole. 1985. *Façons tragiques de tuer une femme*. Paris: Hachette

– 1987. *Tragic Ways of Killing a Woman*. Translated by Anthony Forster. Cambridge, Mass., and London: Harvard University Press

Lucchini, Guido. 1988. *L'istinto della combinazione. Le origini del romanzo in Carlo Emilio Gadda*. Florence: La Nuova Italia

Manzoni, Alessandro. 1971. *I promessi sposi*. Vol. II. Edited by Lanfranco Caretti. Turin: Einaudi

– 1972. *The Betrothed*. London: Penguin Books

Neppi, Enzo. 1992. *Soggetto e fantasma. Figure dell'autobiografia*. Pisa: Pacini

Olivier, Christiane. 1980. *Les Enfants de Jocaste*. Paris: Denoël

The Mark of Cain: Mourning and Dissimulation in the Works of Carlo Emilio Gadda

FEDERICA G. PEDRIALI

E ogni scrittore è un predicato verbale (coordina) che manovra un complemento oggetto (il dato linguistico). E questo complemento oggetto relutta, come
un serpentesco dragone, al dominio e alli artigli del predicato.
      – 'Le belle lettere e i contributi espressivi delle tecniche'

The astounding lexical variety of Gadda's prose is a source of boundless
delight for the reader, in spite of the inconvenience of needing to have
always at hand the most comprehensive dictionary available. Yet, Gadda's
discriminating exactness in the use of language gives way to a moderate,
compulsive repetition of formulas, when, among his various expressive
registers (his *'maniere'*, as he calls them [*RI*, 396]), he activates the lyric
mode. My study will attempt to explain why in this specific area Gadda
fails to defeat convention or, to continue the metaphor of the above
quotation, why the dragon, usually routed with splendid virtuosity, here
achieves victory.

It is true that the fragment is a characteristic form of twentieth-century
art and literature. But in Gadda it dominates the text to a paralysing
extent. Here we have a writer endowed with prodigious technical and linguistic skills. Yet his body of works is remarkably slim, twisted, repetitive,
and truncated well beyond what the spirit of his time could have demanded. As in Kafka's case, literature alone does not explain it. If we want
to make sense out of the *pasticcio* and view that *'gefrorene Meer'* (Kafka
1958, 28) from which Gadda's writing painfully arose, we must be selec-
tive in our choice of means. For us it will be to investigate the intensely
emotional mother-son relationship that culminates in the disquieting
ending of *La cognizione del dolore* in light of a second, but no less severe

and dominating, trauma in Gadda's personal life: that which involves his younger brother, Enrico, who was killed in the First World War.[1] The obvious starting point, the *Giornale di guerra e di prigionia*, has reached us in a rather incomplete state, due to the hazards of war and, we may assume, on account of Gadda's own censorship of memories and thoughts deemed improper or too explicit. It is therefore only partially reliable for our purposes. In the several places where mention is made of Enrico, Gadda generally expresses complete devotion to his brother, intense affection, and extreme protective anxiety.[2] In the letters available to us, references to Enrico are few and far between. Invariably, the tone is one of devastating sorrow at the loss of his 'povero Enrico,' just as intense in 1970 as in 1919.[3] And it will come as no surprise that mention of Enrico in the interviews Gadda accorded when he became a celebrity should follow the same pattern established in the letters.[4]

In a televised interview, given in 1963 when *La cognizione del dolore* was being nominated for the Prix International de Littérature, Gadda explained the title of his novel in the following terms:

Cognizione è anche il procedimento conoscitivo, il graduale avvicinamento ad una determinata nozione. Questo procedimento può essere lento, penoso, amaro, può comportare il passaggio attraverso esperienze strazianti della realtà. La morte di un giovine fratello caduto in guerra può distruggere la nostra vita. Si ricordino i versi disperati di Catullo. (Gadda 1993b, 153)

[Cognition is also the cognitive process, the gradual approach to a particular notion. This process can be slow, painful, bitter. It can entail reliving devastating experiences. The death of a young brother in war can destroy one's life. Remember Catullus's desperate verses.]

Significantly, the novel, usually regarded as 'il romanzo della madre,' is here linked to Enrico. And Catullus's desperate verses, which – we learn from a review Gadda wrote in 1945 – come from *Carmina* 68 and 101 (*SGF I*, 899), direct us towards Gadda's own poems.

Largely unavailable until very recently, and subjected, as Maria Antonietta Terzoli has aptly remarked, to a 'singolare autocensura' (Gadda 1993a, v), his lyric production is limited to twenty-three poems, ten of which were written in early 1919, when Gadda, upon his return from prison in Germany, had learned of his brother's death. Later, set aside in an orange-coloured envelope, they were intended, it seems, to be confidential. Ugo Betti's influence is present throughout them, for it was in those years, when their friendship had peaked, that Gadda found his friend's lyric style particularly appealing.[5] From *Re pensieroso* he drew metaphors and rhetorical devices particularly suitable to his own private obsessions. Gadda's poems make use of a relatively limited complex of images in search of the definitive word capable of expressing his true moral being. They also document his attempts at finding a cure for the painful condition of being a survivor, as revealed in the contrasting moods generated by his mourning for Enrico and the ignominy of imprisonment. Finally, the poems define the 'imaging process' of the Enrico question, integrating its ciphered vocabulary.

One must agree with Gadda when he states that in his work there is no thematic progress; at most there is a thickening of the texture of his writing (Ungarelli 1993, 154). If we cut through the patina of the poems he wrote in 1919, we can find the entire network of symbols later employed in *La cognizione*. Leaving aside for the moment the first poem in the set, 'Sul San Michele' [On San Michele], in 'Alla montagna salire' [Going up the Mountain], dated 5 April, we are greeted with the image of a tower. 'La guerra feroce delle tempeste' [the fierce war of tempests] crushes any desire for moral reconstruction. The passage to health is useless and in vain; the poet's hand falls dead at the attempt (Gadda 1993a, 13, vv 25–32). 'Acqua nascosta' [Hidden Water], composed a day later, still employs a water metaphor to convey the possible reintegration of the suffering subject (14, vv 4–7; 108); its message must not be corrupted by 'il dolce / Silenzio della vendetta' [the sweet / Silence of revenge].

The water imagery runs into the next poem, 'So che v'è un lago' [I Know That a Lake Is There] (9 April), but while in the previous piece the descent of the plane (ibid., vv 13–14) gently led the way for the poet, now jagged and insurmountable mountains imprison him in ice (15, vv 9–10; 108–9). Beyond the 'opaco / Terrore della notte' [opaque / Terror of the night], the poet could drink of the pure, unknown world he senses in the clear mornings (15–16, vv 28–9, 34, 43–4). But the certainty of living one life under one law begins to escape him (16, vv 38–9, 53–7).

The fifth poem in the set, 'Chiara serenità della terra' [Clear Serenity of the Land] is among the most unruffled penned by Gadda, a rare idyll set in the fresh spring air of an Easter Sunday, his first Easter – Gadda informs us in a note – in Longone after the war and the first after Enrico's death (ibid., 109). The distant bells, yet to be demonized as in *La cognizione*, call the living to the sun and clear air (17, vv 11–14). In 1919, Easter Sunday fell on 20 April, a date close to the first anniversary of Enrico's accident. Gadda's *Giornale* entries stop on 1 April with the name of Enrico and after the outburst on 25 March against his family and fate. They resume on 22 May, presumably once the poetic urge had waned (*GGP*, 855–7). But while the diary of those months brims with references to Enrico, Gadda the poet emits no Catullian cry of despair at his brother's death. In fact not until he dictates the epitaph on his tomb will he bring himself to utter his name and to strive for an impossible dialogue.[6] Like Gonzalo in *La cognizione*, Gadda is burying Enrico within himself (*CD*, 682).

If 'Chiara serenità' can be read as a desire for reintegration and a celebration of restored normality, it can also, especially if coupled with the next poem 'Piani di sole' [Layers of Sun], be taken as a 'spectator's lyric.' 'Piani' appears to prolong the mood established in the Easter poem. The idyll continues under a radiant sun, as a street teaming with life is depicted with admiration, until the spell is broken in the final verses: 'L'anima [...] / Conosce oltre la luce / E il lavoro del giorno / Il suo feroce male' (Gadda 1993a, 21, vv 50–6) [The mind ... has knowledge beyond the light / And the daily work / of its fierce affliction]. The fracture is sealed by 'Gli amici taciturni' [Sullen Friends]. Now the world is sterile, forests and mountains shrouded in shadow, the dark silences of still nights shattered by lightning (20–1, vv 6–7, 25–7, 40–1). When memories of things past overcome the emptiness of the present ('altri giorni allora / Vediamo ed altri sorrisi. / E rivediamo le torri / Ed i vecchi castelli' [21, vv 59–62] [other days then / We see and other smiles / And we see again the towers / and the ancient castles]), we have before us an image that will return over and over again as the archetype of Edenic serenity, depicted at the moment of impending loss.

The next poem, 'La sala di basalte' [The Basalt Room], further defines this transition. Inglorious combat, captivity, and bereavement have become additional elements in the conspiracy against the author's marvellous talents (*GGP*, 645). But the accidents of war have merely repeated a pattern which Gadda had experienced since childhood. In 'Sala,' the longest of Gadda's poems, what the consciously public voice attempted to suppress in the *Giornale* now takes over in the disguise of poetry. The opening is serenely nocturnal. Under the September moon, lovers are kissing passionately until – fourteen verses into the poem – a howling wind suddenly breaks the scenic composure as we are plunged into a nightmare: amidst the 'popolo nero / Dei faggi,' a shadow walks along an unknown path (Gadda 1993a, vv 19–23); motionless towers appear (vv 27–8), as the raging tempest obscures the heavens:

Un'ombra passa sul ponte [...] / Come le ombre di quelli / Che sono passati sopra la terra, / Avevano nel viso una luce / E un sorriso. (23–4, vv 31–6)

[On the bridge a shadow passes ... / Like the shades of those / who have walked the earth, / A light and a smile adorned their faces.]

'Sorriso,' a key word associated with Enrico, signals his entrance onto the scene. His ghostlike appearance summons forth the poem's main character, an anxious maiden, living at the mercy of the giants of wind and darkness (vv 49–50). Enveloped in her pain, unaware of her surroundings, she prays for the sweet, pale friend she has lost (v 61). All of her thoughts are absorbed in an impossible conversation with someone who is not there (25, vv 76–9), whose dying moments are relived with morbid desperation (vv 81–90). The girl's descent into the depths of Hades, past the monstrous guardians of the earth, is rewarded by the apparition of a smiling page ('paggio'). Once it evaporates, a third phantom joins in:

Uno sconosciuto soldato / [...] guarda / La fanciulla senza saluto. / Ella chiede per dove si passa / Per dove è passato / Uno dalla dolce nitida faccia. (26–7, vv 145–51)

[An unknown soldier / ... gazes at the maiden without saying hello. / She asks the way / The way taken by / Someone with a sweet, serene face.]

'La sala di basalte' brings to an end the probing process that Gadda began with 'Sul San Michele,' the first poem in the set. Written ten days after he had learnt of Enrico's death, the latter is by far the most realistic piece in the collection. It translates into verse the same heartfelt feelings for Gadda's dead war companions expressed in the *Giornale* and in *Il castello di Udine*. But what is striking is that, in all of the poems written in 1919, Enrico is left out of Gadda's sorrow. Although Gadda invokes the death of his brother throughout the *Giornale* and in numerous public occasions, here, rather than mourn for his brother, like Gonzalo in *La cognizione*, he sublimates the loss in relation to the *'mater dolorosa.'* His own experience is merely qualified by the loss: he is a person who lost his brother in war, just like the characters Grifonetto and Girolamo Lehrer of *Racconto italiano*.

Borges writes in *El Aleph* that our deeds become the symbols of what we are and that one's life reveals its essence in a single act which has taken place at a particular point in time (Borges 1972, 57–8). The poetic act we have just examined is exactly such a pivotal point in Gadda. 'Sala' is no doubt an act of grieving, but it is also an act of unfulfilled desire. The triangle of which Gadda had been part has been dissolved by fate. But the mother keeps going through the motions, refusing to acknowledge that her son has disappeared forever, barely heeding the plea of her other son who has survived. Much has been made of the Oedipal conflict at work in Gadda, but if it is true that it does exist, the third element in the triangle is Enrico, not Gadda's father.[7]

Turning now to Gadda's fiction, we find at its core that very symbolic act about which Borges speaks. In 'La passeggiata autunnale,' a short tale written in 1918, the emotional conflict involving the three main characters is resolved abruptly by the elimination of Stefano (Enrico). But Nerina (the 'fanciulla-madre') continues to avoid Rineri's pleading gaze, her thoughts forever absorbed by Stefano. Although written before Gadda knew of Enrico's death, 'La passeggiata autunnale' is structured very much like 'Sala.' Whether it represents a presentiment or a death-wish is not for us to say. What cannot be ignored is that this scene is played over and over again in Gadda's fiction.[8]

Although Gadda states that his disillusionment and grief are rooted in the war and his imprisonment (*GGP*, 853), the fact of the matter is, if we are to believe his fictional double Gonzalo, that:

Il suo rancore veniva da una lontananza più tetra, come se fra lui e la mamma ci fosse qualcosa di irreparabile, di più atroce di ogni guerra: e d'ogni spaventosa morte. (*CD*, 692)

[His rancor came from a grimmer remoteness, as if between him and his mother there were something irreparable, more atrocious than any war: and than any frightful death. (*AG*, 156)]

This 'remoteness' is partially defined in three of Gadda's short narratives, which could be grouped under the heading of 'Park Stories' since, besides being similar in theme, they all have as their setting the park in Piazza Castello. Densely autobiographical, these narrative exercises were intended as a possible beginning or, better, appropriate setting for *La cognizione*, which Gadda had begun drafting in 1934. The first, 'Una tigre nel parco,' appeared in May 1936, just over a month after his mother's death.[9] It is a bold piece of prose that could be regarded as a kind of 'preemptive strike' at criticism's desire to probe the murky depths of his future novel, deemed by Gadda himself so worthy of psychological analysis

(*SGF I*, 77). In a seemingly irrelevant footnote (76, n1), we learn that the story is set in 1896. The 'tiger' is Gadda as a child, exploring on all fours the enchanted garden of his youth. The child's dream of being a real tiger comes to an abrupt end, as his investigating fingers happen on a strange jam-like substance ('una strana marmellata'). His innocence polluted, he is forced out of his dream into reality. One could say that here Gadda, with extreme lightness of hand, lays the entire repertory of his future novel squarely before his psychoanalyist. Or does he? The garden perhaps contains most of it. The park overrun by nannies and children no doubt represents a time of the senses before the censorship of reason and conscience, the springtime of life, so to speak, an idyllic wholeness protected by a towering castle (75–6). But it is the representation of evil which is uncharacteristic – and incomplete. The 'signorino's' safety, along with his childhood fantasies, are here compromised by the 'ombra de' cupi fossati' [the shadow of the grim moats], by the ruins encircling the castle's broken walls, and by 'l'uomo del sacco' [the bag man], a gorgon-zola-eating outcast (76–9). Missing is the central figure of the maiden and the presence of evil hovering over her. Moreover, the narrator is still an integral part of the action. The towers may conceal the real threat, but, in effect, it has yet to come on the scene. We are in May 1896; in November of the same year Enrico was born.[10]

In 'Ronda al Castello' we move into a higher gear. If in 'Tigre' graceful swallows fill the air, here a swarm of bicyclists invade the peaceful park. The once-sheltered preserve of the tiger has now been made subject to a frantic choreography of 'otherness.' The topography is rearranged on a rational basis; the soldiers courting the nannies are drilled and identified by the narrator with military precision. In a crowding of shadowy images, the military patrol (the *'ronda'*) emerges. The patrol is composed of a lieutenant and two privates – a three-headed reincarnation of the extinct feline – who try to impose some order on the confusion (ibid., 98–9), but are careful to keep at a distance from the dark boulevards and the scented ruins where the women of the night entertain their off-duty companions. Excluded from the dark paths trodden by others, the trio by chance runs into Elsa and Bruno, the latter equipped with a shiny bicycle. The couple is a celestial vision before which they stand with open mouths, as in front of an unexpected masterpiece in an art gallery, divided between admiration and envy. In a revealing simile, Bruno is compared to a hovering hawk (100). In a suppressed passage, later echoed in *La cognizione*, Gadda adorns Elsa with a white and a red rose, while a rain of flowers blesses the idyll within the borders of the 'paradiso perduto' under the siege of the 'lubrificata velocità' (*SGF I*, 1235).

'Al Parco in una sera di maggio' [In the Park on a Late Afternoon in May], which became part of the collection *L'Adalgisa – Disegni milanesi*, contains a further violation of the poised serenity of the setting. The castle is now just a backdrop on a stage populated by motorcycles and every other sort of loud motorized vehicle which, amid the noisy Milanese chatter, deafen any intimation of original purity (*A*, 483, 485). The frivolity of the scene, however, is marked by three undercurrents: the threatening, vengeful figure of the tramp – again the 'uomo del sacco' – encircling the family group; the dapper bicyclist and Elsa's gaze unswervingly fixed on him; the heavenly rain of flowers blessing lovers and children alike (492–7). The children are clearly Carlo Emilio and Enrico, whose father collects chestnut-coloured insects (492). Gadda's mother is split into Adalgisa and Elsa; the former embodying the practical Lombard character of an adult mother, while the latter has all the arresting fragrance and radiance of a 'madre fanciulla.' The lightness of the piece is suddenly encumbered as the narrator abandons his relatively unruffled third-person viewpoint for a no-better-defined 'noi':

Il risultato complessivo era, in noi [...] e in quel declino dell'ora, un disperato sgomento: un male sconosciuto e remoto [...] come il ricordo d'una irripetibile gioia di vivere, d'una luce, che giorni crudeli ne avessero allontanata [...]: poiché tutto di lei, pareva significare senza nostra speranza [...]: 'son io, sì! Quella che avete veduta e sognata.' (499)

[The end result was, in us ... and in that dying hour, a desperate fear: an unknown and distant evil ... like the memory of an irrecoverable moment of joy, of a light, that cruel days made remote ... : since all of her, seemed to mean without our hope ... : 'Yes, it is I! the person you saw and desired.']

Gadda replaces his 'adult' wide-angle lens with a 'child-like,' contour-blurring close-up, focusing now apprehensively on Elsa's unreachable remoteness. She is a 'povera sonnambula, che si affida ai vertiginosi cammini della notte' [a poor sleepwalker trusting in the dizzying paths of the night]; her eyes 'parevano inseguire in idea in un remoto spazio un fuggente: forse uno che ripasserà, sulla sua bicicletta: che rivivrà nella immagine: una seconda, una terza, una ventesima, una cinquantesima volta' (500) [seemed to follow in thought in a distant space someone fleeing: perhaps someone who will come back, on his bicycle, whose image will return two, three, twenty, fifty times]. This musing eventually leads to a long caricatural outburst that leaves the figure of Adalgisa unrecognizable (502).

The three above-mentioned stories, although published in different collections, remained in the forefront of Gadda's interests as he worked on *Fulmine sul 220*, a novel he would never complete. It can be argued that all of Gadda's life and art tended fatally towards the huge 'black hole' of *La cognizione*. His many 'false starts' would be overcome by its strong gravitational pull, in spite of the unmanageable stubbornness of the material. And nowhere is this difficulty more evident than in the *Racconto italiano*, a text which provides us with unique insights into Gadda's working methods.

The *Racconto italiano*, Gadda's first large-scale narrative, is a curious mix of the *Giornale di guerra e di prigionia*, from which it takes its diaristic form and occasional pieces of war literature; *Meditazione milanese*, for its philosophical digressions; and fiction proper. The exposed bluntness of the *Racconto* must have unsettled Gadda, who never allowed such sincerity to surface again until *La cognizione*. The sketchbook, or *cahier d'études*, as he calls it, is arranged in two parallel layers: a novel in progress, and the author's comments and notes on its development. Ultimately, the rational mind behind the notes succumbs to the autonomous will of the narrative.

In the first scene of the *Racconto*, the playful 'tiger in the park' has become quite a different character: 'Il passo era di una belva, sulla coltre del remoto giardino. Il silenzio cortine di velluto, si dischiudeva al procedere del leopardo. Si sentiva lieve, fermo, felice, estraneo ai procedimenti macchinosi e banali con cui gli uomini fabbricano la successione dei loro atti' (*RI*, 402) [The steps were those of a wild beast on the cover of the distant garden. The velvet curtain of silence opened at the leopard's approach. He felt light, secure, happy, extraneous to the banal, machinating procedures with which men fabricate the course of their acts]. The garden we are in now has no Edenic light glowing on its borders. We sense that a crime is imminent and that the excitement of writing has curbed the author's zeal to annotate the action. The opening notes reveal that, although cloaked in universal meaning, the novel's main themes are private and contain specific autobiographical data. The dual topography (Brianza–South America) is established right from the start, and the novel will recount the 'tragedia di una persona forte che si perverte per l'insufficienza dell'ambiente sociale' (397) [tragedy of a strong person who is corrupted because of society's shortcomings]. What is of interest to our inquiry is the way the crime develops. If the character of the protagonist is still undecided (schizophrenically divided into 'Type A' and 'Type B,' each endowed with Gaddian attributes), the scene of the murder is remarkably assured and typical in all aspects (401–2).

As I have argued elsewhere, despite its dazzling and variegated surface, the Gaddian universe is remarkably bare; at its centre we find only the figure of the outcast (Pedriali 1990, 33). Inspired by the Virgilian helmsman, a myth dear to Gadda, I proposed somewhat ironically that in his case we could be dealing with a Palinurus complex. Time and time again, we find in his works a pattern which takes us from the serene contemplation of 'chiari e gaudiosi mattini' to powerless resentment at the realization that his realm, which promised to be well-ordered and intelligently governed, had been invaded and ruled by marauding peons. Then, before the final implosion of his writing, the raging elements envelop normal 'otherness' soon to be overcome by the fury of retribution. In 'Studio No 1' (RI), the curtain rises at nightfall, that is, at the final moment of the sequence just outlined. The garden is dominated by Maria's thoughts of 'lontani dolori' (RI, 401; my emphasis)[11] [distant grief], with the usual counterpoint of the 'gemme del silenzio notturno' (my emphasis) [jewels of nocturnal silence]. When Grifonetto violates the perimeter wall, we are not at all prepared for the sudden burst of violence to come:

La bianchissima preda era presso. Era sua preda, e non d'altri. Basta, basta, o vita [...]. Basta con le stritolanti menzogne, basta con il crudele veleno delle speranze deluse. Il pugnale d'un uomo ti bucherà, menzogna, e il siero verdastro puzzerà come la pancia del coccodrillo. (402)

[The whitest prey was close. It was his prey, and not others.' Enough, enough, oh life ... Enough strident lies, enough cruel venom of unfulfilled hope. A man's dagger will pierce you, lie, and the greenish serum will stink like the belly of a crocodile.]

As he approaches the house, no emotion is allowed to unsettle his resolve, 'poichè nulla di irregolare si compieva nella sua anima, nella sua vita, o in altre anime, o vite' (403) [since nothing unusual entered his mind, or life, in other minds, or lives]. The reference to 'altre vite' kindles a second virulent eruption. A panoramic shot from above quickly surveys the enviable activities of normal men. As the camera enters the bedroom, '[dove] dormono quivi presso la mamma i caldi, profumati bambini [...]

E nei letti profondi dolci donne accolgono il loro maschio e lo saziano con ogni dono' (404) [where warm sweet-smelling children sleep at their mother's breast and where in soft beds loving women satisfy their men's every desire], the heat rises to a second peak:

Nei letti profondi, dove si dissolvono e si ricreano le vane generazioni degli uomini! nei letti profondi v'è la luce dei disciolti capelli che la notte non può spegnere ancora: ma l'oro è utile forse; no, l'oro è utile per la persuasione, come il diadema d'una meretrice di Bisanzio; [...]o mia madre natura [...] è inutile! per i tuoi giochi perversi! (404)

[In the soft beds, where useless generations of mortals die and are recreated! in these soft beds there is the light from dishevelled hair that the night cannot yet put out; but gold is perhaps useful; no, gold is useful as a means of persuasion, like the charm of a Byzantium whore; ... oh mother nature of mine ... it is useless! on account of your perverse games.]

Gadda clustered around this study a series of notes appraising his first steps into the novel, expanding on its implications and trying to fathom the course it will take. When he finally resolves to get down to the business of writing (ibid., 416), he again resorts to those images generated by the subconscious tensions in his inspiration. 'Gemme tremanti nel cielo,' 'punti d'oro e di zaffiro,' 'gole nere dei monti,' 'lontani [...] dolori,' 'male violento e selvaggio,' 'ville' and 'giardini misteriosi' fill his pages (419–21). His eye finally comes to rest on a familiar compositional arrangement: a female figure in an intimate, inaudible conversation with a bicyclist – a scene that elicits wonder in the spectator (423–4). At this point, the novel breaks off again. The author's obsessions temporarily placated, the plot follows its course more steadily, this time proving a little more successful in obeying the dictates of his engineering mind. After about forty pages, the author intervenes again to compensate for the neutral tone of the narration. The notes absorb part of the imagery deleted from the narrative.

Before drawing together all of the elements gathered so far, let us look at two other themes in the *Racconto*: vengeance and remorse. In the Devero river episode (ibid., 535–42), the pristine freedom of the river has been desecrated by busy people (538). Humiliated to the state of a 'working river,' the Devero 'sognava folli vendette' [dreamt dreams of mad revenge], and only the pleasure of vindication would lessen its grief (536). The river becomes thus a steel vein, like Grifonetto's dagger, ready to take revenge for the loss of its prey (535, 539): 'Non più la valle per lui, che nei millenni di sua giovinezza dominò come un esile e dolce donna' (538) [He no longer could roam the valley which in the millennia of his youth he dominated like a slim and sweet woman]. The bright green current (541) takes us back to the green heart of the serpent of the Archangel study (457–60), a dragon with which the narrating 'noi' has identified fully. As we shall see, both of these themes return in *La cognizione*.

In the end, the story falls apart in Gadda's hands. On account of the author's inner tensions, the materials fail to come together. What is important for us here is the emergence of the themes of vengeance and remorse. Before the *Racconto*, haunting Gadda's imagination was the image we find at the end of 'Passeggiata' of a female figure lost in thought who refuses to acknowledge the pleading gaze of the spectator. The object of her devotion is then swept away by obscure forces. This scene returns in the poems of 1919, not as a premonition or wish, but as an irretrievable circumstance. The *Racconto* adds a second victim, for now the figure of woman is the object of hatred and revenge (the mourning Maria is punished with murderous thoughts). Furthermore, the comfort of normality is befouled. Gadda goes to great lengths in arguing that the abnormal is part of the overall design of life, but the underlying message tends to denounce good as nothing more than thinly disguised evil.[12] The bolts that secure Gadda's cage are further tightened; soon they will become irreversibly locked.

Generally speaking, Cain's actions are motivated not so much by sheer envy of his brother as by the unjust preference of him he has had to endure. What is questioned in any Cain-like context is the wisdom of the judge. Two examples come to mind: 'San Giorgio in casa Brocchi' and a crucial passage in *La meccanica*, two works that could be rightly called 'Stories of Preference.' The St George of the title is Gigi, a pampered 'giovin signore,' born of a noble Milanese family. As Gadda himself suggests, under the veneer of social satire lies the symbolic struggle of two saints: St George, the chivalrous womanizer, and St Louis Gonzaga, the ascetic.[13] Countess Brocchi, Gigi's mother, establishes with them a kind of sacred conversation. It is plain that her choice of a patron for Gigi is a choice between two possible sons. Her initial predilection for the safe, righteous St Louis (for two years she has been embroidering an altar cloth in his honour) is progressively eroded by the the alluring charms of the brilliant and athletic St George. The 'figlio bello' triumphs; the cloth will embellish his altar. His attributes, the narrator admits, easily explain the victory: the legendary knight soars undefeated over the springtime tempests and comes to rest, in all the haughty splendour of his full regalia, at the side of the enthroned Virgin. Whether it is in his conquest of the evil dragon or in his proud stance by the Virgin's throne, St George proves to be an irresistible temptation for the mother-Madonna.

Appearance defeats truth, the discriminating faculties of the judge having been blinded by transitory resplendence. It is neither chance nor expediency that places St George at the centre of the Triennale Milanese, presiding over an orgy of the senses against which poor Luigi Gonzaga admonishes in vain: 'Prudenza!' (*RR II*, 657). Addressing the alarmed morality of the countess, he exposes the deceit concealed in St George's dazzling youth. He warns that, although St George appears to provide an answer to our torments, he is but an illusion of spirituality, a false perception. The countess, of course, will disregard the advice, preferring conviviality to severity. Almost instantly, Gigi succumbs to temptation and loses his virginity, betraying his mother's trust, much to the narrator's satisfaction. In echoing Gonzaga's efforts to enlighten the countess, the authorial voice has steadily undermined her adoration for Gigi. Far from being gifted, St George's protégé is just lazy and dense (692). The idea that you could trouble not one but two saints to make something out of such dull material is plainly ludicrous. At the story's end Gigi will fall to the charms of Jole the maid, who, social standing apart, is a perfect match for him. The fall of Gigi (St George) results entirely from – as Gadda put it in the chapter 'Narcisismo giovanile e pedagogia' in *Eros e Priapo* – the 'convoitise eccessiva del pubblico' [excessive cupidity of the public]. But the totally inconsequential continuation of his reasoning suggests an inference of capital importance to to this study:

Si legga il romanzo Destins di François Mauriac, dove l'atto purificatore [...] è un incidente automobilistico. Il giovane e mal concupito protagonista ci lascia la pelle: salvandosi nella morte dalla probabilità di finir male moralmente. (*EP*, 330–1)

[Consider François Mauriac's novel *Destins*, in which the act of purification is a car accident. The young protagonist in a bad bout of concupiscence loses his life: death saves him from the probability of ending up morally unfit.]

This is precisely the fate from which Enrico was saved by death.

If we read 'San Giorgio in casa Brocchi' as a brilliant satire, two victors emerge: the author, who has ridiculed Milanese bourgeois morality, and Gigi, who has overcome his mother's censoring gaze ('gli occhi della mamma, fermi e grigi' [*RR II*, 689] [His mother's still, grey eyes]). But there is a deeper level on which the story can, and should, be understood: as a 'sacred conversation' or confrontation of two saints who measure each other's respective attributes before the altar of the mother. Its real target is not just a set of empty social conventions, but rather the narcissism of the mother. She might appear aloof and unimpeachable, but she is unmasked none the less as she sits in stern judgment. The unjustly demoted son, rightfully angered, overturns the verdict, as he lays bare the profanity of her choice, desecrating forever her assumed divinity. The mother's sin is one of pride: a narcissism that causes her to succumb to flattery and superficiality. Although Gigi may fear punishment for his transgression, it is plain that the fallen idol in the story is not the reprobate son but the ill-judging mother. A tempest builds in the background: St Luigi's revenge is on its way (662); the setting for Part Two of *La cognizione* has already been announced.

La meccanica is unique among Gadda's works in that it contains two fully developed male figures who embody, respectively, the characteristics of Enrico and Carlo Emilio. By contrast, in 'San Giorgio' we have only Gigi (virtually Enrico) and in the *Racconto*, only Grifonetto/Gerolamo (virtually Carlo Emilio). Here the female at the centre is the beautiful Zoraide, around whom gravitate the bright, vitalistic Franco (from whose mechanical propensities the novel's title is inspired) and the dour Luigi – this time a real San Luigi, world-renouncing and austere. The triangle is threatened by Gildo, a snake-like character reminiscent of Iago or Caliban (again the 'uomo del sacco'), to whom the author delegates his vengeful acts (most notably against Franco). As we approach *La cognizione*, it will be useful to dwell on the way the narrator denounces the vacuity of Zoraide. For if *La meccanica* is the place where Gadda has been most daring in depicting his personal tragedy, it is not without significance that he conveys his feelings by means of a painting. The intricate interplay of narrator and characters is embossed on canvas by Giorgione's *La Madonna e Bambino e i Santi Liberale e Francesco*. In a scene that is truly the 'filter,' the moment when the veil is almost lifted, Zoraide, who is being shown around the Cathedral by a group of nuns, stops to look at the masterpiece:

Appariva allora la Purissima con il Bambino, sopra un plinto magnifico [...] ma il demonio subsannante dell'educandato, la Gemma Nuttis [...] aveva suggerito a Zoraide un pensiero diabolico: che quel volto effigiasse l'amante carnale del Zorzòn. Così [...] ella pensava 'l'amante': una misteriosa e torbida felicità, un peccato atroce e meraviglioso, l'amante. (*M*, 491–2)

[Then the Virgin appeared with her Child on a magnificent plinth ... but Gemma Nuttis, that leering, boarding-school demon, had put a diabolical thought into Zoraide's head: that that face was the effigy of Zorzon's lover. Thus ... she thought 'the lover': a torbid and mysterious happiness, a sin both atrocious and marvellous, the lover.]

The ethereal appearance of the Virgin is deftly exposed to the reader as well as to Zoraide. But from the Madonna's sin we quickly move to hers:

A destra della Vergine, San Francesco le andava pochissimo a genio: ma a sinistra San Giorgio, un giovanetto biondo e chiuso tutta la persona nell'arme, le piaceva immensamente: seppe che era un ragazzo dei tempi di allora, morto in una guerra di allora: e il padre, un nobile, non s'era dato più pace; finchè il Giorgione glie lo dipinse per i secoli e santificò nella pala. Zoraide lo sognò di notte. (ibid.)[14]

[To the Virgin's right, St Francis who was hardly to her liking; but to the left, St George, young, blond, and draped in his armour; she liked him immensely and knew he was a boy from that time, killed in a war of that time. His father, a nobleman, could not live in peace, until Giorgione painted him for posterity and sanctified him in wood. Zoraide dreamt of him at night.]

San Liberale is conveniently transformed into San Giorgio to suit Gadda's scheme (ibid., 492).[15] But if we consider the original painting, the scene will look strangely familiar. A strong triangular shape at its centre unites the Madonna, elevated above the two saints. But of the two, San Liberale (San Giorgio) dominates, literally outshining the other in an unfair contest between his glittering armour and Francis's self-denying frock. The composition's symmetry is further subverted by the presence of the spear carried by the warring saint, as well as by the fact that the child is positioned to the side of the canvas. The landscape, moreover, serves to highlight the inequality of the two figures, as a massive tower flanks St George's banner, in stark contrast to the sparseness reserved for Francis. To Gadda's eyes, this is patently a 'family portrait.' In decoding it, Gadda must have shared some of Gemma Nuttis's (diabolical) disenchantment. For the true message is that the Madonna's celestial composure is but a deception: she is only the mistress, not of her maker (Giorgione/Gadda), but rather of her vain postulant, the glittering St George. For Madonna Zoraide, Francis's lack of lustre is no match for the plated carapace of his antagonist. A further subtextual addendum: Gadda, unlike Giorgione, will never offer his patron, the grieving 'bimba,' the commissioned celebration of the dead warrior. For the unjust mechanisms of preference can only generate resistance, vengeance, and remorse.

La cognizione del dolore is a novel of anger, marked by a string of outrageous and desecrating acts, some spectacularly direct (the stamped-on portraits of the father; the final matricide), others embedded deeper in the text. Its locus is 'la casa' (the home), in particular, the 'sala' (dining room), which is the principal site of Gonzalo's malaise. There all the novel's elements converge, all the structural tensions in the narrations reach their peak. It is there that the two main characters meet under the sign of the Dioscuri:

L'alta figura di lui si disegnò nera nel vano della porta-finestra, di sul terrazzo, come l'ombra d'uno sconosciuto: e, dietro a lui, nel cielo, due stelle parevano averlo assistito fin là. Dióscuri spendidi sopra una fascia d'amaranto, lontana, nel quadrante di bellezza e di conoscenza: fraternità salva! (*CD*, 685)

[His tall form was outlined, black, in the frame of the French window, from the terrace, like the shadow of a stranger: and, behind him, in the sky, two stars seemed to have helped him on his way there. Splendid Dioscuri over a strip of amaranth, distant, in the quadrant of beauty and of knowledge: saved fraternity. (*AG*, 148)]

In the middle of Part One, Gonzalo undergoes a medical examination by the good doctor Higueroa. His cry ('Stavo male! non ha veduto? [...] Perché non ha voluto credermi?' *CD*, 632 [I was ill! didn't you see? ... Why didn't you want to believe me?] *AG*, 8) that follows it is a desperate plea for help. But since it is not spoken, it does not reach his interlocutor, locked as it is in Gonzalo's imploring gaze. It is, in fact, not even directed at the doctor, who, in the face of his patient's deep traumas, is truly out of his league. Instead it is Gadda's own cry for help, addressed to the reader, to his own dead mother, and to some universal moral law. It is useful to note here that there is no way that the doctor, either from his examination of Gonzalo or from their conversation, could have ascertained the existence and the nature of this 'male invisibile' (*CD*, 607). Gonzalo's only physical symptom is a duodenal ulcer, while his melancholy could only be the effect of a 'nuova crisi di sfiducia nella vita' (*CD*, 622) [a new seizure of lack of faith in life (*AG*, 69)]. Gonzalo's mute outcry can be explained fully only by clues contained elsewhere in the text. Immediately prior to it, we witness Gonzalo's tantrum sparked by Di Pascuale's grandson on whom his mother had lavished all sorts of gifts (*CD*, 630–1). His appearance in the garden was in turn preceded by Gonzalo's outburst against his mother's visit to the cemetery to tend to his brother's grave (629–30). This indicates a strong correlation between his malady and his dead brother. Even the sceptical (no-nonsense) doctor finally sees that he is preoccupied by something horrible and is beginning to believe the rumours about Gonzalo's misanthropy which have become part of the local mythology (604).

Two openly scandalous acts stand out among Gonzalo's fabled misdeeds: the ingestion of a sea urchin and the torture inflicted on a cat (ibid., 600–4; 598). Of the protagonist's seven capital sins (597), gluttony is the one the people of Lukones seize on the most. Gonzalo is rumoured to have nearly died from having swallowed a sea urchin (601). In the popular imagination, the sea urchin takes on the shape now of a crab now of a sea scorpion or a swordfish, or a brooch fish: 'con quattro baffi, scarlatti pure essi, e lunghissimi, come quattro spilloni da signora, due per parte, oltre alle mandibole (601) ['with four moustaches, also scarlet, and very long, like four ladies' hatpins, two on either side, in addition to the mandibles' (AG, 42)]. Its colour also changes: first black, then scarlet. Ichthyoid, echinoderm, crustacean, throughout its imaginary metamorphosis, the prey never relinquishes the extremely well-fortified defences shielding its flesh, endowed as it is with needles, sword, and mandibles in the form of oars. Only the intervention of a mighty nutcracker (with the leverage provided by Gonzalo's elbows) would finally break through its formidable armour. Violently divested of its crustaceous hardness, the creature is finally swallowed and digested. As local myth has it, its unnoticed main weapon, the sword, would eventually lacerate Gonzalo's duodenum. Ingested with savage lust, the infant-like polymorph proves in the end to be both victim and victor. It should be recalled that during the doctor's visit Gonzalo feels:

un'ansia indicibile sul giro del gastrico, dov'è il duodeno, come piombo: una figurazione di colpa, di inadempienza [...] Nel suo occhio ormai stanco, velato, si adunarono cose dolorose lontane. (CD, 625)

[an undefined anxiety in that part of the gastric system where the duodenum lies, like lead: an image of guilt, of unfulfillment ... In his now-weary, hooded eye, painful things collected, remote things. (AG, 72)]

'Remote' ('lontano') is a key adjective in Gadda's lyrical register that almost always is connected to feelings about Enrico. In the passage under

Carlo Emilio Gadda (right) with his brother, Enrico (left), and his sister, Clara, c. 1900 (Archivio Roscioni)

Gadda (right) with his brother, Enrico, in 1916, together for the last time before Enrico's death at war

Gadda with his sister, Clara, aboard the SS *Principessa Mafalda*, before sailing to Buenos Aires from Genoa, 30 November 1922 (Archivio Einaudi)

Portrait of Gadda by Guido Capocchini, 1934 (Gabinetto Vieusseux)

Gadda (left) with Silvio Guarnieri and Eugenio Montale in Forte dei Marmi, 1941 (Archivio Guarnieri)

Gadda in Ronchi, August 1942 (Fondazione Antonicelli)

Gadda (centre) with Roberto Longhi (left) and Piero Bigongiari (right),
Florence, Villa 'Il Tasso,' April 1950 (Archivio Bigongiari)

Meeting of 'Comunità degli scrittori,' Naples, October 1958, left to right:
Bigongiari, Gadda, Ungaretti, Caproni (Archivio Bigongiari)

Gadda with the first edition of *La cognizione del dolore* (1963)

Gadda, with his assistant, Giuseppina Liberati, in his Roman home, 1969
(Archivio Giuseppina Liberati)

consideration, it appears in the same referential area as the interconnected notions of the perforated duodenum, remorse, and the 'male invisibile.' The obscene rape of the lobster, a veritable 'fiero pasto' of Dantean memory, has a plasticity and richness of detail far surpassing any other of Gonzalo's gastronomic feats. Moreover, while the other victuals are recognizable fare (however paroxysmal the savagery of their treatment may be), the impregnable polymorph defies all classification. And Gonzalo, with the obscene sucker of his mouth, foul entrails, the tail of his quarry dangling from his lips, can only evoke the image of Lucifer (as, say, in Giotto's *Giudizio Universale*), swallowing plump, innocent limbs, shreds of flesh, coloured white or mother-of-pearl. Here, then, it is the dragon that has slain St George, only to be stabbed, posthumously, by his sword. Significantly, Gonzalo's destruction of his father's picture takes place in the dining-room (underscored twice by the narrator [*CD*, 614]), and, in Part Two, it is relived by his mother – this time performed with a table knife – again in the dining-room (689), all to suggest the connection between vengeance and orality, whether linguistic or sensorial.

But the fabled ingestion of that armoured denizen of the sea (whether sea urchin, crab, sea scorpion, or lobster) is a transgression perceived to be more heinous than any other, and, as such, it is more heavily disguised (through its fantastic elaboration in the popular mind). *Eros e Priapo* again comes to our aid. Narcissism, Gadda argues, and the 'meccanismo degli appetiti esofagici' [the mechanism of the oesophagal appetites], are necessary to the development of the ego. Equally essential is the need for an 'eroe-modello della cui immagine [innamorarsi]' (*EP*, 330, 332) [the image of the hero-model to fall in love with]. The last step in the process is then described in these terms:

Più che di innamoramento, si deve parlare di appropriazione o ingestione [...] del modello: così la serpe sente come Io lo stritolato conigliolo. Così come l'antropofago divora il vinto arrostito [...] per incorporarsene la virtù guerriera, l'aggressione vitale della preda. (334)

[More than of becoming enamoured, one must speak of appropriation or ingestion ... of the model; just as the snake feels the slaughtered rabbit as his Ego; just as the cannibal eats his victim roasted ... in order to incorporate the warlike virtues and the vital aggressive practices of his prey.]

We could then say that Gonzalo's truculent consumption of the sea denizen epitomizes metaphorically (and with characteristic ambivalence) the agonizing nature of the Enrico issue, in that it represents both the ritualistic assimilation of the unattainable model of rewarded selfhood and the remorseful elimination of the rival for his mother's love. The punishment, meted out by some vindictive god (the 'Potestà Ultrici del Cielo' [CD, 603]), for his infringement of the social interdict is conveyed psychosomatically through his duodenal affliction. Furthermore, the sword of remorse, now tormenting his viscera, reflects the author's long-standing obsession with the Archangel's weapon of retribution. In fact, if we go back to the 'studio dell'Arcangelo' in the *Racconto italiano*, we find this fixation expressed in relation to a war episode clearly linked to Enrico's death: 'E così come la serpe ci contorciamo in uno spasimo folle, e vano, cui la spada folgorante dell'Arcangelo abbia raggiunto' (*RI*, 457–8, 460) [And just like the serpent, slain by the Archangel's flashing sword, we contort ourselves in a mad but vain spasm].

But in the *Racconto*, there was still the hope that some form of redemption or noble action might come from the serpent's green heart; in *La cognizione* that hope is no longer alive. For now time had been consumed and 'ogni finalità, ogni possibilità [era] impietrata nel buio' (*CD*, 633) [every finality and every possibility had turned into stone in the darkness]. The dream that Gonzalo recounts to the good doctor marks his reality as an anti-hero, outcast from the world, whose tragedy is ignored by others and, especially, by his mother. His condition is sealed in the dream: 'una sera spaventosa, eterna, in cui non era possibile ricostituire il tempo degli atti possibili [...] Tutte le anime erano lontane [...] perse [...] conscie del nostro antico dileggio' (632–3) ['a frightful, eternal evening, in which it was no longer possible to recover the time of possible action ... All souls were distant ... lost ... aware of our former mockery' (*AG*, 82–3)]. In the *Racconto italiano*, the Gaddian counterpart, Grifonetto, believes that as a child he was sabotaged by some demonic or criminal force from which his mother could not save him (*RI*, 487): a betrayal on her part which marks his fall from grace. Children, he later remarks (578), should be brought up with infinite love and tenderness, but what if this, in his case, was not the natural rule of law? What if he grew up sick, with darkness in his heart, as he in fact did? Like Manzoni's Gertrude, Gadda (and all his fictional projections from Grifonetto to Gonzalo) has been dispossessed of his portion of light (594, 597).[16] In *La cognizione*, the outcast's exclusion from light is a major refrain. He has been condemned to darkness by his mother's perfidy, outshone by the blinding smile of his brother; no one acknowledges his moral superiority, neither Gonzalo's mother nor the rabble she loves and protects.

Gonzalo's duodenal ulcer, we believe, firmly establishes the origins of his neurosis, an affliction that forces him to mutilate his adversary, while he continues to suffer its pain. His emptiness – because an exasperated filial narcissism is no solution to the ravages of an exasperated parental narcissism – has no cathartic properties, in other words, but rather is the deep source of his shame, which, like his anxiety, cannot be defined. So his cry for help will go unheeded because it knows no way of direct expression. Gonzalo's neurosis cannot be treated because it cannot be spoken. Every attempt to communicate with the doctor is unsuccessful because of his compulsive urge to disguise the message.

Strongly indicative of Gonzalo's inability to deal with the demons that haunt him and prevent him from disclosing the root of his condition is the wall surrounding the villa, which, significantly, after the dream sequence, becomes the narrative focus. That the wall is useless in keeping out Gonzalo's demons is just as infuriating as the doctor's inability to cure his mother of her narcissism. It is noteworthy that the wall's weakness contrasts with the mother's solidity. Her hands may be skeleton-like, but her brain is as hard as marble. Most importantly, the wall cannot protect Gonzalo from his self-destructiveness; it cannot keep out either the phantoms of the past ('anche le anime dei morti lo scavalcherebbero' (CD, 638) [even the souls of the dead could climb over it (AG, 90)], or the dark, silent shadow who appears in the final chapter (CD, 743), to remind him of what he is not and what he had to be to receive the love that was rightfully his. As a result of his not being the desired other (his brother), and thus his not having what the other has taken and continues to take (his mother's love), he is overcome by a delirium of possessiveness (639). Gonzalo's desperate assertion of his own self (as opposed to his being regarded as the 'other' son or his 'mother's' son) leads him to reclaim the unity of person that has been denied him; but to do so, he must become, against his own will, like Cain.

To a great extent, La cognizione is to Gonzalo what The Tempest is to Prospero: the grandiose delusion of avenging the usurpation of privilege. The 'terra vestita d'agosto' (ibid., 629) of Part One has witnessed the tension rise in Gonzalo on account of his mother's absence (605). Like a late summer storm, he unleashes his rage at the beginning of Part Two at the 'Mater dolorosa.' The 'Madonna di settembre,' the novel's main temporal reference,[17] is the feast of the 'Addolorata,' and, in this sense, La cognizione takes on the features of a 'Pietà,' with the mother stonelike in tearful mourning for her lost son.[18] Gonzalo's fury is directed against her sorrow: the tempest raging outside the villa is the externalization of the son's wrath; the mother, like the ingested sea creature ('un animale giá ferito'), implores helplessly before his all-consuming furor.

Turning now to the second of Gonzalo's outrageous acts, let us again focus on the tactics of dissimulation. As another example of his cruelty to animals, we learn, in a brief paragraph, that Gonzalo hurled a cat from the third floor of the villa to test the theory of impulse, learned from a Jewish doctor who taught mathematics in Pastrufazio. The key words of the passage are 'precipitare' (to fall) and 'campo gravitazionale' (gravitational field), which appear in a discarded footnote.[19] Finally overcome by repeated humiliation, the handsome cat dies from the outrage, because 'ogni oltraggio è morte' (ibid., 598) [every outrage is death (AG, 39)]. In itself, the episode of the cat seems harmless enough, just one among Gonzalo's many legendary acts of cruelty. But seen in the light of the re-evocation of his brother's death in the eighth segment of Part Two ('Peccato che uno si fosse buttato in aria, l'aria bonna, a quel modo: ma la gravitazione aveva funzionato, il 9, 81' (CD, 728) ['It's a pity that one of them had gone up in the air, the fine air, in that way: but gravity had worked, the 9.81' (AG, 204)]), the experiment takes on a new meaning, as well as investing the latter passage with jarring subtextual implications. The dry remark 'aveva funzionato' is at odds with Gonzalo's declared veneration of his dead brother. Not only has Gadda failed to celebrate Enrico in his fifty years as a writer, but the only time he describes how he died he does so in a way that is wholly insensitive and derogatory. We could view the remark as embittered resentment of the aspirations of Gadda's father. But the choice of image cannot help recall not only the cat's misfortune, but also the rather emblematic toss of a demijohn in the Racconto italiano. In this latter case, the 'damigiana proiettile' was used as an instrument of revenge in a petty dispute; the vengeance, totally incommensurate with the offence (a trodden chicory plot) takes place from a window on the top floor of a barracks about twenty-three metres from the ground (RI, 447–8, 459). Gadda's description of the white barracks in the Racconto closely matches the white villa in La cognizione (CD, 628). Cat and 'damigiana' share more or less the same launching pad. But the height is different. Gadda's obsession with numbers is never casual: the twenty-three metres of the Racconto are followed by reference to twenty-three days of drought; Enrico had died on the twenty-third day of April.

'Aprile entrava nella stanza, come il settembre nostro' (CD, 726) [April entered the room, like our September (AG, 201)]. Although it may be true, as Gadda remarks in Meditazione milanese, that astronomy and poetry are not incompatible (MM, 697), for an author as precise as Gadda, who never misses a chance to ridicule poets like Foscolo or Carducci for excessive poetic licence, one would not expect such an artificial equinoctial pairing of April and September. Except that it is all under the sign of Enrico, the dead Dioscuro.[20] Gonzalo, as we have said, must define his identity outside of the Dioscuri bipolarity that his mother has imposed on him. His failure to do so takes the novel to its horrific end, where the mother is finally punished for refusing to put an end to her sorrow. At the beginning of Part Two, thoughts of her dead son fill her mind, but are quickly chastized by the raging storm. When Gonzalo and she meet, she is so preoccupied by the Dioscuri in the sky that she does not recognize him. As he comes into view, she cannot dissociate him from her other son, as she utters the name of the two stars. But here Gadda shows his hand, for the Gemini constellation is not visible at twilight at that time of the year, in either hemisphere. This confirms the obsessive nature of the Enrico issue and the need on Gadda's part to conceal it within the astronomical reference to Castor and Pollux. What is devastating for Gonzalo is that his mother's greeting once again reminds him of his lack: fraternity in truth is not saved in the least. As one on whom 'his parents did not smile' ('*cui non risere parentes*' [*SGF I*, 229; my emphasis]), he would have tolerated playing the role of Cain, if he could have been assured of surviving and taking his brother's place in his mother's life. But the señora's narcissism prevents her from abandoning her preference for her younger son:

Frasi e parole 'scolpite nei cuori.' Si fissano come costellazioni nell'eros caparbio di certe femmine [...] generano [...] gli atti sprrepositati, gli atti inutili, e lo sperpero delle fortune e dei destini: piegano talora verso l'ombra il destino dei figli [...] per una parola ch'era bella da dire, da sentir dire! (*VM*, 450)

[Sentences and words 'engraved in one's heart,' are fixed like constellations in the resilient eros of certain females ... They generate ... useless acts without purpose, and the wasting of fortunes and destinies: often they cast a shadow on a son's future ... for a word that was nice to say and to hear said!]

Gonzalo's mother is indeed one of those 'females'; not only did she fail to protect her children from the serpent's treachery, but driven by her narcissism, she has connived with it. She has incorporated into herself the 'trionfo serpentesco della "sua" villa' (*CD*, 686) [serpentesque triumph of 'her' villa (*AG*, 150)], and now she refuses Gonzalo his last request: to be with her *alone*: 'Le loro anime dovevano, sole, aspettare come il ritorno di qualcuno, negli anni ... di qualcheduno che non aveva potuto finire ...

finire gli studi ...' (*CD*, 729) [Their souls should, alone, wait, as if for the return of someone, in the years ... of someone who hadn't been able to finish ... to finish his studies ... (*AG*, 205)].

As the story moves towards the conclusive matricide, Gonzalo, in desperation, hopes that his perennial condition of lack can be redeemed if he can share in his mother's ceaseless vigil: if he cannot be the Child in the Manger, perhaps he can at least play the role of the humble shepherd (see *RR II*, 872–3). But the filthy crowd that his mother has admitted into the villa – her hope is that the crowd may revive the image of her dead son – rekindles his ancient neurosis. The profanation of his possible serenity is but a replay of the childhood nightmare in which the San Giuseppe fair befouls Gadda's childhood garden of Piazza Castello. Therein, the deceitful serpent drank from his mother's breast ('la femmina aveva la mano attorta da un'aspide a cui porgeva la mammella' [*CD*, 735]); now the maurauding crowd robs her of the last relics of sanctity. In the dining-room, amid the peons, we witness Gonzalo's final outrage against his brother's memory. Here, again, we find the señora in tearful mourning. It is a Friday (Enrico died on a Friday, and the allusion is to a Good Friday service); an enormous, yellow fish (with all-too-obvious anthropomorphic connotations) has been set before the flea-ridden populace. The gravedigger's wife is present, as if to preside at the relived funeral of Gonzalo's brother. The mother's betrayal is complete, and now not even the remaining vestiges of fraternity (the earrings worn by her as symbols of the Dioscuri [611]) can intercede. In a fit of rage, Gonzalo disdainfully throws out the fish from his plate (without touching it), goes up to his room, packs his humble valise, and hurriedly leaves the house to go out into 'un mondo sordo, perduto, già lambito da lingue di tenebra' (737) [a deaf, lost world already licked by tongues of darkness (*AG*, 215)]. When, at the novel's close, Peppa and the other intruders violate Gonzalo's sanctuary, they see a photo of his brother on the table.

In general, the Cain-like qualities we have attributed to Gonzalo are marked by a language that is considerably more incisive than that used to convey unmotivated exile, as for example, 'si era veduto cacciare, come fosse una belva, dalla loro carità inferocita, di uomini: di consorzio, di mille. Egli era uno' (*CD*, 728) [he had seen himself hounded, as if he were an animal, by their infuriated charity, of men, of association, of a thousand. He was one (*AG*, 203)]. The darkness of his soul, full of impious sentiment and sorrowful perturbation that derives from some deep inexpiable zone of hidden truths, would know no peace; with the will of a murderer it would move alone towards the darkness (*CD*, 690–1, 704).

If it is true, as Riccardo J. Quinones states in his *Changes of Cain* (88), that the 'primary experience of the human condition is that of difference and division' and that 'only Cain's awareness, if any, can lead to reintegration,' in Gonzalo's case, cognition is a passive process; no sign of reintegration blesses his questioning rebellion. His supreme confrontation with his mother occurs not at her death by his hand, but earlier, at the beginning of the seventh segment, when his long, desperate kiss – an attempt to suture his severed reality – is interrupted by the intrusion of a peon. But on the previous page, Gonzalo had already denounced that kiss as the 'bacio bugiardo della Parvenza' (ibid., 703) [the lying kiss of Appearance (*AG*, 170)]. The cruel paradox is that if Gonzalo-Cain has been the victim of violence (caused by the 'demenza dei tutori,' which lay at the root of his scandalous acts [*CD*, 642]), the only key to his salvation is held by his forebears, so patently oblivious to his sufferings.[21] Yet, it is impossible to break the vicious circle to which he is doomed. The mother – a King Lear whose destiny only Gonzalo (Cordelia) had divined – is finally abandoned, negated as a mere debased simulacrum. But, in the last analysis, to deny vain images is the same as denying oneself. Hence, Gonzalo's greatness consists in his wilfully lifting his glass in a toast to his bitter, self-destructive end:

rivendicando a sé le ragioni del dolore, la conoscenza e la verità del dolore, nulla rimaneva alla possibilità. (704)

[claiming for himself the motives of grief, the acquaintance with grief and the truth of it, nothing was left to possibility. (*AG*, 171)]

For our erstwhile three-year- old tiger deprived of light, the evil 'uomo del sacco' is the only possible, albeit sterile, therapy, as his own tremulous light has been snuffed out. The deceptive, yet captivating, smile of his dead brother has proved victorious. Having immortally ascended to a heaven that has stopped rotating, he has condemned the other Dioscuro to being submerged in everlasting darkness.[22]

Notes

1 For a study of Gadda's relationship with his brother, see Gioanola, *L'uomo dei topazi*, 22–36.

2 There are two exceptions. He once shows resentment for being unfavourably compared to Enrico (*GGP*, 586–8) and, in another entry, while appearing to

rejoice at his brother's new motorbike, he contrasts his own sacrifices for the
family to Enrico's lack of financial restraint (*GGP*, 628).

3 Among the many examples, see Gadda 1984, 53, 139, 151, 154.

4 See Gadda 1993b, 15, 155, 170, 175, 179, 201.

5 For a study of the friendship, see Pedriali 1994.

6 The epitaph reads: 'ENRICO GADDA / ACCOGLI O ETERNO / NELLA
LUCE DEGLI EROI / CONSACRATA L'ALTA ANIMA / AI DOVERI
SUPREMI – / CI LASCIO' FANCIULLO / E SORRIDENDO VOLLE IL /
SUO FATO – ALPINO, / VOLONTARIO DI GUERRA / NEL 15–16,
PILOTA / AVIATORE NEL 17–18, / DECORATO DI MEDAGLIA / DI
BRONZO E D'ARGENTO / AL VALORE MILITARE, / CADDE IL 23 IV
1918 / IN VOLO DI GUERRA.' See Giuditta Podestà 1978, 212 and the
comments by Terzoli in Gadda 1993a, 55. Gadda also designed Enrico's
tomb: a granite parallelopiped with a knight's sword in relief on the upper
side. I owe this unpublished information to Giuditta Podestà, whom I inter-
viewed in December of 1994.

7 Cf Wieser 1996.

8 Cf *GGP*, 849. See also Dombroski 1987, 148.

9 Published originally in *L'Ambrosiano*, May 1936. Gadda's mother died on 2
April 1936.

10 It is worth noting that Enrico's date of birth does not show in the epitaph
dictated by Carlo Emilio.

11 The lines 'Notte, immobile notte! I tuoi punti di zaffiro e d'oro sono forse
lontani dolori' are a quotation from the closing lines of Gadda's poem 'E nel
viso aveva la luce' (*Poesie*, 37, vv 11–31).

12 See 'Come lavoro' in *VM*, 440–1.

13 'Vi è una lotta simbolica fra S. Giorgio, il Santo cavalleresco e [...] femmi-
nista, contro S. Luigi Gonzaga, il Santo ascetico e rinunciatario' (Gadda 1984,
92) [There is a symbolic struggle between St George, the chivalric and
womanizing saint, and St Luigi Gonzaga, ascetic and given to renunciation.]

14 Cf Zoraide's actual preference for Franco-the-lover over Luigi-the-husband
(*M*, 479, 490–1, 494–5), with the garden as the desired location for her
encounters with Franco. In such an unfair contest, Luigi is further weakened
by illness (*M*, 521–9; 582–6). It is noteworthy that Gadda, on his arrival at
Celle Lager at the end of April 1918 (around the time of Enrico's death), was
mistakenly diagnosed as having tuberculosis. In *La meccanica*, Gadda
rephrases what he had written in his diary, when he thought he would die
of tuberculosis (*GGP*, 768–71).

15 Gadda, 1990, 194–5.

16 It should be stressed that the Gertrude connection refers to the earlier, more

developed character of Gertrude in *Fermo e Lucia*, where the relationship to her brother is discussed more fully. Surprisingly, it seems to have escaped the attention of Gadda scholars that Manzoni used the expression 'cognizione del male' with reference to the Gertrude chapters expunged in the final version of the novel (*I promessi sposi*, 204). Elsewhere I have shown that as early as 1922 Gadda was experimenting with the title of *La cognizione* in a brother-related context; it is not, then, a coincidence that the novel has so much to do with Gonzalo's brother.

17 While the core of Part One takes place on 28 August, from the very start the temporal perspective harks forward to the 'Addolorata' ('si andava già per la Madonna di settembre' [*CD*, 575]). September is also central to 'La sala di basalte' (Gadda 1993a, 23, v 2), and in *La meccanica* Luigi is sent to the front on a September evening (*M*, 526–9).

18 'Ella non poteva più pensare a una madre se non come a un groppo di disumano dolore superstite' (*CD*, 726) [She could no longer think of a mother except as a knot of inhuman pain]. This is obviously Gonzalo's own view of his mother, which explains the temporal obsession with September: Gonzalo has been condemned to play the role of a spectator in a *tableau vivant* in which the mother is eternally bent over in mourning.

19 See Emilio Manzotti's edition of *La cognizione del dolore* (1987), 78–9, lines 1214–1215.

20 In the equation April = September, Enrico's death and the feast of the 'Addolorata,' celebrated on the third Sunday in September, fall quite close together, around the equinoctial date.

21 While Gonzalo saw his mother as a tragically great Shakespearean figure (Veturia [*CD*, 633], King Lear [684], Caesar [724]), she sees in him the petty meanness of a Molière character (682).

22 'Bene-male sono i due diòscuri altalenanti sulla linea d'orizzonte, che quando l'uno sorge, l'altro sommerge' (*VM*, 613) [Good-evil are the two dioscuri on the horizon: when one rises, the other sinks].

References

Borges, Jorge Luis. 1972. *El Aleph*. Buenos Aires and Madrid: Emecé Editores / Alianza Editorial

Contini, Gianfranco. 1989. *Quarant'anni di amicizia. Scritti su C.E. Gadda*. Turin: Einaudi

Dombroski, Robert. 1987. 'La dialettica della follia.' In Marcello Carlino, Aldo Mastropasqua, and Francesco Muzzioli, eds, *Gadda progettualità e scrittura*. Preface by Giuliano Manacorda. Rome: Editori Riuniti

Gadda, Carlo Emilio. 1984. *A un amico fraterno – Lettere a Bonaventura Tecchi*. Edited by Marcello Carlino. Milan: Garzante
- 1990. *Il promi libro della favole*. Edited by Claudio Vela. Milan: Mondadori
- 1993a. *Poesie*. Edited by Maria AntoniettaTerzoli. Turin: Einaudi
- 1993b. *Per favore mi lasci nell'ombra. Interviste 1950–1972*. Edited by Claudio Vela. Milan: Adelphi
Gioanola, Elio. 1987. *L'uomo dei topazi: interpretazione psicanalitica dell'opera di Carlo Emilio Gadda*. Milan: Librex
Kafka, Franz. 1958. *Briefe 1902–1924*. Frankfurt: Fischer
Pedriali, Federica G. 1990. 'Uno studio in nero: "La passeggiata autunnale" di C.E. Gadda.' *Paragone* XLI
- 1994. 'A Trial, Notes on a Friendship through Letters: C.E. Gadda and U. Betti.' *Journal of the Institute of Romance Studies*. London
Podestà, Giuditta. 1978. 'Tre lettere inedite di Carlo Emilio Gadda.' *Lettere italiane* 30, no. 2 (April–June): 212
Quinones, Ricardo J. 1991. *The Changes of Cain: Violence and the Lost Brother in Cain and Abel Literature*. Princeton, N.J.: Princeton University Press
Ungarelli, Giulio. 1993. *Gadda al microfono. L'ingegnere e la RAI*. Turin: Nuova ERI
Wieser, Dagmar. 1996. '"D'un fraterno lutto" (Appunti per una lettura freudiana di Gadda.)' In Maria Antonietta Terzoli, ed., *Le lingue di Gadda*, 81–148. Rome: Salerno Editrice

The Enigma of Grief: An Expressionism against the Self

CARLA BENEDETTI

La cognizione del dolore is the story of Gonzalo Pirobutirro d'Eltino's misdeeds. At first, they come out through the 'bad epos' of the inhabitants of Lukones, but almost all of them target either Gonzalo's mother or the objects and images she cherishes. One episode in particular seems to have captured the general imagination. It was said that the hidalgo-engineer, in a fury, stamped on an old family watch, and later, still angry, trampled on his dead father's portrait before his terrified mother's eyes. The community rumour mill is unable to explain his bizarre behaviour, and takes sides against him, although the perceptions of the various Peppas, Battistinas, Josés, and Palumbos do not shed any light on those events. The peon employed at the villa Pirobutirro maintained that the señora's son carried within him the seven deadly sins entangled in his belly like snakes. Gonzalo's own point of view is no less twisted: while prey to an 'interpretive delirium,' he lays the blame for his grief on the villa, the taxes, the bells, and the charitable gestures of his parents, who are guilty of having given to strangers the money and affection that should have been his. Otherwise, he gets angry at the 'crazy' community which neglects sound economic principles and good, needy fellows, while it showers money on all sorts of rascals, cretins, and sly-stupid people. To complicate matters, the mother's point of view also prevents us from recognizing the real causes of Gonzalo's grief. In other words, Gadda's treatment of grief is far from a clear explanation of how Gonzalo becomes acquainted with it, as the title of the novel seems to promise. Most of all, it is far from providing a satisfactory interpretation of the sorrowful experience it portrays. In his Introduction to *La cognizione del dolore*, Contini compares Gonzalo's desecration of the paternal image to Proust's Mademoiselle Vinteuil, who is an equally stray character, in *Remembrance of Things Past* (Contini 1963, 7). The comparison demonstrates just how 'provisional and poor' Gadda's hermeneutic of grief appears once it is compared to Proust's. Mademoiselle Vinteuil, who forces her woman lover to spit on her father's portrait, displays a sadistic cruelty representative of all such profanations as well as the psychological reasons that provoke them. The monstrous peculiarity of her gesture is connected to the universality of a 'law' of cruelty, and it is represented and interpreted as such. Instead, no universal law – neither psychological nor of any other origin – appears in Gadda's novel to explain Gonzalo's fits of rage against people, animals, and objects. His fury remains enigmatic, neither interpreted nor interpretable. All things considered, the very concept of neurosis, turned as it is into Gonzalo's mysterious and 'obscure' illness (whose causes and forms cannot be analysed), explains nothing. Furthermore, the comparison with Proust demonstrates another feature of Gadda's 'acquaintance with grief,' one that is closely related to the weak hermeneutic Contini referred to. In a sorrowful experience, truth can be found only by he who distances himself from it, who manages to perceive the universal in the observation of small details. As if on a stage, the author of *Remembrance of Things Past* looks at his characters through his 'telescopic' eye, and observes them from a distance. As if he were watching the inhabitants of a different planet, Proust studies human beings and their grief, and tries to deduce the laws that govern their movements. In contrast, Gadda makes Gonzalo's grief undergo the opposite process: he represents it in its stubborn properties, which remain undeciphered, without reference to a 'law' or to a universal. Instead, properties and features are multiplied. His writing plays host to many deforming viewpoints, and it is itself deformed by them. He mixes epic and elegy; the grotesque and the satirical are thrown together into the same pot, though not with a recipe that will permit the truth to come forward. Grief remains unshaped, raw. We are quite far from the tragic conception of knowledge and from one that is able to reassemble fragments.[1] To know does not mean to stand above passions as it would in a Stoic ethics (according to which to know meant only to give voice to one's grief in its immediacy). Acquaintance is not general knowledge, but simply the acquisition of data on this particular grief – but only on *this* one. We should recall that Mademoiselle Vinteuil is just as much an autobiographical projection as Gonzalo is. Therefore, it is not sufficient to point out that Gadda builds his search for knowledge around an all-too-personal matter, unless one prefers to forget his obvious lack of distance. Rather, it is necessary to say that the very concept of *grievous acquaintance* includes and involves the subject who is representing his own grief.

Gonzalo's malady consists of two basic ingredients: anger and melancholy. Hidden behind that angry man seized with 'beastly fits of rage,' one can perceive a secluded, 'melancholic beast' who is constantly ruminating over his ills. However, these two feelings – anger and melancholy – while apparently opposed, are actually very closely connected: both stem from what may be described in the Freudian sense as 'the original loss of the object' that Gonzalo suffers from. His interpretive delirium is based on the fact that, in the reality surrounding him, he sees only *objects* that are not meant for him. Many of the objects in *La cognizione del dolore* share one peculiarity: they are denied to Gonzalo while they are granted freely to others, to all others. At the top of the long list, one can see the 'ossobuchi' that are gobbled down by pompous bourgeois in fashionable restaurants – quite a gastronomic match for the three shrivelled peppers that the hungry hidalgo is given by his mother when he comes home to a poorly lit house. In addition to the 'ossobuchi,' there are gold watches, sweets, figs, cookies, and praise, all of which were denied to Gonzalo in his childhood, while they are now granted by his mother to the colonel's stupid grandson, along with free French lessons. Whenever one of these signs of past offence makes an appearance, Gonzalo bursts into rage. But even harmless objects such as the church bells, the pears in the orchard, onions, the peon's clogs, the laundress's goitre, even hens, fleas, and cicadas, which had nothing to do with what was denied him, may provoke him: the bells are a sign of his father's stupid generosity, which he had paid for; the onions grow in a field beside the villa his father built, to the detriment of his family's wealth; and, like the bells, the cicadas are guilty of celebrating the glory of light, and of life. The sense of loss is metonymically transferred onto all objects, and Gonzalo's melancholy takes in the entire universe, which is but a heap of objects not meant for him and which are therefore meaningless. They enter his field of perception only as bearers of grief. Suffice it to recall the passage that portrays Gonzalo while he is listening to the story of a car accident: a poor mountaineer who used to carry his pannier to the downtown market to sell his home-made cheese, is run over by a car. In the village, he is known as 'the cream-cheese man,' a precision which transforms a meaningless detail into a significant one. However, for Gonzalo, 'cream-cheese' is an unnecessary, incoherent object that, like all others, is only a painful landmark: 'Il figlio dové concedere ai formaggini di entrare anche loro nel cerchio doloroso dell'appercezione. Era il bagaglio del mondo, del fenomènico mondo' (*CD*, 627) [The son had to permit the cheeses to enter the painful circle of his apperception. This was the world's baggage, of the world of phenomena (*AG*, 75)].

Gonzalo's perceptive field is often called, in the novel, a 'cerchio doloroso' [a grievous circle]. Enclosed within are the disconnected elements of the world which remind him of the original loss that tore the cosmos to pieces: 'Le cicale *franàrono* nella continuità eguale del tempo, dissero la persistenza: andavano ai confini dell'estate' (*CD*, 633, my emphasis) [The cicadas collapsed even in the continuity of time: they spoke of persistence: they reached the boundaries of summer (*AG*, 84)]. All unity seems loose and flimsy. The story of the medical examination, for example, is interrupted twice in a row by an unnecessary and insubstantial detail: the creaking of a woodworm. Its reappearance, a few pages later, is worth quoting in its entirety:

[Gonzalo] guardava al di là delle cose, dei mobili: un accoramento inspiegabile gli teneva il volto e anzi quasi la persona. Come quelli che vi hanno un fratello o un figlio: e li veggono fumare, fumare, i vertici dell'Alpe senza ritorni, fioriti di cùmuli, in un rombo lontano. Il tarlo cavatappi non desisteva dal suo progresso; dopo l'accumulo d'ogni intervallo precipitava alla commemorazione di sé. (*CD*, 623)

[[Gonzalo] looked beyond things, beyond the furniture; an inexplicable grief seized his face and, indeed, almost his whole person. He was like those who have a brother or a son: and they see the peaks of the Alp without return smoking, smoking, budding with cumuli, in a distant rumbling. The corkscrew woodworm did not desist from his progress; after the accumulation of every interval he hastened to remind them of himself. (*AG*, 71)]

No matter where the glance of the melancholic falls, it reads the loss of an object, and mourns as if for the loss of someone dear, a child, or perhaps a brother who never returned from war (cf the allusion to 'i vertici dell'Alpe senza ritorni'). In the same vein: 'Un clacson della camionale: e il vuoto delle cose' (*CD*, 678) [The automobile's horn, from the highway, and the vacuum of all things (*AG*, 139)]. Elsewhere, Gonzalo's melancholy is stressed by particular stylistic modulations that aim at dissolving the concrete aspects of objects: 'la cucina era dominata dalla *inutilità lucida del rame in pensione*, appeso ad una parete' (*CD*, 716; my emphasis) [The kitchen was dominated by the gleaming uselessness of the pensioned-off copper, hanging on one wall (*AG*, 188)]. Gonzalo does not see 'shining and useless copper objects' hanging from the wall. He sees 'uselessness itself,' the useless sheen that covers up the object. We find here a turn in style that is very frequent in Gadda's prose. According to Roscioni, it is a turn that characterizes symbolist and post-symbolist prose style: it consists of using an abstract noun (such as 'uselessness') instead of simply an adjective ('useless'), followed, in Italian, by the genitive 'del rame.' In Gadda's hands, Roscioni sees a 'gnoseological' motivation behind this tendency: to seize objects through the perception of objects (Roscioni 1975, 22). However, one should add that the most important feature of this tendency is that it permits Gadda to represent in writing the absence of the object itself, which disappears behind the form, thus becoming an empty phenomenon. In place of concreteness, we find its rich, shiny, yet perfectly useless appearance. Meanwhile, the reduction of the object to a mere appearance is coupled with a mocking remark, an allusion to its being 'in pensione,' a 'retired' object replaced with modern and more functional pots. Gonzalo's anger at the objects is one with the melancholy he feels for their loss.

What Freud called 'mourning' – to detach one's libido from the lost object of love in order to recover it – is, for Gonzalo, the only possible form of 'acquaintance with grief.' It is the same mourning process we find in the pathological mourning typical of depressive or melancholic syndromes (even if in these the loss is removed from consciousness). Mourning is connected to a 'recognition of reality,' as Freud calls it, that is an analysis of all the objects that were linked to the original investment. This process is extremely painful, because the separation from the love object is repeated in an indefinite series of separations. Gadda's acquaintance with grief resembles Freud's 'reality-testing': an examination of 'each single one of the memories and expectations in which the libido is bound to the object is brought up and hypercathected, and detachment of the libido is accomplished in respect of it' (Freud 1963, 245). The fragments of the world surrounding Gonzalo are hypercathected piecemeal, and in reference to each of them is re-enacted the painful detachment from the idea of the plenitude of things. Each object is questioned and excavated, until it becomes an empty image. An example is the villa, which became for the mother almost a new internal organ. In fact, the villa is nothing: taxes, mortgages, an orchard that produces pears hard as stones, lice-ridden chickens, and a precarious wall which should have stood as a mark of private possession but which in fact afforded no protection for him either. Gadda's criticism of private property is a good demonstration of how this mournful recognition of reality works. Gonzalo, who never owned anything because everything was denied to him, manages to treat the wound inflicted on him by showing how illusory possessions are. In an unpublished fragment of *La cognizione*, after explaining how the sense of his family property had become an obsession for Gonzalo (a sort of delirious attachment to domestic objects, even to unmatched glasses), Gadda concludes, apparently contradicting himself:

In realtà nulla egli aveva cercato di possedere nel mondo: e aveva dato tutto come perduto, sempre e preventivamente. Et quod vides perisse, perditum putes. (Cited in Roscioni 1975, 134–6)

[In reality he had tried to possess nothing in the world: and had given everything for lost, always and preventively. Et quod vides perisse, perditum putes.]

By a strange paradox, the grief for a loss can be cured if one believes everything is always lost in advance. This means that the whole world is lost, and that all objects are transformed into an empty appearance. And this is why the distancing glance – always cathartic when it is not conciliatory – plays no role in Gadda's acquaintance with grief. What needs to be expressed is above all the loss along with the deforming perception of it, since this way of processing grief is mourning itself.

Gadda's writing, though, is not limited to simple lamentation. Often, it is enhanced by sudden moments of comedy. One could say that the analysis of reality ends up being fruitful, as if the libido detached itself from the lost object of love to make itself available again. The offended subject, by showing the emptiness of things, sometimes manages to free himself from his anger, to soften his melancholy, and to rebuild the exhilarating 'macaronic' game with the objects he has by now deprived of their immanent meaning. Contini has pointed out that both the comic spirit and the 'maccheronea' perform a pacifying function in Gadda (Contini 1963, 10–11). It is not a complete reconciliation, but a kind of movement that is constantly returning to itself, a sort of alternation of euphoric moments, typical, generally, of manic-depressive states. In Gadda's hands, the 'maccheronea,' as an expressive instrument, is inseparable from his almost obsessive habit of disparaging objects to which his writings seem to be devoted. After all, according to Contini, Gadda does believe (perhaps against his own will) in the outside world. The world which presents itself to the offended writer as a 'richly, greedily desirable world,' is not made of whole objects but can be seen only through the deforming perception of the mourning subject. The 'macaronic' game concentrates on what is left of things once they have been flayed by the melancholic glance, once they have become unable to convey meaning as such. The 'maccheronea' is a divertissement granted to the melancholic, just as is Benjamin's allegory, though in a different fashion. And since it is inseparable from melancholy, 'maccheronea' is always on the point of turning into anger: it is bound to be followed by a destructive gesture.

Gadda himself states, although indirectly, that the 'maccheronea' is an old cure for resentment and grief. In a 1947 article, following Contini's analysis in which Gadda's writing was for the first time defined as 'macaronic' (Contini 1974), Gadda talks of 'merry signs' of 'maccheronea,' which, according to him, should not be confused with the bitter tones of satire, nor with the desolate glance of the melancholic:

Dire per maccheronea è dunque, talvolta, adeguarsi al comune modo e gusto, un rivendicare e un risolvere le istanze profonde contro i piati stanchi, un immergersi nella comunità vivente delle anime, un prevenire o un secondarne in pagina l'ingenito impulso a descrivere, la volontà definitrice del reale, per allegri segni. Tenui sfumature, sottili vincoli o precipitati trapassi, dalla satira alla maccheronea. Dalla malinconia alla maccheronea. (*VM*, 498)

[To speak through the macaronic is, therefore, at times, to adapt to common habits and tastes; it is a way of vindicating and resolving important issues against over-worked disputes; it is an immersion into the living community of souls, an antici-pation or seconding of the innate impulse to describe in writing the defining contours of reality by means of merry signs. Tenuous nuances, subtle links, or precipitous transitions, from satire to the macaronic; from the melancholic to the macaronic.]

In this context, to plunge into the living community of souls is a positive act for Gadda because it implies the mitigation of the exasperated subjectivity which sees only offence in all objects. The 'maccheronea' in fact 'polverizza e dissolve nel nulla ogni abuso' (ibid., 496) [pulverizes and dissolves every abuse into nothingness]. It prevents what is useless or false from passing for valuable or true (in this respect, it fulfils the deforming task that usually belongs to the acquaintance with grief). But it does not become sterile denial. On the contrary, it is 'gioia del dipingere al di là della forma accettata e canonizzata dai bovi: è gioia dell'attingere agli strati autonomi della rappresentazione, all'*umor pratico* della gente' (498) [the joy that comes from depicting beyond the form accepted and canonized by the dimwits: it is the joy that comes from drawing from the autonomous strata of representation, it alludes to the *practical* humour of the people]. Gadda, however, is also alluding to the subtle ties that connect the 'maccheronea' with melancholy and satire (therefore with anger and with undecanted spite). The laughter which punctuates Gadda's mournful recognition with its 'precipitous transitions'[2] is the same as that which may burst out during mourning and which psycho-analysis considers of a maniacal nature. According to Melanie Klein, the typically maniacal triumph over the object hinders not only the pathological mourning of the melancholic, but also normal mourning, as Freud argued. For, in fact, an ambivalence between love and hatred towards the lost object is always at work, and mourning can alternate with the desire to destroy and the desire to debase the object, to annihilate it. When such a conflict of ambivalence takes over, there can be no release: guilt feelings are kept alive, while a persecution complex grows (fear of the object; it may seek revenge) which strengthens maniacal defences. The normal outcome of mourning goes beyond this catch-22 via its painful 'reality-testing.' The subject recovers his/her trust in external objects and, simultaneously, the ability mentally to restore and preserve the lost object. Only at this stage does mourning, like all suffering caused by unhappy experience, become productive. Melanie Klein recalls that 'painful experiences of all kinds sometimes stimulate sublimations' (Klein 1975, 360). In Gadda, instead, precisely as is the case in melancholic states, the conflict of ambivalence is not overcome: the subject loosens the libidinal fixation only by becoming aggressive towards or by destroying the object. It is precisely this triumph that prevents mourning from being a reconstructive process.

Roscioni once pointed out that Gadda's title is reminiscent of a verse in Ecclesiastes: 'He that increaseth knowledge increaseth sorrow' (1:18) (Roscioni 1975, 117). He pointed it out as a confirmation of the pessimism that pervades the novel – a pessimism that conceives of knowledge only as a way to make grief grow. But Roscioni's remark doesn't sufficiently consider Gonzalo's 'cognizione.' We know that, for Gadda, to know does not mean to suffer less: he is actually quite critical of Stoic ethics according to which some good or some happiness is granted to the wise. In the *Meditazione milanese*, he writes that knowledge 'è per ciò stesso confessione e dolore' (*MM*, 893) [is for that reason confession and pain]. But if knowledge does not relieve one of grief, then it is not what grief is originally made of. In Gadda grief is a necessity, it is inevitable. Gonzalo's illness is not the result of an accumulation of knowledge about all things and their vanity, but rather a destiny provoked by an original catastrophe: the consequence of a misdeed or an offence which tore apart the good reality of the ethical organism. His awareness of *vanitas vanitatum*, or better, of the emptiness of all things, is by no means what gives rise to grief. On the contrary, it is the instrument of restoration. Like pale melancholic Hamlet, Gonzalo too is summoned to avenge a wrong he has not committed – a task which is necessary but unjustified. In Gadda's language that is called a 'negazione delle parvenze non valide' [negation of invalid appearances].

For the Spinozian author of the *Meditazione milanese*, the 'good' is inseparable from the principle of 'the common good' which coincides for society (and for any other organism) with the preservation of all wealth and of all potential developments. Evil is whatever dissipates wealth, such as a bad business transaction which wastes capital, or a murder, which terminates not only the victim's life, but also biological continuity, the genetic series. Evil is 'a partial non-being' (*MM*, 692) which endangers the good reality of the organism. The organism reacts by imposing a reconstruction of the broken tissue, a 'reconnection to reality' (693). Thus a bad business transaction provokes a consumption of money: 'quel consumo è elemento riparatore o nemesi [...] dell'affare sballato' (694) [that consumption is the repairing element or nemesis ... for the bad transaction]. The same is true for a murder:

Il poeta e drammaturgo inglese William Shakespeare scrisse un'opera di teatro intitolata 'Amleto, Principe di Danimarca' che è ricchissima di significazioni non ancora tutte, forse, messe adeguatamente in luce. – Egli mostra l'inammissibilità o irrealtà del delitto che perverte la stoffa del reale ingenerando altri delitti espiatori o rammendi della stoffa (692).

[The English poet and playwright William Shakespeare wrote a work entitled 'Hamlet, Prince of Denmark' rich in meanings all of which perhaps have not been adequately considered. He shows the inadmissibility or irreality of the crime that perverts the fabric of the real generating other crimes that expiate or mend the fabric.]

Gadda adds that the process of repair is not meant here in the Christian sense of atonement, but rather as a 'terribile senso di ripristinamento logico-teorico o intrinseco alla realtà' (ibid., 692) [terribly strong sense of logical-theoretical restoration, intrinsic to reality]. The murderer must be punished, or even killed, for he upsets the natural order. About Hamlet, Gadda writes:

Nel dramma l'idea 'vendetta' è chiarita con l'idea (che assume un vero e proprio carattere finalistico) di ripristinamento dell'ordine naturale turbato.[3]

[In the tragedy the idea of 'revenge' is clarified through the idea (which has a truly final character) of restoration of the natural order that had been upset.]

Like Hamlet, Gonzalo is summoned to avenge a crime against the common good. In the 'mondo [...] delle non-borse di studio al buono' (CD, 763) [world ... which grants no fellowships to the good] he sees not only the offence directed against himself, but the offence against economy and reason (CD, 764). The organism, the 'ragioni oscure e vivide della vita' [obscure and vivid reasons of life], calls for compensation. The compensation is, in this case, if not another crime, at least something that has a great deal to do with murder: negation.

La sua secreta perplessità e l'orgoglio secreto affioravano dentro la trama degli atti in una negazione di parvenze non valide. Le figurazioni non valide erano da negare e da respingere, come specie falsa di denaro (703).

[His secret perplexity and secret pride rose to the surface within the woof of his actions in a negation of nonvalid appearances. Nonvalid depictions were to be negated and to be rejected, like false specie, counterfeit money (AG, 170)].

The revenge in which Gonzalo is instrumental consists of unearthing the non-being that the original catastrophe introduced into reality. A 'non-being' no one else can see: no one else is endowed with the grievous perception of it. Therefore, the 'cognizione del dolore' (in which 'dolore,' grief, is not the object but the subject of knowledge) is a distorting eye in charge of an ethical mission. Ethical, that is, from the standpoint of the organism. As Gadda points out: 'la ricostruzione morale operata da Amleto costa a lui e alla sua schiatta la rinuncia alla vita' (VM, 584) [the moral reconstruction introduced by Hamlet costs him and his descendants the renunciation of life]. The organism can reconstruct itself only by annihilating whatever is personal. Totality, which follows its natural necessity, is being 'reconciled' with reality, but the grief-stricken subject is irredeemably threatened by 'non-being,' as well as by the objects that happen to be seen by him. Hamlet's pallor surfaces on Gonzalo's face: it is the 'lento pallore della negazione.'

Cogliere il bacio bugiardo della Parvenza, coricarsi con lei sullo strame, respirare Il suo fiato, bevere giù dentro l'anima il suo rutto o il suo lezzo di meretrice. O invece attuffarla nella rancura e nello spregio come in una pozza di scrementi, negare, negare [...]. Ma l'andare nella rancura è sterile passo, negare vane immagini, le più volte, significa negare se medesimo. (CD, 703–4)

[To seize the lying kiss of Appearances, to lie with her on the straw, to breathe her breath, to drink in, down into the soul, her belch and strumpet's stench. Or instead to plunge them into rancor and into contempt as into a well of excrement, to deny, deny ... But the progress of rancor is a sterile footstep; to deny vain images, most of the time, means denying oneself. (AG, 171)]

To punish and to die: this is what Hamlet was supposed to do in order to complete the repairing process. In contrast, Gonzalo can achieve that goal only through self-denial. The 'cognizione del dolore' does not enrich the subject, but rather empties it. The subject is denied tragic catharsis but also the kind of catharsis towards which tends Schopenhauer's pessimism: catharsis through the elevation of oneself to the role of a pure subject of knowledge, one that has overcome contingency. In Gadda's perspective, to recognize in one's own grief everyone else's grief, to feel horrified before a world filled with suffering, would mean to fail to fulfil the obligation of reconstructing that totality imposes on the subject. The main feature of this 'cognizione del dolore' that condemns the subject to particularity is not negation (which frees one from the will of living), nor ascent, but rancour.

At the core of Gadda's 'gnoseological grudge,' the immanent principle of his writing – the search for multiple causes and for their infinite relations – stands the question and problem of ethics, and the problem of the necessity of evil. When Gadda speaks of causes, he alludes to the causes of evil. The necessary causes slip the limits of subjective perspective. In Gadda, disorder, mess, and chaos are always ethical disorder and chaos, a terrifying distortion which is necessary but not comprehensible. In a note included in the essay 'Abozzi per temi per tesi di laurea,' Gadda notes an interesting remark. ' "The time is out of joint," says Hamlet, "O cursed spite, That ever I was born to set it right!" '[4] Yet, evil is always necessary, even if it seems unjustified. The central idea of Stoic ethics – and Gadda finds it in Spinoza as well – according to which good and evil necessarily coexist, is clearly expressed in Meditazione milanese: 'il male è una coesistenza eticamente periferica del bene' (MM, 681). But men cannot understand the connection that allows what appears to be evil to become good in reference to totality. Gadda's theory of knowledge, based as it is on the Leibnizian idea of 'combination-possibility,' displays the impossibility of the realization of Spinoza's ethical duty: when the world appears as 'la tabella delle infinite combinazioni possibili' (727) [the chart of the infinite combinations that are possible], it becomes impossible to reconstruct the cause of evil, to seize its necessity.

Gadda's work in its entirety is centred on a question concerning evil. Particularly in his early writings, *Racconto italiano* and *Novella seconda*, Gadda seems to feel it is his duty to represent the incredible stories of 'anime difformi' [deformed souls] in order to demonstrate that 'anche i fatti normali e terribili rientrano nella legge, se pure apparentemente sono exlege' (*RI*, 405) [abnormal and terrifying acts, too, are part of the law, even if apparently they are outlawed]. Gadda's early interest in researching the causes of evil is aroused by the ethical duty stressed by Spinoza, which also promises a sort of liberation from passions to acknowledge the natural necessity of all things, including evil, and to comply serenely with it. If we forget this important point, we cannot understand why the failed reconstruction of causes becomes such a dramatic issue in Gadda. The 'cognitive failure' which Gadda's critics mention so often is an ethical failure, not a gnoseological one. The possibility of cathartic knowledge vanishes at the same time as the possibility of reconstructing the necessary causes of evil. The specificity of Gadda's acquaintance with grief lies in the fact that Spinoza's ethics, and the bit of stoicism connected to it, is never completely refuted, only denied. It is kept in mind as an impossible aspiration, an element of unresolved polarity, a blocked tension: on the one hand, the inevitability of the particular, on the other, the aspiration to the universal. Thus, grief can only be absolute negativity. It is unreconcilable, but it is not even the symbol – as Adorno would say – of the falsity of reconciliation in an unreconciled world. For Gadda, grief is a mean particularity, the bitter fruit of human ignorance. The obscure perception, typical of grief, is confused by those passions that Spinoza would have classified among the most negative ones – hatred, wrath, resentment, remorse, and sadness – which can frequently be found in Gadda's writings. There lies the paradox of the 'malignant inker,' as Gadda calls himself, who cannot stand his own malignancy, though he considers it to be inevitable (*VM*, 504).

Gonzalo's grief has therefore nothing to do with the lamentation of the individual who complains about his ephemeral existence or the absence of purpose in life. His tragedy has to be seen at a different level. He does not complain that things have no purpose for individuals, but that the individual – one individual, himself – can neither help the universe achieve its goal, nor preserve the good reality of the organism. The organism can be preserved only through improvement, by passing from the individual to that which is different, or, as Gadda says, from n to $n + 1$. N is the particular that has to be negated to make room for that which is different, the $n + 1$, a still unknown quantity, but which is considered 'better' in relation to reality – by means of a certain teleology that Gadda himself recognizes as Fichtian (*SVP*, 758). Frequently, Gadda uses evolutionistic concepts to explain his ethical thinking:

La funzione crea l'organo: cioè si affacciano nella storia biologica delle relazioni (p. e. relazioni luce, relazioni moto) che poi vengono deferite a sistemi specializzati (occhio, gambe). Ma ciò non avviene di colpo: poco a poco, sine saltu, per tentativi, riprove, correzioni. É l'euresi. É l'intravedere una possibilità sistematica per il moto. Donde gli arti (785).

[Function creates the organ: that is, in biological history relationships present themselves (e.g., light, movement) which are then assigned to specific systems (the eye, legs). But this does not come about all at once: [but rather] little by little, *sine saltu*, by means of trial and error. It is a heuristic process. It is to foresee a systematic possibility for movement. Whereby limbs.]

An individual contributes to this heuristic process by detaching himself from the powerful call of the particular that aims only at self-preservation. For an individual, the only possible happiness (forbidden to Gonzalo) lies in the love of *becoming*, in that kind of heuristic process that drives towards new, unexplored horizons. This is what Gadda calls a heroic feeling: it belongs to the hero who goes to war to sacrifice his own n (life) for 'the country's *becoming*,' but also to the man who procreates to preserve humankind. In his introduction to Hjalmar Bergman's *I Markurell*, Gadda describes old Markurell's self-denying love for his son in these terms:

Bergman esprime nel suo Markurell questo spirito di ascesa, questa tenace volontà di persistenza, di miglioramento biologico e quindi economico: Questa lotta per guadagnare il futuro al proprio sangue [...] Un demone si agita in Markurell: il demone genetico.[5]

[Bergman expresses in his Markurell this spirit of ascent, this tenacious will to persist, to biological (and therefore economic) improvement: this struggle to secure the future for his own stock ... A demon agitates Markurell: the demon of genetics.]

Both ethics and genetics are the sacrifice of the individual to the human species. The particular certainly suffers when it detaches itself from its own particularity, since 'è legge di natura che ogni azione trovi ostacoli e ogni divenire si laceri con dolore e con tormento dal suo essere' (*MM*, 791) [it is the law of nature that every action meets with obstacles and that every becoming is torn with grief and torment from its being]. But this is not Gonzalo's grief, in the same way that it is not Markurell's, when he discovers that his son is not his own child, or Liliana Balducci's who has been condemned to sterility. Markurell, Liliana, and Gonzalo, in different ways, are acquainted with that particular grief that Gadda calls 'second degree' grief. They cannot have access to $n + 1$, they know only 'l'ambascia del non poter divenire' [the anguish of not being capable of becoming], like people forced to stand still instead of building, therefore being only a burden to the community while living within it 'come cosa morta o come perturbazione retrogrediente' [as dead things or retrograding perturbation]. Gonzalo's grief is that of someone who sees himself as a torn member of a larger reality, of a vaster organism, who is ready to sacrifice himself but is bound to his n, to the sterile negation of his 'fragmented self' (744):

Il degenerare verso l'io n immemore del suo possibile ascendere ad $n + 1$, può essere determinato da cause estrinseche ai poteri dell' io personale. Quando ogni compito si chiude oltre il limite raggiunto dall'n, e tutto non per colpa nostra, rovina in una negazione atroce; allora ultimo baluardo di realtà, come talvolta al naufrago, non ci rimane che il nostro misero significato n, il nostro io consolidato negli evi; e su quello esercitiamo la nostra lugubre ora, come chi ha le gambe paralizzate si diverte a risolvere dei 'solitaires' con le carte. (770–1)

[The deterioration to the n self, lifeless in its possible ascent to $n + 1$, may be determined by causes that are extrinsic to the powers of the individual self. When every project terminates beyond the limits reached by n, and not for any fault of ours, it falls into atrocious negation; then our final bulwark of reality, as for the shipwrecked sailor, is nothing but our miserable meaning n, our own self, consolidated with the passing of time, on which we exert our lugubrious sense of the present, like someone who with paralysed legs takes pleasure in winning at solitaire.]

The founding principle of all expressionistic writing is the impossibility of the transfiguration of grief. For, to be able to express the particular in its deformed and deforming immediacy means to hold a subjectivity that is not reconciled nor reconcilable with the universal. In Gadda, the vestiges of subjectivity filter, by their deforming action, everything that is being represented. Moreover, they derive from the very impossibility of mediation between the particular and the universal. But in Gadda, the terms of the problems are overturned: the particular is 'evil' precisely because it tends to persist, while the world, with its lack of a human dimension, is not. Anger against those objects that are not for oneself becomes anger against that very self which is separated from objects. The hurting subject is the 'foul guts,' and is able to say nothing about nothing, as Gonzalo argues in his tirade against personal pronouns:

Io, tu...Quando l'immensità si coagula, quando la verità si aggrinza in una palandrana...da deputato al Congresso,...io, tu...in una tirchia e rattrappita persona, quando la giusta ira si appesantisce in una pancia,...nella mia per esempio...che ha per suo fine e destino unico, nell'universo, di insaccare tonnellate di bismuto, a cinque pesos il decagrammo...giù, giù, nel duodeno...bismuto a palate...attendendo...un giorno dopo l'altro, fino alla fine degli anni...Quando l'essere si parzializza, in un sacco, in una lercia trippa, i di cui confini sono più miserabili e fessi di questo fesso muro pagatasse...che lei me lo scavalca in un salto...quando succede questo bel fatto...allora...è allora che l'io si determina, con la sua brava monade in coppa, come il càppero sull'acciuga arrotolata sulla fetta di limone sulla costoletta alla viennese...Allora, allora! É allora, proprio, in quel preciso momento, che spunta fuori quello sparagone di un io...pimpante...eretto... impennacchiato di attributi di ogni maniera...paonazzo, e pennuto, e teso, e turgido...come un tacchino [...] oppure saturnino e alpigiano, con gli occhi incavernati, con lo sfinctere strozzato dall'avarizia... (*CD*, 637–8)

[I, you ... When the immensity coagulates, when truth becomes wrinkled in an overcoat – of a Deputy in Congress – I, you ... in a mean and shrunken person, when righteous wrath becomes heavy in a belly ... in mine, for example ... which has as its end and only destiny, in the universe, the stuffing of tons of bismuth, at five pesos the decagram ... down, down into the duodenum ... bismuth by the shovelful ... waiting ... one day after the other, to the end of one's years ... When being becomes separated into a sack of foul guts, whose boundaries are more miserable and more foolish than this foolish, taxpaying wall ... which you can climb over in one leap ... when this fine business happens ... then ... that's when the I is determined, with its fine monad upon it, like a caper on the rolled up anchovy on the lemon slice over the Wiener schnitzel. Then, then! That precisely is the very moment! That lousy, incomparable I ... swaggering ... erect ... beplumed with attributes of every sort ... purplished and feathered, and taut, and turgid ...

like a turkey ... or else Saturnine and Alpine, with eyes hallowed in distrust, with the sphincter blocked by avarice ... (*AG*, 88–9)].

Gonzalo's anger is also an anger directed against the expressionist self, the self which lets itself complain about his loss, thus consolidating his poor, sterile negativity. In this respect, as well, Gadda's 'cognizione del dolore' is no different from the pathological mourning of the melancholic, who deals with himself as an object, who directs towards himself all the hostile feelings that were originally directed towards things (Freud 1963, 244–5). Thus Gadda's writing attacks, disparages, and empties the only resource available to expressionists; the comic wrench which turns sad fragments into exciting baroque fantasies is yet another scornful gesture against the self.[6]

The impossibility of unifying multiplicity around an immanent meaning gives way to allegory. Gadda's loss of the object corresponds to the loss of meaning that Benjamin called 'allegorical soullessness' (Benjamin 1977, 183). The painful lived experience is not transfigured through symbol; we are left with an incoherent bunch of uninterpretable fragments. If they have any meaning at all, they expect to be given it from the outside, as redemption. Like Kafka, although by other means, Gadda turns lived experience into an enigma upon which is placed the highest of all enigmas: the necessity of grief. But Gadda, unlike most expressionists, exiles truth into an abyss where no hope of redemption can reach it. Writing fills that abyss with 'merry signs.' Words, their redundancy, dissolve the pathos of truth. The libido, with its voracious desire for accumulation, turns to language:

I doppioni li voglio tutti, per mania di possesso e per cupidigia di ricchezze: e voglio anche i triploni, e i quadruploni, sebbene il re cattolico non li abbia ancora monetati: e tutti i sinonimi usati nelle loro variegate accezioni e sfumature, d'uso corrente, o d'uso rarissimo. (*VM* I, 490)

[I want all the double-sided coins to satisfy my mania for possession and desire for wealth. I want even the triples, and the quadruples, even if the Catholic king has yet to mint them: and all the synonyms in all of their different meanings and nuances, whether of current or very rare usage.]

Gadda's word is not willing to solve the enigma of grief. Instead, it becomes a fantasy, a resonant appearance to be played with by the melancholic. Just as for Benjamin, the fragments to which the melancholic attributes an arbitrary meaning are the 'divertissement' of allegory, the possibility of play with and in language. But this 'divertissement' is a sad one if the euphoric time of the comic mode is not granted to it. The comic is what characterizes Gadda's allegory. What makes Gadda's expressionism so different from that of the other expressionists, his 'maccheronea' from the landscapes of stones and ruins, his violence from the violence of lamentation, is what his 'philosophy' draws from Spinoza: a contempt for vacuous subjectivity. It is also what his writing keeps repeating: the destructive gesture which overwhelms the self and its 'childish vanity.'

Translated by Manuela Bertone

Notes

1 The relationship between knowledge and grief in the novel's title is generally understood by criticism in the tragic sense as knowledge of grief achieved through experience, that is by means of its representation in narrative. The only interpretation that departs from this point of view has been advanced by Gian Carlo Roscioni who refers the title back to a verse from the Book of Ecclesiastes: 'He that increaseth knowledge increaseth sorrow.' As we shall discuss below, in contrast to the tragic sense of knowledge acquired through grief, here it is not grief that generates knowledge, but knowledge that generates grief. I shall argue that neither of these interpretations suffices to explain the relationship between knowledge and grief in Gadda. Grief for Gadda is neither the object nor the instrument of knowledge, nor its product, but rather its subject, in the sense in which it is commonly said that a person who is suffering from grief sees things with a deforming eye. I believe that the 'cognizione del dolore' should be understood as a kind of subjective genitive: as knowledge that has for its subject the deforming eye of grief.

2 Gadda's comment on the ballad by Villon that contains the famous quip 'je riz en pleurs' illustrates better than anything else what he means by 'precipitati trapassi': 'Una meravigliosa capacità di singhiozzare tra le lacrime, la risata che si alterna alla preghiera, alla pietà filiale: la voce più vera del dolore, la desolata contemplazione del proprio destino. La invocazione alla Madonna, nella celebre ballata del "Testamento": e subito dopo la beffa del l'avara meretrice, che non ha corrisposto l'amore. Questa ineguagliata attitudine a cangiar di tono da una strofe all'altra, da un verso all'altro – questa mescolanza – così drammaticamente iridata di pathos e di scherno avvicina François Villon a due grandi poeti: Catullo e Shakespeare' (VM, 527) [[the poet's] marvellous capacity to sob amidst tears, his laughter that alternates

with prayers and filial piety: his most genuine voice of grief and the desolate contemplation of his own destiny. His invocation to the Blessed Virgin, in the famous ballad of the 'Testament': followed immediately by the practical joke of the avaricious whore, who did not return his love. This unequalled aptitude for changing tone from one stanza to another, from one verse to another – this mixture – so dramatically lined with pathos and contempt raises François Villon to the level of two great poets: Catullus and Shakespeare].

3 This passage is taken from an unpublished manuscript ('Abbozzi di temi per tesi di laurea') that Gian Carlo Roscioni cites in his edition of *Meditazione milanese* (1974), 353.

4 *Hamlet*, I.v, cited by Roscioni, *MM*, 353.

5 Introduction to Hjalmar Bergman, *I Markurell* (Turin: Einaudi 1982). Gadda wrote his introduction to the novel in 1944, at the same time or just prior to the magazine version of *Quer pasticciaccio*. In his commentary, he pinpoints what will become the central theme of *Quer pasticciaccio*: the ' sentimento della discendenza' [feeling of hereditary derivation] that animates the Valdarena 'tribe,' and the 'senso di coerenza (oltreché di coesione) etica e genetica proprio delle società chiuse o remote' [sense of ethical and genetic coherence (as well as cohesion) typical of closed and distant societies] that forms the background for the drama of Liliana Balducci's maternity *manquée*.

6 The expressionistic self takes the sadness of objects as its strength. By contrast, in Gadda, all that the self remembers of its inane destiny is transformed suddenly into a 'merry sign.' For example, in *La cognizione*, the hen and the dragonfly at least once are invested with Gonzalo's melancholic gaze, as emblems of loss: the hen does not hatch an egg for him, and the dragonfly soars over the walls surrounding his villa, in mocking denial of his property's inviolable rights to privacy.

References

Benjamin, Walter. 1977. *The Origin of German Tragic Drama*. Translated by John Osborne. London: New Left Books

Contini, Gianfranco. 1963. *Introduzione alla 'Cognizione del dolore.'* Turin: Einaudi

– 1974. *Esercizi di lettura*. Turin: Einaudi

Freud, Sigmund. 1963. 'Mourning and Melancholia.' In *The Complete Psychological Works*. Translated by James Strachey. Vol. XIV. London: The Hogarth Press

Klein, Melanie. 1975. 'Mourning and Its Relation to Manic-Depressive States.' In *Love, Guilt and Reparation and Other Works*. New York: The Free Press

Roscioni, Gian Carlo. 1975. *La disarmonia prestabilita*. Turin: Einaudi

Gadda's Freud

GUIDO LUCCHINI

As far back as the *Meditazione Milanese*, the question of the self has been at the core of Gadda's discontinuously lucid reflections. Gian Carlo Roscioni has pointed out that 'even before Gadda's conceptual world was penetrated by any psychoanalytical idea or notion, it contained all the premises for that particular reappraisal of the self' (Roscioni 1975, 106–7). But the crux of the matter is situated elsewhere: at the time of *Racconto italiano di ignoto del novecento* and the *Meditazione* (between 1924 and 1928), Gadda embraces an anti-substantialist form of criticism that has little, or nothing, in common with psychoanalysis in the strict sense. When he writes that it is foolish to conceive of the individual as a unity (*MM* 649–50), stating that 'ogni pausa espressiva è un io e ogni io è una pausa espressiva' (760) [every expressive pause is a self and every self is an expressive pause], we are to understand these words in relation to his conception of reality as 'a system in perennial deformation' (ibid.). Individuation is a transient, precarious, mostly illusive process, and above all an intrinsically evil one. In its false presumption of autonomy, the self contains in embryo its own perversion, the 'phagic' impulse that Gadda believes to be typical of the instinct of self-preservation.

All of the above is broadly pre-Freudian,[1] but it does not necessarily lead to psychoanalysis. Before discussing the influence of psychoanalysis on Gadda's mature writings, we should ask whether Gadda had a first-hand knowledge of Freud. The answer is a definite yes. In what is left of Gadda's book collection, held at the Biblioteca Teatrale del Burcardo in Rome, there are four volumes of Freud's writings in French translation that to this day, as far as I know, have been completely overlooked. I am referring to: *Essais de psychanalyse appliquée* [*Essays on Applied Psychoanalysis*] (Paris: N.R.F., 1926, 7th edition, translated by Emile Marty and Marie

Bonaparte); *Psychopatologie de la vie quotidienne* [*The Psychopathology of Everyday Life*] (Paris: Payot 1926); *Introduction à la psychanalyse* [*Introduction to Psychoanalysis*] (Paris: Payot 1928); and *Essais de psychanalyse* [*Essays on Psychoanalysis*] (Paris: Payot 1927), all three translated by Saul Jankélévitch. This last collection includes *Au delà du principe du plaisir* [*Beyond the Pleasure Principle*]; *Psychologie collective et analyse du moi* [*Group Psychology and the Analysis of the Ego*]; *Le moi et le soi* [*The Ego and the Id*]; *Considérations sur la guerre et sur la mort* [*Considerations on War and Death*; and *Contribution à l'histoire du mouvement psychanalytique* [*Contribution to the History of the Psychoanalytical Movement*]. On its title page we find written 'Ing. C.' followed by 'April 1924,' probably a reference to when the collection was purchased. This is the only data we have to help us determine when Gadda actually bought and (most likely) read these works.

All four volumes have their leaves cut open; many parts of the introductory lessons and of the essays on psychoanalysis are underlined in more than one place, but sparingly annotated. Even if we consider only these latter essays, which Gadda certainly knew, there is no doubt that we are dealing with one of the sources of his postwar essays. The *Essais de psychanalyse* are particularly valuable, for they support the hypothesis that the author of *Eros e Priapo* became acquainted with Le Bon's ideas on the feminine character of groups through Freud's well-known work *Group Psychology and the Analysis of the Ego*. I shall not treat in detail all of the similarities and analogies that can be drawn between Gadda's relentless tirades against Mussolini (rather than against Fascism) and Freud's prophetic pages; instead, I shall dwell only upon some fundamental passages. It is noteworthy that Gadda has read with great attention the following chapters in particular: 'Suggestion and Libido,' 'Two Artificial Groups: The Church and the Army,' and 'Being in Love and Hypnosis.' They all deal with the erotic bond that links groups to their charismatic leader.

In the first chapter, Gadda has marked in the margin two important passages dealing with the relationship between group psychology and the ego:

The apostle Paul praises love ... He understands it in the same 'wider' sense. But this only shows that men do not always take their great thinkers seriously, even when they profess most to admire them. (Freud 1959, 23)

And also:

One can never tell where that road may lead one; one gives way first in words, and then little by little in substance too. I cannot see any merit in being ashamed of sex; the Greek word 'Eros,' which is to soften the affront, is in the end nothing more than a translation of the German word 'Liebe' [love]; and finally, he who knows how to wait, need make no concessions. (ibid.)

In the second chapter, Gadda focuses on Freud's distinction between natural and artificial groups (that is, groups with and without leaders), as he glosses, with direct reference to Mussolini, the following passage: 'the Commander-in-Chief is a father who loves all soldiers equally' (ibid., 26); in the margin he actually notes: 'hélas! non!.' Farther on, he significantly underlines Freud's entire digression on narcissism as related to rival nationalities, and in this case as well he keeps in mind the desolate reality of the present. 'We are no longer astonished that greater differences should lead to an almost insuperable repugnance ... of the Aryan for the Semite' (33). Finally, it is worth dwelling on at least two more excerpts from the important chapter in which Freud examines the idealization of being in love: 'We love [the object] on account of the perfections which we have striven to reach for our own ego' (44–5), and:

This happens especially easily with love that is unhappy and cannot be satisfied; for in spite of everything each sexual satisfaction always involves a reduction in sexual overevaluation. Contemporaneously with this 'devotion' of the ego to the object ... the functions allotted to the ego ideal entirely cease to operate ... The whole situation can be completely summarized in the formula: *the object has been put in the place of the ego-ideal*. (45)

The sense of Gadda's reading will now become clearer and its results, I would venture to say, predictable. The passages cited no doubt indicate his interest in Freud's theses on the erotic nature of the relationship between groups and their leader, and on the dynamic relationship between narcissistic libido and objectual libido.[2] These concepts return in *Eros e Priapo*, 'Emilio e Narciso,' and in the dialogue entitled 'L'egoista.' It would be especially useful to differentiate Gadda's violent 'political' pamphlet from the thoughtful diptych on narcissism. Even if one were not to venture an appraisal of their respective value (*Eros e Priapo* remains, in my opinion, the least important of Gadda's minor works), I believe that, as far as the former is concerned, we are dealing with the use of psychoanalysis as a libel, an occasion for violent invective. As it is known, Gadda locates the essence of Fascism in narcissism and in the erotic bond connecting the leader to the manifestly 'female' masses. Both theses found their sources more or less in *Group Psychology and the Analysis of the Ego*.

According to Freud, the distinguishing feature of groups consists in the fact that they adopt 'the same object as their ego-ideal' (ibid., 26) and identify one with the other in their ego (note that the same passage is underlined by Gadda in the French translation). The concept of 'ego-ideal' no doubt derives from *On Narcissism: An Introduction*, although Gadda does not use the term in the same way as Freud. 'Ego-ideal' for Freud refers to a step in the psychic process the origin of which is mainly narcissistic ('[The subject] is not willing to forgo the narcissistic perfection of his childhood ... What he projects before him as his ideal is the substitute for the lost narcissism of his childhood in which he was his own ideal' [94]); its model, however, is represented by parental figures, particularly the father.

Curiously enough, such a fundamental connection of the ego-ideal to the Oedipus complex is lacking in Gadda; consider, for example, the following passage taken from *Eros e Priapo*:

L'autolubido esprime la necessaria coesione dell'Io, ed è per il singolo organismo quello che è la forza centripeta o gravitazione per il singolo pianeta. Essa si identifica col pronome Io, accompagna in anticipo di fase lo sviluppo dell'Io, cioè prelude ai singoli e ai variopinti ludi dell'Io, *si sublima* o decede a mano a mano avanti il *sublimarsi* o il decedere dell'Io. (*EP* 323; emphasis mine)

[The individual libido expresses the necessary cohesion of the ego; it is for the single organism what the centripetal or gravitational force is for a particular planet. It identifies with the pronoun I; it accompanies consistently in advance the development of the ego, that is to say, it serves as a prelude to the various, multicoloured games played by the ego; it is *sublimated* or deceased hand in hand with the *sublimation* or death of the ego.]

And elsewhere: 'il modello dell'uomo (in fase di sviluppo) è l'uomo (in fase adulta)' (333) [The model of man (in his developmental phase) is man in his adult phase].

This absence of references to the Oedipal relationship cannot but arouse surprise. Gadda draws on Freud's theory without realizing that his complex utterances on the origins of the ego (the slow, painful movement away from primeval narcissistic perfection) imply that the parental figure of the same sex is assumed as a model, although with ambivalence, precisely on account of the erotic desire directed towards the mother. We are dealing with concepts that are now very well known even outside of psychoanalysis. I will therefore quote only a brief passage from Freud's text which Gadda carefully read: 'The little boy notices that his father stands in his way with his mother. His identification with his father then takes on a hostile coloring and becomes identical with the wish to replace his father in regard to his mother as well' (Freud 1959, 37). Without indulging in facile assumptions regarding the possible reasons for Gadda's total silence on this crucial Freudian hypothesis – Gadda's relationship to his mother, sufficiently transparent in its literary manifestations, goes without saying – let us consider how he relates the concept of narcissism to his fierce criticism of 'il piú lurido dei pronomi' [the foulest of all pronouns].'[3]

When Gadda writes in *Eros e Priapo*:

Nell'uomo normale la carica affettiva o carica erotica normale [...] è suscettiva 1) di impersonarsi in una femina eletta fra le innumeri femine come oggetto, almeno momentaneo, dell'amore e della lubido [...] 2) di 'sublimarsi' in istati dell'animo che tendono a levar su il mastio da le bassezze dell'essere verso la piaggia o l'erta perigliosa del divenire [...] (*EP*, 273)

[In normal men, the love impulse or normal erotic impulse ... is susceptible 1) to becoming one with a female, chosen from the many as object, at least momentarily, of love or libido ... 2) to be 'sublimated' in moods that tend to raise the male up from the depths of being towards the shore or dangerous terrain of becoming ...]

he reiterates what he has stated over and over again in the *Meditazione* about the 'deferring' nature 'of an elective good.' The narcissist's worst sin lies in his inability to sublimate himself in a socially useful activity. One easily recognizes the impassioned reader of Manzoni, hiding behind this usage of Freudian terminology: Gadda, the Lombard, concerned with the 'moral evil' brought to society by men and authorities who fail in their duties.

It would not be unreasonable to speak of a 'mechanistic' reading of Freud: one fully consonant with Gadda's cultural background that accepts and emphasizes the positivistic aspects of Freud's thinking (for example, the rigorous determinism Freud applied to ethics and psychic life, his theory of personality conceived as a system of hierarchically arranged functions, and so on). On the other hand, Gadda misses the 'other' Freud, the founder of a new *ars interpretandi* which he applied not only to dreams but also to the apparently meaningless events of everyday life: slips of the tongue, bungled actions, and witticisms. The limits of Gadda's reading are self-evident and need no further comment. Gadda annexes his imperfect knowledge of psychoanalysis to the philosophy of his favourite authors, Spinoza and Leibniz. Narcissism is, after all, a different name for the ego's unbending belief in its fictitious autonomy, 'a relapse into the infancy of being' as he wrote in a different context about Rimbaud's flight from confinement (*VM*, 561–86). Gadda's reading of Freud does not bring about a true evolution in his thinking with respect to the *Meditazione milanese*. Quite the opposite. The portrait of the 'mad narcissist' he sketches in *Eros e Priapo* (incapable of self-analysis and ethical action, egotistical, and so on), to which he returns in later essays, certainly does not stand out either for depth or originality. If anything, we are again confronted with a vehement form of misogyny. Gadda's discursive inadequacy, already apparent in the *Meditazione*, is even more marked in his later writings. Themes so common in the *Meditazione* – and even before, in the *Giornale di guerra e di prigionia* – such as self-sacrifice, spiritual elevation, and moral action, reappear under the false label of 'sublimation.'[4]

Gadda uses the fundamental theses of *Group Psychology and the Analysis of the Ego* to criticize Fascism. But, as we have shown, his criticism is still embedded in the culture of positivism. It is not by coincidence that even in *Eros e Priapo* dictatorships appear as 'una netta regressione da quel notevole punto di sviluppo a cui la umanità era giunta (in sullo spegnersi dell'epoca positivistica) verso una fase involutiva, bugiarda' (*EP*, 244) [a definite regression from that noteworthy stage of development reached by humanity (at the decline of the age of positivism) towards its degenerative, mendacious phase].

Moreover, the instant connection between Freud's booklet and *Eros e Priapo* should not lead to an overestimation of the latter to the detriment of more meaningful writings, in which, however, Freud's influence is not as easy to trace. In this perspective, Gadda's most interesting texts – those that in some way involve psychoanalysis – belong to the post-Second World War period, with the exception of the short story 'Una tigre nel parco' (*MI*, 74–9). Gadda's interest in Freud is to be situated between the thirties and forties, as documented by the dates of the French translations that are still part of his personal collection, and by the date of the above-mentioned short story (1936), which undoubtedly shows a certain degree of knowledge of some of Freud's writings. But Gadda's deepest reflection on psychoanalysis takes place when he reaches his creative maturity, between 1946 and 1954, the year in which 'L'egoista' was published.

The only essay Gadda explicitly devotes to psychoanalysis, bearing the not-so-original title 'Psicanalisi e letteratura' (*VM*, 455–73), in retrospect is somewhat disappointing. With the traditional opposition of Italian culture to Freud being all but over, Gadda's essay, captivating as it is in many respects, has lost its punch, for the passionate defence of psychoanalysis it contains is now, fortunately, out of date. And yet, in this brief, quasi-journalistic piece we find a series of clues useful to an understanding of Gadda at his best.

While talking somewhat distractedly about Freudian theories on infant sexuality, Gadda quotes in translation two well-known verses by Virgil: 'Begin, baby boy! Him on whom his parents have not smiled, no god honours with his table, no goddess with her bed!' (Virgil 1986, Eclogue IV, 62–3, 33). He quotes them to demonstrate an obvious truth: 'I rapporti tra i genitori e i figli non sono sempre, non sono per tutti così idillici' (*VM*, 460) [The relationship between parents and children is not always, nor for everyone, so idyllic]. This Freudian-like citation from Virgil reappears in 'Dalle specchiere ai laghi,' a short narrative written in 1941, that stands out as one of Gadda's best:

M'ero studiato di ridurre l'ecloga alla terza rima. oh! l'avevo a memoria [...] Ma, in sul chiudere la messianica, Vergilio aveva lacerato il tema, bruscamente: il vaticinio delle pecore pitturate: 'Quello a cui i genitori non hanno saputo sorridere, né un dio vorrà degnarlo della sua mensa, né una dea lo degnerà del suo letto. Nec dignata cubili est.' (*VC*, 301)

[I had tried to render the eclogue in terza rima. oh! I knew it by heart ... But, upon closing this messianic invocation, Virgil had abruptly interrupted his theme: the prophecy of the painted sheep: 'Him on whom his parents have not smiled, nor whom a god would honour with his table, nor a goddess with her bed. Nec dignata cubili est.']

The concordance seems to me very instructive: it is not only further proof of the author's extremely sparing use of words, and frequent, carefully considered, transferral of materials from his fiction to his essays and vice versa, but it is also a definite (although not unexpected) demonstration of the fact that a so-called trauma precedes and explains his interest in Freud.

Gadda reads the end of the fourth eclogue in a Freudian-like fashion because he finds there what he wants to find, namely a clear allusion to the Oedipus complex: to the constant obsession with a frustrated manhood due to parental – particularly maternal – denial and suffocation:

Ero solo: con misere vesti. E al ristare d'ogni folata gli aspetti della mia terra. Avrebbe dovuto riescir *madre* anche a me, [...] come riescí a tutti, al più povero, al piú sprovveduto [...] Ma il dolce declino di quei colli non arrivò a mitigare la straordinaria severità, il diniego oltraggioso, con cui ogni parvenza del mondo soleva rimirarmi. Ero dunque in colpa, se pure contro mia scienza. (ibid. 300–1)[5]

[I was alone: poorly dressed. And with the pause of each gust of wind [I admired] the features of my land. A land that should have been a *mother* also to me ... as it was with everyone else, to the most miserable, to the most incompetent ... But the sweet slope of those hills could not mitigate the extraordinary severity, the outrageous look of rejection, cast on me from all sides. I was therefore guilty, even if I had no reason to think so.]

The best way to understand Gadda's interest in psychoanalysis is no doubt through the autobiographical references in his work. In sharp contrast to his violent treatment of Fascism as a form of 'narcissistic' degeneration, his writings on narcissism display an unstrained and reflective progression of thought. The very title of the first essay on the subject, 'Emilio and Narciso,' suggests a deliberate choice on Gadda's part that implies a definite margin of ambiguity. (The name 'Emilio' clearly alludes to Rousseau, as is attested by a number of quotations from Rousseau's major works, but it could also refer to Gadda himself, 'Carlo Emilio.') In the distinction he draws between 'phagic egoism' and 'egotism' – the most significant *trouvaille* in the whole essay – one can perhaps find the outline of a latent contradiction between the ego's 'normal' development and its morally contemptible pathological involution. The text seems to allow for such an interpretation, with, however, a few reservations.[6]

In this regard, it is useful to read the beginning of 'L'egoista,' the latest and most mature attempt on Gadda's part to define these vague and uncertain notions. 'Egoista è colui che ignora o trascura la condizione di simbiosi, cioè di necessaria convivenza, di tutti gli esseri' (*VM*, 684) [An egoist is a person who ignores or overlooks the condition of symbiosis, that is, the necessary community of all human beings] – thus speaks the first partner in the dialogue, who is, significantly, named Teofilo (almost certainly a reference to Leibniz's Théophile, the person in the *Nouveaux essais* who represents Leibniz's ideas) and continues: 'L'egoista, [...] non ha letto, non ha meditato a sufficienza *la monadologia di Leibniz*' (655, emphasis mine) [The egoist ... did not read and did not meditate long enough on Leibniz's monadology].

The clear and quasi-ostentatious reference to Leibniz at the very beginning of the dialogue is proof of the absolute continuity in Gadda's culture and thinking over a period of thirty-five years. It is hardly worth mentioning a well-known sentence from the *Meditazione*: 'l'individuo umano p. e. Carlo, già limitatamente alla sua persona, non è in effetto ma un insieme di effetti' (*MM*, 649) [the human individual, say, Carlo, himself limited to his own person, is not one effect but a set of effects]; an example that we may compare to the following sentence from 'L'egoista': 'La nostra individualità è il punto di incontro, è il nodo o groppo di innumerevoli situazioni (fatti od esseri) a noi apparentemente esterne' (*VM*, 654) [Our individuality is the meeting-point, the tangle, or knot of innumerable situations (facts or beings) apparently external to us]. The connection between the two passages is evident, since the concordance is almost literal. At a distance of a few decades not only do we not find any development of Gadda's thinking on these matters, but we are made witness to the pure and simple repetition of a few points, themselves incapable of evolution (even the image of 'grumo o nucleo o groviglio di rapporti' [bubbles or nucleus or tangle of relationships] comes back almost identically in the 'nodo o groppo' [the tangle or knot]). On the other hand, in Gadda's definition of the origin of 'natural' egoism, one finds definite traces of Freudian readings that date to more recent times. While egoism

è un impulso istintivo, non riflesso [...] L'egotismo o narcisismo interessa invece la cosiddetta 'vita di relazione' [...] Il narcisista finisce per *vedere* unicamente se stesso. Dimentica l'obiettivo reale dell'amore per cadere innamorato dello specchio [...] A questa immagine il narcisista conferisce il piú idolatrato dei nomi: e questo nome è un pronome: Io. (660–2)

[is an instinctive not reflexive impulse ... Egotism or narcissism involves the so-called 'social life' ... The narcissist ends up *seeing* only himself. He forgets the true object of love in order to fall in love with the mirror ... To this image the narcissist gives the most idolatrous of all names: the pronoun 'I.']

This is how the attempt to contrast 'normal' egoism with 'narcissistic' egoism (that is, 'narcissic' egoism, as Gadda liked to say – a further sign of his having read Freud in French, cf *narcissique*) is settled in a perfectly coherent fashion through the criticism of 'the foulest of all pronouns.' The astonishing immobility of Gadda's reasoning is no doubt one of his characteristic features, but also one of the most important reasons for the intrinsic weakness of his essays. There is no development, no intellectual growth, from the *Meditazione* to his later writings, because he is at once inhibited and overwhelmed by the overpowering need to defend himself from a world he finds hostile and unbearable. In these pages, however, Gadda seems to touch on a fundamental truth. For the distinction between a natural process of formation of the ego and its possible pathological deviation seizes on, or at least points to, a true difficulty in Freud's thinking.

As we know, after originally distinguishing between sexual and self-preservative instincts, Freud was forced to revise his theory, because the very concept of narcissism implied a further distinction within the sexual instincts between objectual libido and narcissistic libido, according to their respective goals: attachment to either an external object or the ego. In other words, the old opposition between sexual and ego instincts (or self-preservation) lost most of its meaning after *On Narcissism: An Introduction*, a turning-point thanks to which even the instinct of self-preservation could be understood as self-love (narcissistic libido). Gadda thinks over carefully the later Freud (*Group Psychology and the Analysis of the Ego* in 1921 is explicitly linked to his paper on narcissism),[7] probably ignoring what happened during the complex and tormented prior years. This is why Gadda's reading sounds extremely out of step with the development of Freud's thinking. As we have noticed, Gadda places the instinct of self-preservation in the nucleus of the ego ('phagic egoism') – it is worth observing the reference to hunger, a primary need: an analogy with Freud, so much more difficult to account for, given the unlikelihood of Gadda's direct knowledge of the early texts in which Freud explains his theory of instincts. Nevertheless, thanks to his reading of the essays cited above, Gadda opposes 'natural' egoism to narcissism, understood in the most obvious and literal sense as love of one's own image. From here comes a somewhat paradoxical conclusion: while in Freud, after 1914, the ego instinct implies the 'narcissic' love of the ego, in Gadda, on the contrary, self-preservation does not go back to narcissism; instead, the latter, far from being at the origin of the ego, seems to be only a pathological deviation from it.

However, Gadda's obsession with the etymology of the word 'narcissism,' which obviously implies a mirror-like relationship,[8] touches on a difficult point in Freud's hypothesis regarding an initial state of human life that precedes the formation of the ego (so-called primary narcissism). This hypothesis, as we know, was presented for the first time in *On Narcissism: An Introduction* and was later included in the introductory lectures on psychoanalysis (1916–17) that are part of Gadda's library in

French translation. The existence of a primary, objectless phase of the ego is questionable – not to mention the other problems it raises – because the very word 'narcissism,' even according to the myth, implies self-reflection and the discovery of one's own image in the other.

When Gadda refers to a 'phase' or a 'narcissistic age,' he uses the French neologism in the sense of 'hypertrophy of the ego' (cf, the passage 'the narcissist ends up seeing only himself, etc.') that seems to correspond to what Freud calls secondary narcissism. A minimal but meaningful clue allows us to state that Gadda had not only bought but also read the introductory lectures. In 'L'egoista,' while discussing the myth of Narcissus, Gadda states that the Greeks

hanno inteso, con duemila anni di anticipo sul *Copernico della psicologia* [che] per il narcisista o egoista il ponte d'amore è interrotto. Il primo dei due pilasti è un io che non può congiungersi al tu. (*VM*, 662)

[understood two thousand years before the coming of the Copernicus of psychology [that] for the narcissist or egoist the bridge to love is blocked. The first of the two pillars is an I that cannot join a you.]

Freud as the 'Copernicus of psychology' is not the product of a typically Gaddian (middle-class and Milanese) rhetorical quip, but rather a direct reference to a well-known passage in *A General Introduction to Psychoanalysis* where Freud points out the causes for the opposition to his theories:

Humanity has in the course of time had to endure from the hands of science two great outrages upon its naïve self-love. The first was when it realized that our earth was not the center of the universe, but only a tiny speck in a world-system ... This is associated in our minds with the name of Copernicus ... The second is when biological research robbed man of his peculiar privilege of having been specially created, and relegated him to a descent from the animal world ... this transvaluation has been accomplished in our time upon the instigation of Charles Darwin, Wallace ... But man's craving for grandiosity is now suffering the third and most bitter blow from present day psychological research which is endeavoring to prove to the 'ego' of each one of us that he is not even master in his own house, but that he must remain content with the scraps of information about what is going on unconsciously in his own mind. (Freud 1974, 252)

The similarity is too striking to be considered accidental. Moreover, beyond such a correspondence, there is a subtler reason to take this well-known passage as Gadda's source. Freud considers his own scientific work as the last stage in a long and complex process of cultural emancipation from common prejudices that, as vestiges of infantile omnipotence, assign to man a prominent position within the universe. This theme shows not only an unquestionable affinity with the problem of narcissism, but it is also part of the young Gadda's thinking (take, for instance, his cold and impassive criticism of anthropocentrism included in the appendix to the first book of Spinoza's *Ethics*, one of the writer's most studied philosophical works).

The results of our archival explorations, along with the modest choice of sample texts presented, describe in some depth the limits of Gadda's psychoanalytical knowledge. A certain margin of doubt remains, not so much about his handling of the sources as about the time-frame of his readings which, as has been shown, cover a long period of time from 1930 to 1940. If we go beyond what is required by protocol towards a brief and provisional attempt at interpretation, our conclusions may reach the same degree of certainty.

The decade we discussed coincides more or less with Gadda's great creative season, which includes *La cognizione del dolore* and *L'Adalgisa*, along with other writings, some definitely minor (*Eros e Priapo*), some more significant or at least interesting (*Il primo libro delle favole*; a few chapters in *Le meraviglie d'Italia, Gli anni*). With the exception of *Eros e Priapo*, the presence of psychoanalysis in Gadda's works is relatively modest. In his major fiction, the Freudian matrix of autobiographical allusions is much more conspicuous than are references to particular psychoanalytical notions. As Contini recently remarked: 'Gadda does nothing but talk about his neurosis, especially in *La cognizione del dolore*. He takes advantage of its cultural equivalent, psychoanalysis (which, on account of being so popularized, had lost its therapeutic credibility), representing it with a maximum of caricature ... in *Eros e Priapo*' (Contini 1987, 3).[9] Contini's opinion is to be accepted in every particular, but with a useful postscript. Gadda's Freudian culture was, in fact, certainly more substantial than we thought. This is another very original aspect of his work which makes him stand out among his mainstream contemporaries. But what is the significance of this originality? If compared to many other writers of his time, who were also fine essayists, Gadda is to be considered a latecomer. His uncommon cultural background, in many respects still late nineteenth century, provided him with a path to psychoanalysis that was still impracticable to most intellectuals of his generation. They could not help being excessively suspicious of this new psychology that was so openly a part of the 'materialism' which shaped the era of positivism, and which, at the same time, could be accused of being 'petty bourgeois.' To use a simplistic formula, we could say that one of the reasons for Gadda's interest in Freud is to be found in his own positivism.[10] A rigorously deterministic psychological theory (although its popularized image is often unsatisfactory) could be made to conform easily with the Spinoza Gadda had studied as a young man.

Of the new psychological theory contained in *Group Psychology and the Analysis of the Ego*, Gadda shares only Freud's dynamic conception of the psyche and the restricted limits he attributes to the activity of the ego. His reading exhibits both misunderstandings and some acute observations, perhaps unintentional, both based on a faulty knowledge of Freud's thought. Gadda is almost completely deaf to Freud's most 'scandalous' position regarding the Oedipus complex, the only part of psychoanalytical theory that circulated in Italy. (Saba and Svevo are to be singled out as exceptions to this rule, and also the literary critic Giacomo Debenedetti, whose presence in Italian culture was exceptional for that time.) Gadda's essays on narcissism not only attest to his lack of development since the *Meditazione*, but above all demonstrate that a huge gap separates his refined, constantly revised, creative works from his inability to expand and refine his ideas. Under the illusion that he could find a conceptually less fragile frame for his old, irrepressible hatred of identity, Gadda annexes Freud to the philosophical notepad of his youth (Pascal's *moi haïssable* sometimes seems to be a remote but indispensable reference for Gadda's invectives against the pronoun 'I').

Without reading too much into Gadda's thinking on narcissism, I believe it more than legitimate to give it a particularly symptomatic value. His unyielding and obstinate denunciation of the moral evils caused by egotism appears at first sight to contradict his extreme and ever-present *autobiografismo*, while, in fact, it is only a complementary aspect of it. His reflection on the ego is disappointing. Although poor in argumentative flexibility and inhibited by neurotic self-defence mechanisms, it carries a definite weight if placed next to his major writings. It throws new light not only on Gadda's cultural background, but above all on his innermost divided self. As everyone knows, another 'character' lives inside the genial, sometimes exceptional author: one exasperating in his attachment to the most banal commonplaces of his time and an inventor of out-dated and infirm narrative mechanisms (for example, *Racconto italiano*). It is not hard to recognize in these two personalities a poor relation of Milan's upper middle class. Gadda becomes a compulsive conformist not so much because of his city's merciless efficiency, but rather because of his lack of financial independence, which led him to undertake tough professional duties, often abroad. Gadda's reading of Freud is somehow the rationalization of this trauma. He uses psychoanalysis as a means of rejecting the Oedipus complex, and as a strong condemnation of egotism. In the first instance, family censorship plays an important role, while in the second lurks the envy he feels towards those, more fortunate in their social life, whose narcissistic desire for recognition is a stimulus to 'success.' Have we not here a Freud read and interpreted in an 'engineer-like' fashion, an undeniably petty-bourgeois Freud? We do, no doubt. But Gadda's Freud is also a definite contribution, albeit not of primary importance, to the understanding of a writer whose cultural interests and exceptional intelligence gave rise to narrative multilingualism rather than to deep and objective self-analysis.[11]

Translated by Manuela Bertone

Notes

1 Cf. Antonio Calzolari 1985, 136, 144–7. Often, however, the author's remarks on the relationship between Gadda and psychoanalysis are wrong or incomplete.

2 It is known that Freud means to indicate by the first term a psychic investment, by the second, an investment directed towards an external object.

3 I am obviously referring to Gonzalo's well-known monologue in *La cognizione del dolore* (chapter 3, Part One). I think it is useful to point out that, in these admirable pages, the words addressed to the doctor are intended for the protagonist himself. His intolerance of the ego-libido turns into a truly narcissistic fixation on the ego. A brief quotation will be sufficient: 'Io non ho mai avuto bisogno di nessuno!...io, piú i dottori stanno alla larga, e meglio mi sento.... Io mi riguardo da me, che sono sicuro di non sbagliare.... Io, io, io! E di nuovo si lasciava prendere da un'idea, e levò la voce, rabbiosamente: – Ah! il mondo delle idee! che bel mondo!... Ah! io, io [...] Il piú lurido di tutti i pronomi' (*CD*, 635) [I've never needed anyone! The farther away the doctors stay from me, the better I feel. I can take care of myself; that way I'm sure not to make mistakes – I, I, I! And again he allowed himself to be seized by an idea, and he raised his voice angrily: 'Ah! the world of ideas! what a fine world! Ah! This I, is [...] the foulest of all pronouns (*AG*, 86)].

4 Gadda does not use the word 'sublimation' in a wholly Freudian way.
Although in Freud the word has a fluctuating and sometimes vague meaning, the main feature of the process termed 'sublimation' lies in the substitu-
tion of originally sexual objectives with others not directly related to sexuality, and (as far as the 1916–17 lectures are concerned) also in the choice of an
object that is judged according to socially higher standards. Gadda uses the
word in the latter sense that evokes spontaneously the notion of moral and
artistic elevation.

5 In this particular case, one could argue that the use of 'mother' in reference
to the land is one of the most obvious of commonplaces and that it should
therefore be considered free from all psychoanalytical connotations. Such an
assumption is definitely plausible in abstract terms. However, the context
provides a clear allusion to the parental relationship (the 'extraordinary
severity,' the 'outrageous denial'). After all, even a superficial reading of *La
cognizione del dolore* would suffice to support my hypothesis. It is important
to recall that one of the unpublished fragments included in the new version
of the novel edited by Emilio Manzotti (Turin: Einaudi 1987) is centred on
the topic of 'maternal sadism': it is significantly called 'Cui non risere
parentes' ['Him on Whom His Parents Have Not Smiled'] (525–35), which
attests to the genuinely autobiographical and obsessive character of the
quotation from Virgil.

6 My reservations concern the distinction Gadda makes between the instinct
of self-preservation (connected to the child's primary need to satisfy 'hunger') and the egotism connected to social life 'il cui supremo scopo e termine
[...] è, in natura, la funzione del sesso, garante della perpetuazione della
specie' (*VM*, 660) [whose main objective and ultimate end ... is, in nature,
sexual reproduction, which grants the preservation of the species]. It is
interesting to compare this passage to a passage included in the twenty-sixth
lecture, 'The Theory of the Libido: Narcissism,' in *A General Introduction to
Psychoanalysis* (Freud 1974, 357–73): 'How is the concept "narcissism"
distinguished from "egoism"? In my opinion, narcissism is the libidinal
complement of egoism. When one speaks of egoism one is thinking of *interests* of the person concerned, narcissism relates to the satisfaction of his
libidinal needs' (361). The comparison clearly shows – putting aside the
obvious and fundamental differences in their style and narration – that for
Freud narcissism implies egoism, not vice versa (since the distinction is
based on the relationship to external objects). For Gadda, however, the
difference between the two notions involves the desire to possess, on the
one hand, and contemplation and identification on the other. This last factor
brings us close to Freud's so-called 'secondary narcissism,' except for one

important detail: according to Freud, narcissism is not only a regressive state, but above all a permanent structure of the ego (in other words, it is part of a 'normality' Gadda is not willing to admit). There is also a small 'philological' query that will be hard to solve. In 'Emilio e Narciso,' Gadda seems to refer clearly to Havelock Ellis as creator of the neologism: 'Ma lo stendhaliano "egotismo," il senso centrico e un tantinello esibito della propria personalità, lui, lo *psicologo inglese*, ne perfezionò il contorno e cavò fuora il nome guisto: che fu "narcisismo." E varò del pari gli aggettivi "narcisistico" o *"narcissico,"* e naturalmente il sostantivo *"narcisista"* (*VM*, 642; emphasis mine) [But Stendhal's "egotism," the eccentric and somewhat exhibited sense of one's own person, was perfected by *the English psychologist* and from its profile he drew the right name: "narcissism." And he also inaugurated *"narcissistic"* and *"narcissic,"* and obviously the noun *"narcissist"*]. Gadda probably got to know Havelock Ellis through Freud who, in his paper *On Narcissism* (a text Gadda almost certainly ignored) stated that Paul Näche had introduced the word. In the introductory lessons on psychoanalysis, which Gadda knew, there is no mention of the origin of the word both in psychiatry and in psychology. Only in a footnote added in 1920 [*sic*. The footnote was added in 1915] in *Three Essays on the Theory of Sexuality*, Freud retracts his own statement, admitting that Havelock Ellis used the word for the first time. We should therefore infer that Gadda found this information in this latter work. However, it is no longer part of his library. One last hypothesis (hardly credible, although impeccable in the abstract): there could be a different source.

7 Towards the end of *On Narcissism: An Introduction*, Freud says: 'The ego ideal opens up an important avenue for the understanding of group psychology. In addition to its individual side, this ideal has a social side; it is also the common ideal of a family, a class or a nation' (101). Chapter VI of *Group Psychology and the Analysis of the Ego*, in which Freud attempts to explain the formation of groups on the basis of the theoretical foundations of psychoanalysis, is explicitly connected to his work on narcissism.

8 The mirror relationship is by far the part of Freud's theory that captures most of Gadda's interest. Consider for example: 'nel prossimo, negli occhi delle belle, nel saluto allegro dei commilitoni, nella parlata grave e nell'arcano verdetto dei sofi, egli [il narcisista] intende avere uno specchio, *e soltanto uno specchio*, dal quale esige l'approvazione, la richiesta d'amore ...' (*VM*, 662; my emphasis) [In his fellow men, in the eyes of the gals, in the cheerful greeting of his comrades-in-arms, in the momentous word and in the enigmatic verdict of the sophist, he [the narcissist] means to find a mirror, *and a mirror only*, to call for his approval, for his demands of love ...].

This passage is repeated almost identically in note 12 in 'Navi approdano al Parapagal,' one of two parts of *La cognizione del dolore* included in *L'Adalgisa*: 'perocché la straripante carica erotica del loro narcisismo ovvero auto-erotismo ella necessita di una adeguata parete di rimbalzo cioè superficie di riflessione: di uno specchio grande, in poche parole. Gli umani funzionano per loro da specchio psichico ...' (*A*, 439). [However, the uninhibited erotic power of their narcissism, or auto-eroticism, necessitates a suitable surface to bounce off, that is, a means of reflecting, in a word, a huge mirror. People are the narcissists' psychic mirror ...].

9 As to autobiographical materials that include Freudian references, let us mention the short story 'Una tigre nel parco.' In it, childhood memories are interrupted by direct references to such psychoanalytical terminology as 'super-ego,' 'narcissic disillusionment,' 'sublimation,' and so on. These are the Freudian terms which occur most frequently in the pages from Gadda's writings considered above.

10 A file on 'Gadda and Positivism' would be almost endless. It is for the most part still to be set up. I would just like to recall a passage of Gadda's conversation with Cesare Garboli: 'Ero portato alla speculazione, ma i libri di filosofia che leggevo non erano molti. Avevo come professore, per la filosofia, *un positivista*. Si chiamava Tedeschi. Dalla sua bocca non c'era mai caso che uscisse un riferimento ai valori dello spirito, alla realtà dello spirito, e simili' (Garboli 1969, 160; my emphasis) [I had a talent for speculation, but I did not read many books on philosophy. My philosophy professor was *a positivist*. His name was Tedeschi. Never once did his mouth utter a reference to spiritual values, to spiritual realities, and the like]. The passage shows some peculiar similarities with other statements by Gadda that are part of a 1963 interview with Alberto Arbasino: 'Avevo già frequentato a Milano [...] i precursori; appunto Charcot, Breuer [...] molti altri [...] a anche gli psicologi positivisti; ricordo *L'intelligenza del regno animale* di Tito Vignoli, psicologo lombardo [...] . A proposito di psicoanalisi, devo dire che mi sono avvicinato ad essa negli anni dal '26 al '40' (Arbasino 1970) [In Milan, I was already acquainted with ... Freud's forerunners – Charcot, Breuer, many others, and also with positivist psychology. I remember *The Intelligence of the Animal Kingdom* by Tito Vignoli, a Lombard psychologist ... As regards psychoanalysis, I must say that I became acquainted with it in the years 1926 to 1940]. Gadda's statement is important for at least two reasons: first, it shows a progress in his readings which, by the way, does not correspond entirely to the dates I extrapolated on the basis of the French translations, but it is close enough to them. Secondly, the name of Tito Vignoli (almost forgotten today) recalls a Tuscan scholar, here defined as a 'Lombard

psychologist,' who was on the editorial staff of the second *Politecnico, Rivista di scienze biologiche*, and the *Rivista di filosofia scientifica*. The quotation is significant: Gadda is referring to a work entitled *Della legge fondamentale dell'intelligenza nel regno animale* (Milan: Dumolard 1877). Another of Vignoli's books, *Mito e scienza* (Milan: Dumolard 1879), caught the attention of an exceptional reader, Aby Warburg. Part of a chapter of this work was recently reprinted in the review *Aut aut* nos 199–200 (Jan.–Apr. 1984): 136–67.

11 This essay was first published as a chapter entitled 'Gadda lettore di Freud' in Guido Lucchini's *L'istinto della combinazione. Le origini del romanzo in Carlo Emilio Gadda* (Florence: La Nuova Italia 1988). It appears here slightly abridged.

References

Arbasino, Alberto. 1970. In *Sessanta posizioni*. Milan: Feltrinelli

Calzolari, Antonio. 1985. 'Gadda filosofo.' *Poliorama* 4

Contini, Gianfranco. 1987. 'Lo strano ingegner Gadda.' *Corriere della Sera* (16 May)

Freud, Sigmund. 1959. *Group Psychology and the Analysis of the Ego*. Translated by James Strachey. New York and London: Norton

– 1974. *A General Introduction to Psychoanalysis*. Translated by Joan Riviere. New York: Liveright

– 1979. *Three Essays on the Theory of Sexuality*. In *On Sexuality*. London: Penguin

– 1991. *On Narcissism: An Introduction*. Edited by Joseph Sandler, Ethel Spector, and Reter Fonagy. New Haven: Yale University Press

Garboli, Cesare. 1969. 'Felice chi è diverso.' In *La stanza separata*. Milan: Mondadori

Roscioni, Gian Carlo. 1975. *La disarmonia prestabilita*. Turin: Einaudi

Virgil. 1986 [1916]. *Eclogues*. Cambridge, Mass.: Harvard University Press, The Loeb Classical Library

Carlo Emilio Gadda and Louis-Ferdinand Céline: Some Considerations on the Novel in Progress

WLADIMIR KRYSINSKI

Nous expérimentons nous-mêmes une multitude dans la substance simple, lorsque nous trouvons que la moindre pensée dont nous nous apercevons, enveloppe une variété dans l'objet.

— Leibniz, *La Monadologie*

La realtà sembra una città e la città è fatta di case; e la casa è fatta di muri: e il muro è fatto di mattoni; e il mattone è fatto di granuli. E il granulo è in sé, è nel mattone, è nel muro, è nella casa, è nella città. Quanto a una gerarchia di significati, l'elaborazione d'un Etica può soltanto occuparsene. Qui ci basta l'aver proposto all'attenzione che il reale si sviluppa per sistemi aventi molteplici significati, secondo il grado di coinvoluzione in cui essi immergono sé medesimi. Se si coinvolgono, per così dire, nel lor solo e proprio mantello non sono ciò che sono quando esprimono una più vasta ragione, coinvolti in mantelli sempre più lati. Granulo.... mattone.... muro....casa.

— Carlo Emilio Gadda, *Meditazione milanese*

... mon truc à moi, c'est l'émotif! le style 'rendu émotif' vaut-il? fonctionne-t-il?... je dis : oui!... cent écrivains l'ont copié, le copient, le trafiquent, démarquent, maquillent, goupillent!... tant et si bien, qu'à force... qu'à force!... mon truc passera bientôt 'chromo'!...
— Moi c'est autre chose!... moi, je suis autrement plus brutal!... moi, je capture toute l'émotion!... toute l'émotion dans la surface! d'un seul coup!... je décide!... je la fourre dans le métro!... mon métro!... tous les autres écrivains sont morts!... et ils s'en doutent pas!... ils pourrissent à la surface, enbandelés dans leurs chromos! momies!... momies tous!... privés d'émotion! leur compte est bon...

— L.-F. Céline, *Entretiens avec le Professeur Y*

What is the assumption underlying a comparison of Céline and Gadda? What are actually the terms of comparison between these two writers? Do their novels and critical observations, their theories and respective narrative practices converge? To what extent can we say that their writing transforms the genre in a similar way?

In attempting to answer these questions, we shall proceed on the assumption that both writers have indeed succeeded in significantly restructuring the novel. In so doing, they follow the way of Joyce, in that, like him, they believe that the mythopoetic, constructive properties of language are the novel's dominant characteristics. Like Joyce, Gadda and Céline perform a significant revision of the novel's structures: their works are founded on the syncretic mixture of such elements as slang, dialect, philosophy (Gadda), and poetry. They both structure their prose by maximizing the tensions inherent in it in such a way that feeling and emotion determine the design their sentences take: either becoming lengthy, marked by enumeration and commentary, as in Gadda, or comprising dissected and fragmented exclamations, most often ending in ellipses, as in Céline.

In *Quer pasticciaccio brutto de via Merulana*, here is the description Gadda gives of Liliana Balducci's corpse:

Il corpo della povera signora giaceva in una posizione infame, supino, con la gonna di lana grigia e una sottogonna bianca buttate all'indietro, fin quasi al petto: come se qualcuno avesse voluto scoprire il candore affascinante di quel dessous, o indagarne lo stato di nettezza. Aveva mutande bianche, di maglia a punto gentile, sottilissimo, che terminavano a metà coscia in una delicata orlatura. Tra l'orlatura e le calze, ch'erano in una lieve luce di seta, denudò se stessa la bianchezza estrema della carne, d'un pallore da clorosi: quelle due cosce un po' aperte, che I due elastici – in un tono di lilla – parevano distinguere in grado, avevano perduto il loro tepido senso, già si adeguavano al gelo: al gelo del sarcofago, e delle taciturne dimore. (*QP*, 58)

[The body of the poor signora was lying in an infamous position, supine, the gray wool skirt and a white petticoat thrown back, almost to her breast: as if someone had wanted to uncover the fascinating whiteness of that dessous, or inquire into its state of cleanliness. She was wearing white underpants, of elegant jersey, very fine, which ended halfway down the thighs with a delicate edging. Between the edging and the stockings, which were a light-shaded silk, the extreme whiteness of the flesh lay naked, of a chlorotic pallor: those two thighs, slightly parted, on which the garters – a lilac hue – seemed to confer a distinction of rank, had lost their tepid sense, were already becoming used to the chill: to the chill of the sarcophagus and of man's taciturn, final abode. (*AM*, 67–8)]

Céline in *Mort à crédit*, a novel full of curious figures who exemplify mankind's degenerate condition, represents his 'secretary,' 'Madame Vitruve,' in the following way :

Mon tourment à moi c'est le sommeil. Si j'avais bien dormi toujours j'aurais jamais écrit une ligne. 'Tu pourrais, c'était l'opinion à Gustin, raconter des choses agréables... de temps en temps... C'est pas toujours sale dans la vie...' Dans un sens c'est assez exact. Y a de la manie dans mon cas, de la partialité. La preuve c'est qu'à l'époque où je bourdonnais des deux oreilles et encore bien plus qu'à présent, que j'avais des fièvres toutes les heures, j'étais bien moins mélancolique... Je trafiquais de très beaux rêves... Madame Vitruve, ma secrétaire, elle m'en faisait aussi la remarque. Elle connaissait bien mes tourments. Quand on est si généreux on éparpille ses trésors, on les perd de vue... Je me suis dit alors: 'La garce de Vitruve, c'est elle qui les a planqués quelque part...' Des véritables merveilles... des bouts de légende... de la pure extase... C'est dans ce rayon-là que je vais me lancer désormais... Pour être plus sûr je trifouille le fond de mes papiers... Je ne retrouve rien... je téléphone à Delumelle mon placeur; je veux m'en faire un mortel ennemi... Je veux qu'il râle sous les injures... Il en faut pour le cailler!... Il s'en fout! Il a des millions. Il me répond de prendre des vacances... Elle arrive enfin, ma Vitruve. Je me méfie d'elle. J'ai des raisons fort sérieuses. Où que tu l'as mise ma belle oeuvre? que je t'attaque comme ça de but en blanc. J'en avais au moins des centaines des raisons pour la suspecter... (Céline 1952, 18-19)

[My trouble is insomnia. If I had always slept properly, I'd never have written a line. 'You could talk about something pleasant now and then.' That was Gustin's opinion. 'Life isn't always disgusting.' In a way he's right.With me it's a kind of mania, a bias. The fact is that in the days when I had that buzzing in both ears, even worse than now, and attacks of fever all day long, I wasn't half so gloomy ... I had lovely dreams ... Madame Vitruve, my secretary, was talking about it only the other day. She knew how I tormented myself. When a man's so generous, he squanders his treasures, loses sight of them. I said to myself: 'That damn Vitruve, she's hidden them some place ...' Real marvels they were ... bits of Legend, pure delight ... That's the kind of stuff I'm going to write from now on ... To make sure they're as good as I think, I rummage through my papers. I can't find a thing ... I call Delumelle, my agent; I want to make him hate me ... to make him groan under my insults. But he's not so easily fazed. It's all one to him, he's loaded. All he says is that I need a vacation ... Finally Vitruve comes in. I don't trust her. I have my reasons. I light into her, point blank: where did you put my masterpiece? I had several hundred reasons for suspecting her ... (Céline 1966, 19–20)]

What is striking in these fragments is no doubt Gadda's analytical drive, which is invested with ambiguity, and Céline's injurious, exclamatory, and picaresque diction. They both transform the Joycean paradigm of a discourse rife with epiphanies into a metanarrative form. In them, the production of meaning draws on the tension that obtains between the narrator's affective subjectivity and the intensity of stylistic expression. In a way, the Joycean aesthetic elements of *claritas, consonantia,* and *integritas* are still functional in both cases, but the narrators' subjective and analytical attitudes shift the focus from the object in itself to place it in the 'eye of the beholder.'

The transformation of the novel is therefore achieved at the levels of style, language, and structure. Equipped with Rabelaisian satirical, stylistic, and macaronically minded verve, as well as with Cervantes' perspectivistic irony, Céline and Gadda are probably the best examples we have of the synthetic novel of modernity in its passage from traditional novelistic discourse to a twentieth-century polyphony that displays an intensity of various stylistic and semantic registers.

In reshaping the language of the novel, Gadda and Céline have given a new status to the relationship between narration, the world, and discourse. Drawing on Benoit Mandelbrot's 'new geometry of nature,' one can describe, by analogy, their sentences as 'fractal,' that is, as 'curved' shapes, 'disconnected "dusts,"' 'or 'oddly shaped' structures (Mandelbrot 1977, 1).[1] In this sense, meaning does not consist only in the cumulative sequence of narrative information, but also in the disconnected or 'oddly shaped' structures. Viewed analogically, sentences in Gadda and Céline contain rhizomatic information. Their fragmented nature attests to their polysemic character. To illustrate, let us take two other examples.

In an important dialogue of *La cognizione del dolore,* Gonzalo confesses to his physician:

'....Sono stato un bimbo anch'io....', disse il figlio. '....Allora forse valevo un pensiero buono....una carezza no; era troppo condiscendere....era troppo!' e l'ira gli tornava nel volto, ma si spense. Poi riprese: '....La mamma è spaventosamente invecchiata....è malata....forse sono stato io.... Non so darmi pace.... Ma ho avuto un sogno spaventoso....'

'Un sogno?.... e che le fa un sogno?.... È uno smarrimento dell'anima....il fantasma di un momento....'

'Non so, dottore: badi....forse è dimenticare, è risolversi! È rifiutare le sclerotiche figurazioni della dialettica, le cose vedute secondo forza....'

'Secondo forza?...che forza?....'

'La forza sistematrice del carattere....questa gloriosa lampada a petrolio che ci fuma di dentro,...e fa il filo, e ci fa neri di bugìe, di dentro,...di bugìe meritorie, grasse, bugiardosissime....e ha la buona opinione per sé, per sé sola.... Ma sognare è fiume profondo, che precipita a una lontana sorgiva, ripullula nel mattino di verità,' (*CD*, 632)

['I was a child myself,' the son said.'Then I deserved perhaps a kindly thought ... no, not a caress, that was condescending too far, it was too much!' And wrath returned to his face, but died away again. Then he resumed', Mama has aged frightfully ... she's ill ... perhaps it was I ... I can't resign myself. But I had a frightful dream.'

'A dream? And what harm does a dream do you? It's a bewilderment of the soul ... a momentary ghost.'

'I don't know, Doctor. Mind you ... perhaps it's forgetting, it's resolving! It's rejecting the sclerotic images of dialectics, the things seen according to force.'

'According to force? What force?'

'The organizing force of character ... this glorious kerosene lamp that smokes us up from inside ... and makes a black wisp, and smudges us with lies, within ... meritorious lies, greasy ones, lying ones ... and has a good opinion of itself, and of itself alone. But to dream is a deep river, which rushes to a distant spring, bubbling up again in the morning of truth. (*AG*, 80–1)]

And in *D'un chateau l'autre*, Céline describes Copenhagen as follows:

Que c'est tout si perfectionné, si mirobolo-sanitaire, Copenhague Danemark, que c'est à se foutre le cul en mille... croyez pas un mot!... la condition du monde entier!... c'est-à-dire... c'est-à-dire: les femmes de ménage qui font tout!... responsables de tout et partout! dans les ministères, dans les restaurants, dans les partis politiques, dans les hôpitaux! les femmes de ménage qui ont le mot!... vous retournent le dossier, un article, un secret d'Etat, comme un agonique!... le monde dort... jamais la femme de ménage!... termites! termites!... le matin vous trouvez plus rien! votre agonique est en boîte!... Yorick! pas d'alas!... s'ils peuvent hurler...! s'ils peuvent attendre! morphine!... sondages! là! là!... moi qu'étais le 'vigilant' de service!... le samaritain à la sonnette!... le dernier soupir? *glinn! glinn!* envoyez! un de moins!... l'Erna... l'Ingrid... m'arrivaient... bâillantes... roulaient le mec hors... je dis, je parle pas du tout en l'air... Sonbye Hospital, chef de service... Professeur Gram... fin clinicien!... subtil, sensible... oh, il m'a jamais dit un mot!... on ne parle pas aux prisonniers!... j'étais moi aussi, en traitement... je partais moi aussi en lambeaux... pas du cancer! pas de cancer encore!... seulement de l'effet de la fosse, la cage, Vesterfangsel... (Céline 1957, 140–1)

[Everything is supposed to be so perfected, so amazingly hallucino-sanitary in Copenhagen, Denmark, enough to hit your head against the wall ... don't believe a word of it! ... it's just like any place else ... I mean, it's the cleaning women who do everything and run everything ... in the ministries, the restaurants, the political parties, the hospitals! it's the cleaning women who have the say ... they're the ones who sweep away records, laws, state secrets, and the dying ... the world sleeps ... not the cleaning women ... termites! ... termites! in the morning you don't find a thing ... your moribund friend is packed away ... Yorick, and no alas! ... let them scream! let them wait! ... morphine ... injections ... to hell with that ... I was the 'watcher' on duty ... the Samaritan with the bell ... The last sigh? tinkle! tinkle! Ship him out! one the less! ... Erna ... Ingrid ... came in yawning ... rolled the guy out ... I know what I'm saying, I'm making it up ... Sonbye Hospital; department head, Professor Gram ... excellent clinician ... subtle, sensitive ... oh, he never said a word to me ... you don't talk to prisoners ... I was undergoing treatment, too ... I was falling apart ... not from cancer, not yet ... only from the effects of the hole, the cage, Vesterfangsel ... (Céline 1968, 113–14)]

In the first passage, the discourse is structured as a rapid flux of associations, while in the second, we have a pulsating monologue whose target is virtually everything to which the narrator's angry psyche reacts. In Céline, the flux of information is discontinuous and, from the outset, highly disconnected, the result being an obsessive system of information involving the narrator's unconscious feelings as well as the conscious attitude of his mind. In this analytical and playful rewriting of the novel, the relationship between narration, the world, and discourse draws entirely on the subjectivity of the narrator.

Céline and Gadda bring about their revolution in the novel form by highlighting the emotional aspect of perception and information. In so doing, they revise the novel's codes and conventions to enable us to grasp the novel as process and thus as open-ended in the 'fractal' sense of the term. Yet at the same time they adhere to such conventional structures as narrative continuity and cohesion. What is specific about these texts is that their newly expressionistic prose covers the entire space of the narrative. The effect of their writing is cognitive: it draws the reader's attention to the irregular line of a narrative whose status is constantly being redefined.

In Céline and Gadda, style, language, speech, and discourse re-enact a complex mimesis of the world and its referents, which has the effect of relativizing the theories on the novel developed since the 1920s. The work of such theorists as Lukács and Bakhtin fails to account for the innovations in the novel form brought about by Belyi, Joyce, Musil, Broch, and, more recently, by Julio Cortázar, Augusto Roa Bastos, Reinaldo Arenas, Eduardo Galeano, and Thomas Pynchon. Instead of trying to identify what in a given novel is 'dialogical,' 'polyphonic,' 'carnavalesque,' 'monological,' 'homophonic,' and which character represents a 'demoni-acal hero' in a society of downgraded values, one has rather to come to grips with the text itself, which in addition to harbouring the narrator's voice, displays a differential surface of words, sentences, images, metaphors, and changing rhythms. The differential surface of the text gives us an open perspective on the novel, regulated by the constant tension between narration, representation, and sentence: a tension that will never be completely resolved, since it is rooted in ambiguity and instability. The novel evolves through the signs that produce its meaning. And in the process of producing meaning, its language is constantly fluctuating between prose and poetry, on the one hand, and narration and representation, on the other.

Gadda and Céline belong to a literary family which in modern times boasts such writers as Sterne, Diderot, Carlyle, Dostoevsky, and, in our century, Belyi, Joyce, Broch, and Beckett. Their common traits include the dominant position of the narrator, strong digressive tendencies, self-irony, and epiphany. It has often been said of Gadda that the 'pre-established disharmony' of his worldview is identical to his discursive practice. That is to say, it reveals basic human entanglement. In Gadda's vocabulary of concepts, 'groviglio' expresses the idea of a chaotic universe. To account for the 'groviglio,' the narrator commits himself to a baroque manner of expression that incorporates the tension between order and systematization, on the one hand, and chaos and flux, on the other. For Gadda, sentences are pauses in the flow of cognition ('Le frasi nostre, le nostre parole, sono dei momenti-pause [dei pianerottoli di sosta] d'una fluenza [o d'una ascensione] conoscitiva-espressiva' [VM, 437]); they systematize and at the same time show the fault lines of the structure they have produced.

Céline, on his part, collapses the problem of sentences into the question of style. For him, the style of French literature is too conventional and conservative. It is the 'pupil's style,' ('le style du bachot'), the 'conventional style' ('le style admis'), the 'style of the everyday newspaper,' the 'style of licence' ('le style de la licence'). His purpose is to effect a stylistic revolution in literary French, openly attacking the sentence 'bien filée' of Voltaire, Bourget, and Anatole France. Céline explains his way of producing sentences thus:

Je reviens à ce style. Ce style, il est fait d'une certaine façon de forcer les phrases à sortir légèrement de leur signification habituelle, de les sortir des gonds pour ainsi dire, les déplacer, et forcer ainsi le lecteur à lui-même déplacer son sens. Mais très légèrement! Parce que tout ça, si vous faites lourd, n'est-ce pas, c'est une gaffe, c'est la gaffe. Ça demande donc énormément de recul, de sensibilité; c'est très difficile à faire, parce qu'il faut tourner autour. Autour de quoi? Autour de l'émotion. (Céline 1987, 66–7)

[I come back to this style. This style is made out of a certain technique of forcing the sentences to go slightly beyond their usual meaning, of putting them, so to speak, out of joint, displacing them and forcing the reader to displace the meaning. But very little! Because if you do it too heavily, it will be a blunder, it will be *the* blunder. It therefore requires an enormous distance, a lot of sensitivity; it is very difficult to do, since you have to turn around. Around what? Around the emotion.]

Characteristically enough, Gadda, as though he were echoing Céline, dedicates one of his philosophical reflections in *Meditazione milanese* to feeling ('sentimento'), observing:

In realtà il sentimento opera spontaneamente sintesi più vaste fra essere e divenire – che non siano le sintesi essere-divenire che la ragione opera per schemi e astrazioni, rivolgendosi a temi determinati. (*MM*, 798)

[In fact, the feeling achieves spontaneously broader syntheses between being and becoming – they are not the syntheses of being-becoming which are made by the reason by way of schemes and abstractions, addressing some determinated themes.]

In Gadda and Céline, emotions and feelings are sentence regulators which produce a 'spasmodic' effect. Representation amounts to presenting the real as deformed (that is, known) through the emotional vibrations of the subject. For Céline the narrator must:

descendre dans l'intimité des choses, dans la fibre, le nerf, l'émotion des choses, la viande, et aller droit au but, à son but, dans l'intimité, en tension poétique, constante, en vie interne, comme le 'métro' en *ville interne* droit au but, une fois le choix fait, il faut rester dans la même conviction, dans la tension intime, une fois pour toutes, dans l'intimité de la vie, tenir ainsi l'histoire. (cited from Merlin 1979, 81) [descend into the intimacy of things, into the fibre, the nerve, the feeling of things, the flesh, and going straight on to the end, to its end, in intimacy, in maintained poetic tension, in inner life, like the *métro*, through the *inner city* straight to the end, once the choice is made, it's essential to stay in the same conviction, in the same intimate tension, once and for all, in the intimacy of life, to seize the story in this fashion. (Merlin's translation, ibid., 81)]

The self-awareness shown by Gadda in his dealings with reality is quite similar. Acting on the assumption that the 'grotesque' and the 'baroque' are internal to both nature and history, he declares:

La sceverazione degli accadimenti del mondo e della società in parvenze o simboli spettacolari, muffe della storia biologica e della relativa componente estetica, e in moventi e sentimenti profondi, veridici della realtà spirituale, questa cérnita è metodo caratterizzante la rappresentazione che l'autore ama dare della società: i simboli spettacolari muovono per lo più il referto a una programmata derisione, che in certe pagine raggiunge tonalità parossistica e aspetto deforme: lo muovano alla polemica, alla beffa, al grottesco, al 'barocco': alla insofferenza, all'apparente crudeltà, a un indugio 'misantropico' del pensiero. Ma il barocco e il grottesco albergano già nelle cose, nelle singole trovate di una fenomenologia a noi esterna: nelle stesse espressioni del costume, nella nozione accettata 'comunemente' dai pochi o dai molti: e nelle lettere, umane o disumane che siano: grottesco e barocco non ascrivibili a una premeditata volontà o tendenza espressiva dell'autore, ma legati alla natura e alla storia: la grinta dello smargiasso, ancorché trombato, o il verso 'che più superba altezza' non ponno addebitarsi a volontà prava e 'baroccheggiante' dell'autore, sì reale e storica bambolaggine di secondi o di terzi, del loro contegno, o dei loro settenarî: talché il grido-parola d'ordine 'barocco è il G.!' potrebbe commutarsi nel più ragionevole e più pacato asserto 'barocco è il mondo, e il G. ne ha percepito e ritratto la baroccaggine.' (*CD*, 759–60)

[Sorting out the events of the world and society into appearances or magnificent symbols, the mold of biological history and its relative aesthetic component, and into the motive forces and the deep, truthful feelings of spiritual reality – this is the sorting out characteristic of the method lovingly deployed by the author in his representation of society. The magnificent symbols open the register to programmed derision that on certain pages reaches paroxsymal tones and deformed appearance: moving it to polemic, mockery, the grotesque and the 'baroque,' to intolerance, to apparent cruelty, to a 'misanthrophic' hiatus of thought. But the baroque and the grotesque exist already in things, in the individual discoveries of a phenomenology external to us: in our very customs, in the 'common' sense of the few or the many: and in letters, be they humane or dishumane. Baroque and grotesque are not attributable to authorial premeditation or expressive propensities, rather they are linked to nature and to history ... So much so that the rallying call 'G is baroque' could be expressed in the more reasonable and serene assertion 'the world is baroque, and G. has perceived and depicted its baroqueness.']

Hence the perception, for Céline as well as Gadda, that the baroque and the grotesque are ontological properties of the world dictates the guidelines for their respective representations. Both writers imitate what they regard as objectively deformed and deface that object-reality further through the pressure and stress demanded by subjective impulse.

While defining Gadda's *Weltanschauung* as a 'system of systems,' Italo Calvino remarks that:

The seething cauldron of life, the infinite stratification of reality, the inextricable tangle of knowledge are what Gadda wants to depict. When this concept of universal complication, reflected in the slightest object or event, has reached its ultimate paroxysm, it seems as if the novel is destined to remain unfinished, as if it could continue infinitely, creating new vortices within each episode. Gadda's point is the superabundance, the congestion, of these pages, through which a single complex object – the city of Rome – assumes a variegated form, becomes organism and symbol. (Calvino 1985, vi)

Here Calvino identifies the determinacy of Gadda's style and narrative technique by referring to 'universal complication,' 'ultimate paroxysm,' 'new vortices,' and 'superabundance.' Although Céline's work cannot be defined, strictly speaking, in the same terms, it exhibits some notable similarities. For 'universal complication' all we need to do is substitute 'universal hatred and violence,' while the notions of 'ultimate paroxysm,' 'new vortices,' and 'superabundance' are plainly applicable to Céline, in that his writing, like Gadda's, is broadly convulsive. It gives the sensation of whirling around distinct objects with an excess of expression. The object is trapped within the tension, or vortex, generated by the narrating voice that determines (a) 'what gets to be narrated' and, psychoanalytically speaking, (b) 'what implies a double relationship between the subject and the world.' That is to say: (1) a correlative of instinct, understood as a specific type of satisfaction that fulfils itself when instinct seeks to fulfil its purpose. It can be a person, a partial object, a real object or a phantasmal object; (2) a correlative of love or hate. The relationship which is presupposed implies a total person or an instance of the self or of the object (person, entity, ideal). (Laplanche and Pontalis 1967, 290)

A good example of the narrated object is Mussolini in *Eros e Priapo*. In this unique pamphlet, the Duce is the object of a grotesque satire which pleases the narrator so much that he cannot release his hold. As a result, Mussolini becomes the subject of infinite predication. Here is one of many possible examples:

Alla 'recettività' singulare della femina egli portò l'unica oblazione di sé medesimo. Ed ebbe faccia da proferire, notate, da proferire verbalmente, con l'apparato laringo-buccale la sporca e bugiarda equazione: io sono la patria; e l'altra: io sono il pòppolo. Lui solo, a sentirlo, impersonava la patria, lui solo impersonava la causa de i' su' poppppolo con quattro p. Egli si autopromosse e si anteprepose ad eponimo della patria e del popolo che soli il sacrifizio de' sacrificati aveva e il travaglio de' travagliati arebbe, per quanto fortunosamente, portata a salvezza. E questo per esser venuto a luce, secondo il poeta d'Annunzio, con testa di ciuco e codonzolo di verro. Per aver 'sofferto' cioè imbroccato al malcantone la nottìvaga da du' lire che gli versò nel cervello i destini imperiali della patria.

Lui si anteprepose alla recettività di alcune femine. Andò verso di loro. Parlò loro, mascelluto, stivaluto, la sua bugiarda sinéresi: io Patria. E suggerì al loro inconscio (ma non tanto inconscio) quell'altra sinèresi che poi le ossedé per un ventennio. Io non sono un cornuto, anzi il contrario. (*EP*, 257)

[He brought to the singular 'receptivity' of the female the unique offering of himself. And he had the courage to proffer, note, to proffer verbally, with his tankard larynx the filthy and mendacious equation: I am the Fatherland; and the other: I am the people. He alone, to listen to him talk, embodied the Fatherland, he alone embodied the cause of his people (pronounced with four p's). He promoted himself to and proposed himself beforehand as the eponym of the Fatherland and of the people who alone the sacrifice of those sacrificed had and the hardships of those who suffered would have, albeit by luck, brought to salvation. And this for having come to light, according to the poet D'Annunzio, with the head of a jackass and the pecker of a pig. For having 'suffered,' that is, picked up in an ally a five-dollar street walker who poured the imperial destiny of the Fatherland into his brain.

He proposed himself beforehand to the receptivity of certain females. He moved towards them. Spoke to them, big-jawed and booted, his mendacious syneresis: I Fatherland. And he suggested to their unconscious (but not that much unconscious) that other syneresis which then obsessed them for twenty years.]

This is one small segment of Gadda's endless reiteration of the object, yet it displays all the features of his style: the mixture of high and low, irony, erudition, the comic, and the poetic. Mussolini unfolds through the various registers of Gadda's voice. We see in full light the obsessive manoeuvring by Gadda of this element of his fantasy, suffer its cognitive effect, and thus seize on it completely. In the process, the object of narration reaches the utmost limit of its totality, becoming at once an object of scorn and fascination.

In Céline we note a similar relation to the object that tends to take on the qualities of a phantasm. In spite of his violent tone and the trenchant brevity of his sentences, the narrative line is retained, albeit as a secondary and conventional element. What really matters are inventiveness, poetry, and intensity, traits which give his prose its unique physiognomy. It is in such a perspective that we can best appreciate in *Voyage au bout de la nuit* the description of the journey to Africa:

Notre navire avait nom: l'*Amiral-Bragueton*. Il ne devait tenir sur ces eaux tièdes que grâce à sa peinture. Tant de couches accumulées par pelures avaient fini par lui constituer une sorte de seconde coque à l'*Amiral-Bragueton* à la manière d'un oignon. Nous voguions vers l'Afrique, la vraie, la grande; celle des insondables forêts, des miasmes délétères, des solitudes inviolées, vers les grands tyrans nègres vautrés aux croisements de fleuves qui n'en finissent pas. Pour un paquet de lames 'Pilett,' j'allais trafiquer avec eux des ivoires longs comme ça, des oiseaux flamboyants, des esclaves mineures. C'était promis. La vie quoi! Rien de commun avec cette Afrique décortiquée des agences et des monuments, des chemins de fer et des nougats. Ah non! Nous allions nous la voir dans son jus, la vraie Afrique! Nous les passagers boissonnants de l'*Amiral-Bragueton*!

Mais, dès après les côtes du Portugal, les choses se mirent à gâter [...] Dans cette stabilité désespérante de chaleur tout le contenu humain du navire s'est coagulé dans une massive invrognerie. On se mouvait mollement entre les ponts, comme des poulpes au fond d'une baignoire d'eau fadasse. C'est depuis ce moment que nous vîmes à fleur de peau venir s'étaler l'angoissante nature des Blancs, provoquée, libérée, bien débraillée enfin, leur vraie nature, tout comme à la guerre. Etuve tropicale pour instincts tels crapauds et vipères qui viennent enfin s'épanouir au mois d'août, sur les flancs fissurés des prisons. Dans le froid d'Europe, sous les grisailles pudiques du Nord, on ne fait, hors les carnages, que soupçonner la grouillante cruauté de nos frères, mais leur pourriture envahit la surface dès que les émoustille la fièvre ignoble des Tropiques. C'est alors qu'on se déboutonne éperdument et que la saloperie triomphe et nous recouvre entiers. C'est l'aveu biologique. Dès que le travail et le froid ne nous astreignent plus, relâchent un moment leur étau, on peut apercevoir des Blancs, ce qu'on découvre du gai rivage, une fois que la mer s'en retire: la vérité, mares lourdement puantes, les crabes, la charogne et l'étron.

Ainsi le Portugal passé, tout le monde se mit, sur le navire, à se libérer les instincts avec rage, l'alcool aidant, et aussi ce sentiment d'agrément intime que procure une gratuité absolue de voyage, surtout aux militaires et fonctionnaires en activité. (Céline 1994, 112–13)

[Our ship's name was the *Admiral Bragueton*. If it kept afloat on those tepid seas, it was only thanks to its paint. Any number of coats laid on, layer after layer, had given the *Admiral Bragueton* a kind of second hull, something like an onion. We were heading for Africa, the real, grandiose Africa of impenetrable forests, fetid swamps, inviolate wildernesses, where black tyrants wallowed in sloth and cruelty on the banks of neverending rivers. I would barter a pack of 'Pilett' razor blades for big long elephant's tusks, gaudy-colored birds, and juvenile slaves. Guaranteed. That would be life! Nothing in common with emasculated Africa of travel agencies and monuments, of railways and candy bars. Certainly not! We'd be seeing Africa in the raw, the real Africa! We the boozing passengers of the *Admiral Bragueton*.

But as soon as we'd passed the coast of Portugal, things started going bad ... It didn't take long. In that despondent changeless heat the entire human content of the ship congealed into massive drunkenness. People moved flabbily about like squid in a tank of tepid smelly water. From that moment on we saw, rising to the surface, the terrifying nature of white men, exasperated, freed from constraint, absolutely unbuttoned, their true nature, same as in the war. That tropical steam bath called forth instincts as August breeds toads and snakes on the fissured walls of prison. In the European cold, under gray, puritanical northern skies, we seldom get to see our brothers' festering cruelty except in times of carnage, but when roused by the foul fevers of the tropics, their rottenness rises to the surface. That's when the frantic unbuttoning sets in, when filth triumphs and covers us entirely. It's a biological confession. Once work and cold weather cease to constrain us, once they relax their grip, the white man shows you the same spectacle as a beautiful beach when the tide goes out: the truth, fetid pools, crabs, carrion, and turds.

Once we had passed Portugal, everybody on board started unleashing his instincts, ferociously; alcohol helped and so did the blissful feeling conferred, especially on soldiers and civil servants, by the knowledge that the trip was absolutely free of charge. (Céline 1983, 95–6)]

The narrator encircles here two significant objects: 'Africa' and 'white men.' His cruel, realistic vision is filtered through the accumulation of their specific traits, conveyed through metaphor and violent imagery. Three registers dominate: irony and mockery, accusation and judgment, metaphor and poetry – procedures that are frequent in Gadda's prose. Moreover, it is the narrator's relationship to his objects that determines the specificity of Gadda's and Céline's prose. Here, Robert Dombroski's insight on Gadda's style can be generalized and extended to Céline:

The principal characteristic of Gadda's style is that his images do not imitate any form of objective reality; rather they exhibit objects, already culturalized by use and convention, that are lodged as ideal constructs within the collective psyche. The result is that actions and characters are twice removed from the real, for what Gadda parodies is not their reality, which remains intact and constant as a violated norm, but their cultural representation in language. (Dombroski 1994, 136)

This process of exhibiting objects and characters 'already culturalized by use and convention' marks Gadda's and Céline's writings as deviations from the narrative norm. Their novels, rather than tell a story, organize around the narrative different materials and tensions proper to the narrators' visions, ideas, and fantasies. They are paranarratives in the sense of their being commentaries, and metanarratives, since they reflect (implicitly and explicitly) on the narration as an incongruently posited gesture before the world's complexity. Gadda's writing establishes a significant distance between referent and language. Céline's method resides in a systematic, poetic expansion of the material.[2]

At this point, it is useful to ask how a reader should approach these works. To answer this question one has to assume that reading becomes a cognitive operation on the condition that one can identify the specific features of the narrative process and of linguistic expression. It entails intellectual curiosity on the part of the reader who has to capture meaning in its ever-growing complexity. It also requires a relational imagination and an understanding of discontinuous novelistic processes. Moreover, it presupposes the goal of capturing a vision in which narration and representation are at the centre of a dialectical tension between the intentionality of showing and imitating, and the impossibility of a 'willing suspension of disbelief.' Finally, the reader must also recognize the fact that whatever the wealth of expression, it does not shroud the distinctiveness of the narrative voice. In his *Poetique de Céline*, Henri Godard argues that, notwithstanding its plurivocalism, Céline's voice remains 'unique':

[Céline's voice] imposes itself, then reasserts itself from book to book; identical to itself, thoroughly present and unmistakable no matter where it is found. Its plurivocalism is but one of its characteristics ... Beyond all of its effects, however rich and subtle they may be, there is one manner, different from all others, and that is the work's substance, of writing French, and it is to this that we give the name Céline. (Godard 1985, 181–2)

The voice's textual embodiments are language and style, the specificity which enables us to 'hear' the voice attached to one particular person. Hans-Magnus Enzensberger has made essentially the same case for Gadda in his postscript to the German edition of La cognizione del dolore:

Erudition and originality, subtle knowledge of the tradition and the pleasure of destroying constitute here a strange couple ... In Gadda, language stems from the labyrinth, a linguistic Babel, sovereignly organized; it is a system and, at the same time, a composed set of individual languages, written and spoken languages, living and dead ones, peasant and foreign, a mixture of chatter, slang, jargon and the language of class affiliation, of every possible terminology and nomenclature, of epic- para- and meta-languages: where memory, document and an absolute ear weave the cocoon. (Enzenberger 1992, 314–15)

With respect to Céline, we can deduce from the following description of his idiolect its vocal qualities:

The Célinian idiolect realizes an astonishing performance of serving almost all the levels of language with the same effect of intonation, since he goes deliberately against the linguistic 'rituals' accepted by the implicit competence of the reader. Thus, to the sustained style ('style soutenu') and to its compatible tones (literary, precious, urbane, learned, etc.) he will make corresponding desublimizing connotations. Or, inversely, he will try to impose on the social and cultural registers, qualified as 'vulgar,' a lyric and almost incantatory countertone. (Latin 1988, 66)

In Gadda and Céline, the prevalence of voice and idiolect subordinates the other elements to secondary, albeit necessary, structures. The finality of the voice amounts to a sustained intensity of subjective writing and systematic narrative deviation. The message of these authors is never complete since it cannot be separated from the network of relations that determine the flux and duration of sensory data. For Gadda, who retains his belief in the Kantian noumenon, the object world is nothing but appearance. Each component of this world is for him a system employed by the real: 'Un sistema ci si rivela come un operatore del reale (ossia, in generale, esso è un qualche cosa, diviene un qualche cosa, è un è-divenire)' (*MM*, 822) [A system reveals itself to us as an operator of the real (or, in general, it is something, becomes something, it is an is-becoming)]. Nevertheless, inasmuch as it is a system, it can become something else, but what it becomes is never clear beforehand; its 'becoming' is obscure, as are its functions and its effects: 'l'oscuro divenire, l'oscuro "dover trasformarsi," l'oscuro compito e esito' (ibid., 827).

What Gadda assumes about a given system is based on the presupposition that consciousness is not perfect, being as it is only that which 'systematizes or relates or refers.' He states in *Meditazione*:

L'atto della coscienza è un atto di polarizzazione (almeno): è una crisi euristica o giudizio euristico contrapponente alcunché ad alcunché, anche sé a sé. (*MM*, 829)

[The state of awareness is an act of polarization (at least); it is a crisis in the heuristic process or a judgment that counterposes something to something else, even itself to itself.]

While Gadda's epistemology delivers a precise meaning of the world as perception, system, and awareness, it allows for the presence of the unknown, the obscure, and, above all, the complex. As in Leibniz's *Monadology*, 'We experience a multitude in the simple substance, when we notice that the smallest thought which we perceive envelops a variety in the object' (Leibniz 1963, 149). Gadda assumes therefore that the Invisible Form acts in some obscure fashion on the world and that our perceptions of the real are based on 'inscrutable appearances.' 'Noi vediamo quindi che i grumi di realtà si annodano secondo apparenze imperscrutabili' (*MM*, 823) [We see therefore that the clots of reality are connected on the basis of inscrutable appearances].

This form can only be approximated. In spite of Gadda's extraordinarily dense style and precise descriptions, the Invisible Form and the Idea are received as both mystery and essence. Let's recall how in *Quer pasticciaccio* Gadda describes the 'baroque' abode of Zamira Pàcori: a description that contains all the stylistic features of Gadda's voice. It begins with a series of material notations:

La cantina, o sala seminterrata, era provveduta d'un orinale: e, più, d'un lettuccio: che però crocchiava per un nulla, sto coglione, e aveva tegumento d'una 'coperta da letto' verde-stinta: con damascatura di indecifrabili maculazioni: le quali, nel loro autentico ermetismo, tiravano al barocco: a un barocco pieno e fastoso e di primo getto, per quanto poi lavata e rasciugata nell'orto, la coperta: e parevano escludere già in ipotesi ogni tardo stento neoclassico [...] Ma quela manna doveveno contentasse d'annasalla appena, senza poterla in altro modo raggiungere che con l'olfatto: fiutavano l'Idea, la presenza d'una Forma invisibile. Forma de pecorino bono de montagna, de quando nun c'era ancora cascato addosso l'impero: sì, sur groppone. (*QP*, 150–1)

[The cellar, or half-basement room, was equipped with a urinal: and, more, with a cot: which however creaked at a mere nothing, the bastard, and had the tegument of a 'counterpane' of faded green: damasked by undecipherable maculations which, in their authentic obscurity, had a baroque tendency: a full, pompous baroque of the first jet of imagination, though it was washed and dried in the garden, the coverlet: and it seemed to deny even hypothetically any belated, neoclassical restraint ... But they had to be content with a bare smell of that manna, unable to reach it in any other way than with their olfactory sense: they whiffed the Idea, an invisible Presence. The presence of good mountain pecorino, a whole cheese of the days before the Empire landed on us: yes, right on the neck. (*AM*, 204–5)]

Zamira's cellar is also represented as a place in which a 'drop of Probability' could become manifest:

Tutto quello che ce voleva, c'era. Un luogo, insomma, il laboratorio della Zamira, da non si poter incontrare il più opportuno a distillarvi una goccia, una goccia sola e splendida della eternamente proibita e eternamente inverisimile Probabilità [...] Un punto d'incontro dei vitali compossibili: magia, maglieria, sartoria, pantaloneria. (*QP*, 151)

[There was everything you could want. A place, in short, this workshop of Zamira's whose like you would never find, still less its better, for distilling a drop, a single and splendid drop of the eternally prohibited or eternally unlikely Probability ... A point of contact of the vital compossibilities: magic, knitting, tailoring. (*AM*, 205)]

The Probability, 'the eternally prohibited or eternally unlikely,' as well as the 'vital compossibilities,' allude to, but are not an exact application of,

Leibniz's ideas of 'possible worlds.' For Leibniz, 'a possible world is a set of mutually compossible complete individual concepts. It is "maximal" in the sense that it contains every complete individual concept that is compossible with the ones it contains' (Mates 1976, 340). One can say that Zamira's 'laboratory' is a grotesque occurrence of a possible world in which 'there was everything you could want'; a possible world without a harmonious organization, a grotesque transformation of philosophically thought 'possibilities' into the conventional novelistic frames of narration and description.

In contrast to Gadda, Céline has not been influenced by Leibniz nor for that matter by any other philosophical system. His dark vision of the world needs no philosophical support. The horrific world he, as narrator, inhabits and constantly suffers is sufficient cause for his response. As his stories emanate from the centre of his emotions, he does not need a philosophical touchstone to give a coherent and systematic account of his vision. It is in this sense that Céline's outlook is metonymically inscribed in his discourse. It emerges as a mundane totality, and gives the impression of being 'incidentally' added to his storytelling. Here is an example from the *Voyage*, the story of Musyne, one of Ferdinand's girlfriends of whom he has become desperately jealous:

Dans mon désespoir tremblotant, j'avais entrepris, pour comble de gaffe, d'aller le plus souvent possible, je l'ai dit, attendre ma compagne à l'office. Je patientais, parfois jusqu'au matin, j'avais sommeil, mais la jalousie me tenait quand même réveillé, le vin blanc aussi, que les domestiques me servaient largement [...]

Quand nous nous retrouvions au matin devant la porte elle faisait la grimace en me revoyant. J'étais encore naturel comme un animal en ce temps-là, je ne voulais pas la lâcher ma jolie et c'est tout, comme un os. On perd la plus grande partie de sa jeunesse à coups de maladresses. Il était évident qu'elle allait m'abandonner mon aimée tout à fait et bientôt. Je n'avais pas encore appris qu'il existe deux humanités très différentes, celle des riches et celle des pauvres. Il m'a fallu, comme à tant d'autres, vingt années et la guerre, pour apprendre à me tenir dans ma catégorie, à demander le prix des choses et des êtres avant d'y toucher, et surtout avant d'y tenir. (*Voyage*, 81)

[In my jittery despair, I had taken to waiting for Musyne in the butler's pantry as often as possible, a stupid thing to do. Sometimes I waited until morning, I was sleepy, but jealousy kept me awake, and so did the quantities of white wine the servants poured out for me ...

When she saw me at the door in the morning, she made a face. I was still as natural as an animal in those days. I was like a dog with a bone, I wouldn't let go. People waste a large part of their youth in stupid mistakes. It was obvious that my darling was going to leave me, flat and soon. I hadn't found out yet that mankind consists of two very different races, the rich and the poor. It took me ... and plenty of other people ... twenty years and the war to learn to stick to my class and ask the price of things before touching them, let alone setting my heart on them. (*Journey*, 67)]

Céline's narratives are governed by one basic principle: the world in its very nature is bad, violent, and subjected to the death instinct and to the law of reciprocal destruction. In contrast to Gadda, instinctive violence operates in his work as an element of the integral chaos displayed by a humanity committed to self-destruction. Céline's dark and profoundly pessimistic vision, which plunges the narrator into the substance of mankind's destructiveness, is marked by a reflexive and generalizing tone. In the *Voyage*, while trying to define the condition of exile, Céline remarks:

Tout en pérorant ainsi dans l'artifice et le convenu je ne pouvais m'empêcher de percevoir plus nettement encore d'autres raisons que le paludisme à la dépression physique et morale dont je me sentais accablé. Il s'agissait au surplus d'un changement d'habitude, il fallait que j'apprenne une fois encore à reconnaître de nouveaux visages dans un nouveau milieu, d'autres façons de parler et mentir. La paresse c'est presque aussi fort que la vie. La banalité de la farce nouvelle qu'il faut jouer vous écrase et il vous faut somme toute encore plus de lâcheté que de courage pour recommencer. C'est cela l'exil, l'étranger, cette inexorable observation de l'existence telle qu'elle est vraiment pendant ces quelques heures lucides, exceptionnelles dans la trame du temps humain, où les habitudes du pays précédent vous abandonnent, sans que les autres, les nouvelles vous aient encore suffisamment abruti.

Tout dans ces moments vient s'ajouter à votre immonde détresse pour vous forcer, débile, à discerner les choses, les gens et l'avenir tels qu'ils sont, c'est-à-dire des squelettes, rien que des riens, qu'il faudra cependant aimer, chérir, défendre, animer comme s'ils existaient. (*Voyage*, 214).

[While perorating thus artificially and conventionally, I couldn't help realizing that there were other reasons than malaria for my physical prostration and moral depression. There was also the change in habits; once again I was having to get used to new faces in new surroundings and to learn new ways of talking and lying. Laziness is almost as compelling as life. The new farce you're having to play crushes you with its banality, and all in all it takes more cowardice than courage to start all over again. That's what exile, a foreign country is, inexorable perception of existence as it really is, during those long lucid hours, exceptional in the flux of human time, when the ways of the old country abandon you, but the new ways haven't sufficiently stupefied you as yet. At such moments everything adds to your loathsome distress, forcing you in your weakened state to see things, people, and the future as they are, that is, as skeletons, as nothings, which you will nevertheless have to love, cherish, and defend as if they existed. (*Journey*, 184–5)]

Although Céline is more aphoristic and digressive and Gadda more analytical, the affinity that connects them consists in the wholly negative character of their respective worlds. Gadda sees reality as a chaotic structure and as entanglement ('groviglio'), while for Céline it is a morbid and mortuary mechanism. Both writers purport to invent an adequate literary form that would give symbolic meaning to the universal failure of humankind to understand and justify the world. The following observation by Gadda underlines the necessity to learn that the world is entanglement:

Ci educheremo a concepire ogni cosa come un groviglio o somma di rapporti nel senso più lato. (*MM*, 634)

[We will educate ourselves to conceive of everything as a tangle or a sum of relations in the broadest sense.]

And Céline remarks:

La rue des Hommes est à sens unique, la mort tient tous les cafés, c'est la belote 'au sang' qui nous attire et nous garde. (1987, 115)

[The Street of Men is a one-way street, death owns all the coffee shops, it is the game 'of blood' that tempts us and keeps us.]

Both authors denounce and analyse; both reveal the world's opacity and cruelty. But there is a clear line that separates Gadda's almost compulsive will to understand and to explain the world from Céline's conviction that it is negatively organized without any supreme reason and thus immutable.

In *Meditazione,* the problem of the world is posited along with the problem of the system, its functioning, and its stability or instability. It must be seen in the context of Gadda's 'groviglio conoscitivo,' that is to say, the conviction that knowledge is necessarily caught up in the complex network of relationships and signs:

Il mondo è sì anche un guazzabuglio o salsa di furbi, con ogni genere di cattive spezie: ma ciò apparentemente. In realtà è creazione o deformazione logica, è trapasso dal noto all'ignoto: o meglio dal noto a ciò che 'divien noto,' e questo che divien noto si crea o determina o fabbrica come supercoscienza di un superdato dalla coscienza del dato. (*MM,* 761)

[The world is also an entanglement or a sauce of scoundrels with all sorts of bad spices: but it is so apparently. In fact, it is a creation or a logical deformation, it is a passage from what is known to what is unknown or better, from the known to what is 'becoming known,' and what is becoming known is creating itself or determines or produces a superconsciousness of a superdatum from the consciousness of the datum.]

The disorder is therefore apparent. It defines the world at the very first level, but to fathom the meaning of the world requires the conviction that it is a constant passage from what is known to what becomes known. Gadda seems to advocate a search for certitude. Above the datum there is a superdatum. Compared to Céline, his 'philosophy' attempts to throw light on the world's disorder and to understand it as a process of creation and logical deformation. In this sense, each of Gadda's works may be considered a search for knowledge from within the chaos of the world.

Céline's vision stems from the conviction that the dynamics of human society are determined by the death instinct.

Dans le jeu de l'homme, l'instinct de mort, l'instinct silencieux, est décidément bien placé, peut-être, à côté de l'égoïsme. Il tient la place du zéro dans la roulette. Le casino gagne toujours. La mort aussi. La loi des grands nombres travaille pour elle. C'est une loi sans défaut. Tout ce que nous entreprenons, d'une manière ou d'une autre, très tôt, vient buter contre elle et tourne à la haine, au sinistre, au ridicule. Il faudrait être doué d'une manière bien bizarre pour parler d'autre chose que de mort en des temps où sur terre, sur les eaux, dans les airs, au présent, dans l'avenir, il n'est question que de cela. (1987, 114)

[In man's game, the death instinct, the silent instinct, is decidedly well positioned, perhaps, next to self-love. It holds the place of zero in roulette. The house always wins. So does death. The law of great names works for death. It is an unfailing law. Everything we undertake in one way or another quickly runs up against death and becomes hateful, sinister, and ridiculous. You'd have to be very clever to talk about anything other than death in these times, when on land and waters, in the air, for the present and for the future, it is only a question of that.]

The characters and the plots of the novels are emblematic signs of interrelated structures in which man strives desperately for knowledge. If Gadda conceives of the world in terms of system and of complex, quasi-monadic organization, undermined by irretrievable chaos, Céline sees it as the continuous operation of the death instinct. If reality in Gadda's texts is full of 'fili' and 'grumi,' if it is profoundly and monadically 'aggroviglia-ta,' Céline's world persists in its chaotic, sloppy, and violent dynamics of brutality and destructiveness. In Gadda, we have the tendency to fore-ground the narrative by means of a panoramic description of the general state of the human condition, as at the beginning of *La meccanica*:

Ma per piani aridi e illuni o nell'aggrovigliata paura delle giungle immense udrà forse taluno di là da ogni voce de' viventi come segui il torbido fiume delle generazioni a devolversi e penserà che sciabordi contro sue prode le rame e li steli dalle selve divelti; e verdastre, con i quattro piffari all'aria, le carogne pallonate de' più fetidi e malvagi animali, quali furono in vita e saran pecore, jene, sanguino-lenti sciacalli, saltabeccanti scimie, asini con crine de' lioni e gran baffi: e il branco lurido e tronfio arriverà nelli approdi lutulenti a travolgersi, dove è soltanto la vanità buia della morte.
Ma la sacra corrente seguiterà defluendo, con una mormorazione delle tenebre, verso lontane stelle. E resupino sulla cóltrice nera del flutto e come adagiato nel silenzio e nella solitudine della sua morte, trapasserà segno o corpo che parerà fatto di cerea luce: greve per tutte le membra della fatica mortale, di che solo avrà voluto vestir il fulgore di sua giovinezza: e avrà il capo stancamente nel flutto, il viso rivolto verso i cieli gelidi. Così composto nella sua morte parerà un fiore pallido della eternità. (*RR II*, 469)

[But perhaps, across dry and moonless plains or in the tangled fear of the jungles, someone will hear, beyond the voice of any living being, how you follow the flow of the torbid river of generations and [that someone] will think that you are swashing against your shores the branches and the stalks from uprooted forests; and the swollen, greenish upturned carcasses of animals just as fetid and malicious as they were in life: sheep, hyenas, bloodthirsty jackals, hopping monkeys, donkeys with lions' manes and large whiskers. This lurid and vain flock will arrive on muddy landings to be swept away to where there is only the black emptiness of death.

But the sacred current will continue flowing with a murmur in the dark towards distant stars. And facing upward again on the black bed of its swell and as if comforted by the silence and solitude of his death, that someone will pass through sign or body that will seem made of pale light: heavy in all his members from the mortal labour of which he would have wanted to dress the splendour of his youth: and he will rest his head wearily on the wave, his face turned upwards towards gelid skies. So composed in his death, he will seem a pale flower of eternity.]

This cosmic and organic vision of the world, expressed in its atemporal being, is based on an accumulation of strata containing both botanic and biological entities. It comprises a series of metaphors and images that hold the complex meaning of a liminal presentation of the world, seen as archaeological strata that contain both what has been destroyed and what is in the process of reproduction, being placed between the 'black emptiness of death' and the permanent flowing of the 'sacred current.' The hypothetical 'someone' who 'will seem a pale flower of eternity' embodies symbolically both the separation of the cosmos from humankind and the inclusion of the human in eternity.

In some aspects, Céline's vision of Fort-Gono in *Voyage* is quite similar to Gadda's description. What distinguishes, however, Céline's vision from that of Gadda is a strong anthropomorphization of nature's forces. They act as though they were humans with an aggressiveness that defines their specific character; hence the 'swollen, wildly aggressive vegetation,' 'delirious lettuces,' and 'some jaundiced European':

La végétation bouffie des jardins tenait à grand-peine, agressive, farouche, entre les palissades, éclatantes frondaisons formant laitues en délire autour de chaque maison, ratatiné gros blanc d'oeuf solide dans lequel achevait de pourrir un Européen jaunet. Ainsi autant de saladiers complets que de fonctionnaires tout au long de l'avenue Fachoda, la plus animée, la mieux hantée de Fort-Gono. (*Voyage*, 143)

[The fences could hardly contain the swollen, wildly aggressive vegetation of the gardens; the rampant foliage molded delirious lettuces around the houses, those chunks of dried-out egg white, in which some jaundiced European was rotting away. All along the Avenue Fachoda, the liveliest and most fashionable street in

Fort-Gono, there were as many overflowing salad bowls as Government officials. (*Journey*, 122)]

This penetration into the African universe describes a sort of perpetual, all-encompassing destruction, seen as an anthropomorphic action. The narrative which follows is therefore an active illustration of what is said about the universe in terms of nature perceived as aggressive and destructive human energy.

The novel that stems from these premises has to be most attentive to the relationship between the commentary and the story's unfolding. Gadda endorses the same intention of enriching the novelistic material with a series of philosophical or quasi-philosophical observations. The position of Céline is relatively similar. The subjective clauses of meaning are the cellular units of his compulsion to reveal the various configurations of the states of being. These units, such as sentence or paragraph, build upon the emotion, the vision, the phantasms, the analytical tendency to scrutinize objects, characters, and situations, and to promote specific plots, that underlie a representation of the world caught up in its mechanisms of destruction, cruelty, and barbarian violence.

After the stylistic differentiation of *Ulysses* and the self-analysis achieved through Proust's 'mémoire involontaire,' Gadda and Céline, by the strength of their individual styles, bring a new structure to the novel. They do it by expanding the stylistic principle, the complexity of its idiom, and the dynamics of narrative subjectivity. Both Gadda and Céline demonstrate the extreme richness and the efficiency of syncretically composed languages in expressing the complexity of the world. The specific features of their style and techniques contribute to the novel's progress towards the infinite space of multiplicity that they inhabit in order to show how this open-ended genre neither knows the limits of its idiom, nor can stop the expansion of the subjective principle embodying poetry, emotion, and passions. From Gadda and Céline the novel has progressed a good deal on the way of discovery and knowledge.

The similarities and differences that we have surveyed between Gadda and Céline help us realize that their expressive worlds diverge rather than converge. Gadda's manner of writing is analytical; it deals with the world in its presupposed and sought-for totality, and in this way it accounts for its complexity. By contrast, Céline's intensity builds on the principle of stylistically conveyed emotion. His all-encompassing negative viewpoint excludes Gadda's quest for understanding the world as systematic complexity and potential chaos. In their differences, however, Céline's existential anger corresponds to Gadda's Leibnizian wisdom. Together they contribute to the development of the novel by engaging in the molecular production of meaning that works according to the principle of multiplying fragments of style and meaning.

Notes

1 Mandelbrot remarks: 'I coined *fractal* from the Latin adjective *fractus*. The corresponding Latin verb *frangere* means "to break": to create irregular fragments. It is therefore sensible-and how appropriate for our needs! – that, in addition to "fragmented" (as in *fraction* or *refraction*) *fractus* should also mean "irregular," both meanings being preserved in *fragment*' (1977, 4).

2 Julia Kristeva remarks that Céline achieves an important transformation of the syntax and accomplishes a significant segmentation of the sentence: 'No doubt his SYNTACTIC invention contributes, most radically, to the heterogeneity of the signifying process' (Kristeva 1977, 48).

References

Calvino, Italo. 1985. Introduction to *That Awful Mess on Via Merulana*. Translated by William Weaver. London: Quartet Books

Céline, Louis-Ferdinand. 1952. *Mort à crédit*. Paris: Gallimard

– 1957. *D'un chateau l'autre*. Paris: Gallimard

– 1966. *Death on the Installment Plan*. New York: New Directions

– 1968. *Castle to Castle*. New York: Delacorte Press

– 1983. *Journey to the End of the Night*. New York: New Directions

– 1987. *Le style contre les ideés. Rabelais, Zola, Sartre et les autres*. Brussels: Editions Complexe

– 1994 [1952]. *Voyage au bout de la nuit*. Paris: Gallimard

Dombroski, Robert S. 1994. *Properties of Writing: Ideological Discourse in Modern Italian Fiction*. Baltimore and London: Johns Hopkins University Press

Enzensberger, Hans Magnus. 1992. Introduction to *Die Erkenntnis des Schmerzes*. Munich and Zürich: Piper

Godard, Henri. 1985. *Poétique de Céline*. Paris: Gallimard

Jamet, Claude. 1945. *Images mêlées de la littérature et du théâtre*. Paris: ELAN

Laplanche, Jean, and Jean-Baptiste Pontalis. 1967. *Vocabulaire de la psychanalyse*. Paris: PUF

Latin, Danielle. 1988. *Le 'Voyage au bout de la nuit' de Céline. Roman de la subversion et subversion du roman*. Brussels: Palais des Académies

Kristeva, Julia. 'Actualité de Céline.' *Tel Quel* Nos 71–3 (Fall 1977): 48

Leibniz, Gottfried Wilhelm. 1963. *La monadologie*. Paris: Librairie Delagrave

Mandelbrot, Benoit B. 1977. *The Fractal Geometry of Nature*. New York: Freeman

Mates, Benson. 1976. 'Leibniz on Possible Worlds.' In H.G. Frankfurt, ed., *Leibniz, A Collection of Critical Essays*. Notre Dame, Ind.: University of Notre Dame Press

Merlin, Thomas. 1979. *Louis Ferdinand Céline*. New York: New Directions

Roscioni, Gian Carlo. 1975. *La disarmonia prestabilita. Studio su Gadda*. Turin: Einaudi

Fascism and Anti-Fascism in Gadda

PETER HAINSWORTH

This essay attempts to clarify the relationship between two stages in Gadda's career as a writer which have tended to be ignored or have not been given an appropriate weight, either together or in isolation. Though there have been exceptions,[1] Gadda has been discussed chiefly in literary terms, that is, in terms which, if they have a historical dimension, locate it overwhelmingly within the terms of literary history, allowing political questions to remain marginal or generic. There are good reasons for reading Gadda as literature before everything else, and he himself gives strong nudges in this direction. Yet something important seems to be missing from accounts with too literary an emphasis. He was, after all, a convinced Fascist, and then, in the immediate aftermath of its fall, he wrote vitriolically against Fascism. Unlike most who denounced Fascism he did so from a strikingly right-wing viewpoint, not from the left. All of this requires comment, the more so since the time for a certain *pudeur* seems to be past, while the possibility of Fascist resurgence seems increasingly more real. It is also more possible now than before to make informed comment, thanks to the edition of Gadda's works recently completed under the general editorship of Dante Isella. It will become evident that my debt to this edition is immense.

My bald statement above that Gadda was a convinced Fascist needs to be substantiated. Gadda himself gave the impression in some of his comments that he began to be disillusioned with Fascism quite early on. In the early 1950s he told Carlo Cattaneo that he had already seen through Mussolini by the time of Matteotti's murder (Cattaneo 1973, 63). Later, in his generally mendacious and bizarrely neurotic interview with Dacia Maraini of 1968, he claimed to have had the first idea for his principal anti-Fascist work, *Eros e Priapo*, in 1928 and to have written it in the 1930s,[2] though it is now certain that the book was begun in the later part of 1944.[3] In fact he was a Fascist party member from the early 1920s.[4] From 1939 onwards – this was the year when his career as a journalist really began – he wrote articles supporting the regime's policies and institutions, especially in the fields of science and economics. These are serious articles, some of them quite technical, others more popularizing. Some may well have been written rather grudgingly and mainly for economic reasons,[5] but none can be easily dismissed as opportunistic journalism.[6] The last two were late indeed. 'L'Istituto di Studi Romani,' a celebrative but considered piece on the perpetuation of the Roman tradition through the activities of the institute mentioned in the title, appeared in *Primato* for 15 August 1942. 'All'insegna dell'alta cultura,' which appeared on 1 February 1943, also in *Primato*, applauds the rebirth of the Milanese 'Istituto dell'alta cultura' under the auspices of Bottai, and the central events it promotes, notably and (given the circumstances) significantly, concerts of German, Hungarian, and Italian music.[7]

Nor can we make a clear distinction between Fascist journalism and non-Fascist, let alone anti-Fascist, literary work. Though there is clearly no overt propaganda intent, the early fiction – the *Racconto italiano di ignoto del novecento* of 1924–5, *La meccanica* of 1928–9, and the *Dejanira Classis* or *Novella seconda* of the same period – all show an appreciation of the daring and decisiveness of Fascism as opposed to the opportunism of socialism and the bathos of liberalism. The title story of *La Madonna dei Filosofi*, Gadda's first published book (1931), is set in 1922 and is almost an allegory of Italy in the period immediately following the First World War. The sufferings of Maria are not to be resolved through the falsities of fashionable internationalism (represented by her French friend, Mademoiselle Delanay) nor by bourgeois stolidity (Pertusella, whom her family wish her to marry). Her improbable union with the tormented Baronfo represents a recovery of life and also a return to the healthiest traditions of the past, after the sacrifices of the First World War and the despair which followed it.

There are similar analogical, if not allegorical, implications in the *Meditazione milanese*. Its main areas of concern are general problems of cognition, as has been brilliantly expounded by Roscioni (1969), but it has a social and political dimension which shows itself principally in the elaborate, often surprising comparisons which Gadda draws to illuminate the strictly philosophical theses and which in places become subjects for discussion in their own right. In these passages an optimistic vision emerges of what could be a good society, and in particular a good Italian society. It is one dynamically pressing forward, scientifically educated and respectful of knowledge, harmonizing its contradictions and the rich diversity of its culture and traditions, untrammelled by restrictive regulations, and asserting its will, a society which gives priority to action over paralysing reflection and self-justification. There is no discussion of Fascist ideology as such, but the consonance is plain.

The *Meditazione* would remain unpublished until 1974. *Le meraviglie d'Italia*, in its 1939 version (the 1964 version is quite different),[8] finds explicit and specific realization of these ideas in Fascist Italy, with plain enthusiasm, for instance, for autarchic policies ('Il carbone dell'Arsa'), Italian technological advances ('Apologo del Gran Sasso d'Italia'), the 'giovinezza nuova d'Italia' ('La funivia della neve,' [*MI*, 127]), the sturdy vitality of local practices and traditions ('Delle mondine in risaia'). There may be irony and playfulness, there may be moments of metaphysical pessimism, but the overriding mood is of measured optimism. The last piece ('Sull'Alpe di marmo'), on the quarrying at Carrara, ends with a salute to 'il coraggio e la fatica dell'uomo' (198) [the courage and the labour of man], in which the very substance of the Apuan mountains, inherited skill, and new technology and discipline are seen as coming together in the dynamic present of the new Italy.

La qualità delle maestranze carraresi, come un'eredità morale dei padri: la nuova tecnica; la nuova volontà e la nuova disciplina del lavoro: ecco i mezzi per il perfezionamento dell'impresa latòmica, che dalla Bianca Luni ha impegnato, traverso i millennî e fino all'Italia recuperata, questa gente apuana. (199)

[The quality of Carrara master-craftsmanship, like a moral inheritance left to them by their fathers, and the new techniques, the new strength of will, and the new discipline in work – these are the means for bringing to perfection the enterprise of quarrying which has employed this Apuan people through the ages since the time of now whitened Luni to these days of a renewed Italy.][9]

There is one work from the Fascist years which has often been credited with carrying an anti-Fascist charge, that is, *La cognizione del dolore*, which first appeared in *Letteratura* between 1938 and 1941.[10] Gadda himself suggested in the 1968 interview with Dacia Maraini mentioned above that the nightwatchmen who play a large part in the novel symbolize the Fascists, at least up to a point, and the equation has also been made by some interpreters.[11] But such a reading is hard to justify. The novel makes it clear that the 'Nistitúo de Vigilancia para la Noche' is emblematic of administrative corruption.[12] Gadda's specific target in Mahagones or Palumbo is the ex-soldier who pretends to be a hero and war victim and, having failed to obtain a pension, finds a niche for himself in a state police organization which he can use as a protection racket. It is a conventional polemic, in complete accord with policies for bureaucratic reform which Fascism publicly proclaimed and which won it a great deal of popular support. As for the satire of the bourgeoisie that figures in *La cognizione* and even more in *L'Adalgisa*, that was also a standard theme of orthodox Fascist writing, which continued to be rehearsed throughout the *ventennio*, however remote from reality it may have become, or may always have been.

Gadda's Fascism was obviously nonconformist, nor was it an incidental or accidental feature of his experience and work during the *ventennio*. Though he might seem now to have been naïve or self-deceiving, he clearly saw himself as giving measured, thoughtful support to the regime. Fascism responded to his need for order and dignity in a world which his own traumatic experience during and after the First World War indicated was bereft of both. It held out the prospect of harmonizing diversity in the social and political spheres, even if the fundamental disharmony of life and the self could not be eradicated, and of restoring order and dignity to Italy after the chaos of liberalism, with its culmination, as far as he was concerned, in Caporetto.[13] Historical events seem to have done nothing to disabuse him until 1943.[14] If there were difficulties and dangers, then the good soldier stood his ground, spiritually at least, even if he were too old to fight.[15] This did not mean total agreement with the policies of the regime. Like many other loyal Italians, especially those who had fought against the Austrians and Germans, he was disturbed by the alliance with Hitler, the 'eredo-alcoolico Fuhrer' [inheritedly alcoholic Fuhrer] and his assassins, as he puts it in a letter to Bonaventura Tecchi of 29 October 1939 (Gadda 1984, 139). More importantly, there remained, alongside the doubtless sincere expressions of optimism, that visceral pessimism and scepticism which ensured that the real fragility and uncertainty of his literary enterprises was obliquely but unremittingly acknowledged in the very process of carrying them through.[16] Even *Le meraviglie d'Italia* has passages on the vanity of all things human, such as the lyrical meditation of the 'Frammento – sostando nella necropoli comunale,' which forms the muted conclusion to the first section of the book.

Gadda gave up his engineering work in 1940 and established himself in Florence, determined at last to live by the pen. Clearly, the early years of the war were not particularly difficult. Indeed, things went relatively well, compared to the economic and other uncertainties of the pre-war years. There were relaxed summer holidays in Forte dei Marmi with other *letterati* (Montale, Vittorini, Guarnieri, and others), with bicycle rides along the sea front and lazy days on the beach (Guarnieri 1989, 96–100; Gadda 1983a, 122–3; Gadda 1988, 41). And some time in early 1942, largely through the efforts of Riccardo Bacchelli, to Gadda's evident satisfaction, came a prize for his work from the Accademia d'Italia.[17] But the next year was a different story. In mid-1943 he escaped into the countryside, staying for a while with Luigi Russo, until apparently a chance encounter with a partisan sent him hurrying back to Florence, in what may have been the terror of being somehow compromised, or disapproval of the partisan struggle, or a mixture of both (Guarnieri 1989, 104ff; Gadda Conti 1974, 62–3; Cattaneo 1973, 109). He seems to have lived as best he could in Florence through the difficult months that followed, but then he was swept south with hosts of other refugees whom the British sent away from the battle zone soon after they reached Florence in summer 1944. Writing or publishing were clearly out of the question, as the gap in the bibliography of his writings between early 1943 and early 1945 testifies.[18] In fact his comments in interviews and letters,[19] though few and brief, make it plain that for him, as for innumerable others, this whole period was a time of extreme fear and horror. In some ways he seems to have felt that it was Caporetto all over again, to judge from the strange blurring of the First and the Second World Wars that takes place at some moments of *Eros e Priapo* (292–3), as if Fascism had followed Liberal Italy in creating an image of Italian military power and organization, whilst in reality it was equally inefficient and inept, or even more so. He was terrified by the bombardments, impoverished, hungry, uncertain of where he could safely sleep. But he found refuge in Rome in August. He was helped out financially by friends and was able to stay in a room in a pensione run by the sister of Alfredo Gargiulo. He remained in Rome until some time in 1945, when he returned to Florence.[20]

It was during his stay in Rome that he began to write against Fascism, impelled by what apparently became an uncontrollable need to find expression for his feelings.[21] As was usual for him, though no doubt the circumstances were an additional factor, the various writings of this period overlap, and none progressed in a straight line to completion and publication. First came the three short *I miti del somaro*, as they were entitled by Alba Andreini, who was responsible for publishing them for the first time in 1988.[22] They were written (and, unusually for Gadda, apparently completed) between September and December 1944. *Eros e*

Priapo was begun during the same period, but its composition dragged on well after Gadda's return to Florence in 1945, eventually petering out as Gadda devoted more and more of his attention to the third text begun during this period, the much more famous *Quer pasticciaccio brutto de via Merulana*. The novel began to appear in *Letteratura* in 1946 but was not published in book form until 1957. In spite of contracts with Mondadori for an early publication, *Eros e Priapo* first appeared as *Il libro delle furie* in *Officina* in 1955–6 and then in book form in 1967.

The common genesis of the three books (as I shall call them for simplicity's sake) is plain in spite of subsequent redrafting of two of them. The passages in *Quer pasticciaccio* explicitly concerned with Fascism are close in tone and (in places) in phrasing to *I miti del somaro* and *Eros e Priapo*, with the same violence, outrage, sarcasm, comedy, and exaggeration, and the same antiquarian mixture of vulgarity and rhetorical elaboration. Obviously in other ways the novel diverges, whilst *Eros e Priapo* and *I miti del somaro* are explicitly given over in their entirety to the discussion of Fascism and are more discursive, making claims to intellectual rigour with arguments to unfold and with quasi-scientific theses to defend, especially in *Eros e Priapo*.

Indeed, *Eros e Priapo* asks to be considered as a treatise in the first instance. It claims to be an investigation into the reality of Fascism, 'un atto di conoscenza' [a cognitive act] relating to a historical *male* [evil] which will contribute to national rebirth (*EP*, 223, 231). Though the project is undermined by the book's own rhetoric almost from the start, one of its most interestingly ambiguous aspects is that at least the central arguments have a certain persuasive force, even an intellectual one. Broadly speaking, they are psychosexual, and are clearly of Freudian derivation. They have something in common with the arguments first put forward in the 1930s by Wihelm Reich in *The Mass Psychology of Fascism*,[23] which also stressed Fascism's exploitation of irrational, half-conscious desires. Still, whatever his idiosyncrasies, Reich is plainly far more systematic and expert than Gadda, whose Freudianism is probably better seen as that of an intelligent layman, rather like Moravia's in his fiction of the postwar years, especially in *Il conformista* of 1951.

Gadda's fundamental thesis is that Fascism corresponds to the stage of infantile narcissism. In normal development (what he calls 'autocostruzione' [ibid., 340] – self-construction), it is a stage which is passed through, though it inevitably continues to be present in more or less submerged form and may come to the surface in the mature individual. Under Fascism there was in the Italian nation as a whole a regression to infantile narcissism, or a refusal to go beyond it and reach full psychological maturity. Up to a point the regression rested on reciprocal deception. To the Italian people Fascism offered fantasy fulfilments of infantile needs through parades, uniforms, fantastical rhetoric, and theatrical displays of all kinds. At the same time, Mussolini and his henchmen were able to indulge in self-deluding, infantile exhibitionism which the applauding crowd fed and identified with. Like other writers looking back to the Fascist period in the immediate aftermath of its fall, Gadda softens the blame to be laid on Italians as a whole. The constant focus of his verbal attacks is Mussolini himself, the prime agent and promoter of regression: 'a cinquant'anni egli sventola ancora il sesso alla facciazza del publico – coram populo – come un regazzino che fa la pipì a fiumi sotto a i'naso a la balia' (367) [At the age of fifty he still flaps his sexual organ in the face of the public – yea, before the people – like a small kid who pours out a river of pee under the nose of his nurse]. The most obvious form which the phallus (or Priapus of the title) took was the pathetic dagger the Fascists wore as part of their uniforms. The 'inargentato pene' [besilvered penis] served no purpose in modern warfare, but it fascinated the eye as a sign of power and virility (285; cf *QP*, 73, and *MS*, 919–22). Socially and politically the result was criminality masquerading as legal authority and power (cf *QP*, 80–2) and psychologically a condition similar to schizophrenia (*EP*, 324–6). Hence such phenomena as the ridiculous cult of youth (246), the false patriotism (327), with its absurd slogans, such as 'L'Inghilterra deve scontare i suoi delitti' (294) [England must pay for its crimes], and the deluded belief in Italian military might. Together such crass delusions masquerading as substantial truths led to the destruction of the best of Italy's young men.

It was not just real virility and strength that were missing, but also the vital process of sublimation. As is constantly rammed home by the comically desublimating rhetoric, there was no rising above immediate psychological and material needs. Eros dominated Logos, when the opposite is the major sign of psychological maturity. This does not mean that a pedestrian rationalism is the solution. As a supreme example of what can be done, Gadda cites Dante (ibid., 340), who transformed the pains of exile and bereavement into the greatest of positive achievements in the *Divina Commedia*. Though he offers few other clues in *Eros e Priapo* as to what might be the general modern equivalent, in *I miti del somaro* he is a good deal more explicit. Here he acknowledges the need for myth to motivate and inspire human action, but dismisses the idea that all myths are of equal value. A myth that works cannot be, as Fascism was, a 'mito qualunque' [any old myth], or 'un mito d'accatto, un giucattolo adocchiato a caso in una bancarella' (*MS*, 904) [a myth picked up cheap, a plaything that happened to draw the eye on a street stall]. The myth that is needed is summed up in the title of the second piece, 'La consapevole scienza' – scientific knowledge, but not unthinking and inhuman submission to technology or to brute scientific data. Scientific knowledge must go with self-awareness and be constantly adapted to the psychological and other changes that we must inevitably live through and at the same time regulate.

Consapevolezza potrebbe essere l'accettazione d'un senso di vigilia tecnologica, d'un incarico demandato alle funzioni operatrici dell'anima; d'un impiego della propria vita che non contrasti ai modi associativi della umanità. (915)

[Awareness might mean accepting the need for a sense of technological vigilance, for fulfilling a duty demanded of the operational functions of the soul, for an engagement of one's own life which is not at odds with the associative ways of humanity.]

He concludes a few lines later:

Un certo rispetto del dato, una certa osservanza del meccanismo del Mondo, è insito in ogni forma del pensiero e della operazione umana. Ed Ermes il Macchinatore ci potrà guidare al riposo ben più dolcemente che le Erinni. (916)

[A certain respect for the given fact, a certain observance of the mechanism of the world, is innate in every form of thought and operation of humanity. And Hermes the Devisor will be able to guide us to our rest much more gently than the Furies.]

All of which mythology the mythology of Fascism has clearly contravened.

Restricted to these elements, Gadda's argument is probably recuperable within the borders of familiar discussions of Fascism, Freudian and non-Freudian alike. But Gadda breaks the rules. In some places he says things which are questionable or unacceptable within accepted intellectual discourse. More generally, rather than aspiring to an ideal univocal language, he constantly displays the polyvalence that is characteristic of his literary work as a whole and sets before the reader a sometimes bewildering set of interpretive possibilities. The rhetorical mode which he adopts for much of *Eros e Priapo* and which is evident in *I miti del somaro* and *Quer pasticciaccio* too – that of *vituperium* – favours overstatement, trivialization, and abuse which may or may not have some basis in fact but may equally well be prejudiced or fantastical in its turn and may threaten the validity of the intellectual analysis which is also being conducted. Rhetoric may assert its own fascination; comedy may outweigh analysis. And other more problematic consequences may follow. Rather than expose Fascism the writer may expose himself. Though he does so on the page and therefore arguably in a quite different manner from that of the principal object of his opprobrium, some uncomfortable analogies between the two forms of exhibitionism may emerge.

In places there is what looks like a simple mechanism at work. It is particularly evident in the passages dealing with Mussolini. Gadda almost always refers to Mussolini using some absurd periphrasis or nickname, such as 'il primo Racimolatore e Fabulatore ed Ejettatore delle scemenze e delle enfatiche cazzate' (*EP*, 224) [the prime Collector and Fabricator and Emitter of drivel and emphatic bollocks], 'presidente del Conziglio in bombetta e quanti giallo canarino' (227) [the Prime Minister in bowler and canary-yellow gloves], 'principe Maramaldo' (228) [Prince Maramaldo], 'Scipione Affricano del due di coppe' (228) [a two-of-spades Scipio Africanus], 'il Napoleone fesso e tuttoculo' (229) [the cretinous, all-ass Napoleon], together with briefer appellations, such as 'il Bombetta,' 'il Somaro,' 'il Baffo,' 'il Gran Maestro.' All of the above are taken from *Eros e Priapo*, chapter 1. Though they and many others like them reiterate the constant message of *Eros e Priapo* – that of the gap between rhetoric and reality – they also lend themselves to being savoured for their comic hyperbole. The macaronic mixture of the popular and the learned draws the attention, almost submerging the referent (Mussolini) in language, much as the silver dagger fascinated the attention of Mussolini's audience. It is a kind of name-calling, a childish game, though a highly literary one, and one that at any given moment may seem to situate itself at some ill-defined point on a notional scale between theatrical display and the expression of real rage and frustration. But the gamble is unstable, as childish games are. When Gadda says, as he does repeatedly, that Mussolini was syphilitic, it is quite unclear whether this is more abuse or whether, in the old-style positivist manner that is characteristic of his thinking, he is taking up something that was commonly said and proposing it as the necessary physical cause for a psychosexual disease.

In other words, Gadda oscillates between analysis of Fascism as an objective phenomenon and a mode of writing which is itself contaminated with at least some of the features he lays at Mussolini's door. Does this

signify some acknowledgment of guilt or of having himself been mistaken? I think not. Let us take another image of Mussolini which also
appears in *Eros e Priapo*, chapter 1, and then is reworked in *Quer pasticciaccio*.

Con que' du' grappoloni di banane delle du' mani, che gli dependevano a' fianchi,
rattenute da du' braccini corti corti: le quali non ebbono mai conosciuto lavoro e
gli stavano attaccate a' bracci come le fussono morte e di pezza, e sanza aver che
fare davanti 'l fotografo: i ditoni dieci d'un sudanese inguantato. (228; cf *QP*, 55–6)

[With those two great bunches of bananas of his two hands, hanging down at his
sides, held up by his two shrunken little arms – hands that had never known work
and were fastened to his arms as if they were dead and reduced to rag, with
nothing to do in front of the photographer, the ten lumpish fingers of a Sudanese
with gloves on.]

Here there is plainly a problem. The comedy and the attack on Mussolini
are from a racist perspective. It is not that Mussolini is at fault for his
imperialist ventures, but that he looked like an uncivilized African
dressed up as a European. The writer exposes not merely his childishness
but political attitudes which were part and parcel of Fascism as of the
European right generally in its traditional forms.[24]

Let us take a theme which is much more insistently present in *Eros e
Priapo* than the racist elements. Gadda introduces a powerful strand of
anti-feminism, in places couched in terms that are as strong as his
vilification of Mussolini. It was particularly Italian women, the Sophonis-
bas, as he insistently calls them, who responded to the false male in
Mussolini, who found sexual excitement and gratification in his displays
and promises and egged him on. At some points the discussion is plainly
metaphorical and might, I suppose, be allowed some justification on those
grounds. It is the feminine element in society (notably the crowd, the
despised 'moltitudine' [ibid., 224]), and in individual males which has
been allowed the upper hand. That which is naturally passive, subordi-
nate, material, which is animal, emotional, hysterical, has been allowed to
overrule the male, to overrule rational consciousness and conscience, the
shaping, directive will which the female naturally wants to be led by and
which is the agent of sublimation.

At times the images are Rabelaisian in their incongruity. To take but
one example, there is quite a long passage describing 'una distintissima
e dimolto agiata donna e signora' [a most respectable lady of considerable

means], who takes advantage of the blackout as she passes between the cathedral and the *campanile* in Florence. Crouching down, she emits 'in una gran birra quel tepente fiume la l'aveva in fontana' (ibid., 287) [in a great beery froth that river of warm water that she had springing up inside her]. It is a transgressive image, an image which reveals a difficult conflict in the writer between notions of the ladylike and the unladylike, the ideal and the real, but an image whose charge is probably exhausted in the act of comic transgression.

But neither the comedy nor the metaphors override the constant reiteration of what we might call traditional values. Women may have souls, they may have intelligence of a sort (though intellectual females typified by Margherita Sarfatti are a perversion of nature [ibid., 253]), they may be admired and desired, but their place is in bed and in the home, their sexuality and their hysterical needs firmly under male control. 'Non nego che la Patria chieda alle femine di adempiere il loro dover verso la Patria che è, soprattutto, quello di lasciarsi fottere' (245) [I do not deny that our country asks women to carry out their duty to the country, which is, above all, to let themselves be fucked]. Under Fascism, female sexuality was encouraged not to be materially satisfied and ordered but to find fantasy, narcissistic fulfilment, which might take the form of deliquescence in sonorous abstractions (253) or imagined congress with Mussolini himself. At its worst – though again there may be self-deflating hyperbole here – through a redirection outward of the need to be the recipient of male violence, perverted and indulged female narcissism found gratification in the idea of the youth of Italy being destroyed by war.

The tone may now be deliberately absurd, but there are obvious overlaps with Gadda's representations of women elsewhere before and after Fascism. The positive image is to be found in a piece in the 1930 *Meraviglie d'Italia*, entitled 'Casi ed uomini in un mondo che dura quindici giorni,' which includes a description of an ideal family, concluding:

Tu vedi la vecchia mamma dell'industriale assistere amorosamente le fortune del figlio, o la sposa accompagnare, al suo posto d'onore e di fatica, il marito. La donna è da noi presente alla vita de' suoi uomini, vicina ai loro adempimenti ed alle speranze. (*MI*, 72)

[You see the aged mother of the businessman lovingly aiding in the fortunes of her son, or the wife at the side of her husband at his place of labour and honour. In our country woman partakes actively in the life of her menfolks, is close to their achievements and their hopes.]

But it is the negative stereotype which dominates Gadda's fiction. Woman is associated most inevitably with forbidden and dangerous desires, provoking, perhaps inadvertently, an aggression which may be directed against others or against herself. Obviously the most powerful instances, though they are not exclusive, occur in the two major novels. In *Quer pasticciaccio*, Liliana – beautiful, childless, perverse, self-deceiving Liliana – is murdered. What is more, one of the possible murderers is another woman, the aggressively sexual maid, Virginia, whose violence is depicted with particular force in the first, *Letteratura*, version of the novel. In *La cognizione* the mother is the object of murderous filial rage, displaced towards the end of the novel onto an attack by others in the course of a burglary. But in the fiction the association between the female and the *male* [evil] of life is generally left implicit. Only in *Eros e Priapo* is the link made explicit and developed at length. One may surmise that, under the pressure of the expressive need that dictated the first writing of *Eros e Priapo*, something or some things were said which Gadda did not bring himself to say elsewhere in quite those terms. Certainly in the version published as *Il libro delle furie* there was a brief moment when the homosexual component that may be surmised in his anti-feminism became almost explicit: 'No, no, non c'intendiamo, ottimi educatori e buoni padri di famiglia! buoni scrittori eterosessuali, non c'intendiamo!' (*EP*, 37) [No, no, we do not understand each other, you excellent educators and virtuous family men! you virtuous heterosexual writers, we do not understand each other!], where the later version has 'moraloni' [paragons of virtue] instead of 'eterosessuali.'

But the implications of that stance are not ones that Gadda chooses to follow out. Indeed the urge to self-expression is dissipated or controlled as much as it is indulged. As *Eros e Priapo* proceeds, Gadda shelters increasingly behind an *alter ego*. Alì Oco De Madrigal, as he anagrammatizes his name, is partly spoken of in the third person and is presented as the writer of the book. He emerges, particularly in later pages, as a sad, old-fashioned Italian of the right, a genuine nationalist who appreciates the positive moral and physical qualities of his countrymen (283–5) and the courage and sacrifice of those who died fighting for Italy in the two wars (296) but who has seen his values traduced and what was best in his country destroyed. Now he has to face the inauthenticity of modern culture, with its new forms of narcissism – fashions, publicity, newspapers, and the like (351–6). In a way De Madrigal is a figure of fun, with his fairground name – a comic mix of the pseudo-exotic and the aristocratic, with an allusion not to the 'Patria,' but to the mother or motherland emerging from its very syllables. Gadda can foist any or all of the views expressed on to him, and yet he maintains the ambiguity. In so far as he does not completely differentiate himself from De Madrigal, he half-closes the door which he also half-opens.

What are we to make of the criss-crossing interpretive possibilities that he offers us? There are obviously particular solutions available in abundance. If one is selected, it will be because the text comes to be located in a particular genre by the interpreter. It seems possible to see *Eros e Priapo* as a genuine polemical treatise, and to discount the literary, comic, and self-deflating features. Gian Paolo Biasin, writing soon after its first appearance in book form, saw it as achieving the 'atto di conoscenza' initially proposed and potentially being socially beneficial (Biasin 1969, 476). With rather more subtlety and with more attention to the historical gap between the end of Fascism and the first publication of Gadda's denunciations, Carla Benedetti sees both *Quer pasticciaccio* and *Eros e Priapo* as probings into the nature of the *male*, seeing Fascism less in historical terms than as a continuing 'metahistorical' presence (Benedetti 1980, 81–99)[25] – though one might think that Mussolini, as Gadda sees him, is only very loosely identifiable as a metaphor for the *male* of postwar Italy. Mirko Bevilacqua takes more account of the complexity of the problems. All the same, he presses towards the moral, perhaps moralizing, conclusion that the final result is a form of fiction with a strong ethical component (Bevilacqua 1987, 181–8). At the opposite extreme are interpretations which privilege the literary aspects. These are not exclusive to literary critics. Renzo De Felice, plainly unconvinced by Gadda's analysis of Fascism, could still appreciate the book as a divertissement (Ledeen 1985, 109–10). He is certainly not alone.

The difficulties of interpretation can seem very large indeed. In Gadda's work generally there is always something that calls into question any particular values and beliefs that might seem to be proposed. Historical reality, problems of articulation and definition, philosophical aporia, self-doubt, repressed drives and inner conflicts, and other ostensibly negative forces – any and all of these seem to rend his writing and thinking, preventing the completion (in a conventional sense) of any of his major projects from the *Racconto italiano* onwards and leaving openness inscribed on every page. The very theorization in the *Meditazione milanese* of the irreducible many-sidedness of any phenomenon, literary or not, and the idea of the act of knowing being, like any other act, a form of deformation automatically problematize even the simplest act of interpretation. Indeed in *Eros e Priapo*, perhaps even more than in *Quer pasticciaccio* and other novels where some degree of generic expectation and restriction still obtains, freedom is drastically imposed on the reader. As Gian Carlo Ferretti (1987, 124–41) implies, no convincing categorization of the work in terms of genre can be found: it is the reader who has to choose what parts of the text to take as ethically valid or valid as literature, to pick up some of Bevilacqua's phrasing – at least up to a point.

In fact there are restrictions. The fan of receptive and interpretive possibilities is not large. The hyperbole and comic deformation create question marks, or inverted commas, around whatever is being argued or stated. But, if there are values and beliefs that can be affirmed, it is plain what they are – a traditional or reactionary view of women (with its hypocrisies and contradictions) and of non-Europeans, a patriotism which sets store by national traditions and national strength, a confidence in the social utility of science if correctly regulated and in the utility and value of rational knowledge generally, though with a recognition of the power of the irrational in human behaviour and the impossibility of achieving total order in society. It is also plain what is not believed in: unregulated irrationality, self-delusion and the delusions of others, arrant and wanton violence, not to mention women getting above themselves, modern life, and the cult of youth. And it is interesting to note the gaps, given the context of the years 1944–6. There is no interest in the idea of democracy or in democratic institutions. There are only passing and, of course, negative allusions to socialism, and there is no mention of the Partito d'azione (which would draw Montale and other liberal *letterati* who glimpsed, briefly, the chance of real national renewal),[26] nor of the Christian Democrats, for that matter. The 'atto di conoscenza,' if it occurs at all, occurs in a void. De Madrigal belongs to the past, as Gadda the writer can plainly see.[27]

And what of the really glaring omissions? Nowhere in *I miti del somaro*, *Eros e Priapo*, and *Quer pasticciaccio* is there any reference to Gadda's own involvement in Fascism, though in one or two places he perhaps comes close to some sort of admission. Near the start of 'mito e conoscenza,' the first of the *I miti del somaro*, he lays down the basic premise that: 'un mito è pur necessario a travolgere gli umani verso il futuro' (*MS*, 901) [a myth is certainly necessary to whirl human beings towards their future]. Without naming Fascism, he seems to admit to a qualified acceptance of it on these terms: 'Una tesi del genere (1922–1944) venne accolta con qualche riserva dalla nostra circospetta tendenza al meglio' (ibid.) [A thesis of this sort (1922–1944) was accepted with some reservation by our circumspect tendency to betterment]. 'La consapevole scienza' has a paragraph lamenting how easy it is to dismiss positivism in which Gadda seems to suggest, flickeringly and antiphrastically, that he was one of those who did not see through the charade: 'noi che abbiamo assaporato il conferenziere unico e funerario con tibie in croce sul fez: noi che abbiamo riconosciuto la spia, e lo sgherro travestito, in ogni biblioteca e in ogni fabbrica' (911) [we who have savoured the unique funereal lecturer with his crossed tibiae on his fez, we who have recognized the spy and the disguised agent in every library and in every factory]. Similarly, at the very end of *Eros e Priapo* Gadda seems to hint that his *alter ego*, De Madrigal, might at some point have something in common with the believers, when a 'carica narcisistica' [narcissistic charge] is sadly (and fiercely) acknowledged to be at work in him too (*EP*, 374). But these are scant appeasement to the puritan eye, which is all too aware that for the most part the denunciations and analyses are general. Ostensibly, the targets are others, primarily other Italians, who allowed themselves to be deceived or who did the deceiving. Self-reference is reduced, consciously or unconsciously, to what is not said, to the implications of blotting out that might be picked up by the reader alert to Freudian ideas of negation or to analogies already mentioned between the narcissistic play of the text and Mussolini's antics.[28]

Whatever unconscious motivation might be at work, it is worth considering the repression in a wider context. In not being able to admit to having supported Mussolini in so many words, Gadda behaved in the same way as the great majority of Italians. To say the least it was impolitic, not to say dangerous, to make any such admission in 1944 and 1945 and remained so in a country where the Fascist party was illegal and formal anti-Fascism a *sine qua non* for public acceptance in almost any field. Most intellectuals and writers who emerged from the Fascist years kept silent about the past in the immediate postwar period, though of course many were eager to establish their anti-Fascist credentials. Gadda had some scathing comments to make about painters and writers of the latter sort.[29] He himself was unusual, especially among those of the right, in feeling impelled to write about Fascism at all, and of course he did so at length and with considerable force almost as soon as it collapsed. Since he was only persuaded to publish *Eros e Priapo* and *Quer pasticciaccio* when Mussolini's Fascism was well in the past (and *I miti del somaro* would not appear until after his death), he obviously had no opportunistic motive. The nearest he comes to public pronouncements in the immediate postwar years are some letters to Milanese friends which have a similar tone and phrasing to *Eros e Priapo* (Gadda 1983b, 50-57). All in all, it is tempting to give primary importance to motives of pain and anger for what is said about Fascism and to motives of understandable prudence for what is not said.

Yet there is obviously more to it than that. If we look back to the pre-1943 Fascist Gadda, the contrasts with the Gadda of 1944–6 can be reduced to the central fact of denouncing Mussolini and Fascism, whereas previously he was positive about both. The values of *Eros e Priapo*, *I miti del somaro* and *Quer pasticcaccio* are ones which Gadda had consistently subscribed to and written about since the 1920s, with and without irony. Even on secondary matters the changes are few. *Eros e Priapo* satirizes Fascist rhetorical demands that England must pay; but Gadda had always been suspicious of English perfidy, and remained so.[30] He had accepted the Fascist rhetoric of youth; now he rails against it. But, anticipating some American presidents, it was a youthfulness of spirit which he professed to admire, not mere youthful years. Perhaps the only change of note is the waning of his anti-bourgeois satire, which is absent from *Eros e Priapo* and much reduced in *Quer pasticciaccio* in comparison with *La cognizione del dolore* and *L'Adalgisa*. He had seen Fascism as a vehicle for furthering what he believed in. Now he sees it as having been entirely destructive.

Writing against Fascism is a form of 'autocostruzione' and of self-justification. It is a way of constructing a negative past, circumscribing Fascism, and cordoning it off as the definitive Other, alternately barbaric, female, and absurd charade. In the process Gadda can reaffirm, up to a point, values he has always subscribed to and hence his own moral identity. Irony and absurdity are acknowledgments of the insubstantiality of that identity and of its incongruity within the historic order. But they are also the means whereby one further value can be unequivocally reaffirmed on every page. That value, which had been crucial throughout Gadda's career, is the value of literature, seen as an end in itself, whatever the ambiguities of its role and its meanings.

Gadda's manoeuvre or operation (as it may be termed) has resemblances to that more frequently and publicly carried out by younger left-wing writers, who also contributed to the image of Fascism as something inhuman or subhuman. Looking back, they interpreted their own pre-war populism as a form of anti-Fascism that led naturally to the resistance and membership in the Communist Party. In some ways the political differences are insignificant. Gadda was apparently prone to make cutting remarks about Vittorini posing as a 'santone' [goody-goody] and disapproved of *Il Politecnico* (Cattaneo 1973, 32). But Vittorini wrote approvingly of Gadda (Vittorini 1956, 22–4, 70, 418) and had a hand in the progress of *La cognizione* towards publication in book form (*RR I*, 851n). The cultivated *letterato* that was present in all of the significant writers of the early postwar years made for powerful bonds. Both Vittorini and Gadda had emerged from *Solaria*, which had wished to include a wide range of practices in its highly civilized republic of letters. The one essential was literariness. Neither had changed in that respect, just as they felt fundamentally they had not changed as regards their political ideology. They and others like them were the embodiment of the intellectual and literary continuity that managed to objectify and distance a still-threatening past. Similar delicate and potentially dangerous operations took place in many other areas of Italian culture and society and, thanks to the cooperation of almost everyone, the vast majority were successfully completed.

Notes

1 The one essay devoted to Gadda's Fascism is Robert S. Dombroski 1984, 91–114. Other studies which include considerations of the subject are cited below. The earliest discussion of the limits of Gadda's anti-Fascism appears in Cesare Cases, 'Un ingegnere in letteratura,' originally published in *Mondo operaio*, supplemento scientifico-letterario, 5 (May 1958): 7–17. The bulk of this text is in Giorgio Patrizi ed., *La critica e Gadda* (Bologna: Cappelli 1975), 169–80.

2 Interview with Dacia Maraini: 'Solo nel '34 ho capito cos'era il fascismo e come mi ripugnasse. Prima non me n'ero mai occupato. Le camicie nere mi davano fastidio e basta. D'altronde il libro *Eros e Priapo* l'ho scritto nel '28 e mostra tutta la mia insofferenza per il regime. Ma solo nel '34, con la guerra etiopica, ho capito veramente cos'era il fascismo. E ne ho avvertito tutto il pericolo' (Gadda 1993, 168) [Only in 1934 I understood what Fascism was and how it disgusted me. Before then, I was never concerned about it, the Black Shirts bothered me, but that's all. Besides, I wrote *Eros e Priapo* in 1928 and it displays all of my intolerance for the regime. But only in 1934, with the Ethiopian war, I truly understood what Fascism was. And I cautioned against all its danger].

3 For an account of the composition and publishing history of *Eros e Priapo*, see Giorgio Pinotti's note to the text in *SGF II*, 992-1023.

4 A letter to his sister of 3 September 1923 speaks of Gadda's efforts 'come membro del direttorio' [as a member of the directorate] to strengthen the *fascio* of Buenos Aires and of his intention not to write anything further for the Italian paper there, *La Patria*, until it stopped criticizing Fascism. Men-

tioning the Albanian crisis of that summer, he expresses a highly positive view of Mussolini: 'speriamo che il senso di responsabilità e di misura di Mussolini, la sua rapidità d'azione e la sua energia, facciano trionfare, come merita, la ragione d'Italia' (Gadda 1987, 84–6) [Let us hope that Mussolini's sense of responsibility and restraint, his rapidity of action and his energy, will make the Italian cause triumph, as it so deserves].

5 'Per tirare avanti e per guadagnare qualcosa, ho accettato di sobbarcarmi a qualche fatica pamphletaire tecnico-propagandistica, cavandone gloria nessuna, denaro poco e noia molta' (Gadda 1983a, 129: 26 Feb. 1941) [To make ends meet, I agreed to take on some work as a pamphleteer of technical-propagandistic [articles], from which I gained no glory, little money, and much annoyance].

6 For Gadda's integration as an 'organic' intellectual into Fascism and in particular his enthusiasm for autarchy, see Greco 1983, 51–98.

7 Texts of the articles are now in *SGF I*, 863–74 and 874–81. Dombroski (1984, 101–2) finds a sarcastic note creeping into the second, but the expressive element in Gadda's prose here seems to me good-natured and relaxed.

8 See notes in *SGF I*, 1248 and 1289–95.

9 All English translations are mine.

10 For a summary of the growth of *La cognizione*, from the first nucleus intended apparently for *Le meraviglie d'Italia*, see *RR I*, 851–80.

11 'Deve tener presente, ma questo non so se è bene che lo scriva, che in questo libro io ho creato una confusione narrativa, fra l'idea dei fascisti e l'idea dei vigili notturni. Non vorrei però avere dei fastidi. Crede che potrò avere delle noie?' (Gadda 1993, 171) [You must keep in mind, but I don't know whether it's good that I write this, that in this book I created a narrative confusion between the idea of the Fascists and the idea of the nightwatchmen. I would not want this, however, to become troublesome. Do you think it will cause me trouble?]. Cf Seroni 1969, 33, and Flores 1973, 64.

12 The appendix ('L'Editore chiede venia del recupero chiamando in causa l'Autore'), which, for all its ironies, is closer to the novel than the interview with Maraini, makes it plain that the satire is generally anti-bureaucratic, with at most reference to the plight of the ex-soldiers from the First World War. See *RR I*, 763.

13 For a considered personal assessment of Gadda's attitude to Fascism in the 1930s by a friend of those years, see Guarnieri 1989, 68–119, esp. 72–4.

14 There is no evidence of disillusionment in the later 1930s, as is argued, for example, by Papponetti 1994, 34.

15 One of Gadda's fears in the later 1930s was that, as a reservist, he would be recalled to military service.

16 For a penetrating examination of Gadda's and Montale's registration of the status of literature in the 1930s, see Luperini 1987–8, 41–50.

17 He wrote to his cousin on 28 April to thank him for his congratulations, adding: 'all'adunanza capitolina le cose si sono svolte in modo molto semplice e secco, come è ovvio, dato che gli altri offrono alla loro nazione ben altra attività che le lettere in questo momento!' (Gadda Conti 1974, 55) [at the gathering in the capital things went along very simply and matter-of-factly, as they obviously should, since at this time others are offering to the nation an activity very different from belles-lettres].

18 See *Bibliografia e Indici*, 34.

19 Cattaneo (1973; 108–9) reports conversations about the pains of hunger which were particularly intense for a man of Gadda's appetites and enjoyment and the devaluation of Gadda's remaining shares. A letter of 12 July 1945, re-establishing contact with Lucia Rodoconachi, refers to 'un tempo e uno spazio disegnati di orrore' (Gadda 1983a, 152) [a time and place of horror]; cf Gadda's words in Gadda Conti 1974, 63: 'Quest'ultimo orrore [la guerra] mi ha demolito' [This last horror [the war] has demolished me].

20 For a fuller account of Gadda's movements in this period, with references, see G. Pinotti's note to the text of *I miti del somaro* (*SVP*, 1370–1).

21 See Pinotti's note to the text of *Quer pasticciaccio* (*RR II*, 1139).

22 Andreini ed., 1988; now in *SVP*, 895–923. Giorgio Pinotti's 'Nota' (1369–1400) details their publishing history and their composition (1370–1).

23 Reich 1975. The first German version of *Massenpsychologie des Faschimus* was published in 1933.

24 For prejudice against blacks, see *Eros e Priapo*, 290 and 373; against Jews, 252; against foreigners generally, 343–4.

25 See also Dombroski 1984, 112–13.

26 For some ironic allusions to the Partito d'Azione see the letter to Contini (who was a member) of 20 December 1946 (Gadda 1988, 50).

27 Not surprisingly, Gadda voted for the monarchy in the 1946 referendum (Gadda Conti 1974, 66).

28 So Dombroski argues that *Eros e Priapo* and *Quer pasticciaccio* are both concerned with rejecting 'il male di cui l'Autore stesso si sente colpevole, cioè l'egoismo che ha condizionato il suo consenso al fascismo' (1974, 111) [the evil of which the author himself feels guilty, that is, the egoism that conditioned his acceptance of Fascism].

29 'Per quattro sgorbi che compicciano sulle loro tele, per quattro raccontini che hanno cacato su una rivistucola studentesca nel lontano 1937 si gonfiano più del tacchino di Predappio' (Gadda Conti 1974, 67) [For those few blots that they manage to put together on their canvases, for those few meagre little

stories that they shat out on a student rag in the distant 1937, they swell more than the turkey from Predappio].

30 Gadda was capable of scathing sarcasm about England in pre-war days, for instance, in his autarchic piece, 'Il carbone dell'Arsa,' included in the 1939 version of *Le meraviglie d'Italia*, which celebrates efforts to free Italy from dependence on 'zia Inghilterra e l'elogio della manna d'Inghilterra' (*MI*, 182) [Aunt England and the praise of England's manna].

References

Benedetti, Carla. 1980. *Una trappola di parole. Lettura del 'Pasticciaccio.'* Pisa: ETS

Bevilacqua, Mirco. 1987. '*Eros e Priapo*: trattato, romanzo o divagazione parodistica?' In Marcello Carlino, Aldo Mastropasqua, and Francesco Muzzioli, eds, *Gadda progettualità e scrittura*. Rome: Editori Riuniti

Biasin, Gian Paolo. 1969. 'L'Eros di Gadda e il Priapo di Mussolini.' *Belfagor* 24, no. 4

Cases, Cesare. 1975. 'Un ingegnere in letteratura.' In Giorgio Patrizi, ed., *La critica e Gadda*. Bologna: Cappelli

Cattaneo, Carlo. 1973. *Il gran lombardo*. Milan: Garzanti

Dombroski, Robert S. 1984. *L'esistenza ubbidiente. Letterati italiani sotto il fascismo.* Naples: Guida

Ferretti, Gian Carlo. 1987. *Ritratto di Gadda*. Bari: Laterza

Flores, Enrico. 1973. *Accessioni gaddiane. Struttura, lingua e società in C.E. Gadda.* Naples: Loffredo

Gadda, Carlo Emilio. 1983a. *Lettere a una gentile signora*. Edited by Giuseppe Marcenaro. Milan: Adelphi

– 1983b. *Lettere agli amici milanesi*. Edited by Emma Sassi. Milan: Il Saggiatore

– 1984. *A un amico fraterno. Lettere a Bonaventura Tecchi*. Edited by Marcello Carlino. Milan: Garzanti

– 1987. *Lettere alla sorella 1920–1924*. Edited by Gianfranco Colombo. Milan: Rosellina Archinto

– 1988. *Lettere a Gianfranco Contini*. Milan: Garzanti

– 1993. *Per favore mi lasci nell'ombra. Interviste*. Edited by Claudio Vela. Milan: Adelphi

Gadda Conti, Piero. 1974. *Le confessioni di Carlo Emilio Gadda*. Milan: Pan

Greco, Lorenzo. 1983. 'L'autocensura di Gadda: gli scritti tecnico-autarchici.' In *Censura e scrittura. Vittorini, lo pseudo-Malaparte, Gadda*. Milan: Il Saggiatore

Guarnieri, Silvio. 1989. 'Il doloroso travaglio di Carlo Emilio Gadda.' In *L'ultimo testimone*. Milan: Mondadori

Ledeen, Michael A. 1985. *Intervista sul fascismo*. Bari: Laterza

Lucchini, Guido. 1988. *L'istinto della combinazione. Le origini del romanzo in Carlo Emilio Gadda*. Florence: La Nuova Italia

Luperini, Romano. 1987–8. 'Il fascismo e "la repubblica delle lettere": storia e simboli nelle *Occasioni* e nella *Cognizione del dolore*.' In *Rivista di studi italiani*, 2 (Dec. 1987) and 6, no. 1 (June 1988)

Papponetti, Giuseppe. 1994. 'L'opera al nero di Gadda.' In *Otto/Novecento*, 18, no. 6

Reich, Wilhelm. 1975. *The Mass Psychology of Fascism*. Harmondsworth: Penguin

Roscioni, Gian Carlo. 1969. *La disarmonia prestabilita*. Turin: Einaudi

Seroni, Adriano. 1969. *Gadda*. Florence: La Nuova Italia

Vittorini, Elio. 1956. *Diario in pubblico*. Milan: Bompiani

Towards a Biographical Study of Gadda's Novel of Entanglements: The Intricate History of the *Pasticciaccio*

ALBA ANDREINI

Tracing the complicated journey of the *Pasticciaccio* and disentangling the jumble of contacts made by Gadda on the way to its publication means entering into a maze worthy of the book's own title, one which establishes complexity and imbroglio as characteristics of the author's poetics. Only after the accumulation of a considerable amount of relevant documents in recent years has it become possible to disentangle the snarl of vicissitudes involved in the publication of this text.

The principal stages in the travail of publishing the novel are: (1) its first, partial appearance in serial form in *Letteratura* during 1946; and (2) its subsequent publication in book form by Garzanti in 1957.[1] The book version included ten chapters, the last four of which were new, while the first six corresponded to four of the five original magazine instalments.

In each case, there was some force beyond the usual circumstances that worked to overcome Gadda's normal inclination towards procrastination. Giving birth to this novel, in both its versions, was by no means a serene or spontaneous effort, but rather one which was quite painful. Having put it off for as long as possible, Gadda seems to have delegated the responsibility for his work's seeing the light of day to others, and even referred to their efforts as a kind of imposition. On each occasion, coercive pressures forced him to release the text: indeed, the chapters published in *Letteratura* reached the public only through the midwifery of Bonsanti, and behind the Garzanti volume was the 'pointed gun' of the publisher (Gadda Conti 1974, 91). In short, with the *Pasticciaccio* we have another instance of the old story of Gadda's producing a literary work under pressure, almost under compulsion, and despite his congenital reluctance to let go of what he had written. The peremptory threats with which the author was enjoined to deliver both the instalments and the book are, among other things, then transformed in his imagination into experiences of actual torture: writing to friends, he emphasized his own imagined role as victim, and spoke of the attentions of his sponsors as having been helpful to the point of being persecutory. If it is to the credit of Bonsanti to have understood Gadda's greatness and to have miraculously sprinkled the baptismal water upon his friend's future masterpieces, extracting them from him piece by piece (*Letteratura* was also where a number of sections of *La cognizione del dolore* appeared in 1938), it remained on the other hand for Garzanti to launch Gadda into view of the broader reading public.

With *Quer pasticciaccio*, Gadda attained wide recognition; its publication marked the beginning of his fame and the popularization of his books. The connection with a major publisher like Garzanti rekindled interest in his earlier writings and thereby aroused the 'libidinous fury' (ibid., 126) of other publishing houses, which set about vying with each other for the exclusive rights to his complete works as if they were hunting down a long-sought trophy. It is for this reason that *Quer pasticciaccio* and *La cognizione del dolore* (published by Einaudi in 1963) came out in a chronological order inverse to that in which they were written.

The year 1957 also brought what amounted almost to the 'invention' of the writer, as if he had never before existed, creating the 'Gadda phenomenon.' Up to that time, if not exactly unknown, Gadda had been familiar only to a critical élite, with his books printed in very modest editions. Amidst the sudden honours heaped upon the author, the very person who had urged Gadda on towards his calling in the face of his mother's opposition and the demands of his engineering work found himself left outside in the cold and deprived of what he considered his just reward. Gadda's friend and patron, Bonsanti, at the explosion of enthusiasm for the writer, reacted like a pioneer whose homestead has been expropriated. Bonsanti, who had served as point man of Gadda's literary career, decried the short memory of the times in which forgetfulness of the origins of things came close to outright dishonesty. For him, the 'Gadda phenomenon,' based as it was on the recycling of older writings, ran the risk of passing off, as new, material that was really a product of an earlier period. Years after the events of 1957, during the heat of which he had refrained from speaking out publicly, Bonsanti reflected on them in an entry from 25 September 1974 in his commonplace book:

For many readers, and for a great number of the critics, Gadda belongs to this postwar period; to those who knew him a good deal further back, back to the outlying fringes of another postwar period, after a war that increasingly proved to have upset and reshaped his nature, [...] the current discoveries being made with respect to his work arouse something less than charitable smiles among those who knew him then. And yet, we have to get used to seeing our friends, as well as ourselves, as posthumous; [...] and nothing is more difficult, for that matter, than to convince people that the world existed even before now. [...] Alas, we will never be able to know the unpublished Gadda, we who came through it all with him and who savoured at the moment of their birth, word by word, his writings and idiosyncrasies. (Bonsanti 1978, 239–40)[2]

It is precisely this discrepancy between two different times that is translated here into Bonsanti's uneasiness and distress. As the first promoter of the undiscovered original, untainted by the least suspicion of having merely hopped aboard the bandwagon, he ended up having to live through it all over again, this time as a mere spectator of the prodigiously elaborated replay of the past, set in motion by the machinery of success.

Historically speaking, it was only on account of the newly expanded market of the publishing business in the 1950s that Gadda could be turned into a popular author. Now that the 'Gadda phenomenon' has become common knowledge even down to the secret crevices of his legendary eccentricity, it may seem strange and impossible that he achieved success only when he was already in his sixties (he was born in 1893), since he had been at work for almost half a century (his first writings go back to 1915). The arrival of celebrity status astonished him: 'I have been here right along,' he said, marvelling at the change. It caught him unprepared, and he reacted with irritation to all the noisy publicity of a world which was duplicating his likeness in every popular magazine, and distributing it to the waiting-room of every dentist in Italy. The 'hullabaloo of interviews' and the 'circus of popular magazines' annoyed him. He would not willingly participate in the ceremonies of recognition, which, precisely because they were long overdue, were characterized by triumphalism and noise; he resisted the assaults of popularity: 'I have become a kind of Lollobrigido, a kind of Sofio Loren, though I am lacking in the gifts of these two incomparable champions' (Gadda 1983, 60–1).

As a writer, Gadda bore within him the same sense of injury that weighed upon him as an individual. On account of the sufferings that had marked his existence and had brought him to 'biografando' [writing down his life] as a way of 'flying over the thorny patches' (VM, 427), attaining the glory of success turned out something less than the model of it which had taken shape in his own mythography. As with the original rejection suffered as a child, '*cui non risere parentes*' [him on whom his parents have not smiled],[3] the conquest of victory was reduced, in summing up his career, to simply a long trudge through adversity and hardship. A sense of the difficulties endured by Gadda along his way to affirming himself as a writer literally explodes, at the moment of his success, with reference to the interminable *Pasticciaccio*, which he defined as 'infernal' and 'eternal' (Gadda Conti 1974, 74, 92), using two adjectives which sum up all the travail of a long and difficult gestation, the diachrony of his exertions.

The tribulations of that endless labour went on just as intensely during the interim between the two dates of publication. Getting the text of the *Pasticciaccio* settled down took ten years, from 1946 to 1957. They were years of torment, both personally, as a result of his relocation from Florence to Rome and his interval of employment from 1950 to 1953 at RAI, and creatively, because of the goading need to wrap up a work in which he had invested so much of his energy. In sudden moments of discouragement, he would confess these sufferings to friends; not even success could ever entirely make up for them.

When the *Pasticciaccio* finally appeared as a book and the acclaim of the public had at last arrived, he was too exhausted to be appeased by the clamour of being a celebrity. Consciously, he understands the paradoxical workings of this 'stupid fame' that had arrived so late, not without some unpleasant moments (Gadda Conti 1974, 128).[4] He was timid and fearful amid the worldly din, and he was reluctant to turn over a work of high quality to that kind of marketplace. In his own mind, he attached a value to the book based on the personal price he had paid in writing it, and he stressed the history of these sufferings in fiercely defending it:

The novel cost me years of mortifying labour in a poor state of health and with heart trouble on top of it all. And now, there is this avalanche of novels on Roman, Sicilian, and Jewish subjects which has overtaken it and submerged it in the din of the howling and general idiocy of the readers. (Gadda Conti 1974, 104)

Unfailingly, every time he touched upon the *Pasticcciaccio*, Gadda obsessively harped upon the effort and time spent in producing it. This was also a way of declaring 'I am different,' of eschewing the presumed extemporaneity claimed by other writers, and of removing himself from any suspicion of having flirted with the literary fashions that quarrelled over him. Cautiously, he navigated between the Scylla of a waning neorealism and the Charybdis of a burgeoning neo–avant-garde, mistrusting those who tried to associate him with these movements, and distinguishing himself as remaining faithful to the highly cherished tradition of Manzoni and Dossi.

Gadda's quarrel was not with literary seasons; it was rather a private quarrel with the times: his new-found status as a celebrity caught him unprepared, and he would have preferred to have been spared its constant interruptions. It may have been only through Garzanti's goading, expressed in their correspondence in the form of jesting, peremptory threats, that the *Pasticciaccio* eventually attained publication as a book. For his part, however, Gadda suffered a kind of post-partum anguish, while concealing it behind endless complaints of physical and nervous illnesses in his epistolary jeremiads. In fact, his reluctance to write an ending, felt to be improbable in itself, testifies to his attachment to perfectionism. Every threatening ultimatum would upset him, since it was only the provisional, the uncertain, that was appropriate to the practically endless narration of this story: 'slowness' and 'reticence' (Cattaneo 1973, 116), which defined for him the untimeliness of his own literary fate, connote also his nature as a writer inclined to temporize. The *Pasticciaccio* was the work that gave him the worst time of all. Thus, in his later account of its development, the sufferings of his whole life are fused with those endured in the creation of the novel, entangled in a way that they mirror each other:

Let them be indulgent, share in my pain, my labour, the humiliation and hunger I had to endure silently for years, interminable years, in the effort to flee from their claws, to fly 'towards the times of freedom.' The toll I shall pay to Charon is called grief.

With the act of writing thus understood, separation from the text achieves no liberating effect:

'I sent it to the printers': yes, 'I sent it to the printers.' If I had an ounce of sense, I should really be preparing for that final staunching of the tongue, of the pen, I mean, for which I ardently pray: for that definitive silence which will stand as the best of my works. (*VM*, 506, 511)

Gadda's leave-taking from the *Pasticciaccio* seems comparable to that of one of its characters, Liliana, from the world of the living: in both cases there is the need to make sense of one's temporal existence, the former through writing, the latter through having a child. There is also symmetry in their common attraction to silence and nothingness. Tracing the links in this chain of similarities, one may also hazard the thought that Gadda's weariness and Liliana's psychic alteration can lead to a further analogy: Liliana's failure to give birth has its equivalent in the travailed parturition of the *Pasticciaccio*, torn from Gadda despite his dilatory instinct. Both abrogate finality and demonstrate an excess of idealism, hindering the completion of the project or leading to the transfer of responsibility for its completion to others. The *Pasticciaccio*, in short, has the complexity of a last will and testament, the drafting of which has been repeatedly postponed, and the delivery of which not even the coinage of success could ever recompense.

Jealously guarding the phases of his creative elaboration, Gadda also stressed the importance of his method of work. When he contrasted his own deliberate pace to the incontinent haste of others, he implied, with bitter vexation at the chance similarities and presumed concordances noted by others, that there was actually a unique quality to his procedure, whose tangible sign was the variants, in keeping with the principles expressed in his attacks on the ineffability of so-called literary prophets.

No other work of Gadda's accompanied him for so long, no other demanded so much energy and material sacrifice. The five sections which appeared in *Letteratura* in 1946 were born out of 'an uncontainable and explosive urgency' (*VM*, 506) of his spirit, amidst the hardships of the war: its hunger, bombardments, and terrors. This was the most difficult period of his altogether unfortunate residence in Florence, which lasted from the 1940s to the 1950s. The announcement in the thirty-first issue of *Letteratura* of a sixth chapter, even though not yet written, testifies to this initial creative momentum, attributed in the gossip of his acquaintances to an outpouring of creative energy. The legendary impossibility of finding the original manuscript makes it impossible to verify; however, the seriousness of his intention to continue is documented by the subject headings shown under the 'To be continued' notice at the end of the fifth instalment, an intention contradicted by the absence of its continuation in the next issue, despite the journal's advertising to the contrary.

The years from 1946 to 1950 were marked by great poverty, ironically self-defined by Gadda as the predicament of 'an elect spirit,' yes, but one 'stuck [...] in a body that must live on bread.' The answer for this situation was found in 1950 through a 'paid editing job' obtained for him by G.B. Angioletti at RAI (Gadda 1983, 68), but the resumption of writing the *Pasticciaccio* meanwhile fell victim to his miserable circumstances. From 1946 on, Gadda dedicated himself to its continuation irregularly, in fits and starts, waiting to find, after a number of advances, financial backing substantial enough to permit him to finish it off. It is difficult to determine exactly which parts of the continuation were got under way during this period, to which Gadda refers with the term 'interrupted application':

I continued to work on my *pasticcio* with some perplexities, with some intermissions, and from time to time with vigour, during the first months of 1947. I had other sudden fits of writing in '48 and '49. (ibid.).

The publication of the 'Sogno del brigadiere,' which is a precursor to the opening of the future chapter 8, is definite evidence that he did continue to write during the interval of his 'office work' (ibid.).[5]

From 1946 to 1953, up to the time, that is, when Garzanti underwrote him with a subsidy that would permit him to quit the office job and seriously devote himself to finishing the book, economic necessity drove Gadda in search of a publisher. The result was a multiplicity of negotiations with various prospective editors which served to further confound his own already overextended plans of work.

Careless promises, the failure to keep them on time, and the resulting extra burden of making up for these lapses all contributed to the making and unmaking of his writing schedule, entangling him in a heap of 'works in progress.' The list of publishers approached unsuccessfully grew long. First, there was Parenti himself, who was in charge not only of the review *Letteratura*, but also of the collection of texts connected to it. The *Pasticciaccio* was to have appeared in this collection as a complete novel. In fact, the only thing which actually appeared (between 1946 and 1947) was an advertisement holding out the promise of an edition 'enriched with copious notes – those characteristic Gaddian *notes* – PREVIOUSLY UNPUBLISHED.' Next, Vallecchi took the book over, having succeeded the Parenti brothers in running *Letteratura*; with the completion of the novel, among other points, Gadda was to have paid off a debt to Vallecchi for another work (*Racconto italiano*) which was never published under Vallecchi's imprint (Gadda 1984). Immediately afterwards, in mid-1948, Gadda offered Mondadori the novel under a title slightly different from that by which it is known today: *Il delitto di via Merulana*. Then, there was Longanesi, as well. Finally, there is evidence in an unpublished letter from May 1953 of subsequent negotiations with Einaudi in direct competition with Garzanti for the rights to the *Pasticciaccio*. In the letter addressed to Luciano Foà, Vittorini formulated the basis of a strategy for complete, step-by-step publication intended to extricate Gadda from old obligations while tying him to new ones. Vittorini proposed to meet the author's demands by 'making a substantial advance payment for the *Pasticciaccio'*:

we would seek to get hold of this whenever it's finished [...] the very day that Gadda [...] gave us a free hand to enter negotiations; however, I would try to obtain at least some moral commitment from Gadda to consider us his future publishers, for this book which, if completed, will be among his best.[6]

Perhaps more for financial reasons than for any real interest in the medium, Gadda also wrote a film treatment of the *Pasticciaccio* and was paid for it by Lux Film, to the head of which Gadda had been introduced by his friend Bonsanti in the latter's constant concern to find a solution to Gadda's economic straits. From the text, which was titled *Il palazzo degli ori* and which remained unpublished until 1983, it is possible to date the writing to 1947–8.[7] In it we have a unique and unexpected work written by Gadda specifically for the screen, though from its technical characteristics (scope, arrangement of scenes, and so on), it would appear to be a treatment rather than a true and proper film script.

Despite the fact that this treatment was based on the only work of Gadda's which, among all his writings, ever made it to the screen, neither Germi nor Schivazappa, the two directors associated respectively with the screen version of 1959 (titled *Un maledetto imbroglio*) and the television version of 1983, was able to make use of Gadda's own work-up. While demonstrating through the author's own hand the cinematic possibilities of the novel, the trial script remained unused; it never became a movie. It is more interesting as a further twist in the complex internal and metamorphic history of the *Pasticciaccio* than for its singularity in the Gadda canon.

Apart from the history of the novel, Gadda's interest in cinema may also have something to do with its prehistory: *Il palazzo degli ori*, which falls chronologically between the appearance of the *Pasticciaccio* in *Letteratura* and the novel's publication as a book, picks up an idea which predates both. This was an early idea for a detective movie datable to around 1940: the author, who discussed it with Bonsanti and Forzano, put it in writing for Tirrenia-Film, in whose archives it must have been lost.[8]

As with Gadda's interest in film, which goes back to 1928, to this predecessor of the *Il palazzo degli ori*, the theme of the 'detective story' also has an antecedent in the form of some notes written in 1928 concerning a sketch for a detective novel, *Novella seconda*. Its possible use as a literary vehicle is discussed theoretically in an epistolary confession to Carocci:

[...] a mood of weariness, of boredom with life [...] leads us to seek in dreams – in art, popular art, art accessible to the masses – a momentary escape from these evil times. One must recognize that this is what underlies artistic productions aimed at a mass audience (carnivals; popular theatre; crime stories; and now, the Cinema).[9]

La cognizione del dolore, if one traces it back to the actual date of its drafting, is proof that even in the thirties Gadda continued in various ways and contexts, to follow that thread of thought. In all probablility, the *Pasticciaccio* itself was originally no more than a 'detective story': the only one to have actually been done, and then immediately expanded to the size of a novel, of twelve stories that had been planned for the review *Letteratura* and its associated publishing house.[10]

Gadda's intense interest in court cases and crime reports, which is a commonplace in reminiscences about him, led him to try playing alternately upon the dual keyboards of film and detective story in pursuit of a popular appeal which he recognized as their common denominator in the letter to Carocci. At the outset, the *Pasticciaccio*, too, may in fact have been connected to an actual crime, the Stern case.[11]

Gadda's goal of reaching a 'mass audience' is, however, most evident in the film treatment, due to this medium's accessibility and appeal to a broad public. The objective of reaching ordinary people prompted Gadda to indulge in a sympathy for the common man. The expository form of the treatment, which is necessarily stripped down to highly economical camera directions, reveals this intention with unusual clarity, setting it down in its pure, ideational state.

The demands of writing for film account for the principal differences between the two versions of the novel, on the one hand, and the excursion into cinema, on the other. A comparison of the three moments of the *Pasticciaccio* must be done on the level of structure.

The five chapters which appeared serially in *Letteratura* were converted into six chapters for the novel.[12] The periodical's first instalment is equivalent to the novel's first chapter; the second instalment was divided and became chapters 2 and 3; similarly, the third instalment was divided into two chapters for the novel, 4 and 5. The fifth instalment became chapter 6, while what had been the fourth instalment was entirely dropped. Of the four new chapters which appeared in the novel in 1957, the content of chapter 10 parallels that of chapter 1 (both concern the two crimes); the others (chapters 7, 8, and 9) centred on the investigation of the theft. In the final form of the *Pasticciaccio*, then, four chapters are devoted to the investigation of the robbery (chapter 6, as taken from *Letteratura*; and chapters 7, 8, and 9); four other chapters (the second, third, fourth, and fifth) deal with the investigation of the murder. In terms of the structure, the revision, including the changes made to the *Letteratura* material and the addition of new chapters, is intended to achieve a careful balance of the overall design of the novel, by dividing chapters equally between the theft and the murder. The splitting of the two *Letteratura* instalments to create four book chapters serves precisely this purpose. The result is that as a book, the novel contains equal numbers of chapters devoted to the two investigations, and because of the parallelism, its structure is static.[13] Furthermore, Gadda eliminated the fourth instalment (of the *Letteratura* text), which might have cast light on the murder through an allusion to the guilt of Virginia; the author's ulterior motive was thus to leave the mystery unsolved, to forego a conclusive ending. Gadda opted for the open-endedness of the work; he contrived to achieve a leisurely and diffracted discursive movement in contrast to a direct forward thrust towards a conventional resolution. It is not by chance that he defended the compelling artistic reasons which forced him to ignore the publisher's suggestion to limit the novel's digressions:

Your impression concerning the excursus which may seem unrelated to the narrative is perhaps justified. But if I were to delete certain passages [...] I would end up changing the whole design of the work. [...] That is more or less the way I write. In any case, permit me to continue with this design, complicated though it may be. (cited in Andreini 1988, 133)

The plotting of *Il palazzo degli ori* differs from that of the *Pasticciaccio* as published in *Letteratura*, where only the investigation into the murder approached, though with similar results, a conclusion. It differs also from that of the book, in which there is an investigation of both crimes, but the guilty go unapprehended: the jewels are recovered in one case, but nothing more than questions are raised concerning Liliana's last niece. In 1947 Gadda found a ready-made idea for a detective film precisely in the portion of the *Pasticciaccio* that had already appeared in *Letteratura* the year before. What did the writer do? He took the plot out of those five instalments and modified it, outlining further incidents and above all pursuing it to a solution of the two crimes. Entirely constructed of actions, the treatment skilfully prepares for its sudden twofold resolution after having posed the hypothesis of a single perpetrator. Virginia, who is one of Liliana Balducci's maids, thus becomes in *Il palazzo degli ori* the person responsible for the murder: a kind of matricide, given the maternal feelings that the childless Liliana had for her. Retalli, who commits the robbery, is pursued through the Pontine countryside and pays with his life for the sole crime of having robbed the Countess Menegazzi: hunted down, he is killed by the carabinieri Pestalozzi and Santarella.

The resolutive catharsis typical of the detective mystery which occurs in *Il palazzo degli ori* results from its having been conceived for the movie screen. The demands of the film genre not only call for an ending with a bang, but also impose a certain process of development. When in 1957 it appeared that the 'old screenplay' was about to come out in *Settimo Giorno*, Gadda, in asking for its authorization from Garzanti, considered the 'solution of the mystery' to be an obstacle to his plan for a 'second volume.' In fact, although a sequel to the *Pasticciaccio* was the subject of correspondence with his publisher until 1959, nothing ever came of it.[14] The events in *Il palazzo degli ori* were set up, with its double solution and dynamic rhythm, towards achieving its climactic ending. The two crimes, in fact, are distanced from each other in the presentation so as to constitute a crescendo, to help create which several new episodes have also been inserted (for example, the theft of Liliana's little dog, Lulu, and its later strangulation). Thus, there is some play with foreshadowing devices, through which events take on a linear progression. *Il palazzo degli ori* consequently attains a pyramidal structure, which is later shattered by the static construction of the novel in 1957, in which, after the initial parallel between the crimes, there follows the parallel between the two police investigations, and everything gets blocked in the stasis of entanglement. The architecture of *Il palazzo degli ori* confirms that Gadda's renunciation of solving the crime in the novel, though having thought about it as 'material' for an eventual sequel, is not the consequence of that organic incapacity to write a novel which his critics accused him of.[15] The ending of the film treatment responds rather to his desire to end 'the story line that was tending to deform itself with a dramatic apocope':

The knot comes loose all at once; it ends the story brusquely. To go on at length about the hows and whys seemed to me to be no more than vain mumbling, a pedantic and, in any case, posthumous dragging out of the narration. Such dithering would have dampened the sudden shock, not to mention the trauma, of the unexpected ending. (*SGF I*, 1213)

While he aims, using the form of the police investigation, at the specificity of the detective story, Gadda fractures it, throwing out the standard seal of an epilogue and reducing the finale to a flash of intuitive sagacity on the part of Ingravallo. Whether or not the intention had been to discipline his own creative magma with the corrective of a tried and proven literary form, Gadda then went on to undermine the form's traditional optimistic ending. Thus the genre's principal characteristic is negated, as if in Gadda's view, the creative magma of reality is resistant to the order and systematic control of reason. The non-finite is the refusal to follow the convention; it is not simply the product of the author's fatigue, for having got stuck in the confusion of his own narrative. The incomplete is, on the contrary the 'structural emblem' of the work, the sign not of its 'limit' but of the 'potency [...] of the [Gaddian] investigation' (Guglielmi 1986, 240), through which the writer makes us understand that it is the creative magma of the world itself that condemns him to the impossibility of a neat ending (ibid.)

Il palazzo degli ori, furthermore, because of the historico-cultural moment in which it was written, exalts that desire to understand the lower classes which, by self-definition, is the mainspring of Gadda's narration. The evident antithesis between rich and poor which serves as the motor for the plot is doubtless attributable to neorealistic taste and the influence of the times as well as to the medium of film itself, which is, of course, aimed at a mass audience. Beauty, with its exuberant and aggressive vitality, is almost openly called upon for the realization of a revenge against poverty, by posing beauty as poverty's figurative correlative:

In general, all the characters are young, and males and females must be extremely attractive to signify the thriving health and beauty of the people of Lazio, despite their poverty ... This youthful beauty is, however, thirsty not only for life, but also for ... jewels, which happen to be owned by the rich. (*SVP*, 952)

In one scene, when the focus is on explaining the yearnings of the characters, the director is instructed to create an atmosphere that is one of respectful and participant seriousness:

There follows separation and a farewell scene with light romantic-heroic emphasis, in the manner of poor people, for whom crime is sometimes an act of sacred rebellion, etc., and the police who are chasing them are equivalent to the persecution of fate, etc. A serious scene, with aesthetic and sentimental nuances of the director's choice. (ibid., 969)

These directives serve to clarify the whole load of explosive provocativeness that Gadda later pours out in the untamed attractiveness of the 'impoverished country beauties' (Lavinia, Assunta, Ines) of his novel. What also is apparent is the desire to understand the 'humiliated and offended,' with which the new chapters of the novel would be embroidered. In the novel, they are brought into focus against the backdrop of the dilapidated outskirts of the city, in an agricultural *habitat* already prefigured in the movie treatment with its core of desolation, expressed in occasional descriptive cues:

Dolly shots of the maresciallo fleeing on motorcycle through the fields and dirt roads and some remote corners of the countryside, towards the residence of Retalli Enea. Some passersby, some greetings, some oxen. Vineyard workers or pruners. [...] The wretched little house, picturesque in the Italian style, of the Retalli family: uncles or parents working, old women somewhat frightened and curious little girls, chickens, piglets. (ibid., 959–60)

In the screenplay, the factor of poverty as the sole mainspring of the chain of 'revenge-humiliation-cupidity' (ibid., 985) that is unleashed in the palazzo lies behind both crimes. It is at work in Virginia, who is guilty of the murder there, as well as in Retalli, who is responsible for the theft. It is poverty, especially as regards the theft, that tightens the knots of the story, and heightens its tension, due to Enea Retalli's love for Lavinia:

The spectator must be seized by the tragic sense of poverty and of the impending night, of life exposed to the elements. The spectator is induced to 'sympathize' momentarily with the two young people because of their love, which the dangerous encounter suddenly reveals. (968)

And elsewhere:

The love that they have freely exchanged made its bed upon the poverty of the bare earth, rather than on the mattresses of the rich, and was protected not by votive candles and the Madonna, but by the thicket of shrubs agitated by the storm. (969–70)

Indeed, precisely upon the binomial poverty-love, which softens the negativity of nail-hard greed, there evolves a dramatic crescendo (the death of Retalli) which is meant to rouse the audience's interest and stir up their passions:

In the movie viewer: a) sense of sharing the fate of the two, love and the salvation of the treasure. The dramatic interest passes for a moment from the police investigation to the 'fortunes' of the two lovers. (ibid., 970)

That the greed of the poor should take on the tones of a justified revenge against their fate is already suggested in the title of the treatment, where it is not by chance that what dominates is the image of wealth as seen through the eyes and fantasies of the people.

From Gadda's unpublished correspondence with Garzanti we know that the writer had thought about changing the title to *La casa dei ricchi* or *Er palazzo dell'oro*[16] for both the movie and the novel. Utimately, however, he discarded these in favour of the original *Quer pasticciaccio brutto de via Merulana*, which stresses, above all, the entangling confusion of reality, according to a notion of complexity that can be extended to his entire narrative universe, one that, as with all great writers, makes us see the world according to his own image and likeness, which is to say, *pasticciato* [all messed up] and Gaddaesque. Not accidentally, the term *pasticciaccio*, which powerfully evokes the intrinsic nature of this vision, is now used in everyday language. In effect the centrality of the poverty-wealth theme and its propulsive role in the narrative mechanism dwindle in the novel. The economic factor also wanes from being the exclusive motive for the murder to one which is presumably merely an accessory. The 'mystery' of the *Pasticciaccio* leaves altogether unsolved its rebus of motivations, pursuing them into a kind of investigative jumble.

The *Pasticcaccio* does not negate the rich-poor antithesis; it attenuates its importance without, however, altogether dissipating it. Social consciousness in Gadda's writing is not the immutable and indisputable element one might suppose from the frozen image one gets of him as a conservative; it is rather a strand, thus far neglected by critics, which the magnifying lens of *Il palazzo degli ori* allows us to examine more closely, revealing its consistency.

If, in the autobiographical *La cognizione del dolore*, the personal account of the outrages inflicted upon Gadda by destiny includes a sarcasm aimed at the humble (as personified in the characters who deprive him of his mother's affection), in the *Pasticciaccio* the poor are instead viewed with sympathy. The objectivity of the narration, along with the variegated reality which it is meant to depict, registers the poor as 'human "types"' with 'their priceless turns of fate' (*VM*, 503) whom Gadda seeks to understand and with whom he intends to empathize. Such concerns, which are the warp upon which the entire *Il palazzo degli ori* is spun out, with its explicit formulations concerning emotional solidarity, become, in the *Pasticciaccio*, merely a watermark, legible only when held up to the light. The centrifugal power that words have in the novel, intensifying and overloading themselves with agglutinated meanings particularly in the last added-on chapters, conceals, by dressing it up in the garb of literary effect, the clarity of the novel's retributive contents. The whole process of creating variations also leads towards complexity. The revision of the text's language was not limited to a technical improvement in the reproduction of dialects (with numerous variants, in spelling and pronunciation, and otherwise). It was undertaken by Gadda in consultation with experts like Mario Dell'Arco, involving above all the fine-tuning of the Roman dialect. Gadda did not want to reproduce, with neorealist or ideological coherence, a cosmos of monolinguistic regionalism, but to remain faithful to his idea of a heterogeneous and messy world. According to the greater space the narrator assigns to himself in the new chapters, the emendations are aimed at attaining the strongest possible density of expression. Every expression that is merely factual or informational is taken out; for example, there is an almost systematic replacement of the generic verbs *avere* and *fare* in favour of those which are more specific and more expressive. There is also a more compact, condensed form of writing that accompanies an extensive revision of punctuation; indeed, the use of ellipsis points is greatly reduced while there is a broad turn to that of the colon. The writing, considerably more layered in 1957, is made dense by the author's taste for recaps, homages, citations, and plays on words. To this taste is related the delight Gadda takes in altering the names of his characters, hardly one of whom escapes untouched; similarly, dates and addresses are never the same twice. It should be noted that Gadda's ongoing concern with the origin of names goes hand in glove with all this play upon variations. Nor do the changes always turn out to be easily explained; it is almost as if something maniacal were at work, and we were being asked to make psychophilological conjectures in order to decipher them.

The numerous revisions constitute an intricate thicket of variants whose individual and specific purposes and motivations, whether involving cuts or additions, can at times be explained by a detailed analysis of the text. The complex of variants unfolds in interpretation, with the flexible rules of philosophical and linguistic values, upon whose intertwining the act of interpreting casts light.[17]

In any case, the heavy labour of correction, entailing a careful attention to detail, in keeping with the 'poetics of rubbish' (Andreini 1988, 88) expressed in his *Primo libro delle favole*, is united with his pursuit of perfection via a tendentially infinite process of re-elaboration. Even after 1957, Gadda continued to go through each new printing of the *Pasticciaccio*, not only correcting mistakes and typographical errors, but going through the anguished labour of revision each time (*RR II*, 1155–62).

The mechanism underlying this interminable process of correction, to which he could never put an end, was his neurasthenia combined with the meticulous habits typical of professional engineers. His neurotic behaviour was always taking him to the edge of psychosis, but would then be completely resolved in frenetic bursts of activity, in attention to every detail, in lucidity, planning, and a restless quest for exactness, as if he were working on an engineering project.

Gadda's fragility and anguish are transmuted into plain, patient, unremitting laboriousness;[18] in this painful, exhausting dedication to being concrete is encapsulated all the modernism that the writer was endowed with, his 'Come lavoro,' a method which ran contrary to that of the inspired seers whom he deprecated. Such patient creativity is unwilling to adorn itself with the magical powers of the 'artifex,' to which, by reminding us of the exertions and torments of the workshop, it seeks to offer, in the form of meticulous drudgery, the broadest and most coherent reply. Gadda expressed something similar in a theoretical essay entitled 'Come lavoro,' where he attacked the divinatory poses of certain types of writing.

Moreover, the characteristics of Gadda's methods of work indicate his distance from the literary currents of the years during which he wrote the different versions of the *Pasticciaccio*, whatever possible indebtedness historical contemporaneity might suggest. In so far as neorealism is concerned, the distance is mental rather than chronological. Just as he did not want to sacrifice reality to ideology, Gadda did not want to sacrifice his art to a conception of art as the reflection of a unique and immutable reality, which he viewed as the 'faecal residue of history.' His voracious dedication to open-endedness and to inclusion, along with his playing with variation, proof of his restless drive to work out and rework everything he wrote, were all aimed at discovering the 'quid più vero,' the 'truer thing' that stands behind things, 'like the mechanism hidden behind the face of a clock' (*VM*, 629–30). On the levels of structure and of detail, Gadda showed his faith in the principle of indeterminacy, and with his endless revisions, he pursued ambiguity, uncertainty, and the secret mystery in things. He achieves this precisely by martyrizing words so that the detail might come to life, by subjecting things to revised etymologies, and by declaring war on obviousness so that language is set free from the banality and alienation of the commonplace. The constant shifting at the heart of each single emendation demonstrates that his purpose was to inquire into 'the possible,' the 'rationality or irrationality of the fact,' precisely what neorealism did not do.

Similarly, Gadda is distinguished from the neo–avant-garde because his ability to manipulate language fed upon all his intense moods, upon his despair, his fears, his affections, upon all of his highly complex instincts and humanity. The indefatigable energy demonstrated by his ever-renewed efforts to make corrections sprang from the bond between the act of writing and his very being. Therefore, in 1957, when he he was being acclaimed for the explosive novelty of his style, and all kinds of 'followers' were hopping aboard his bandwagon, Gadda was not entirely wrong to disclaim them, saying 'they somewhat arbitrarily set themselves down in the shade of *his* umbrella, as if with a passport or reference' that he had never issued them (Gadda Conti 1974, 111).

Translated by Arnold Hartley and William Hartley

Notes

1 All but one part of *Quer pasticciaccio* published in *Letteratura* appeared in 1946: the first instalment in number 1, 26: 47–81, the second in 2, 27: 42–71, the third in 3, 28: 35–76, the fourth in 4, 29: 27–54; the final in 6, 31: 51–67 appeared in February 1947.
2 On the role played by Bonsanti in regard to Gadda, see Andreini 1990, 99–111.
3 This verse from Virgil is the heading of a fragment of *La cognizione*. See Emilio Manzotti's edition of *La cognizione del dolore* (Turin: Einaudi 1987), 525–35.
4 Gadda was not awarded the Premio Marzotto for which he was a candidate, and Cecchi, in order to compensate for Gadda's having been slighted, set up the 'Premio degli Editori.'
5 'Il sogno del brigadiere' appeared in *L'Apollo errante*, Almanacco for 1954. Edited by M. Dell'Arco. (Rome: Il Belli 1953), 19-20.
6 For the text's editorial adventures, see Andreini 1988, 131–7, and, mainly for the stages involved in the actual delivery of the manuscript to Garzanti, which can be reconstructed through Gadda's correspondence with Garzanti, see Giorgio Pinotti's note on *Quer pasticciaccio* (*RR II*, 1137–69). For the link with Longanesi, see Gadda Conti 1974, 74. I am grateful to Einaudi for permission to cite Vittorini's letter.
7 *Il palazzo degli ori* appeared for the first time in 1983, published by Einaudi, with a note by Alba Andreini and is now contained in *SVP*. In addition to

the note mentioned above, for the dating of the work, see Andreini 1988, 138–52, and Pinotti's note in *SVP*, 1401–24.

8 The history of this movie has not been written, lost as it is in the files of the film company. What I know of the discussions that led to the project I have learned from Alessandro Bonsanti.

9 In Gadda's first attempt to write a detective story, he states that he wants to interest the general reading public in order to reach a selected public: 'Interest the masses in order to achieve a high expressive style that good minds will appreciate. It is a way of publishing that requires quality (Manzoni, Pr. Sposi), and good, hard method' (*RR II*, 1318). Gadda's interest in detective fiction goes back even farther to *La passeggiata autunnale* (1918). In the 1930s Gadda edited several detective stories for Mondadori. See Roscioni 1969, 36–7.

10 Gadda speaks of a 'Book of 12 detective stories to appear in the review "Letteratura" within two years (1946 and 1947), and then to be assembled in book form for the "Edizioni di Letteratura" (1948),' in a letter of December 1945 to Alberto Mondadori (5 Dec. 1945), published in the commemorative volume *Alberto Mondadori* (Milan: Il Saggiatore 1977). And a few days later, the same intention is conveyed to Bompiani, but with the number of stories reduced to six. See Valentino Bompiani, *Via privata* (Milan: Mondadori 1973), 229–30.

11 On the articles that refer to the crime, published in 'Risorgimento liberale,' see Andreini 1988, 140, 145.

12 On the different subdivisions of the *Letteratura* instalments that Gadda proposed to Garzanti, see Pinotti's notes (*RR II*, 1146). Chronologically, the structural revision of the first *Pasticciaccio* was undertaken after the addition of the new chapters.

13 On the arrangement of the stories of the robbery and murder, see Ceccaroni 1970, 57–85.

14 See Gadda's letter to Garzanti (25 Sept. 1957), cited by Pinotti in *RR II*, 1141. Gadda discusses the prospects of continuing the novel in a second volume in a memo to Garzanti dated 6 Sept. 1957 and in successive letters (ibid., 1153–5). On the importance of Gadda's correspondence with Garzanti, see Andreini 1988, 131–7.

15 See Alberto Moravia's interview with Gadda in *Corriere della Sera*,' 17 Dec. 1967. Gadda is constantly afraid of being considered incapable of finishing his novel; see Gadda Conti 1974, 86.

16 For the first of the titles, see Gadda's letter to Garzanti of 27 Feb. 1956 in *RR II*, 1147; for the other variants, his letter of 14 May 1957 (ibid., 1152).

17 For an ample critical examination of the variants, see Andreini 1988, 94–131.
18 Cf Asor Rosa 1987, 16–17.

References

Andreini, Alba. 1988. *Studi e testi gaddiani*. Palermo: Sellerio
– 1990. 'Bonsanti e gli scrittori. Il caso Gadda.' In Paolo Bagnoli, ed., *Alessandro Bonsanti scrittore e organizzatore di cultura*. Florence: Festina-Lente
Asor Rosa, Alberto. 1987. 'Perché Gadda.' In Marcello Carlino, Aldo Mastropasqua, and Francesco Muzzioli, eds, *Gadda. progettualità e scrittura*. Rome: Editori Riuniti
Bonsanti, Alessandro. 1978. *Portolani d'agosto*. Milan: Mondadori
Cattaneo, Carlo. 1973. *Il gran lombardo*. Milan: Garzanti
Ceccaroni, Arnaldo. 1970. 'Per una lettura del *Pasticciaccio*.' *Lingua e stile* 5, no. 1: 57–85
Gadda, Carlo Emilio. 1957. Interview with Alberto Moravia. *Il Corriere della Sera* (17 Dec.): 11.
– 1983. *Lettere agli amici milanesi*. Edited by Emma Sassi. Milan: Il Saggiatore
– 1984. 'Lettere all'editore.' Edited by Mario Marchi. *Nuovecarte* 1, no. 2
Gadda Conti, Piero. 1974. *Le confessioni di Carlo Emilio Gadda*. Milan: Pan
Guglielmi, Guido. 1986. *La prosa italiana del Novecento*. Turin: Einaudi
Manacorda, Giuliano. 1979. *Lettere a 'Solaria.'* Rome: Editori Riuniti
Roscioni, Gian Carlo. 1969. *La disarmonia prestabilita*. Turin: Einaudi

Gadda in the Sixties: A 'Sofio Loren' among the 'Fat Asses' of Via Veneto

PAOLO ARCHI

Gadda's adventure in Rome had its first turning point in the 1950s, when he was hired there as a journalist and consultant by the state-controlled radio-TV network. He had finally landed what he considered to be a really decent position, his '*cadrega*' as he called it, using the Milanese term for a 'big comfortable chair.' It was during the years at RAI (1950–5) that he wrote 'Standards for Editing a Text for Radio Broadcast,' the contents of which testify to the meticulous, efficient, and exact application of that positivistic and scientist ideology which he took so much pride in. But it was only a matter of years before he started to complain about being 'crushed' by the job's burdens, and to insist that he could no longer go on with this life of hard labour: 'I couldn't remain as an "employee" at RAI: it would not have been the decent thing to do to myself' (Gadda Conti 1974, 90). Certainly the rupture with the RAI had its roots in the advance moneys provided by Einaudi for *I sogni e la folgore* as well as the monthly stipend coming in from Garzanti for *Quer pasticciaccio*. From this point on, Gadda assumed the role of professional writer, capable of earning a living by means of his pen; he had finally won the wager made with his departed, though ever-severe, mother.

He summed up how he felt about his early years in Rome in a letter to his friend Silvio Guarnieri: the days at the RAI had been 'five lost years.' And thus they needed to be added in with the melancholy accounting of an existence that had been plagued throughout:

Deductions from the life of a man:		
10 hours a day at the Polytechnic:	years	5
Engineering for 10 hours a day:	years	11
Hunger – two catastrophic wars:	years	6
Total amount of time wasted:	years	22

To this summing up, if one were to adhere to the dramatic calculations made by the author, for whom the years 'seem to go right down the tube' (Ungarelli 1974, 30–1), Gadda might have added another 'bloc' – at least six years – from 1957 to 1963, when *La cognizione del dolore* was published. Thereafter, existential weariness would overcome to a certain extent his remaining strength. However, during these six years, which were also in some ways tied to the mythic number 14 (the house in Via Blumenstihl, number 19, where he moved in 1957, was exactly fourteen kilometres from the centre of Rome; he had been born on the fourteenth of November, and had received his degree on the fourteenth of July), the Gaddian 'traumas' took on a substantially different guise in comparison to the ones usually associated with his home life and early adulthood.

Critics and biographers tend to regard the entire residence in Rome as a single, homogeneous trajectory, as an ongoing intensification of his private sufferings, made worse by old age:

By contrast, now began the age of prosperity ... Colleagues who used to arrive in a pick-up or on an old rusty tram, later by bus or even Vespa, were now stepping out of cars, and from models that were increasingly luxurious. For Gadda, however, life hardly seemed to have changed. (Cattaneo 1991, 128)

However, the engineer's years in Rome during the 1960s were by no means all characterized by isolation from society, as is evident in both what he wrote and how he conducted his daily affairs. Rome as the centre of governmental power, the Rome depicted in Fellini's films of that decade, when Italian politics were evolving from centrism to the centre-left coalition, and an emergent culture was increasingly aimed at the masses, were all elements that had a powerful impact on Gadda's work.

Most of all, Gadda took notice of the centrality of Rome (and therefore of its language, but even more of the government's political ideology and abuse of power) in the transformation of Italy into a neocapitalist society. In the process, it was losing what he considered to be certain fundamental values: what the Milanese bourgeoisie called the sense of commitment and dedication to one's work, *lavurà*. With anguish he confronted the demands made upon the writer to turn himself over to the media and public-relations people, and was horrified as political circumstances drew the clerical–Christian Democratic government first towards Fascism (the Tambroni administration), then towards the progressive opening to a centre-left coalition. This moment of violent modernization paradigmatically coincided with the moment in which Gadda, for the first time ever, achieved the status of a 'writer' officially supported by his publisher (Garzanti), and free from any obligation to labour other than at the production of literature. Gadda's apparent independence paralleled the explosion of mass culture in Italy, of high-circulation magazines, of television, of the distribution of novels in unprecedented numbers. These were the days of 'the sack of Rome,' and of the broadening of the government to include the Socialist party, on the heels of the disquieting alliance with neo-Fascists. Under these extreme conditions, the engineer wrote, published, and struggled through the last battle of his prose, ironically designating himself as the 'Sofio Loren' of literature, a celebrity of the literary world who, having been discovered, was now being followed and fondled both by the critics of 'high,' bourgeois culture (through the blessings of Contini) and by the illustrated magazines, which were intrigued by the 'Roman' content and other more trivial aspects of his narratives. In addition, there were his more famous leftist 'followers,' in search of some kind of personal blessing to support their new 'committed' literature, which had been born out of the crisis of neorealism.

Gadda lived this defining passage to Italian modernity in the first person: on one side he assumed the new role of writer–literary image as a true and proper duty, with the same patient attention to detail that he had shown as a young officer in command of his troops, or as a mature engineer working at the Vatican, or as a 'displaced person' scrupulously repaying the loans he had received, or as a zealous editor establishing the guidelines for radio broadcasts. And so, if the publisher so desired, there was Carlo Emilio on the pages of the picture magazines, photographed in Via Merulana, or next to the ads for women's underwear in 'Grazia,' ready to play the game of literary prizes, to accept the mechanisms of the literary marketplace. This public posturing produced various internal reactions: above all was the desire to wipe away the traces, to cover the tracks of his own experience, to hide from everyone outside the circle of the few trusted friends who remained: Citati, Contini, Bassani. With the paranoiac and persecutional fears that typified the setting-in of his old age, he strove to suppress every reference to real people while preparing the new editions of his Milanese works.

His judgment on the Italy of the sixties and its great leap forward arose from this new situation of profound desperation: the nascent hegemony of the left in the sphere of culture, the neo-Fascist regurgitation, the oppressive Catholic clericalism, the continuous polemics between Rome and Milan, the spread of new consumer goods like cars, the inroads made by TV as an instrument of the globalization of consent. Some intellectuals had taken to the new reality like fish to water (Pasolini, for example); others, like Gadda himself, remained permanently attached to their 'putrescence and obsolescence,' the two words that best characterized the final stage of Gadda's life.

To Gadda, the sixties above all suggested a new ideological conception of Rome as the capital of the modern 'pandemonium,' that confusion of power and intrigue which, in the era of ascendent neocapitalism, would destroy the logico-rational order of the northern, Milanese spirit. Thus arose the language question, the problem of the relationship between standard Italian and its dialects, one which was also tied to the reworking of *Quer pasticciaccio.* Although it is certainly extremely important in regard to this period, a thorough discussion of the language question is beyond the scope of this essay. Naturally, however, there was a link between Gadda's privileging of the Roman dialect and the ideological-political importance of the capital in those years. The Roman dialect, he felt, was 'topographically and lexically at the centre of gravity,' whereas the dialect of Florence was 'too subtle and refined to adequately express the crudity and brutality of the times in which we live, write, think and speak' (*SGF I*, 1144).

Gadda commented upon the inevitable geopolitical upsurge of the language of the capital in various places:

The advance of Roman dialect is due not so much to our efforts as to certain geographical and social facts that are beyond us, and we can neither be blamed nor praised on their account ... Besides, there are certain manifestations of modern culture, for example, the cinema, which today are headquartered in Rome. (Gadda 1993, 70)

Thus, Rome was the *caput mundi* of a new reality that could no longer be identified as 'Mussolinian,' but rather was clerical-Fascist-Marxist besides being crude and brutal. 'Gaddus' watched it going up all about him, on the hills of Monte Mario, and heard it in the noise that surrounded him and drowned out the peace of his house at number 19 Via Blumenstihl. Paradoxically, he felt himself to be an integral part of this new power, and looked upon some of the prizes he had won and even the filming of his novel as the fruit of favours and recommendations bestowed upon him for the very fact that he had become, by then, Roman. He was in the right place at the right time, and he was ready and willing to have himself photographed, to have his privacy violated anywhere and at any time, even in his own home. Even so, he thought of himself as an intruder in a land of infidels; at bottom, he still identified himself as a representative of the 'moral capital' of the north, as a Lombard, and despite his recognition and adoption of the baroque tongue of the southern capital, he feared that sooner or later he would be found out. In his 'Vocabolarietto dell'italiano: furberia' (1958), Gadda identified two types of cunning. His own personal type was that of a person who lives in a dangerous world where it is always necessary to protect oneself from aggressors and thieves of every sort. These are people who are:

cunning in the way they get away from the enemy, the persecutor, the violent, in the way they avoid a dangerous threat by circumventing it. A cunning and quick-witted person is one who slips his wallet to the ground before it has been seen and declares to those who have assaulted him that his pockets are empty; another is the wounded man who pretends to fall dead so as to avoid further wounds that might kill him. Morality permits cunning as long as it is motivated by the necessities of defence and flight; it is practical and vindicated when used by the weak, by the underling whose very existence is threatened by a cunning and powerful oppressor. (*SGF I*, 1151–2)

In fact, Gadda felt very close to one of the characters in *I promessi sposi*: 'Among the humble, there is no doubt that I feel a sympathy for the character of Don Abbondio, who really committed no immoral act other than to have yielded to the violence and terror of violence' (Gadda 1993, 90). And so, Gadda was living in Rome as a kind of sly 'Sofio Loren,' even if his cunning was the defensive, moral, 'Milanese' type because it was justified by the need to escape from the attacks of those who were 'wickedly cunning,' by whom he was surrounded and perpetually threatened in the capital:

Apart from defence and escape, I would say that cunning is an attitude and even a spiritual quality and mode of behaviour which is definitely wicked ... Cunning is an evasion of one's own duties and of the universally recognized limits which define every activity, limits which must be implacably observed in their entirety, in their necessary, logical, and even mathematico-logical combination and inter-connection. Cunning conspires towards the cancellation and destruction of social life, by substituting historical activity with a pseudo-history, or worse, with a non-history. In any case, it produces a vile and fraudulent concoction, a base narrative that leads to meaninglessness, in fact, to nullity. (*SGF I*, 1152)

Gadda's cunning was the honest kind, the defensive kind, not the Roman variety of *escroc*, that quintessentially Italian art of swindling other people.

In a subsequent article, 'Il latino nel sangue' (1959), the anti-Roman polemic continued. Rome had, absurdly, become the centre of a new way of thinking that was both anti-Latin and anti-rational; the new reign was characterized by a cloying *pathos*, which constituted the cipher of modern Italy:

Rationality, logos, do not get good press, I know, I know, in this throbbingly pathetic, theatrical world of ours, a world which has become gratuitously distracted or abstract. Logic and reason have become repulsively rancid stuff in this land of throbbing hearts, and so Latin and mathematics are to be 'abolished' from the duties of teaching as well as of learning. (*SGF I*, 1162)

The most complete and precise picture of Rome in these years was provided by Federico Fellini's *La dolce vita* (1960), which moved Gadda to an obstinate defence of its most essential themes and motifs:

Here too there is the issue of Fellini's film (*La dolce vita*) and the related bacchanal. Our fellow citizens get overly excited about the 'revelations' concerning our modes of behaviour. I agree with you. I, too, find it to be a work of value, and it irritates me the way his accusers and detractors, with all their gratuitous insults, fail to realize that these modes of behaviour, which are so bitterly and desolately portrayed by Fellini, were by no means invented by him. In his own way, Fellini tends to get himself into this mess by creating this *pasticcio*, which is to say the synthesis of inane or divergent figures, because he is trying to represent human life and all of its contradictory elements within the confines of Rome. Among the modes of behaviour which he depicts, some are at bottom amusing and reminiscent of Petronius (drunk American women dancing with young men, old women nodding off in their chairs, etc.), others are simultaneously pathetic and elegant (the scenes of the castle of Sutri being cared for by genuine but penniless nobility); others are perhaps mildly unpleasant. However, these images are to be seen everywhere, and not only among the nobles and the wealthy, in Via Veneto, etc.; they can be seen all over Italy and Europe, in Jamaica, in Brasil and elsewhere. (I witnessed similar scenes with my own eyes on the faces and in the streets of Rio de Janeiro, on a twelve-hour stopover there). (Gadda Conti 1974, 90, Letter of 1 February 1960)

For Gadda, Rome was the privileged home of the 'pasticcio' (as seen in the two varieties of the pathetic and the grotesque), but also of the hypocritical Christian-Democratic attitude which would have liked to repress this fact. There actually was a 'senator-and-father-of-four' who wanted to have the film withdrawn. On the other side of the coin, it was also the city of the slum dwellers as seen by 'Pasolo' (Pier Paolo Pasolini) in the film *Accattone*: 'The subject matter is somewhat novel; the scenes are completely authentic. There are five or six hundred thousand desperate people living like this in Rome' (ibid., 115: spring 1961). Thus the cinema, too, acknowledged the centrality of Rome, and it was perfectly useless for his cousin, Piero Gadda Conti, to repudiate in his ironic manner the pleasures and perquisites which Carlo Emilio believed he had received by living there. His adopted city had become the realm of a reverse paranoia, where power, even though detested, was generous with its favours and benefits. Symbolically, Gadda made the daily fourteen-kilometre com- mute to its centre to demonstrate his passive submission to this perverse mechanism.

Gadda's situation changed after he left the job at the RAI, but the status of the writer in the era of neocapitalist Rome had also changed. Another of his articles introduces us to the sixties and to his new role of a funded, though by no means independent, professional writer: 'Can a Writer Earn a Living from His Pen?' (*SGF I*, 1146). Naturally, his personal answer was negative. Having for so many years spent ten hours a day working as an engineer instead of writing ('Since I was really penniless, I was forced to alternate between periods dedicated to the art of letters and periods that were totally unlettered'), he had arrived at literary success only to discover that his hours were again being drained away, this time by the obsessive attention of the media. Thus, according to the way he viewed it, his situation had paradoxically remained the same: in place of the duties which he performed at the RAI, there was now 'a literary prize, an editor, a picture magazine,' always something that kept him away from the work he loved. A letter to Contini announced the inception of the literary craze that had exploded about him:

Reviews, interviews, and photographs at home conveying my non-existent graciousness; there are also telephone calls although I don't own a telephone. My generous Russian concierge, Katia, receives them on hers and is kind enough to relay them to me, so there's a constant running up and down between her ground floor quarters and my third floor flat. (Gadda 1988, 96: 25 September 1957)

Even so, immediately following his experience at the RAI, financial insecurity began to plague him more than ever before. Like any respect- able member of the middle class, Gadda always invested his savings in the stock market, and as a result, he had already lost his pension payment from RAI in 1955: 'The collapse of the market has reduced my miserable savings, which is to say what I had left from the Viareggio prize after paying two years of rent' (Gadda Conti 1974, 88–9). He had a very precise notion of the culprit behind this personal misfortune: it was the centrist government of the DC, which kept oscillating between right and left instead of setting up a stable liberal regime. This was only the outset of the 'Sofio Loren' period, and yet his sense of being economically 'humiliated and offended' has very clear origins in Roman politics. On one side, there was Christian Democracy, especially those currents in favour of renewal, which would lead the country to the centre-left; on the other side, this very same DC was centred in Rome, a city where anyone who worked or had ever toiled for a living was looked down upon and marginalized:

You can imagine what my feelings are about these 'loosenings' and 'openings to the left!,' the prophets of 'a better tomorrow,' the 'radicals' (neo-separatists), the fat asses of Via Veneto. You are the son and grandson of men who have always worked, but the fat asses of café society on Via Veneto call you 'slavedriver from the North,' 'kilowatthour monopolist,' and so forth. So let them put up a lightning rod! They are nothing but a bunch of filthy, drooling swindlers. (ibid.)

The government in Rome was not only leftish, it was also tendentially anti-Milanese, and, in so far as he was being supported by a northern publishing house, Garzanti, to live in the southern capital, Gadda had to manoeuvre in order not to be caught in the pincers; he was forced to make compromises in order to get along.

Gadda's politics corresponded to the old liberal-monarchist tradition, one which cherished a stable, conservative regime; from this anachronistic position, he looked upon the ruling classes and their governing parties (DC and PSDI), as well as the Roman Catholic church, as the objects of his visceral class hatred. He wrote ferocious attacks against Saragat and Segni, whom he envisioned in the next world with Dantean imagery:

I spend the night in the most agitated dreams about sending the whole pack of them into hell, into their own Catholic inferno, and I imagine obscene devils intently driving them back down, with pitchforks and grappling hooks, into the boiling tar. Please excuse my blowing off this wretched steam! But it just isn't right that the financial and economic affairs of a country be placed at the mercy of these braying donkeys, who really know absolutely nothing about how to set up or run anything that works ('el lavora'). (ibid.)

Having failed to garner the Marzotto prize in December 1957, and following his attack upon the government, he launched another against the cultural establishment. This time, he railed against the hegemony exerted by former Fascists, who weren't about to pardon him for his attack on Mussolini:

I really couldn't give a flying fig about receiving a Zanellian laurel wreath from former black shirts or from black marketeers. Formally, I was passed over after serious deliberation by that clique of academic snobs with their suave southern decorum so typical of the Italian soul. There was certainly no lack of 'formal' pretexts and reasons. I'm sure that I was found guilty of a 'cowardly offence' against that defunct bastard who ruined Italy and tarnished forever the name 'Italian.' (ibid.)

'Gadda's cause' had not gone well; Citati informed him of 'the lost laurel' that had gone to Saba: 'that Fascist clique that handed out the prize today wouldn't even have dared mention Saba's name when he was alive and persecuted and on the run' (Gadda Conti 1974, 92–3). Gadda had a reputation for being a bitter antagonist of the 'steel-jawed Duce,' and the ruling cultural figures, those who gave out the prizes, were still by and large tied to the old regime, which had been physically based in Rome. The MSI was already quite strong there even in those days; however, it was a somewhat ironic retaliation to award the prize to Saba, who was a Communist sympathizer and a Jew to boot.

When Gadda finally did win a major prize, he immediately began to calculate how much money the poet Luzi and the Florentine Pratolini had been given with theirs. The former had won four million lire, even if this was 'somewhat weighed down by having to maintain his residence in Florence' (ibid.), and the latter had won five million from the Academy of the Lincei. But it was the comparatively modest two-and-a-half-million lire that went to Gadda that set off a storm of anger against him:

They'll probably say that I'm a Milanese and that I suck the blood of the poor; that my novel isn't even finished, that it's 'extravagant,' 'baroque,' etc., etc.; that there are a thousand candidates who are more worthy than I am, and not rich like I am with my name Gadda; that I belong to the rich and pitiless 'northern bourgeoisie,' etc., etc.; that I was an engineer at the Vatican and built the throne, which is to say the toilet, for that bourgeois Pope from Milan. (ibid., 94–5)

To receive an award was for him to experience a moment of anguish. On this occasion, all his enemies seem to unite against him: the Fascists against the denigrator of *il Duce*, the left against the rich bourgeois, the Romans against the efficient northerner from Milan, the anti-clerics against the Vatican's engineer. In the end, however, the worst of all turned out to be the voracious tax-collector; Gadda wished he could have 'taken the money on the sly, stuck it in my pocket without letting anyone see, least of all, the revenue agents' (ibid., 95: December 1957).

The theme of neo-Fascism, this time Italian and European, reappeared in 1961, during the struggle over Algeria in France. In one article, 'Hand a Rifle to a Boy ...' he responded to the question raised by Giancarlo Vigorelli ('Is Fascism Over?'), by calling it a

sudden undermining of the laws of social life, laws which assist and comfort human development and the democratic state as constitutionally defined. The events in Algeria and in Paris certainly give one cause for bitter reflection, especially when this kind of subversion is enacted with overwhelming violence by a group of citizens who seek to excuse themselves from a social contract that has been freely accepted by the nation. (*SGF I*, 1181).

These agitators had, however, acted 'in defence of the territorial integrity of France and Algeria.' Gadda's incurable pessimism reasserted itself: 'Hand a rifle to a boy, and within the space of an hour, he will have shot it at his sister, his mother, and his best friend.' Gadda opposed the new Fascism:

We must overcome the Fascism inside ourselves, in the mind of every citizen, by despising, condemning, and ridiculing it. And by considering with disgust the cult of force, the iniquitous lust of the self to dominate, the 'physical' ambition to be above others, and the typically Fascist 'faith' in our presumed capacity to decide the fate of the community and lead it to 'victory' by means of certain ideas of power which, like weeds in a neglected garden, could proliferate only in the minds of our cretinous supermen or genuinely out-of-their-heads head-men. (ibid.)

Yet right alongside this anti-Fascist polemic, there also emerged in the early sixties an intense rage against a leftist culture that was progressively spreading in Italy. The emblem of this new hegemony that was driving Gadda to distraction was Visconti's renowned film *Rocco and His Brothers* (1960). The story of southern emigrants living in Milan, the film became the symbol of an Italian proletariat that was on the move:

As for Visconti's film, I haven't seen it and it's possible that I never will because the poverty-stricken Sicilian-Calabrian-Sardinian from the South and the vile bourgeois from (I can imagine) the North are two clichés that I am frankly sick of (aesthetically) and angered by (morally). So much the more so because these stereotypes have been used to make millions in novels and films promoted by editors and producers who are bourgeois to the core, capitalist through and through, and rolling in dough! (Gadda Conti 1974, 112)

Even the cherished Pasolini wallowed in this new climate favourable to the left; as described by Gadda, the Friulian poet was 'working a lot all the way from Aeschylus to De Laurentis, and he is preaching to the left and, it seems, he's raking in tons of old money from the coffers of the northern bourgeoisie' (ibid., 110: 24 March 1959).

More and more he felt besieged by the culture of the left: Repaci wanted to take him to Porretta to consult on a film 'that will probably be paracommunist' (ibid., 111: 23 June 1960). He even advises his dear cousin Piero Gadda Conti to move towards the left, so as to get into the good graces of the official culture: 'Just think that with a single dirty novel, one, moreover, that is "open to the left," you could lift yourself above the din created by the "Book Festival at the Grand Hotel," inserting yourself among the "great narrators," which is to say, the utmost cretins (or cretinesses) of the present state of pandemonium' (112: 30 October 1960). It is thus apparent that the same term ('cretins and cretinesses') is applied equally to Fascist and to Socialist-Communist politics and culture; both are at bottom allied and complicit with that Democratic-Christian power centred in Rome which is opposed by the liberal-monarchist Gadda, the 'free citizen of a self-styled free and constitutional, not to mention bigoted, papal republic' (114: spring 1961).

This was on the eve of the centre-left alliance; but the Tambroni government, supported by the MSI, was hanging overhead, and Gadda was as fearful of a Fascist rebirth as he was of the new opening to the left. 'There was that storm of taxes, and I am still petrified, as I will explain to you. My heart starts pounding whenever I think of what's going on: both the crisis of the government and that of the public' (ibid., 104). This is from 1959, when the Fanfani wing of the DC was preparing the centre-left coalition while the right was preparing to use the Tambroni government for a surprise attack to marginalize Fanfani's left. The latter had begun 'to push for a fundamental shift in the pattern of the DC's political alliances ... [in order to construct] a firm base for social planning, for moderate reform and for further government intervention in the economy' (Ginsborg 1990, 255). Thus the ruling party left ever farther behind the ideal of an orderly and conservative liberal regime, which had always been Gadda's dream.

In 1964, after the famous new introduction to *La cognizione*, we find Gadda's final comments on the sixties as formulated in that period. This time, his expressions unite North and South: 'the sack of Rome,' the construction of villas which was devastating the hills of the city, had now struck even the green slopes of Brianza, the Lombard region that was so dear to Gadda:

Reinforced concrete, plastic, and tin cans have covered even the soil of Lombardy, and the green trees are all gone. We are living in an infernal gloom, the so-called 'miracle' has arrived everywhere! ... and Via Blumenstihl is like a cement works enveloped in a permanent cloud of dust; here too the olives and pines are being destroyed, and everything green is disappearing. (Gadda 1983, 224–6: 29 May 1964)

By this time, the centre-left coalition was in full swing; the 'miraculous-infernal' burst of construction activity observed by Gadda was providing the motor for the new 'boom.'

It was not only on the external world that the author projected his childhood 'traumas.' Between 1957 and 1963 he went about creating for himself and his correspondents (and the same image oozed out of his interviews also) a new persona, that of someone 'humiliated and offended.' As a writer, he was being forced to insert himself into this new cultural market, while internally, he felt ever more alone and ill. This dichotomy, the external photograph with his haughty smirk and the internal horror and exhaustion with life, reappears over and over again and provided the natural 'humus' for his final works. This gave rise to an important turn in the production of his prose. Gadda was constrained to pull everything he had written before out of his drawers, but he did so with the constant terror that he would be discovered and exposed by the people whom he had turned into characters in those pages.

The theme of his own psycho-physical decay goes back to 30 March 1956, when he noted in his diary that 'my brain no longer responds to "marching orders," as that stinker Mussolini used to call them' (Gadda Conti 1974, 89). But the issue of personal health, which is joined to his attitude towards modern reality, is different from the various 'traumas' (mostly psychological) that had afflicted him in the preceding years. From this point on, he would use a specific binomial phrase, 'putrescence/ obsolescence,' in order to characterize his progressive state of decay:

My health is poor. I do not get around at all. Bassani took me to Antignano [...], (he was away from Florence since 1954 and from Milan since 1951). With your deep sense of *pietas*, and with your equally deep intelligence, I am sure that you will want to note to my credit, which is to say, to exonerate me of any lack of courtesy towards such gracious people, and yourself in particular, the fact of this gradual obsolescence, this putrescence which is slowly drawing me towards silence. (Gadda 1988, 96: 25 September 1957)

Most of all, he had to suffer through the siege of photographers who were tormenting him:

Right now I am very busy with the new work, with the avalanche of thank-you messages which I need to get a start on, with the intrusions of photographers who want to take my picture in my studio or in Via Merulana; in addition, I am having troubles with the tax collector, that infernal dragon on whose back rides the spectre of the late-but-not-lamented Vanoni. It might be better to live the life of an old man, like those abandoned figures who haunt the public parks and gardens: seated on a bench in the park twirling my Garibaldian mustachio and rattling on disconnectedly with a fellow veteran of Abba Garima. (Gadda Conti 1974, 93: 26 September 1957)

The contrast between the outer image and internal wear and tear could not be more jarring: 'wretched health, stuck with needles every day, I'm tired, I'm old, and here is this circus of picture magazines going on all around me' (ibid., 96: 3 January 1958); Gadda, moreover, protested that he was not responsible for the photos that continued to appear in the press. This was the essence of the 'Sofio Loren' persona: this parodistic combination of physical degradation and charmingly posed photographs in popular magazines. By the end of the summer of 1958, Gadda was still being harassed by Garzanti for the next novel, and he felt besieged: 'proposals for films during the hottest days of the summer, proposals for translations into French and German.' But most of all, he feared encounters with the world of the capital, where he had assumed the role of a dangerous subversive, and he was worried that what he had written about Foscolo might end up by hurting him:

This farce which was put together by Channel Three ought to 'go over.' But there are still reservations having to do with prudence and modesty, and I myself am a bit shaken over it, after the myriad accusations of lack of respect for the 'Idols' of our literature and for the presumed history of our fatherland. (99: 25 October 1958).

Gadda–Don Abbondio had an almost physical hatred for the image of Foscolo, steeped as it was in an exuberant lust for life and sexuality.

He felt himself to be the target of an ongoing aggression, constrained as he was to lend an ear to what seemed an excessive and demanding public:

There are just too many people in Rome who want to meet and speak with me. I have neither the time nor the energy to chatter away for the edification of all the little assistant professors of literature at the University, and the whole mob of journalists in this capital of two million inhabitants. (ibid.)

Now that he was a fashionable writer, life had become a torture; he was forced to participate in the National Congress of Writers at Naples, and while the others were busy 'arguing, proposing, and sometimes braying like asses,' he preferred to keep to his 'fatigue, old age, and the consequent dumbfounded silence,' and so: 'I didn't chime in' (ibid.).

In Rome the mania for words was combined with a frenetic, though aimless, activity on account of which the intellectual had always to be present, and to assume 'new and always extremely urgent tasks; there is always this great hub-bub (*fru fru*) as we say in Milan in our Milanese way' (ibid., 100). He ended up feeling ashamed at all the exposure he was getting in the popular magazines:

If (by misfortune) you happen to see an article about me in 'Grazia,' just keep in mind that I am not the one who is responsible for it. They used 'brute force' to enter my home, just as the *Corriere d'informazione* had. I am just the opposite of Moravia and Pasolini in regards to exhibitionism. Just seeing my face among the ads for bikinis and women's underthings on the models who grace the pages of 'Grazia' is enough to put me beside myself with rage for three weeks! I suffer it, I put up with it, that's all; just so as not to damage the interests of my publisher. (ibid., 113: June 1960)

Eventually, Gadda would adopt a pun which, as an old conservative, was dear to him, that of 'folla/follia,' a combination that links 'the crowd' and 'folly.' He spoke of a suffocating and perverse arena which the public (though in actuality it was really the journalists) had drawn around him. 'A gust of imbecility, puerility and folly sweeps through the crowds wherever I am concerned [...] every day the pressure, I could almost call it blackmail, which is crushing me, seems to increase' (ibid., 102: 18 March 1959). A little later he refers to 'an incessant siege of editors, interviewers, women, friends, etc. I feel sick and I am close to disappearing either by death or flight' (103: April 1959).

In contrast, the doctors, whose attention he would have liked to have had more of, either ignored him or treated him badly. 'They're not curing me; they're poisoning me. I have reached the point of desperation, not just solitude. None of those con-artists out there, male or female, seems to understand that I really am sick and ought to be left alone' (ibid., 110: 24 March 1959). The cultural scene demanded a Gadda who was in top form while he himself was feeling at the end of his rope: 'I am alone and tired now; but don't tell anyone. I have to pretend to be healthy, youthful, and intellectually vigorous' (105: 22 September 1959).

No less violent was his opinion of the cultural world in Rome, that 'circuit of scribblers,' to which the major part of Italian writers at that moment had gravitated. The disputes between Einaudi and Garzanti over his books, the anguish of not making any headway on *Quer pasticciaccio*, caused him 'a very serious nervous exhaustion, the consequence of many troubles brought on by the editors and by (mea culpa) my own books.' And it was all beginning to appear to have been in vain. Despite the effort to remain on the front pages of the newspapers and magazines, a flood of novels in dialect had followed after and overtaken his own:

My life appears to me in all its horror, from childhood to Carso, to the years following the first war, to the incredible exhaustions of working as an engineer abroad, to the many renunciations imposed upon me by fate and by poverty, to the sorrows of my family life. The novel cost me years of mortifying labour in a poor state of health and with heart trouble on top of it all. And now, there is this avalanche of novels on Roman, Sicilian and Jewish subjects which have overtaken it and submerged it in the din of the howling and general idiocy of the readers (ibid., 104: 11 August 1959)

In fact, it was his coterie of enthusiastic 'followers' that was drowning out his own work. Even though he was completely against the idea of opposing dialect to the national language, he had been accused of supporting dialect, and therefore of favouring the dissolution of Italy.

Gadda saw the Nobel Prize awarded to Quasimodo as an act of concession to the superficial fashion of the moment, to the most boorish and anti-national form of dialect literature:

I am feeling a bit wearied and annoyed these days by the rather heavy attacks aimed at those who write in dialect, attacks in which there is a confusion between philological events and questions of morality. I am responsible for the work I produce, as well as for my actions in general. This landslide of novels in dialect (Testori in the dialect of Lombardy and Pasolini in the dialect-jargon of the outskirts of Rome) cannot be blamed on me. My work is embroidered on a background which is Italian, indeed, '*Italianissimo*,' as Signor M. would say. Giving the Nobel to Salvatore Turiddu is nothing more than another instance of Italian and Swedish asininity. (ibid., 106: 20 October 1959)

Furthermore, he refused to have contacts with his leftist supporters (Pasolini), denying that he was in fact their tutelary deity:

They will not leave me in peace here, especially the swarm of neoterics, from P.P.P. [Pier Paolo Pasolini] on down, who, somewhat arbitrarily, have sat themselves down in the shade of my umbrella, producing something like a licence or passport that I certainly never issued them. [...] Livio Garzanti is unhappy; he's quite vexed with me. (ibid., 111: 23 June 1960).

Another category of distraction threatening to disturb his solitude was constituted by women writers or those in search of a husband. Some of them could sit down and write out two novels a year: 'they must be specially equipped to be able to put off going weewee more than once a semester. Myself, I could never do it; I suffer too much from the retention of urine' (ibid., 106: 20 October 1959). His misogyny was easily aroused: 'There are a lot of beautiful and available forty-year-old women here who would like to marry me, under the impression that I have a fat wallet stuffed with endless amounts of money. They haven't got a clue!' (110: 24 March 1959).

Against journalists, cultural figures, avant-garde writers, against those who, in short, represented this new type of neocapitalist society in the Rome of the sixties, 'Sofio Loren' sought a refuge for himself in solitude while rejecting the cultural and political evolution underway. Many critics have noted the mimetic process through which, prior to this period, Gadda had often adopted and copied the language of the world in which he was living. At the RAI, as a technician of mass communication, he expressed himself plainly and clearly; when writing to Contini, he exhibited a 'Continian' style, deep and refined. In the sixties, Gadda reversed the pattern; he avoided and distanced himself from his friends because he feared they might become contaminated by his horrors, by his decadence. For Contini to help win a prize for the engineer amounted to a *'trauma linceo'* (the Academy of the Lincei awarded Gadda five million lire); it meant entering a mire which should have been suffered only by Gadda himself. He therefore asked his dearest friend to:

abandon me to the pandemonium with all my misfortunes and bad luck, or rather this brutal destiny of a *dilettante vexé par l'imprévu, tracassé par l'horreur* [a dilettante vexed by the unforeseen, shaken by the horror] of his own life and of the era that it was our lot to traverse. And you must believe that even in my desperation I want nothing so much as to get as far away as possible, to escape from the *huée* [racket] without dragging anyone else's name, and least of all your own, which is spotless, into the ruinous (for me) uproar. (Gadda 1988, 99–100: 7 November 1962)

But when the very same Contini, in 1963, was preparing the Introduction to *La cognizione del dolore*, Gadda's horror of the sixties re-exploded in an outburst of annoyance and rage typical of better times. 'Sofio Loren' had seen a comparison to Proust in his friend's fine analysis, and he vociferously asked to have the phrase 'an autobiography of Mademoiselle Vinteuil,' which clearly tied the novel to his own place of birth, taken out. Such a connection would only bring upon poor Gadda 'the resentment and outrage' of the people he had grown up with, including, perhaps, his 'unfortunate sister' (ibid., 103). Contini honoured his friend's request, seconding his paranoia. At that moment, the 'inhabitants of Lukones,' 'my living relatives,' were becoming the symbols of his difficult relationship to the world, divided as they were between those who attacked him within 'the narrow enclosure of national hypocrisy and bombast,' and those who suffered with him from 'wounds deep enough to pierce the heart.' Thus Gonzalo resurfaced again, but he also attempted 'to throw the reader off the track of his real existence' (103), and Contini, informed by Roscioni about Gadda's fears, complied with 'the desire of the author, first substituting a cryptic periphrasis in place of the name of Mademoiselle Vinteuil at the beginning, and then altogether suppressing the place name, which had been suggested by circumlocutions' (Contini's note, ibid., 104). But even as he was hiding himself away, Gadda could not help but leave a *'senhal,'* a trace of his own presence. The beautiful letter that reopens the maternal wound of *La cognizione* is dated 'Rome, 9 April 1963, 2 p.m. (*ore*

14),' hinting at the famous and fatal number of his own dolorous existence.

Translated by William Hartley

References

Cattaneo, Giulio. 1991. *Il gran lombardo*. 2nd ed. Turin: Einaudi.
Gadda, Carlo Emilio. 1983. *Lettere a una gentile signora*. Edited by Giuseppe Marcenaro. Milan: Adelphi
– 1988. *Lettere a Gianfranco Contini*. Milan: Garzanti
– 1993. *Per favore, mi lasci nell'ombra*. Milan: Adelphi
Gadda Conti, Piero. 1974. *Le confessioni di Carlo Emilio Gadda*. Milan: Pan
Ginsborg, Paul. 1990. *A History of Contemporary Italy: Society and Politics 1943–1988*. London: Penguin Books
Ungarelli, Giulio, ed. 1974. *Gadda al microfono*. Turin: Eri

Bibliography

Novels and Short Stories

La Madonna dei Filosofi. Florence: Edizioni di Solaria 1931; reprinted by Einaudi 1955

Il castello di Udine. Florence: Edizioni di Solaria 1934; revised edition by Einaudi 1955

Le meraviglie d'Italia. Florence: Parenti 1939; reprinted by Einaudi 1964

L'Adalgisa – Disegni milanesi. Florence: Le Monnier 1944; revised edition 1945; reprinted by Einaudi 1955

Il primo libro delle Favole. Venice: Neri Pozza 1952

Novelle dal Ducato in fiamme. Florence: Vallecchi 1953

I sogni e la folgore. Turin: Einaudi 1955

Quer pasticciaccio brutto de via Merulana. Milan: Garzanti 1957

Accoppiamenti giudiziosi. Milan: Garzanti 1963

La cognizione del dolore. Turin: Einaudi 1963; revised edition by Einaudi 1970

Gli anni. Florence: Parenti 1964

Le meraviglie d'Italia – Gli anni. Turin: Einaudi 1964

Eros e Priapo (da furore a cenere). Milan: Garzanti 1967

La meccanica. Milan: Garzanti 1971

Le bizze del capitano in congedo e altri racconti. Milan: All'insegna del pesce d'oro 1981; reprinted by Adelphi 1981

Il palazzo degli ori. Turin: Einaudi 1983

Racconto italiano di ignoto del novecento (Cahier d'études). Turin: Einaudi 1983

Essays

I viaggi la morte. Milan: Garzanti 1958

Verso la Certosa. Milan-Naples: Ricciardi 1961

I Luigi di Francia. Milan: Garzanti 1964

Meditazione milanese. Turin: Einaudi 1974
Il tempo e le opere – Saggi, note e divagazioni. Milan: Adelphi 1982
Un radiodramma per modo di dire e scritti sullo spettacolo. Milan: Il Saggiatore 1982
Azoto e altri scritti di divulgazione scientifica. Edited by Vanni Scheiwiller. Milan: Libri Scheiwiller 1986
I miti del somaro. Edited by Alba Andreini. Milan: Libri Scheiwiller 1988

Journals
Giornale di guerra e di prigionia. Florence: Sansoni 1955; revised edition by Einaudi 1965
Taccuino di Caporetto – Diario di guerra e di prigionia (ottobre 1917 – aprile 1918). Edited by Sandra and Giorgio Bonsanti. Milan: Garzanti 1991

Poetry
Poesie. Edited by Maria Antonietta Terzoli. Turin: Einaudi 1993

Theatre
Gonnella buffone. Parma: Guanda 1955

Translations
La verità sospetta – Tre traduzioni di C.E. Gadda. Milan: Bompiani 1977

Correspondence
Carteggio dell'ing. C.E. Gadda con l' 'Ammonia Casale S. A.' (1927–1940). Edited by Dante Isella. Verona: Stamperia Valdonega 1982
Lettere a una gentile signora [Lucia Rodocanachi]. Edited by Giuseppe Marcenaro. Milan: Adelphi 1983
Lettere agli amici milanesi. Ed Emma Sassi. Milan: Il Saggiatore 1983
A un amico fraterno – Lettere a Bonaventura Tecchi. Edited by Marcello Carlino. Milan: Bompiani 1984
L'ingegner fantasia – Lettere a Ugo Betti 1919–1930. Edited by Giulio Ungarelli. Milan: Rizzoli 1984
Lettere alla sorella – 1920–1924. Milan: R. Archinto 1987
Lettere a Gianfranco Contini. Milan: Garzanti 1988

Contributors

Alba Andreini is Associate Professor of modern and contemporary Italian literature at the University of Turin. She has worked extensively in the area of twentieth-century narrative, especially on Carlo Emilio Gadda and Elio Vittorini, and is the author of *La ragione letteraria. Saggio sul giovane Vittorini* (1979) and *Studi e testi gaddiani* (1988). She has also edited two previously unpublished works of Gadda, *Il palazzo degli ori* (1983) and *I miti del somaro* (1988), as well as Elsa Morante's *Diario* (1989). More recently, her interest has been centred on women's writing, particularly on the works of Sibilla Aleramo and Elsa Morante.

Paolo Archi, who has a *laurea* from the University of Florence and a PhD from the University of Connecticut, teaches in the *liceo classico* in Florence. He is the author of *Il tempo delle parole: saggio sulla prosa di Pirandello* (1992) and articles on Parini, Moravia, Gadda, and Pasolini. He has also published the CD-ROM essay *I giorni e l'opera di Giovanni Verga* (1997).

Carla Benedetti is Associate Professor of modern and contemporary Italian literature at the University of Pisa. Her books include *La soggettività nel racconto* (1984), *Una trappola di parole. Lettura del 'Pasticciaccio'* (1987), and, as co-author, *Modi di attribuzione. Filosofia e teoria dei sistemi* (1989) and *Figure del paradosso. Filosofia e teoria dei sistemi 2* (1992). She is also co-editor of the volume *A partire da 'Petrolio.' Pasolini interroga la letteratura* (1995) and author of a book-length study of the figure of the author in contemporary literature currently in press.

Manuela Bertone is Associate Professor of Italian at the Université de Savoie-Chambéry. She is the author of *Il romanzo come sistema. Molteplicità e differenza in C.E. Gadda* (1993) and *Tomasi di Lampedusa* (1995). She has also written on Gadda, Moravia, Landolfi, Primo Levi, Tabucchi, Maraini, Guibert, Anissimov, Gruppo 93, and C. Paglia for the *Harvard Review*, *The Italianist*, *Narrativa*, *Allegoria*, *Franco-Italica*, *Gradiva*, *MLN*, and *Baldus*.

Gian Paolo Biasin is Professor of Italian at the University of California at Berkeley. He has written numerous books on contemporary Italian literature, both in Italian and in English. The most recent of them, *The Flavors of Modernity. Food and the Novel* (Princeton 1995), received the Presidental Book Award of the American Association for Italian Studies. And *Le periferie della letteratura. Da Verga a Tabucchi* is scheduled to appear in 1997.

Robert S. Dombroski is Distinguished Professor of Italian and Director of Italian Graduate Studies at the City University of New York. He has written extensively on Gadda, Pirandello, Manzoni, intellectuals and Fascism, and Gramsci. His most recent book, *Properties of Writing: Ideological Discourse in Modern Italian Fiction* (Johns Hopkins 1994), was awarded the Modern Language Association Howard R. Marraro and the Aldo and Jeanne Scaglione Prizes for Italian Literary Studies.

Guido Guglielmi is Professor of Contemporary Italian Literature at the University of Bologna. His principal interests are in the area of literary theory and criticism. Among his more recent publications are *La prosa italiana del Novecento. Umorismo, metafisica, grottesco* (1986), *Interpretazione di Ungaretti* (1989), and *La parola del testo. Letteratura come storia* (1993). A second volume on twentieth-century fiction is slated for publication by Einaudi.

Peter Hainsworth lectures in Italian at Oxford University and holds a Fellowship at Lady Margaret Hall. He has published *Petrarch the Poet* (1988) and a range of articles on medieval and modern poetry in Italian.

William Hartley received his PhD From the University of Chicago with a dissertation on the cultural politics of Antonio Gramsci. Besides having contributed to various research, editorial, and translation projects, he has published articles and reviews in *The Chicago Reader*,

Praxis, Italian Quarterly, Italica, and *Socialism and Democracy.* His students on the south side of Chicago say he is 'un buen maestro de inglés.' His father, Arnold Hartley, helped in the translation of Alba Andreini's essay.

Wladimir Krysinski is Professor of Comparative and Slavic Literatures at the University of Montreal. Among his numerous publications are the books *Carrefours de signes. Essais sur le roman moderne* (1981), *Le paradigme inquiet. Pirandello et le champ de la modernité* (1989), and *La novela en sus modernidades. A favor y contra Bajtin* (1997).

Guido Lucchini has degrees from the universities of Milan and Pavia. He is one of the editors of Gadda's *Opere,* directed by Dante Isella, and the author of *L'istinto della combinazione. Le origini del romanzo in Carlo Emilio Gadda* (1988), from which his chapter on Gadda and Freud has been taken, and *Le origini della scuola storica – Storia letteraria e filologia in Italia (1866–1883)* (1990). He has edited the volume *Pio Rajna-Francesco Novati. Carteggio (1878–1915). Tra filologia romanza e mediolatina* (1994). Currently he is working on a study of Graziadio Isaia Ascoli and Judaic culture in Italy.

Emilio Manzotti, Professor of Italian Linguistics at the University of Geneva, has published widely in the area of discourse analysis. His many contributions to Gadda criticism include his critical edition with commentary of *La cognizione del dolore,* published by Einaudi in 1987, *Le ragioni del dolore – Carlo Emilio Gadda 1893–1993* (1993), and a long chapter on *La cognizione* contained in the fourth volume of *Letteratura italiana* published by Einaudi.

Federica G. Pedriali lectures at Edinburgh University on nineteenth- and twentieth-century Italian literature. She has published articles on Gadda, Calvino, Montale, Baretti, and Virginia Woolf.

Gian Carlo Roscioni is Professor of French at the University of Rome, La Sapienza. He has written widely on French, German, English, and Italian literature. On Gadda he has published *La disarmonia prestabilita* (Turin 1969, 1995) and *Il Duca di Sant' Aquila* (Milan 1997), a biography of the young Gadda. He is also the author of *Sulle tracce dell' "Esploratore turco"* (Milan 1992), a study of literature and espionage in libertine Europe.